The Last Years of the
GEORGIAN MONARCHY
1658-1832

STUDIES OF THE RUSSIAN INSTITUTE, COLUMBIA UNIVERSITY

The Last Years of the
GEORGIAN MONARCHY
1658-1832

DAVID MARSHALL LANG

COLUMBIA UNIVERSITY PRESS
NEW YORK   1957

The Russian Institute of Columbia University

THE Russian Institute was established by Columbia University in 1946 to serve two major objectives: the training of a limited number of well-qualified Americans for scholarly and professional careers in the field of Russian studies and the development of research in the social sciences and the humanities as they relate to Russia and the Soviet Union. The research program of the Russian Institute is conducted through the efforts of its faculty members, of scholars invited to participate as Senior Fellows in its program, and of candidates for the Certificate of the Institute and for the degree of Doctor of Philosophy. Some of the results of the research program are presented in the Studies of the Russian Institute of Columbia University. The faculty of the Institute, without necessarily agreeing with the conclusions reached in the Studies, believe that their publication advances the difficult task of promoting systematic research on Russia and the Soviet Union and public understanding of the problems involved.

The faculty of the Russian Institute are grateful to the Rockefeller Foundation for the financial assistance which it has given to the program of research and publication.

Studies of The Russian Institute

Columbia University

For Janet

Note on Transliteration

THE TRANSLITERATION system used in this series for Russian words and proper names is based on the Library of Congress system, with modifications in the case of Russian Christian names having common English equivalents, or names of celebrities familiar in the West, and so forth. For Persian, Turkish, and Armenian names, a simplified system has been worked out based on that in use at the School of Oriental and African Studies, University of London, but with diacritical marks omitted. The method of transliterating the Georgian is the same as that adopted by the author for his monograph, *Studies in the Numismatic History of Georgia in Transcaucasia,* published by the American Numismatic Society, New York, 1955. This system is summarized in the following table of the Georgian alphabet. The first column in each set of three represents the Khutsuri, or ecclesiastical capitals; the second, the Mkhedruli, or modern alphabet; and the third, the transliterations.

Khutsuri	Mkhedruli	Translit.	Khutsuri	Mkhedruli	Translit.	Khutsuri	Mkhedruli	Translit.
ⴀ	ა	a	ⴌ	ნ	n	ⴕ	ყ	q
ⴁ	ბ	b	ⴐ	ჲ	y	ⴘ	შ	š [sh]
ⴂ	გ	g	ⴍ	ო	o	ⴙ	ჩ	č [ch]
ⴃ	დ	d	ⴎ	პ	p	ⴚ	ც	c [ts]
ⴄ	ე	e	ⴏ	ჟ	ž [zh]	ⴛ	ძ	dz
ⴅ	ვ	v	ⴐ	ღ	r	ⴜ	წ	ç [ds]
ⴆ	ზ	z	ⴑ	ს	s	ⴝ	ჭ	č [tch]
ⴡ	ჱ	ey	ⴒ	ტ	t	ⴞ	ხ	ḫ [kh]
ⴇ	თ	tʿ	ⴓ	უ	u	ⴤ	ჴ	h [kh]
ⴈ	ი	i	ⴣ	ჳ	w [vi]	ⴟ	ჯ	j
ⴉ	კ	k	ⴔ	ფ	pʿ	ⴠ	ჰ	h
ⴊ	ლ	l	ⴕ	ქ	kʿ	ⴢ	ჵ	ho [oy]
ⴋ	მ	m	ⴖ	ღ	ġ [gh]			

Preface

UNDERSTANDING the nationality problem of the Soviet Union is impossible unless it is realized that many of the constituent republics of the USSR were, until relatively modern times, independent states, with their own traditions of national achievement in statecraft, war, the arts, and letters. For many centuries Georgia was such a state. At the present time, as the age-old Russian drive for power in the Near East enters a new and acute phase, the tsarist empire's absorption of Georgia and the other once-independent nations of Caucasia takes on fresh historical perspective, and shows how Near Eastern disunity and tension can profit the masters of Russian foreign policy.

Everybody knows, of course, that Stalin was a Georgian, but he was not the only Georgian prominent in modern Russian history. The names of Nicholas Chkheidze and Irakli Tseret'eli stand out in the annals of Russian Social Democracy, while those of Orjonikidze and Beria are conspicuous in the history of Bolshevism. The careers of these men might have been expected to focus attention on their native land and to encourage Slavists and students of current affairs to make serious study of their Caucasian background. But with the notable exception of Deutscher's biography of Stalin, disappointingly little has been done along these lines.

Politics apart, even the skeptic must admit that Georgia's economic resources and industrial potential make the country important for study. The ancient Greeks drew largely on the Caucasus for their supply of iron and precious metals, as is symbolized in the myths of

Prometheus and the Argonauts. Today, Georgia's production of manganese is indispensable to Soviet industry, while substantial deposits of coal, iron, copper, silver, lead, zinc, molybdenum, cobalt, quicksilver, and arsenic are being opened up for exploitation. Fast-flowing rivers are harnessed to a series of hydroelectric stations, and on the Black Sea, Batum plays a vital role in refining and distributing oil from Baku. The Georgian district of Atchara (Ajaria) produces almost the entire tea crop of the Soviet Union, as well as quantities of citrus fruits and tobacco. The wine of Kakhet'i is drunk throughout the USSR, while the spas and health resorts of Georgia are visited annually by many thousands of Soviet citizens.

*   *   *

The present work is concerned chiefly with the history of Georgia on the eve of the Russian annexation in 1801, and with the years immediately following the Russian occupation. The last years of the Georgian monarchy include the period of the last two dynasties: the Mukhranian Bagratids, who ruled at Tiflis from 1658 until 1723, and the Bagratids of Kakhet'i, who reigned in Eastern Georgia from 1744 until the kingdom was abolished in 1801. As an epilogue, the story of the first three decades of Russian rule has been included, in order to describe the earlier effects of tsarist domination on Georgia, as well as to give an account of the final attempt to restore the Bagratids to power in Georgia—an attempt crushed by Emperor Nicholas I in 1832. This latter year marked the end of Georgian royalist hopes.

The interest of this period of Georgian history is enhanced by the country's role as a focal point in Near Eastern power politics. In the seventeenth century Georgia was uneasily divided between the Turkish and Persian spheres of influence; at the same time the advancing power of Russia in the north was raising the Georgians' hopes of a crusade against the Mohammedan empires. In the following century Georgia occupied a key position in Peter the Great's grand but abortive strategy for Russian conquest of Persia and the Indian trade routes. Under Catherine the Great, Georgia was used as a pawn in Potemkin's ambitious plan for reestablishing a Christian empire at Constantinople. And finally, Georgia was occupied by

Alexander I in 1801, who thus drove a wedge between two of Russia's main foes in Asia, Persia and the Ottoman Empire, involving Russia in a long drawn-out struggle against the mountaineers of the Caucasus. The repercussions of Russia's advance in the Caucasian isthmus were world-wide. The fears and suspicions of France and Great Britain were aroused, and with the arrival of a permanent Russian garrison at Tiflis, the Eastern Question may be said to have entered a new phase. The present study, by tracing the history of the Georgian principalities within the framework of Near Eastern power politics, aims to contribute to the general picture of Russia's Oriental policy during this eventful period.

Within Georgia itself the period under discussion provides much of interest to the social, economic, and cultural historian. The legal system of Georgia, with its emphasis on ordeals and payments of blood-money, provides valuable material for the student of comparative law. Study of the disintegration of the Georgian feudal monarchy may be helpful to the student of mediaeval institutions, who can compare and contrast the symptoms of this decay with those observed in comparable phases of the political evolution of Western Europe. The pattern of Georgian social life at this time, with its superimposed Persian and Turkish elements, is a fascinating amalgam of East and West, of Mohammedan and Christian manners and customs.

This is the first detailed study of this period of Georgian history to appear in English. In W. E. D. Allen's *History of the Georgian People* (1932), a landmark in Georgian historical studies, the period under review is overshadowed by the glories of the earlier mediaeval kingdom. Other contemporary Western writers on Georgian history, like the author's friend and colleague Professor Cyril Toumanoff of Georgetown University, Washington, D.C., are concentrating on placing the early periods of Georgian history on a new scientific basis, or else, they are attempting, like Dr. Firuz Kazemzadeh in his *Struggle for Transcaucasia,* to throw new light on the brief years of Transcaucasian independence which followed the First World War. A survey of Georgian history on the eve of Russian occupation may therefore fill a gap in the history both of Georgia and of Russian expansion in the Near East.

Among the pioneer writers who have made my research possible, a special debt is owed to M. -F. Brosset, who saved the fundamental Georgian chronicles from loss or oblivion by translating and publishing them with every refinement of careful scholarship. Butkov, Tsagareli, and others have edited much of the Russian archive material concerned with Georgia. The Georgian school of historians have lately done fine work in advancing knowledge of their national past. In addition to making use of Georgian and Russian material, the present work incorporates extracts from diplomatic and missionary reports in the unpublished archives of the French Ministry of Foreign Affairs. For access to these, grateful thanks are expressed to the Librarian and the Director of the Archives of this Ministry.

Grateful acknowledgment is made to the Russian Institute of Columbia University for the generous grant of a Senior Fellowship, making possible a year's profitable work in New York. The Library of Congress, the Dumbarton Oaks Research Library at Washington, D.C., and the Widener Library at Harvard University gave free access to their important collections of Georgian books. The Georgian coins in the American Numismatic Society's museum in New York were kindly made available for study, and yielded useful data on Georgian fiscal and economic policy. The author is particularly grateful to Professor Geroid T. Robinson of Columbia University and to the staff of Columbia University Press for much good counsel in the preparation of the manuscript; special thanks are due to Miss Barbara Melissa Voorhis of the editorial staff of Columbia University Press. The map was kindly drawn by Mr. J. Tremblay of the American Geographical Society, and the Georgian royal arms by Mr. Albert Adams; to both these skilled artists thanks are expressed.

DAVID M. LANG

School of Oriental and African Studies
University of London
October, 1956

Contents

Illustrations

ENSIGN ARMORIAL

ROYAL ARMS OF THE BAGRATID DYNASTY   title page
From a sketch made for the author by Albert Adams
> CENTRAL PANEL: the Tunic of Our Saviour Jesus Christ (according
> to an ancient legend, this was recovered after the Crucifixion, brought
> to Georgia, and preserved there)
> TOP LEFT PANEL: the sling with which David killed Goliath and
> David's harp, symbolizing the Bagratid dynasty's claim to descent
> from King David of Israel
> TOP RIGHT PANEL: the royal orb and crossed swords
> BOTTOM LEFT PANEL: the scales of justice
> BOTTOM RIGHT PANEL: St. George killing the dragon
> (St. George is the patron saint of Georgia)

MAP

GEORGIA AND THE CAUCASUS ABOUT 1800   page 7
Map drawn by J. Tremblay of the American Geographical Society
New York

PORTRAITS AND TREATY

The following illustrations are reproduced from *Letopis' Gruzii,*
edited by B. S. Esadze, Tiflis, 1913. The portraits of King Erekle II,
Queen Darejan, and King Giorgi XII are from contemporary paintings and that of David Batonishvili from a contemporary engraving,
all formerly in the Main Archives of the Russian Imperial Ministry

of Foreign Affairs, Moscow. The photographs of the treaty are from
the original, also formerly in the Foreign Ministry's Archives,
Moscow.

The Last Years of the
GEORGIAN MONARCHY
1658-1832

I

The Historical Background

THE lands inhabited by peoples of Georgian stock border to the north on the main Caucasus range, to the west on the Black Sea, and to the south on the Armenian plateau. Eastward, they extend roughly to the junction of the rivers Alazani and Kura, over halfway across the Caucasian isthmus. At its greatest extent, this territory measures some five hundred kilometers in length. The portion included in the present-day Soviet republic of Georgia has an area of 76,200 square kilometers. This does not include large territories to the southwest which once formed the Georgian principalities of Tao and Samtskhe. These have been in Turkish hands since the sixteenth century, though the population remains predominantly Georgian. In addition, the Moslem Lazes or Tchans, a people of Georgian descent, inhabit a coastal strip extending from Batum to the region of Trebizond. Though long under Byzantine and Turkish rule, they still retain their distinct nationality and language, and incidentally provide the Turkish navy with some of its finest seamen.

Georgia is a country of hills and valleys, with a wide range of climatic conditions. The Black Sea coastal area and the Rion valley, comprising the districts of Abkhazia, Mingrelia, Guria, and Atchara, have a subtropical climate with luxuriant vegetation, but, until recently, malaria and other swamp fevers took a heavy toll of the populace. On the far side of the line of hills known as the Suram Range, Eastern Georgia enjoys more Mediterranean conditions, not unlike parts of Spain or Italy. The summers are exceptionally hot and

dry in low-lying parts, though the country's many rivers insure ample water supplies for irrigation. Kakhet'i and much of K'art'li are renowned for their orchards and vineyards. Where the Georgian domains extend northward into the Greater Caucasus and its foothills, alpine conditions prevail. Sheep and cattle-rearing, hunting, and, in olden days, banditry used to be the mountaineers' main occupations. In a number of scattered areas, deposits of iron, copper, and precious metals were worked by traditional and, prior to Russian occupation, primitive techniques.

As a physical type, the Georgians are generally tall and well proportioned, with strong features: "Stately, upstanding, erect, square-built, strong folk of swarthy complexion, fearless, valiant warriors," as a sixteenth-century German pastor described them.[1] Dark hair predominates, an abundant growth of beard being common. The beauty of Georgian women is proverbial. Most Georgians have what anthropologists term the "Anatolian" nose, fairly thick, curving in toward the tip. In Western Georgia, however, an aquiline nose is often seen, combining with other features to produce an almost Latin type of countenance. This may be the result of mingling with Greek and Genoese settlers around the Black Sea coast.

In spite of some superficial resemblance and intermingling, however, the Georgians, ethnically and linguistically, have been shown to be basically unrelated to the Latin peoples of Indo-European origin. They form a group of their own, termed "Ibero-Caucasian," "South Caucasian," or "K'art'velian" (the latter is the Georgians' own name for their nation). The late Professor N. Y. Marr brought into use the term Japhetic to designate the Georgians together with other surviving remnants of the ethnic group which he believed to have inhabited the Mediterranean basin before the arrival of the Indo-Europeans on the scene. Of this group of peoples, the Georgians and the Basques are the sole survivors (the extinct Etruscans may have belonged to a kindred family). The Georgians and the Basques managed to survive by strategic withdrawal to the inaccessible woods, marshes, and mountain fastnesses of Transcaucasia on the one hand and to the Pyrenees on the other. Certain affinities between

[1] Schweigger, *Ein newe Reyssbeschreibung,* p. 86.

the Basque and Georgian languages, as well as resemblances between the two peoples in physical type and even in popular customs
help to confirm this reconstruction of their ancient past. The languages of both peoples are quite unrelated to any of the Indo-
European or Semitic tongues.

Generalizations about peoples are always dangerous, and the
Georgians are no exception to this rule. But most observers would
agree that, along with a high level of intellectual ability, they are
quick-witted and prone to volatility and change of mood. They are
gifted in dance, song, and poetry, and Georgian folklore is an in-
exhaustible mine of invention. They tend to take an optimistic view
of life, are generous in hospitality and fond of wine.

The Georgians have always been renowned for chivalry and for
skill in battle. In Roman times, the East Georgian King Artag put
up a spirited resistance to Pompey. King Farsman II of Georgian
Iberia paid a visit to the court of the Roman Emperor Antoninus
who, we are told, was deeply impressed by Georgian equestrian feats.
Their martial prowess was later praised by the Crusaders. Jacques
de Vitry, Latin Patriarch of Jerusalem, described them as "very
warlike and brave in battle, being strong in body and powerful in
the countless number of their warriors." Whenever they came on
pilgrimage to the Lord's Sepulcher, they would march into the
Holy City with banners unfurled and without paying tribute or
toll to anybody. The Saracens dared not molest them for fear of
reprisals. The Patriarch observed that their hair and beards were
worn about a cubit long.[2]

Natives of different provinces of Georgia, in popular belief at
least, all have their regional traits. The K'art'lians, in whose country
the capital city of Tiflis is situated, have a reputation for aristocratic
breeding. The Kakhians are known for a certain stolid resoluteness.
In Western Georgia the Mingrelians are singled out for astuteness
and the Gurians for boastfulness as well as ruthlessness and tenacity
of purpose. In upland Imeret'i, the Ratchans are known for thrift,
industry, and physical strength. The Svans of the Caucasian mountain fastnesses used to have a reputation for savagery. The P'shav,

---

[2] Jacques de Vitry, *The History of Jerusalem,* Vol. XI of Palestine Pilgrims' Text
Society (London, 1897), pp. 83–84.

Khevsur, and T'ush mountaineers of Eastern Georgian hold to curious ancient rites and costumes, including the wearing of medieval chain armor. They were noted for their fidelity to the Georgian monarchy.

Since the fourth century a great national unifying influence has always been the Georgian Church, an autocephalous body following the Eastern Orthodox rite. It is by membership in the Georgian church as much as by nationality that the Georgian distinguishes himself from the many other peoples and tribes of the Caucasus— Gregorian Armenians, Russians, Moslem Persians, Turks, Daghestanians, and so on. The conversion of Georgia is ascribed to St. Nino of Cappadocia, who came to Georgia during the reign of Constantine the Great. Her miracles so impressed King Mirian and his consort that they and all the people were, according to the legend, converted from Zoroastrianism and paganism to Christianity. The Persians, and later the Arabs and Turks, strove to suppress the new faith. Many Georgian Christians were martyred. The Georgian Church was at first subordinate to the patriarchs of Antioch, but was later raised to the status of autocephaly. Its catholicos-patriarch resided at Mtskhet'a, the ancient capital. In some periods an independent catholicos of Abkhazet'i pontificated in Western Georgia, but these prelates were generally considered secondary to the patriarch at Mtskhet'a. The church was a great vehicle for spreading the cultural influence of Byzantium, as well as a bulwark of patriotic consciousness in times of alien rule. Curious rustic rites and pagan beliefs handed down from prehistoric days have lived on side by side with Christianity and even Marxism to this day. Demon giants (*devebi*) and wood and mountain sprites (*k'ajebi*) have to be propitiated, and the universal cult of St. George has always retained elements of primitive idolatry.

The institution of monarchy in Georgia goes back to the age of myth and legend. Jason and the Argonauts, for example, found Colchis, the present-day Mingrelia, ruled by Medea's father, King Aietes. The Greek geographer Strabo at the very beginning of the Christian era relates that the Iberians (East Georgians) were divided into four classes: the royal family, the priestly caste, the freemen and warriors, and finally, the slaves. During the Sasanian period, the

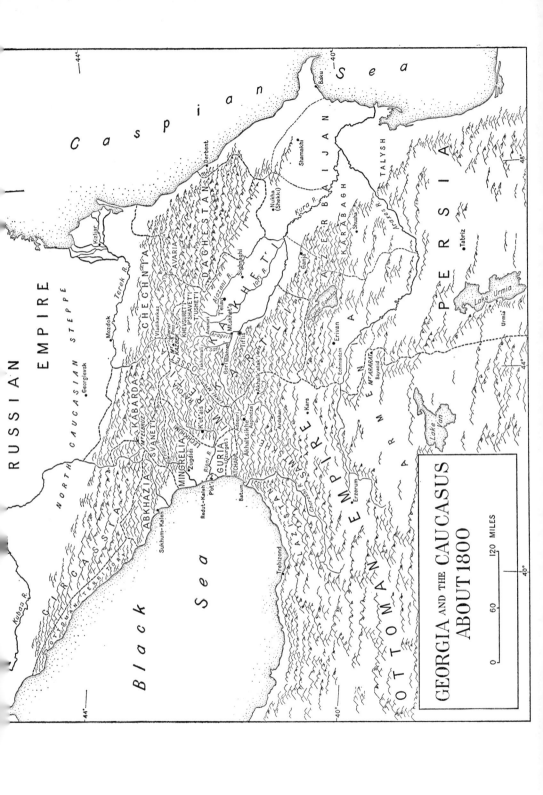

GEORGIA AND THE CAUCASUS
ABOUT 1800

0   60   120 MILES

Iberian monarchy was suppressed by the Persians, who engaged in a bitter but unsuccessful struggle to drive the Byzantines from their dominant position in western Georgia on the Black Sea. The rise of Islam abruptly changed the whole situation in Transcaucasia. The Arabs occupied Tiflis in A.D. 654, and an emir ruled over most of Georgia in the name of the caliph.

While the Georgian monarchy was thus in eclipse, a vigorous ruling family was rising to eminence in the marchlands of Georgia and Armenia. This was the clan of the Bagratids who were to unify Georgia and reign there for over a thousand years. For purposes of prestige they and their chroniclers proclaimed the dynasty's descent from David and Solomon of Israel. It is generally conceded, however, that the Bagratids originated in Sper (Ispir), in the upper Chorokhi valley, north of Erzerum. The first Bagratid prince of whom we have historical record is Sumbat I, who was master of the horse and coronant of Armenia between A.D. 288 and 301. In Georgia, the power of the Bagratids dates from the end of the eighth century, when Ashot the Great settled at Artanuji in Tao (southwestern Georgia), receiving from the Byzantine emperor the title of *kuropalat,* or guardian of the palace.[3]

The first king of anything approaching an all-Georgian monarchy was Bagrat III (975–1014), who succeeded in uniting under his rule the principalities of Tao, Samtskhe, Abasgia, K'art'li, and Kakhet'i. An exception, however, was the capital city of Tiflis itself, which was still ruled by independent Moslem emirs, the Jafarids. Tiflis fell at last to David the Builder (1089–1125), who was aided by the arrival of the Crusaders in the Levant and who won brilliant victories over the Seljuk Turks. The highest pitch of Georgian power was reached a century later in the reign of Queen T'amar (Tamara), whose realm stretched from Azerbaijan to the borders of Circassia, from Erzerum to Ganja, forming a pan-Caucasian empire, with Shirvan and Trebizond as vassals and allies.

At its zenith, the Georgian kingdom was a political organism of great complexity. The monarch ruled by divine right, though the

[3] See T'aqaishvili, "Georgian Chronology and the Beginnings of Bagratid Rule in Georgia," in *Georgica,* Vol. I; Javakhishvili, *K'art'veli eris istoria,* Vol. II (1948); Toumanoff, "The Early Bagratids," in *Le Muséon,* LXII (1949), 21–54.

existence of vigorous feudal institutions prevented the royal power from becoming sheer despotism. A movement at the outset of T'amar's reign to limit the royal prerogative and set up a legislative body with authority equal to that of the sovereign came to nought, unlike parallel developments in England at the time of King John. Nevertheless, the power of the great nobles and ecclesiastics represented on the council of state had always to be reckoned with, as had that of the provincial tribal chiefs. The government machine rested on a highly developed feudal system, the nobility, in theory at any rate, holding their domains in trust from the sovereign in return for allegiance and for support in time of war. The central administration was headed by five vazirs or ministers, the chancellor (an office long associated with the ecclesiastical dignity of archbishop of Tchqondidi), the war minister, the lord chamberlain, the chancellor of the exchequer, and the *atabag* or lord high constable, each with a staff of subordinate officials.[4] The provinces were governed by the dukes or *erist'avs* (literally heads of the people), nominated until about the thirteenth century as viceroys of the king, but tending later toward hereditary status and provincial autonomy.

By the time of T'amar (1184–1213), the structure of Georgian society had evolved into the form it was to retain, with some modifications, until the end of the monarchy in 1801. This paragraph aims to give only the broadest outline of that structure. By T'amar's time, most of the nation was divided into the categories of *patroni,* or lord, and *qma* (vassal or serf, according to context and social position). The term *patroni* signified both protector and master. Supreme in this class was the monarch, to whom the powerful *didebulni,* or grandees, and the other *t'avadni,* or princes, owed immediate fealty. A similar relationship in turn linked the princes with their *aznaurni,* or squires. The squires were the direct lords and masters of the peasant serfs who dwelt and worked on their estates. With certain exceptions and restrictions, serfs could be sold to other proprietors, either with or without the land they tilled, though it was considered shameful to sell serfs into slavery abroad. Special categories of peasants belonged directly to the king and to the estates of the church, and some possessed royal or princely charters giving them

---

[4] The full list may be found in Allen, *History of the Georgian People*, pp. 258–62.

perpetual exemptions and privileges. The church estates also had squires attached to them. There were, in addition, free yeomen, who were usually tenant-vassals of the great nobles. In the hills, peasants lived in free communities, often governed by dukes set over them by the king. Somewhat apart from the main social hierarchy stood the *msakhurni,* or retainers, who performed court duties and held administrative offices. They were in many cases elevated to the squirearchy. There were also the *vatcharni,* or merchants, and the *mok'alak'eni,* or burghers. The chief merchants took part in affairs of state and provided economic advice and financial support. Most of the burghers and merchants were of Armenian descent, and formed special communities in the cities of Tiflis, Gori, and Dmanisi. While nominally *qmani* (vassals) of the monarch, the burghers enjoyed special status and were exempt from military service.[5]

The reigns of David the Builder and Queen T'amar comprised the "golden age" of the arts in Georgia. The national poet Shot'a Rust'aveli was a contemporary of the great queen. His romantic epic, *The Man in the Panther's Skin,* allegorically paints an idealized picture of the splendor and chivalry of Georgia in its heyday. Noteworthy is the cult of courtly love, in which one seems to hear the strains of the Western troubadours in a more exotic Eastern setting. Church architecture, too, reached its zenith of perfection. The Georgian style was by now fully evolved. It is characterized by grace and purity of line, avoiding the luxuriant excesses sometimes affected in Byzantium, as well as the bulbous exuberance of mediaeval Russian churches.

After Queen T'amar, decline set in. The thirteenth century saw successive incursions by Khwarazmian and Mongol hordes from Central Asia. The Mongol Il-Khan rulers of Persia exhausted the country with their exorbitant demands for tribute in cash and kind. There was a period of partial resurgence under Giorgi the Brilliant (1314-46), but the chaos following the collapse of the Il-Khanid empire in the mid-fourteenth century exposed Georgia to the ravages of marauding tribal chieftains. Then the onslaughts of Tamerlane

---

[5] More will be said in a later chapter about the class structure of Georgia in the seventeenth and eighteenth centuries. The foregoing brief account of the social system of T'amar's time is based on Berdzenishvili, Javakhishvili, and Janashia, *Istoriia Gruzii,* pp. 185–88. See further K. Grigolia, *Akhali K'art'lis tskhovreba,* pp. 24–29; Gvritishvili, *P'eodaluri Sak'art'velos,* pp. 5–29.

between 1386 and 1403 dealt blows to Georgia's economic and cultural life from which the kingdom never fully recovered. The countryside was strewn with the ruins of churches, castles, and towns, the people fled to the hills, and the once busy roads were overgrown with grass and bushes.

The last king of united Georgia was Alexander I (1412–43), under whose sons the realm was divided into squabbling princedoms. The disintegration of the monarchy was accelerated by the fall of Constantinople in 1453 and the resulting isolation of Georgia from Western Christendom. The attempt of Popes Calixtus III and Pius II to organize a crusade of the European powers together with Persia and the Georgian princes to liberate Constantinople was abortive. The Black Sea became a Turkish lake, and the land routes from the Caucasus to the Mediterranean and the West through Erzerum and Syria were all in hostile hands.

In Eastern Georgia, K'art'li and Kakhet'i formed separate kingdoms. West of the Suram mountains was the kingdom of Imeret'i, nominally subject to which were the autonomous dynasts of Mingrelia, known as the Dadians, and the Gurieli, rulers of Guria, on the Black Sea coast. To the southwest, the Atabag of Samtskhe ruled independently at Akhaltsikhe.

Disunity prevented Georgia from resisting the expansionist designs of Turkey and Persia. In 1510, Ottoman troops invaded Imeret'i and sacked K'ut'ais. Tiflis was ravaged twelve years later when Shah Ismail Safavi of Iran invaded K'art'li. Ismail's successor, Shah Tahmasp, undertook four campaigns against King Luarsab I of K'art'li, who perished at the battle of Garisi in 1558.

From the north the Grand Princes of Muscovy had already begun their drive toward the Caspian and the North Caucasian steppe. In 1492, King Alexander of Kakhet'i sent an embassy of friendship to Ivan the Great of Moscow. Kazan fell to Ivan the Terrible in 1552, Astrakhan in 1556. The tsar then placed King Levan of Kakhet'i under Russian protection and sent him a Cossack bodyguard. Persian threats and protests, however, soon led to the Cossacks' withdrawal.

The death of Shah Tahmasp and subsequent anarchy in Persia enabled the Turks, then at the summit of their power, to invade and overrun the whole of Transcaucasia. Ottoman troops occupied Tiflis in 1578, while to the south they seized Tabriz and all Azerbaijan.

Their triumph was short-lived. The Persian monarchy soon rose to new heights of power under the ruthless and brilliant Shah 'Abbas I (1587–1629). No sooner, however, did Shah 'Abbas the Great succeed in expelling the Turks from Western Persia than a new era of oppression began for Georgia. King Alexander II of Kakhet'i was murdered in 1605 by his own son, Constantine, a renegade brought up in Persia. This parricide was engineered by the Shah as a reprisal both for Alexander's suspected pro-Turkish leanings and for his action in establishing diplomatic relations with Tsar Boris Godunov. Constantine was shortly afterwards killed by the loyalist nobility. His successor, T'eimuraz I, pursued a policy of seeking Turkish support against the Persians.

'Abbas's plans for complete subjugation of Georgia were furthered unexpectedly by the flight to Isfahan of the prefect, or *mouravi,* of Tiflis, Giorgi Saakadze. This able soldier had risen from modest origins to a position of prominence in the K'art'lian kingdom (his sister was married to the king, Luarsab II). Saakadze's meteoric rise aroused the jealousy of the old nobility, who conspired to murder him. In 1614 the Persians, led by 'Abbas and Saakadze, invaded Georgia. Many thousands of the Christian population were deported to distant regions of Persia, where their descendants live to this day. Almost every town and village of Kakhet'i was razed to the ground. King Luarsab was lured into the Persian camp and later murdered in captivity, in spite of Russian intervention on his behalf. King T'eimuraz of Kakhet'i escaped, but his mother, Queen K'et'evan, was martyred at Shiraz, and his two sons, hostages in Persia, were castrated. Puppet rulers from the Georgian royal family were appointed to govern Georgia under Persian dictation.

Shah 'Abbas the Great died in 1629. In the resulting confusion, it was a Georgian prince, Khusrau Mirza, prefect of Isfahan, whose energetic action resulted in the elevation of Sam Mirza, grandson of 'Abbas, to the throne of Persia, under the title of Shah Safi. This Khusrau was an illegitimate scion of the K'art'lian royal family, brought up in Persia and converted to Islam. In recognition of his services to the new sovereign, he was given the title of Rustam Khan, and sent in 1632 as the shah's *vali* or viceroy to Tiflis.

King Rostom, as Khusrau-Mirza came to be known in Georgia, is an attractive figure, and certainly one of the most accomplished of the later Georgian kings. Already sixty-seven years old on his accession, he had gained valuable administrative experience in governing the Persian capital. He was a subtle politician and a man of the world, with the additional advantage of possessing a substantial private fortune. The new shah placed unbounded confidence in him, and even, we are told, regarded him as a father. He was given a free hand in governing Georgia, and had a Persian army at his disposal.

The country needed an administrator of Rostom's caliber. After being ravaged by the minions of Shah 'Abbas, the land had suffered still further from the effects of popular rebellions against the Persian overlords, and from civil wars between rival patriotic factions and "resistance movements." Much of the arable land was now under forest. Trade was almost at a standstill. The population was decimated by deportation, famine, and disease.

Rostom applied his political skill to healing the country's wounds. He persuaded the shah to allow many of the Georgian deportees to return from exile. Himself a Moslem, Rostom took to wife the daughter of a leading Georgian aristocrat, and was married by both Christian and Moslem rites. He reorganized the administration and court after the Persian style, but without completely suppressing Georgian tradition. Members of both nationalities and creeds were received at court on an equal footing. Rich presents were given to influential grandees. Rostom endeared himself to the Christian populace by restoring the Patriarchal Cathedral at Mtskhet'a.

The king had to overcome strong hostility on the part of the patriotic extremists. Many of them regarded him as a traitor to Georgia, and resented his addiction to Persian ways and habits, luxury and high living, dissipation, unchastity, dishonesty, love of pleasure, baths and unseemly attire, lute and flute players," as the eighteenth century historian Wakhusht disapprovingly comments.[6] Opposition to Rostom centered on T'eimuraz, the king of Kakhet'i, the Persians' inveterate enemy. T'eimuraz maintained himself more or less precariously in the hills from which he used to sally forth and inflict reverses on Rostom and his Persian auxiliaries. He was finally defeated and driven out of Eastern Georgia in 1648, but then he

[6] Wakhusht, "Histoires particulières du Karthli," in M.-F. Brosset, tr. and ed., *Histoire de la Géorgie,* II, Part 1 (1856), 66.

tried to arouse the king of Western Georgia (Imeret'i) against
Rostom. The latter countered this adroitly by concluding an alliance
with the powerful Levan Dadian, prince of the neighboring province
of Mingrelia.

The international situation at this period tended to favor Rostom
and give him a free hand. None of the three great powers surrounding the Caucasus was in a position to intervene strongly in that area.

To begin with, the two Mohammedan empires were still at odds
with one another. Sultan Murad IV of Turkey (1623–40) was intent on reconquering Baghdad from the Persians, who had captured
it from Turkey at the time of 'Abbas the Great. He raided western
Persia, and forced Shah Safi to return much of the territory won by
the successful campaigns of Shah 'Abbas. The peace settlement following the fall of Baghdad in 1638 confirmed the traditional division
of Georgia into Persian and Turkish zones of influence in the eastern
and western provinces of the country respectively. To the north of
the Black Sea the Turks were hard pressed on their frontier with
South Russia. In 1637, the Don and Dnieper Cossacks captured Azov
and retained it for several years. The ministers of Sultan Murad's
successor, the imbecile Ibrahim I (1640–48) had little inclination
for adventures in the Caucasus. Ibrahim was devoted to pleasure,
and began a tedious war against the Venetians. The early years of
Ibrahim's successor, Mohammed IV (1648–87), were fully occupied
with operations in Transylvania and Central Europe.

In these circumstances, the Ottoman court was usually content to
leave Western Georgian affairs in the hands of the pasha governing
Akhaltsikhe, capital of the former Georgian province of Samtskhe.
This district had been in Turkish hands since the late sixteenth
century. In 1625, Bek'a Jaqeli, head of the local ruling family, and a
prominent Georgian feudal potentate, adopted the Mohammedan
faith and the title of Safar Pasha. From his strategic position and
with the help of Turkish janissaries stationed in Batum on the Black
Sea coast, he could threaten the Western Georgian king of Imeret'i
at K'ut'ais, exploit the latter's feuds with his own vassals, and extort
from Western Georgia an annual tribute of cash and slaves for the
sultan's seraglio. Throughout Rostom's reign, the pashas of Akhaltsikhe were careful to maintain good relations with the court at

Tiflis. This meant that Rostom had little to fear from his Turkish neighbor, which was naturally very helpful to his administration.

Another of Rostom's major preoccupations was his relationship with his suzerain, the shah of Persia. Here again, Rostom's hand was strengthened by Persia's difficulties on other fronts. In Afghanistan, for instance, the key fortress of Qandahar was captured from Persia by the Mogul emperor of India, and later had to be retaken at great cost to the Persian army. Nor did the successors of Shah 'Abbas the Great have the outstanding qualities of that formidable man. Behind the gilded façade of Safavi splendor, Persia was drifting into indolence and decay.

Significant for the future of Georgia was the consolidation of the Grebenskii and Terek Cossack settlements in the North Caucasian steppe. Under Tsar Boris Godunov (1598–1605), an attempt had even been made to gain possession of the strategic fortress of Tarku in Daghestan, capital of the powerful dynasty of the Shamkhals. This ended in disaster for the Russians, but the presence north of the mountains of these vigorous outposts of Muscovy remained an important factor in Caucasian politics.

In Rostom's time, the Russian court avoided full-scale military intervention in the Caucasus. The flourishing trade relations between Astrakhan and the Caspian provinces depended on peace with Persia. Apart from this, the Polish war of 1632–34, the great riots of 1648–50, the Ukrainian problem, the Nikonian schism in the Russian church, and the war with Sweden of 1656–58 gave the Russian government constant cause for anxiety. A Caucasian war would have been an unwelcome and unnecessary burden.

This did not mean that at this time Russia showed no interest in Georgian and Caucasian affairs generally. Between 1630 and 1660, peaceful penetration was especially intense. The Dadian or prince eignant of Mingrelia and the king of Imeret'i, both in Western Georgia, were taken under nominal Russian suzerainty, and several embassies were exchanged with the valiant King T'eimuraz of Kakhet'i. Great emphasis was laid on the community of religion between the Russians and the Georgians, and every advantage was taken of the Georgians' hostility to the Mohammedan powers.

Rostom was fully alert to these developments, and had his own

agent active at the Russian court.[7] But in any case, Tsar Alexis
Mikhailovich had no real desire to precipitate a formal rupture with
the shah of Persia. When T'eimuraz came in person to Moscow in
1658 to beg for military support against the infidel Persians, and
their creature, King Rostom, he received only gifts and fair words.
The Russians, in short, were for the time being happy to pose as the
champions of Christianity in Georgia, so long as this did not involve
them in any real unpleasantness with the Mohammedan powers.

Rostom's neighbor and contemporary, in Western Georgia, was
King Alexander III of Imeret'i (1639–60), whose realm was showing
disquieting signs of disintegration. His nominal vassal, the hereditary
prince of Mingrelia Levan II Dadiani (1605–57), far from acknowledging the king's suzerainty, persistently attempted to seize control
over the whole of Western Georgia. He galvanized his subjects into
unaccustomed industrial and military activity, engaged a French
engineer to cast cannon for his army, and in 1645 came to bombard
K'ut'ais, the royal capital—but unsuccessfully. In spite of these
vicissitudes, the narrative of the Russian envoys Tolochanov and
Ievlev, as well as the sketchbook of the contemporary Italian missionary Castelli, make it clear that the West Georgian court at
K'ut'ais still retained considerable splendor and magnificence. When
foreign ambassadors approached the royal palace, for example, they
were welcomed by three hundred musketeers, who shot off volleys,
while thirty cannon fired a salute. On either side of the ambassadors
rode nobles and equerries on racing stallions. At state banquets, the
food was served on gold and silver plates and the wine in gold and
silver goblets.[8]

As Rostom's reign went on, it became increasingly clear that the
East Georgian succession would become a thorny problem if the king
took no measures to appoint a successor since he was childless. To
avoid an outbreak of civil war after his death, Rostom adopted as
his son a junior scion of the K'art'lian royal family, his cousin
Luarsab. But in 1653, Luarsab was killed in a hunting accident.

[7] This fact was established by M. A. Polievktov in his article "K voprosu o
snosheniiakh Rostoma Kartalinskogo s Moskvoiu," in *Bulletin de l'Institut Marr,*
V–VI, 523–31.

[8] Allen, *History of the Georgian People*, p. 349.

There remained no other eligible member of the senior line of the royal house willing to accept the succession. The king's choice therefore fell on the representative of a collateral branch of the royal family, Bakhuta-Beg, otherwise known as Wakhtang, Prince of Mukhran. The prince was sent to the court of Shah 'Abbas II at Isfahan to pay homage and receive official recognition as heir presumptive. The shah granted him the honorific title of Shah-Navaz (Shahnavaz), signifying "the shah's well-beloved."

Rostom was by now over ninety years of age. In 1658 he died peacefully at Tiflis, after bringing Georgia a return of much-needed tranquillity and settled administration. "Everywhere," as the French traveler Chardin records, "he reestablished peace and order, and governed with much clemency and justice." [9] He was one of the few far-sighted Georgian statesmen of the time who preferred conciliation to gallant but often suicidal patriotic ardor.

But in spite of Rostom's achievements, it cannot be denied that in 1658, on the accession of Rostom's adopted heir Wakhtang as the first sovereign of the Mukhranian dynasty, Georgia had declined greatly in power and prosperity since the great days of Queen T'amar. The country had never fully recovered from the crushing blows dealt her by the Mongols in the thirteenth and fourteenth centuries. Just as reunification had seemed possible, the rise of the Ottoman Turks and the fall of Constantinople had cut Georgia off from Western Christendom and exposed her to the full impact of Turkish and Persian hostility. The economic decline of the country had aggravated the restiveness of the feudal nobles. The machinery of central government sapped, each duke aspired to be lord over his own province. The triumph of the feudal magnates, paradoxical as it may seem, led to the decay of feudal institutions. The principle of loyal service and allegiance to the sovereign gave way to an anarchical pattern of provincial separatism—a system, or lack of system, sometimes referred to in Georgian as *t'avadoba,* or the rule of princes. With this went a deterioration in the relations between lord and peasant, to the detriment of the latter's rights and privileges.

A national rebirth was prevented by the country's division into Turkish and Persian spheres of influence. The Turks looked on

[9] Chardin, *Voyages en Perse,* II, 149.

Western Georgia merely as a source of slaves and booty, and did their best to keep the land internally divided and demoralized. The Persians, after the ruthless campaigns of Shah 'Abbas I, were content to integrate Eastern Georgia as far as possible into the Safavi empire as a semiautonomous viceroyalty. To Eastern Georgia, this brought both advantages and disadvantages: the loss of sovereignty and national liberties was to some extent offset by economic and administrative benefits derived from association with the prosperous realm of the seventeenth-century shahs. But this division of Georgia into two camps, each dominated by one of the great Mohammedan powers, casts an ever-present shadow over Georgian social and political life during the period to be surveyed. As a result, the Georgians, like the Balkan Slavs, looked confidently to Orthodox Muscovy as a potential deliverer. The consequences of this touching but at times misguided confidence will be demonstrated more fully in subsequent chapters.

2

The Government of the Mukhranian Viceroys, 1658-1723

COMPARED with the mediaeval kingdom of Georgia, the Georgia of the seventeenth century in its disunity was a political patchwork, and only the mountain clans of the Georgian highlands were free from some form of alien suzerainty. As has been observed, the formerly united kingdom was now divided at the Suram Range into Eastern Georgia under the Persians (consisting of the kingdoms of Kakhet'i and K'art'li, with the city of Tiflis) and Western Georgia (with its capital at K'ut'ais), which was usually known as Imeret'i, meaning "the land on the far side" (i.e., from Tiflis). Under intermittent Turkish overlordship, it was weakened by the secession of several of the principal provinces, which had become separate principalities.

This cleavage had its origin in ancient times, when Iberia to the east was quite independent of the kingdom of Colchis-Lazica bordering on the Black Sea. It was only at the beginning of the eleventh century that the concept of an all-Georgian state could be put into effect, but Mongol invasions soon broke the unity. From the tyranny of Hulagu Khan, King David Narin fled to K'ut'ais in 1258, and set up a separate court there, leaving his cousin, King David Ulugh, "Big David," to reign under the Mongol governor general in Tiflis. The feudal magnates were encouraged by the Mongols to assert their independence of the Georgian crown.

This trend continued, in spite of attempts at permanent reunification in the fifteenth century under King Alexander I. By the end of that century, the disintegration of the central monarchy was complete. This was at a time when the general trend in Europe and the Near East was toward centralization and reinforcement of state authority. In 1485 the Tudors in England emerged triumphant after the Wars of the Roses. In France, the ruthless Louis XI had stamped out the remnants of feudal turbulence. The Grand Princes Ivan the Great and Basil were swallowing up the independent duchies and free cities of Muscovy, and laying the foundations of modern Russia. The sultans of Turkey on the Bosphorus were building up an empire straddling, menacingly, the Orient and the Occident. In Persia, Shah Ismail Safavi founded a new, national dynasty, giving vent to his people's reborn religious and patriotic fervor. But in Georgia, cut off from the upsurge of Renaissance civilization and deprived of the sinews of power, the political clock was turned back rather than forward. Here, there was no sturdy middle class to provide kings with the resources to vanquish feudal pretension. If any Georgian sovereign attempted to head a movement of national revival, he soon found his way blocked by the jealous particularism of his vassals, ready even to lend a hand to some foreign invader sooner than sacrifice precious privilege for the nation's good.

Tiflis was the seat of the senior branch of the Bagratid royal house, which had ruled in Georgia without interruption since the eighth century. At the breakup of the Georgian kingdom in the fifteenth century, K'art'li with Tiflis had devolved on the senior line, Kakhet'i on another branch, and Imeret'i on yet a third. Tiflis continued to rank first in national esteem as Georgia's Dedak'alak'i, or Mother-City. Indeed, the K'art'lian capital and court at Tiflis always retained a certain metropolitan character. Tiflis was situated at a focal point where there was ready access to Persia via Tabriz or else via Baku and the Caspian Sea; to Russia via the Caspian and Astrakhan, or over the Caucasus through the Dariel Pass; to Turkey via Kars and Erzerum. Under an ordered administration, Tiflis tended to predominate as the principal commercial and cultural center for all Georgia, irrespective of political divisions. This became even more noticeable when the West Georgian kingdom centered on K'ut'ais became prey during the seventeenth century to civil war. The Dadian of Mingrelia with his capital at Zugdidi, the Gurieli prince regnant at Ozurget'i, and the Sharvashidze dynast at Sukhum, became virtually independent monarchs, rendering fealty to the sultan of Turkey rather than to their own king at K'ut'ais.

After subjugating K'art'li and Kakhet'i in his ruthless campaigns of 1614–16, Shah 'Abbas I did not completely suppress the royal Bagratid line. The Persians contented themselves in K'art'li with arrogating the right to nominate as their *vali* or viceroy in Georgia (or Gurjistan, to use the Turco-Persian name for the country) whichever of the Bagratid princes seemed most amenable to Persian interests. In the Persian official hierarchy, the viceroy of Georgia ranked as the third of the grand emirs, immediately following the viceroys of Arabistan and Luristan.[1] The shahs made it a condition that the viceroys of K'art'li, outwardly at least, abjure Christianity and embrace Shi'a Mohammedanism. Persian garrisons were stationed in the citadel of Tiflis and at a few other key points. Among the Georgians, the shah's viceroy was still known by the title of *mep'e* or king, as previously. Internally, he retained virtually absolute power over his subjects, within the limits of custom and the barriers imposed by local institutions, but had to refer questions of war and foreign affairs to his overlord, the shah. According to the French traveler Tournefort, who visited Georgia in 1701, the Georgians paid a capitation tax to the shah of Persia at the rate of 6 silver 'abbasi a head (equivalent to 1 ruble and 20 copecks silver of the time). The collection of this capitation tax was farmed out to a contractor at 300 tomans a year.[2] The Georgians of K'art'li, Tournefort adds, presented to the shah as homage 4 hawks every year, 7 slaves every three years, 24 cartloads of wine annually, and other gifts. Besides all these, many of the most handsome girls were reserved for the shah's harem.[3]

In the other Eastern Georgian kingdom, Kakhet'i, the Persians were less indulgent toward the people's national proclivities. After King T'eimuraz I of Kakhet'i had been defeated and expelled from his domains by King Rostom in 1648, a succession of Persian gov-

[1] Minorsky, ed., *Tadhkirat al-Muluk*, p. 44.

[2] Equivalent at that time to £900 sterling, or 3,000 rubles silver (see Rabino, *Coins, Medals, and Seals,* Table IV), or 18,000 gold marks in modern money (see Hinz, in *Der Islam,* XXIX, 132).

[3] Tournefort, *Voyage into the Levant,* III, 149–50.

ernors were appointed. Their rule proved highly vexatious to the Christian population.

The position was somewhat different in the Turkish zone of influence. The kings of Imeret'i did not officially recognize Turkish overlordship. Indeed, both King Alexander of Imeret'i and Levan Dadian of Mingrelia attempted in 1650 and 1638 respectively to place themselves under Russian suzerainty and protection. But though they did not receive investiture from the sultan, they were forced to pay a tribute to the sublime Porte (the sultans' court at Constantinople), partly in the form of slaves. All the Western Georgian princes were so weakened by civil war and economic decline that they were at the mercy of the sultan's frontier representatives, the Turco-Georgian Jaqeli pashas at Akhaltsikhe, who often played a decisive role in the political intrigues of the Western Georgian kingdom. These pashas were adept at exploiting the internal rivalries between the kings of Imeret'i and their nominal vassals. The Ottoman government could probably have annexed the country outright, but preferred to keep it as a sort of nursery for slaves and for women for the sultan's seraglio.[4] Professor B. Lewis points out that this excellent source of slaves and eunuchs would have been lost to the Turks had Western Georgia been placed under direct Ottoman rule, since Islamic law forbids the enslavement or mutilation of even Jews and Christians once they are living under the direct aegis of Moslem rule.[5]

Internally, the system of public administration in the various Georgian kingdoms and principalities was still modeled on the pattern evolved in the great days of Queen T'amar. The principal difference, of course, was that instead of one court and government for all Georgia, there now existed several, with the result that each department of state was much shrunk in its functions and jurisdiction. Economic decline and exhausting wars had also resulted in a general deterioration of the standard of administration.

In Eastern Georgia, a seventeenth-century innovation was the

[4] Chardin, *Voyages en Perse,* I, 252–53; "Wanderer," pseud., *Notes on the Caucasus,* pp. 238–39.

[5] For the orthodox Islamic doctrine on slavery, see the article " 'Abd" in the *Encyclopaedia of Islam.* Of particular interest is the fiction of a constant Holy War prevailing between the Islamic and non-Islamic worlds, including Georgia, rendering legitimate the importing of captives from lands outside the pale.

renaming of the Georgian high officials in accordance with the usage of the Persian capital. This change was introduced by King Rostom, who had long served as prefect of Isfahan. As a result, the titles of the principal functionaries at the court of Tiflis, as enumerated by the eighteenth-century authority, Prince Wakhusht, in his classic treatise on the geography and customs of Georgia, correspond to those found in the official hierarchy of Safavi Persia.[6] The head of the administrative hierarchy and paymaster general of the armed forces became the *qorchi-bashi;* he corresponded to the Persian officer of the same title, who was "the most important of the Pillars of the Mighty State." The head of the royal bodyguard of the Georgian kings at Tiflis was now called the *qullar-aghasi,* or lord of the royal slaves, and he too corresponded precisely to the Persian dignitary of that name. The Georgian commander in chief bore the Persian title of *sardar,* or general. Other important functionaries who are enumerated by Prince Wakhusht, or whose names occur in documents of the period, are the grand master of ceremonies, the master of the royal table, the lord chamberlain, the lord chief justice or *mdivan-begi* (meaning head of the high court or senate—another Persian title), the *mehmandar* (an officer charged with the reception of distinguished visitors), the chief scribe, the keeper of the royal seal, the chief usher, and the head porter of the palace.[7]

Outside the capital, the provincial administration of Georgia was carried on mainly by the dukes or *erist'avs* (a Georgian title meaning literally heads of the people). In olden times, these dukes had been designated at will by the monarch to govern each province on the royal behalf. Prince Wakhusht specifically states that until about the fifteenth century, these offices were not hereditary: when a duke or other royal officer died, his sword and steed were delivered to the king, to be handed on to the eldest son of the deceased if the king saw fit, or else to some other nobleman of the king's choice.[8]

With the final partition of the monarchy in the fifteenth century, the royal power was dispersed among three branches of the Bagratid house. It was now impossible to prevent the duchies from becoming

---

[6] Wakhusht, *Description géographique de la Géorgie,* pp. 38-41; Minorsky, ed., *Tadhkirat al-Muluk.*

[7] A more complete list of officials is given in M.-F. Brosset, *Histoire de la Géorgie,* Introduction, pp. CLXIV–CLXX.

[8] Wakhusht, *Description géographique de la Géorgie,* pp. 38-39.

hereditary. The dukes set themselves up as autonomous potentates. In Eastern Georgia, the most influential were the duke of the K'sani valley and the duke of the Aragvi valley, both nominally subject to the king of K'art'li. These dukes used to carry on private wars, and even at times enter into independent negotiations with neighboring chieftains and princes. Their power was not broken until the mid-eighteenth century. In Western Georgia, after the princes regnant of Mingrelia, Guria, and Abkhazia, the most formidable magnate was the duke of Ratcha, a district on the upper reaches of the River Rioni. At the end of the seventeenth century, we even find a duke of Ratcha delivering his sovereign, King Alexander IV of Imeret'i, into the hands of Alexander's enemy, the king of K'art'li, who put him to death.[9] In the 1760s we shall find Duke Rostom of Ratcha heading the opposition to King Solomon of Imeret'i, until Solomon crushes the duke and abolishes the autonomy of the duchy.

As a counter to the usurpations of the dukes, the kings of Georgia often had recourse to the appointment of *mouravs,* or deputy governors, who answered directly to the central government. In Kakhet'i, the most easterly of the Georgian kingdoms, this important change was carried out in the fifteenth century, when Giorgi I "abolished all the dukes of Heret'i and Kakhet'i, and replaced them by deputy governors in each locality of any importance." [10] In K'art'li and Imeret'i this process was far slower and less complete. Though many of the deputy governors gradually acquired more or less hereditary status, they provided the state with a valuable prop to withstand the encroachments of the dukes.

The mountain and nomad clans retained their old tribal and patriarchal organization. The Khevsurs, for example, acknowledged the authority of a chief half-spiritual, half-temporal, known as the *khevis-beri* or archdeacon (literally, "monk of the glen"), who acted as arbiter in legal as well as ecclesiastical matters. The Tatar nomads who grazed their flocks in Borchalo and other steppe districts in Georgia's southeastern marches had their own headmen, who some-

---

[9] Wakhusht, "Histoires particulières . . . de l'Iméreth," in M.-F. Brosset, tr. and ed., *Histoire de la Géorgie,* II, Part 1, 294–99.

[10] Wakhusht, "Histoires particulières . . . du Cakheth," in M.-F. Brosset, tr. and ed., *Histoire de la Géorgie,* II, Part 1, 148; "Code de Vakhtang VI," in Karst, ed., *Corpus Juris Ibero-Caucasici,* II, 264–65.

times functioned in consultation with deputy governors appointed
by the Georgian king.

The power of the kings depended, of course, on the loyalty of
their armed forces. Apart from occasional troops of mercenaries, the
Georgian royal armies consisted of feudal levies. These were organized in each of the three kingdoms in territorial groupings referred to as "banners." The men of each banner or standard were
recruited from the domains of one of the principal grandees.[11] Each
banner was commanded by either the grandee himself or by a member of the Georgian royal family. For example, in the reign of
Wakhtang VI (1711–23), the four banners of K'art'li were those of
Sabarat'ashvilo (domains of the Orbeliani and Barat'ashvili families),
Mukhran, Samilakhoro (Amilakhori family), and Satsitsiano
(Tsitsishvili family). They were commanded by members of the
royal house, the last named by the king in person. When fully
mobilized, each banner was composed of nine or ten thousand
effectives. When a campaign was imminent, the head of each banner
was ordered to assemble his men at a given time and place. It was
usual for the constituent units to provide their own food and forage
for a month, after which they either lived off the country or received victuals from the king. Pay seems to have been irregular, if
not nonexistent, plunder the principal incentive. A Russian observer
of the time records that military organization was rather loose and
informal, but morale and discipline good. The levies were armed
with muskets, lances, and swords, and most of them were mounted.[12]

A similar system prevailed in the kingdom of Kakhet'i, as witnessed by a charter of King David (Imam-Quli-Khan) of the year
1710, defining the battle order of the banner commanded by the
archbishop of Rust'avi, who headed the left wing of the Kakhian
army.[13] It is noteworthy that the princes of the church were still
leading their vassals into battle up to the end of the eighteenth
century.

The revenue of the Georgian kings was derived from a large

[11] Further details may be found in Wakhusht, *Description géographique de la
Géorgie,* pp. 14–15 and 34, and Index, under Bannières.

[12] Report of Ivan Tolstoy (1722), published in M.-F. Brosset, "Notice historique
sur . . . Wakhtang VI," *Bulletin Historico-Philologique,* III (1847), 336–37.

[13] Edited by Karst, in *Corpus Juris Ibero-Caucasici,* II, 362–71.

number of different sources. Most substantial was the income from crownlands. About the year 1700 the private domains of the king of K'art'li were bringing in an annual revenue of over 600 tomans in cash, equivalent at the exchange rate of that time to 6,000 rubles silver. The shah of Persia further granted his viceroy the king of K'art'li an annual cash subsidy of 300 tomans. Among other sources of revenue may be mentioned the state brandy monopoly, farmed out at 35 tomans (350 rubles silver); the income from the famous thermal spa waters of Tiflis, amounting to 12 tomans; and the municipal tax paid by Tiflis shopkeepers. Special dues were levied on irrigation channels, poultry, vineyards, and other sources of agricultural income. The peasantry were liable to a poll tax, payable to the king or to their feudal lords according to whether they belonged to crown or private domains. A levy of 3 silver 'abbasi (abazi), equivalent to 60 copecks, had to be paid to the exchequer by newly married couples. Fines for various offences also helped to enrich the treasury. Another substantial item was the receipts of the customs-houses situated on the frontiers between Eastern and Western Georgia, between Georgia and Persia, and at the gates of the principal towns. In 1701 the municipal customs of Tiflis alone were worth nearly 500 tomans. A special tax was levied when serfs and prisoners of war were sold into slavery.

In the Georgian civil service no regular salary was paid to the officers of state, but each one had the right to certain specified fees and perquisites. Thus, the royal secretaries had a sliding scale of fees for drawing up charters and documents, varying according to the sums involved and the wealth of the client. The prefect of Tiflis had his share of the city customs dues. Other functionaries were rewarded in a similar way, in accordance with ancient custom, or on the basis of charters of privilege granted by the king.

Augmenting the cash income of the Georgian court at Tiflis, the king's household was fed and maintained almost entirely by offerings in kind from his loyal subjects. Each peasant family, for example, provided annually one sheep for the king's table, which might total some 40,000 sheep a year. The king also received, according to contemporary observation, the prodigious quantity of 40,000 loads of wine. We find in the Dasturlamali, or Manual of Administrative Practice, drafted by King Wakhtang VI, a note that market gardeners were expected to keep the royal table supplied with vegetables; those who failed to do so were forbidden to offer their produce for sale in the public market.[14]

With regard to the revenues of the other Eastern Georgian kingdom, Kakhet'i, our information is less detailed. For much of the period under review, this district was ruled directly by governors appointed by the Persian shah. Persian sources list the total emoluments of the Persian military governor at Zagem in Kakhet'i at just under 6,000 tomans; out of this the governor had to maintain a garrison of 1,200 Persian regular troops. The Persian commandant at Qara-Aghach, also in Kakhet'i, had an income of 636 tomans, and had to maintain a garrison of 210 men. These figures are evidently made up of army pay received from the Persian central treasury, combined with what the Persian governors were able to extort from the local Georgian population.[15] At other periods, when the legitimate dynasty of the Georgian Bagratids of Kakhet'i ruled the kingdom, taxes and contributions in kind were levied on much the same basis as in K'art'li.

On passing to Western Georgia, one finds that the financial resources of the state had been much impaired by the virtual secession of the autonomous princes regnant of Mingrelia, Guria, and Abkhazia. This meant, of course, that the income of the kings of Imeret'i was greatly reduced. The autonomous princes regnant do not appear to have contributed anything to the royal treasury at K'ut'ais, but as there is little material in Georgian sources, it is necessary to rely on the estimates of foreign travelers for an appreciation of the financial position of Western Georgia. In the sixteenth century, for example, Ogier Ghiselin de Busbecq, ambassador of the Holy Roman Empire in Constantinople from 1554 to 1562, noted in his *Turkish Letters,* that very little money was in circulation in Western Georgia. In

[14] These financial data are drawn from M.-F. Brosset, *Histoire de la Géorgie,* Introduction, pp. CIII–CIX (Fortune du roi; Économie de sa maison); Karst, *Corpus Juris Ibero-Caucasici,* II, 317–55 (Des impôts en général); Tournefort, *Voyage into the Levant,* III, 149.

[15] The figures are taken from Minorsky, ed., *Tadhkirat al-Muluk,* pp. 101–2.

Mingrelia, taxes were paid in kind, liberally providing the local ruler, who bore the title of Dadian,

with all that his mode of life requires in the way of food, drink, and clothing, and for rewarding his household and those who serve him well. He has inexhausible supplies both from the tithes and other royal dues, and also from the presents which are continually showered upon him.[16]

A hundred years later, the French traveler Chardin related that the Mingrelian Dadian of his time had an income equivalent to 20,000 French crowns. This was derived from customs dues on imports and exports, from the sale of slaves to the Turks, and from plunder and pillage. This sum represented net gain to the prince as his retainers served him without pay and the ruler's private domains furnished the court sufficiently with food and wine. It was also the custom for each village to entertain the Dadian and his following for a few days each year. These visits were made the opportunity for collecting taxes.[17]

As will be related subsequently, Western Georgia was ravaged from the mid-seventeenth century onward by a particularly savage civil war. This had a disastrous effect on the country's governmental and economic system. As a result, the income of the king of Imeret'i and those of the autonomous princes regnant were drastically curtailed. No official figures are available for the early eighteenth century, but significant evidence of economic decline is provided by an important unpublished document in the French Foreign Office archives. This document, a resolution of the Chamber of Commerce of Marseilles, dated May 25, 1747, is concerned with a suggested French commercial station which the French ambassador at Constantinople wished to set up in Western Georgia. From information laid before the chamber of commerce, however, it transpired that the Georgians were reluctant to provide facilities for foreign merchants to settle among them, and that Georgian merchants who

[16] E. S. Forster, tr. and ed., *The Turkish Letters of Ogier Ghiselin de Busbecq,* pp. 128-29.

[17] Chardin, *Voyages en Perse,* I, 137-38, 149-50. According to the Russian envoys who visited Mingrelia in 1639-40, Levan Dadian received at that time an annual subsidy of 1,000 tomans from the shah of Persia; on the other hand, he was expected to pay a tribute to the Sultan of Turkey amounting to 800 arshins of linen cloth and 30 or 40 slaves a year. (Likhachev, *Puteshestviya Russkikh poslov,* pp. 212, 217.)

visited Constantinople, bringing wax, leather, and other local commodities to exchange for French cloth and manufactured goods, incurred far less expense than would European merchants settling in Georgia itself. Furthermore, the Marseilles Chamber of Commerce reported to the French Foreign Ministry that Western Georgia was an extremely poor country. Money was so scarce there that trade was conducted principally by bartering cattle or slaves. It was impossible to recover debts in cash. Even the patriarch of Western Georgia had had to settle his debts with a French creditor by giving him slaves in payment.[18] The report quoted here thus gives an eloquent picture of the decline, both economic and social, into which Western Georgia had sunk by mid-eighteenth century, when it seems clear that the public revenue had shrunk to a fraction of even the modest figures quoted earlier by Chardin.

Under the subject of finance, it may be of interest to include some details on the coinage of Georgia during the period under review. From the time of King Giorgi X of K'art'li (1600–1605), Eastern Georgia had been minting silver in the name of the shahs of Persia. The earliest specimens of this type were minted in Tiflis in the year A.H. 1013 (corresponding to A.D. 1604). These coins were of standard Persian Safavi design, and carried the values of the whole 'abbasi (called in Georgian, "abazi"), the mahmudi (or half 'abbasi), and the shahi (in Georgian, "shauri"). The value of these coins in European currencies naturally fluctuated according to the Persian exchange rates, but the 'abbasi or abazi was reckoned in 1701 as worth 1 French livre, 20 copecks silver, or slightly over a shilling sterling.[19] These silver coins did not bear the names of the kings of K'art'li, but were inscribed with those of the shahs of Persia, embodied in poetic couplets in flowery Persian. On the other side of the coin would appear a pious Mohammedan formula with the names of the twelve holy imams. The mint town and date were also inscribed.

The minting of silver was controlled by the central Persian mint,

[18] Archives of the French Foreign Ministry, "Réflexions de la Chambre de Commerce de Marseille sur la proposition de faire un Établissement de Commerce en Géorgie," in Correspondance Politique, Perse, VII, 202–4.

[19] See the chart in Rabino, Coins, Medals, and Seals, Table IV, Value of Iranian Coins in Foreign Currencies.

but the striking of copper coins, often called "autonomous coppers," was left to local finance departments. Every town of importance in the Persian empire had its own special issue, with characteristic designs. The autonomous coppers of Tiflis show a lion, a ship, and several other devices. Later in the Safavi period, under the feeble rule of Shah Sultan Husayn, the K'art'lian viceroys at Tiflis reverted to a more specifically Georgian type of coinage. While not infringing on the shah of Persia's monopoly of the silver coinage, new patterns were introduced for the copper, incorporating the initials or monogram of the Georgian ruler of the time. Thus, the Prince Regent Simon minted copper coins in the year A.H. 1124/A.D. 1712, showing a dragon, with the Georgian letters S.M.N., the abbreviation for Svimon. Simon's nephew Bak'ar struck in 1717-18 some handsome copper pieces with a peacock design, with the letters B.K'.R, for Bak'ar.[20]

In Western Georgia, the minting of money had almost ceased during this period. It is true that Chardin and Tavernier speak of the striking of coins by the Dadian of Mingrelia and the kings of Imeret'i,[21] but this was done on a very small scale. It is probable that the coins struck in Western Georgia consisted of crude imitations of Persian silver: Father Lamberti notes that Levan Dadian of Mingrelia (1605-57) struck some coins "with Arabic inscriptions, resembling those current in Persia, called 'abbasi, but the local people prefer Spanish Reals and foreign currency." [22] This indication is confirmed by the collection of the American Numismatic Society, which includes a few crude imitations of silver coins of the type struck at Tiflis.

Gold coins were not minted in Georgia, nor indeed to any great

[20] This brief survey of Georgian currency of this period is based on the writer's personal examination of the collections of the American Numismatic Society in New York, and of the British Museum Coin Room. See further: Langlois, *Essai de classification des suites monétaires de la Géorgie;* Karst, *Précis de numismatique géorgienne,* and the literature quoted therein; Poole, *Catalogue of the Coins of the Shahs of Persia in the British Museum;* Lang, *Studies in the Numismatic History of Georgia,* pp. 90-97; Kapanadze, *K'art'uli numizmatika,* pp. 91-96.

[21] Chardin, *Voyages en Perse,* I, 148; Tavernier, *Les six voyages,* I, 449-50.

[22] Lamberti, "Relation de la Mengrellie," in Thévenot, *Relations de divers voyages,* I, 43. See also Likhachev, *Puteshestviya Russkikh poslov,* p. 217.

extent throughout Persia. Gold pieces struck by the shahs were intended mainly as commemorative medals. Larger transactions were carried on in Venetian and Hungarian gold ducats, Turkish sequins, Dutch crowns, German thalers, and other foreign currencies.[23]

Legislation and the dispensing of high justice were personal prerogatives of the Georgian kings, who constituted in their person the supreme tribunal in the land. Laws and administrative decrees were signed and sealed by the king, and countersigned by the chief scribe and perhaps one or more witnesses. After the division of the kingdom in the fifteenth century, the domains of each of the Georgian monarchs were quite small enough to make this practicable.

Appeals and cases of importance were heard by the king in person. The Georgian chronicler Sekhnia Chkheidze records that Wakhtang VI when regent (1703–11) held sessions of his royal tribunal every Wednesday and Friday, and "used to dispense justice to great and small." [24] Under a less able and just sovereign, this system might have disadvantages. We hear of a case where Wakhtang's predecessor, Erekle I, condemned a notorious murderer to death, but then reprieved him on the entreaties of the criminal's wife. One of the king's favorites persuaded Erekle of the bad effect this pardon would have on public opinion. Erekle then ordered the murderer's hand to be cut off, which was done. Changing his mind again, the king dismissed the executioner for not waiting for confirmation of the royal pleasure.[25]

Cases of secondary importance were decided by the court of the *mdivan-begi* or lord chief justice, and then often referred to the king for formal approval. In this connection, it is worth outlining an ordinance of Prince Levan of K'art'li, father of King Wakhtang VI, and himself lord chief justice of Iran, promulgated for Georgia in 1704. The ordinance provides that the *mdivan-begi* should judge

[23] Tournefort, *Voyage into the Levant*, III, 149–50; Rabino, *Coins, Medals, and Seals*, pp. 14–15.

[24] Chkheidze, "Chronicle," in Brosset, tr., *Histoire de la Géorgie*, II, Part 2, 28.

[25] Tournefort, *Voyage into the Levant*, III, 147–48.

all cases of violence among tribesmen and nomads, as well as among the burghers of Tiflis. The lieutenant of police, on the other hand, was given powers of summary jurisdiction when on tour in the provinces. In the city of Tiflis, the prefect was to act as the lord chief justice's deputy when the latter was away. When disputes arose between the serfs or personal retainers of the queen, the queen's major-domo was to settle the affair, unless the king or the lord chief justice were on the spot to administer summary justice. No military commander was to interfere with the course of civil law in his military district without the king's authority. Proceeds of fines were to go to the royal treasury after the deduction of fees due to the appropriate officers of justice.[26] For civil cases and local disputes, there was also a special municipal tribunal, presided over by the *mourav* or prefect of Tiflis, and a bench of two or three burghers, assisted by the city provost, his lieutenant, and a staff of ushers and bailiffs.[27]

In an emergency, the king might appoint an extraordinary commission to proceed to the scene of some outrage or conspiracy and deal with it on the spot. Such a proceeding, for example, was adopted by King Simon in 1590 to deal with an outbreak of brigandage.[28] A similar procedure was sometimes used to settle land disputes between the provincial nobility. The kings themselves might hold touring assizes. This was especially common in Western Georgia. The subjects of the Dadian of Mingrelia would wait by the roadside for the ruler to pass, and then kneel before his horse to hand him petitions. The Dadian would either decide the matter on the spot, or else direct the disputants to appear at his encampment in the evening.[29]

With regard to the laws themselves, the outstanding monument of Georgian legislation for the period is the code of Wakhtang VI

---

[26] Karst, *Corpus Juris Ibero-Caucasici*, II, 60–62.

[27] See the statute defining the rights and duties of the prefects of Tiflis, in Karst, *Corpus Juris Ibero-Caucasici*, II, 274–75. Further details about the prefect's duties are given in Ioseliani, *Goroda, sushchestvovavshie i sushchestvuiushchie v Gruzii*, pp. 82–86.

[28] T'aqaishvili, ed., *Sak'art'velos sidzveleni*, II, 23–24.

[29] Chardin, *Voyages en Perse*, I, 138; Lamberti, "Relation de la Mengrellie," in Thévenot, *Relations de divers voyages*, I, 38.

of K'art'li, who governed as prince regent from 1703 to 1711 and as king, with interruptions, from 1711 to 1724.

Wakhtang's regency was a period of intense administrative activity and reform. He felt himself much hampered by the lack of a complete legal code. Earlier royal codes had become obsolete, and no longer corresponded to the conditions of the time. The long series of ordinances and decrees issued at various times by succeeding monarchs merely made the confusion worse. It was clearly essential that no time be lost in drawing up a comprehensive legal code which would embody the best features of traditional Georgian usages and define the rights and duties of each class of citizens.

With this in view, Wakhtang set up an advisory commission which included his brother the Catholicos Domenti III and other church dignitaries, Prince Erekle of Mukhran, Duke Giorgi of the Aragvi and Duke David of the K'sani, the commander in chief, General Luarsab Orbeliani, the Grand Constable Avt'andil, and other dignitaries.[30]

This commission began by collecting and recording certain non-Georgian bodies of law which had been introduced into Georgia and adopted in earlier periods. It was intended that these should give precedent and guidance for judges in cases for which Wakhtang's own code failed to provide, and should also serve as a basis for comparison in the drafting of a new code.[31] These non-Georgian codices consulted and set down by the commission include the laws of Moses and those of the Byzantine Emperors Leo VI the Wise (886–912) and Constantine Porphyrogenitus (913–59).[32]

[30] Wakhtang VI, "Code de Vakhtang VI," in Karst, ed., *Corpus Juris Ibero-Caucasici*, I, 42–43. This is the standard translation of Wakhtang's code. The six fascicles of Karst's work comprise Wakhtang's own code, in French translation (Vol. 1); commentary (Vols. II and III); the codes of Bek'a and Aghbugha, grand constables of Samtskhe in the fourteenth and fifteenth centuries (Vol. IV); the laws of King Giorgi the Brilliant, c.1314–46 (Vol. V); the Nomocanon of the Georgian catholicos-patriarchs (Vol. VI). The Georgian text of Wakhtang's laws was edited by T'. Enuk'idze at Tiflis in 1951.

[31] See Vacheishvili, *Narkvevebi k'art'uli samart'lis istoriidan*, I, 18.

[32] Wakhtang's version of the Byzantine laws is printed only in the Russian translation of Frenkel and Bak'radze, *Sbornik zakonov Gruzinskogo tsaria Vakhtanga VI*, in the section headed "Zakony grecheskie" ("Greek laws"); for background and bibliography, see Vasiliev, *Histoire de l'Empire Byzantin*, I, 448–52.

Wakhtang and his advisers also incorporated a Georgian translation of the ancient laws of Armenia, as preserved and handed down since the fall of the Armenian kingdom in the eleventh century by the catholicoi of Echmiadzin.[33] These Armenian laws had special relevance because of the large and privileged Armenian communities that existed in Tiflis, Gori, and other principal towns.

Turning now to the ancient laws of the kings of Georgia, Wakhtang reedited those of Giorgi the Brilliant (c.1314–46),[34] and reedited as well the code of Bek'a II and Aghbugha, both of whom governed as grand constables of Samtskhe c.1361–91 and c.1444–51, respectively. The latter compilation also embodies laws attributed to King David the Builder (1089–1125). Advancing to more recent times, Wakhtang incorporated the Nomocanon of Catholicos Evdemon of Abasgia (sixteenth century), as revised by the Catholicos Malak'ia (c.1603–39). It should be borne in mind that this Nomocanon is not confined solely to matters of church discipline, but constitutes an important body of civil and criminal law tending to reinforce the authority of both catholicos and king.[35]

This somewhat heterogeneous body of legislation is crowned by Wakhtang's own laws, in 267 articles. These give definitive guidance to lay judges and take precedence over all the other codes previously enumerated, apart from those embodying canon law. Study of Wakhtang's laws aids understanding of the spirit and structure of Georgian society, while the student of comparative institutions cannot fail to be impressed by the many curious features of Georgian criminal procedure.[36]

The system of judicial ordeals in use in Georgia to the very end

---

[33] This Armenian code translated under Wakhtang's instructions embodies the twelfth-century Armenian version of the so-called Syro-Roman code (paras. 1–150) and the laws of the twelfth-century legislator Mkhit'ar Gosh (paras. 151–431). See Karst, *Armenisches Rechtsbuch* (Strasbourg and Venice, 1905–6); "Code de Vakhtang VI," in Karst, *Corpus Juris Ibero-Caucasici,* I, 10; Melik'set'-Begi, *Corpus Juris Armeniaci, versio Georgica.*

[34] See the English version by Sir J. O. Wardrop, "Laws of King George V of Georgia," *Journal of the Royal Asiatic Society,* July, 1914.

[35] See further on Georgian canon law, Karst, "Recherches sur l'histoire du droit ecclésiastique Carthvélien," in *Archives d'Histoire du Droit Oriental,* Vol. I–II (Brussels, 1937–38).

[36] See Holldack, *Zwei Grundsteine.*

of the monarchy is remarkable, and seems a relic of some bygone age. The ordeals prescribed in Wakhtang's code, following ancient national custom, are strikingly similar to those in force in mediaeval Europe, including Russia and the Latin kingdoms of the Levant.[37] The main Georgian ordeals were: (1) ordeal by single combat; (2) the ordeals of boiling water and red-hot iron; (3) solemn oath on an icon; (4) the ceremony known as saddling oneself with sin, an ordeal apparently peculiar to Georgia.

For the application of these modes of trial, precise rules were laid down. Single combat was reserved for cases of high treason, felony, spoliation of the royal treasury, and sacrilege. Accuser and accused had to fast and pray for forty days, and draw up and sign a prayer of the following tenor: "O God just and equitable, I pray and implore Thee not to hold me this day to account for my other sins! But if I have been innocent of what this man falsely lays to my charge, then deliver up his head to me; in the opposite event, I am ready to abandon my head to him!" This prayer was to be attached to the combatants' necks, or the sheaths of their lances. The king and his army were to maintain fair play at the combat, the former pronouncing judgment in accordance with the verdict of arms.

That ordeal by single combat was far from a dead letter in Wakhtang's time is attested by several cases in the annals of the period. Thus, in 1653, the heir presumptive of K'art'li, Prince Luarsab, was killed during a hunt. A certain Georgian noble was accused by another knight of murdering the prince. Trial by single combat was ordered. The duel took place opposite the royal palace in Tiflis, and both parties were gravely wounded. The accuser was judged vanquished, and imprisoned.[38] Again, Chardin tells of another instance about 1670, when rumors spread by a former lover

---

[37] See Haxthausen, *Transkaukasia*, II, 267–77; H. C. Lea, *Superstition and Force* (4th ed.; Philadelphia, 1892), Book III; "Sud Bozhii," in Brokgaus-Efron, *Entsiklopedicheskii Slovar'*; G. Vernadsky, *Medieval Russian Laws* (New York, 1947), p. 12; P. W. Topping, *Feudal Institutions as Revealed in the Assizes of Romania* (Philadelphia, 1949), p. 163.

[38] Karst, *Corpus Juris Ibero-Caucasici*, II, 107–9, citing Brosset, *Chronique géorgienne;* Zacharie le Diacre, "Histoire des Sofis," in M.-F. Brosset, *Collection d'historiens arméniens,* II, 119–21.

resulted in the rupture of the engagement of a noble lady affianced to a scion of the royal family. It was decided that only a duel could elicit the truth of these allegations. The lady's champion, her brother, was about to engage the slanderer in single combat when a squad of soldiers arrived and separated the combatants. Chardin adds that the Georgians called trial by single combat "going to the tribunal of God," and were convinced of its reliability.[39] We also have the authority of Father Lamberti that ordeal by single combat was regularly practiced in seventeenth-century Mingrelia.[40]

The ordeals of boiling water and red-hot iron were prescribed in Wakhtang's code for offences of treachery, church-robbing, and adultery. The normal method of administering the first ordeal was to drop a copper or silver cross into a cauldron. After the accused had pulled it out of the boiling water, his arm was enclosed for three days in a bag, and if it showed no sign of scalding he was acquitted. That this ordeal was also current in seventeenth-century Mingrelia is attested by Father Lamberti.[41] For the hot iron, the defendant's hand was covered with a sheet of paper on which the iron was placed; he then had to take three leaps with the iron on the paper before throwing it from him. If unburnt, he was considered innocent.

Perhaps the most singular of these ordeals was that known as saddling oneself with sin, prescribed for trivial offences involving property worth less than a marchil, or sixty copecks. The accused was to take the plaintiff upon his back and make this declaration: "May God hold me responsible for thy sins at the Last Judgement, and may I be judged in thy place, if this deed has really been committed by me." Readiness to perform this ritual was regarded as proof of innocence. Among the Georgian mountain clan of the Khevsurs, a variation of this ordeal was used in cases of dispute over land. The plaintiff had to place a clod of earth on his neck and say, "May the sin of the earth be upon me if I lie; the field in dispute belongs to me." [42]

[39] *Voyages en Perse,* II, 154–55.
[40] Lamberti, "Relation de la Mengrellie," in Thévenot, *Relations de divers voyages,* I, 37.
[41] *Ibid.*
[42] Karst, *Corpus Juris Ibero-Caucasici,* II, 39.

It has been conjectured that some of these forms of ordeal may have filtered through to Georgia from the Frankish kingdoms established by the Crusaders in the Levant.[43] But it is more likely that they evolved independently, though sometimes they paralleled the system practiced in Western Europe. We may rather see in the ordeals employed in Georgia survivals of a far earlier era, when Georgia was under the sway of Mazdeist Persia. The Georgian annals and early lives of saints, together with the findings of archaeology, all point to a profound influence exerted by Arsacid and Sasanian Persia on the evolution of Georgian institutions in pre-Mohammedan times.[44] It is well known that the administration of justice in ancient Iran involved many types of ordeal.[45] In Achaemenid times the judgment of Mithra was invoked by the ordeal of boiling water.[46] Under the Sasanians, the ordeals of fire and molten metal were in current use.[47] It is thus highly probable that the Georgian system of ordeals of Christian times derived from those practiced in pagan Transcaucasia under Persian suzerainty. Certain features, of course, were modified to harmonize with Christian beliefs. This was also the case in the West, where many of the ordeals current in mediaeval Europe had been adapted from the heathen judicial rites of the ancient Teutons.[48] In the remote hill districts of Georgia, where Russian influence was slow in penetrating, the ordeals prescribed in Wakhtang's code have remained in use almost until the present day.[49]

Another important feature of Wakhtang's code is the elaborate system of wergild or blood-money, prescribed for every conceivable variety of tort from murder downwards. A specific monetary value was assigned to the blood of members of any given class of society, a certain proportion of which went to the exchequer as a fine, the remainder to the injured party or his heir.

[43] M. Kovalevskii, *Zakon i obychai na Kavkaze,* I, 180.

[44] Berdzenishvili, Javakhishvili, and Janashia, *Istoriia Gruzii,* pp. 106–10.

[45] Lea, *Superstition and Force,* pp. 265–67.

[46] A. T. Olmstead, *The History of the Persian Empire* (Chicago, 1948), p. 130.

[47] A. Christensen, *L'Iran sous les Sassanides* (Copenhagen, 1936), p. 299; S. J. Bulsara, *The Laws of the Ancient Persians* (Bombay, 1937), p. 715, giving further instances and references.

[48] Lea, *Superstition and Force,* p. 276.

[49] A. Grigolia, *Custom and Justice in the Caucasus,* pp. 154–57.

The payment of wergild was regarded less as a form of punishment than as due compensation to the sufferer or his dependents. The element of moral condemnation scarcely entered into the matter. The rather primitive legal philosophy behind the wergild system has been well defined by Sir James Fitzjames Stephen, who remarks in connection with its application among the Anglo-Saxons:

It should be remembered that in early times the really efficient check upon crimes of violence was the fear of private vengeance, which rapidly degenerated into private war, blood feuds, and anarchy. The institution of the *wer* in itself implies this. . . . It belongs properly to a period when the idea of public punishment for crimes had not yet become familiar; a period when a crime was still regarded to a great extent as an act of war, and in which the object of the law-maker was rather to reconcile antagonists upon established terms than to put down crimes by the establishment of a system of criminal law, as we understand the term.[50]

Sir James's comments help one grasp the significance of the wergild system in seventeenth- and eighteenth-century Georgia. Its persistence reflects the failure of the Georgian kings to crush the feudal magnates and set up a centralized judicial and administrative machinery. In most of the countries of Europe, as well as in the Ottoman Empire, aristocratic turbulence had been thoroughly subdued. Kings and judges wielded power capable of striking terror into the most powerful malefactor. In Georgia, however, provincial separatism, with resultant anarchy, was the rule. It was hopeless for Georgian kings to try to assert regular powers of life and death over their unruly vassals. The traditional wergild system, consecrated by centuries of usage, offered the best hope of maintaining a semblance of law and order. It also has to be remembered that the system of blood-money payments was prevalent in contemporary Persia, with which Georgia had such close political links. For instance, a murderer was obliged to pay 800 piastres to relatives of the victim at

[50] Sir J. F. Stephen, *History of the Criminal Law of England* (London, 1883), I, 59–60. Parallels between the Georgian and Teutonic wergild systems are drawn by Karst, in *Corpus Juris Ibero-Caucasici*, II, 166–70. The laws of Ethelred (tenth century) are instructive in the study of the wergild system in England, while the Njal Saga shows that Icelandic tradition provides further points of comparison. See G. W. Dasent, *The Story of Burnt Njal* (Edinburgh, 1861).

the town of Shiraz in 1787.[51] In remote Persian tribal areas, especially in Kurdistan, murders were settled by blood-money payments until the beginning of the present century.

In setting up a table of wergild rates, Wakhtang was introducing no innovation. It is hard to say exactly when the system of blood-money payments became generally accepted in Georgia. The fourteenth- and fifteenth-century codes of King Giorgi the Brilliant and of Bek'a and Aghbugha contain detailed provisions for the assessment of blood-money, though here the right of the injured family to resort to vendetta is not yet completely abolished. Throughout the Middle Ages Georgian monarchs used to reward devoted service from their subjects by granting charters promoting them to a higher blood-money category.[52] These charters were taken into account by Wakhtang when he drew up his own table of wergild rates. He specified that if the families to whom such charters had been granted in ancient times had since then increased or waned in wealth and importance, this fact would have to be considered in calculating the scale of blood-money to which they were entitled.

Wakhtang's regulations for wergild payments related to the killing of one man by another of equal social standing and blood-money rating may be summarized as follows:

1. No rate of wergild is laid down for the slaying of the king or the catholicos patriarch, who are deemed to have equivalent status as heads of the temporal and spiritual hierarchies. Any crime committed against either of these amounts to high treason.[53]

[51] W. Francklin, *Observations Made on a Tour from Bengal to Persia* (2d ed.; London, 1790), pp. 128–30.

[52] Karst, *Corpus Juris Ibero-Caucasici*, I, 74, and the charters published in the same work, II, 132–48. It should be noted, however, that the earliest of the charters edited by Karst, purporting to date from 841, has been exposed as a partial forgery, and in reality dates from the fourteenth century. See T'aqaishvili, ed., *Sak'art'velos sidzveleni*, II, 12–13. Another important collection of wergild charters is published by S. Kakabadze, in *Saistorio Moambe*, Vol. I, Part 2.

[53] We should note, however, that the wergild system could on occasion become operative as between reigning sovereigns. A remarkable instance of this occurs in the Georgian annals for the year 1645. Some years earlier, King Simon of K'art'li had been slain by partisans of King T'eimuraz of Kakhet'i. King Simon's relative and successor, King Rostom, now threatened to ravage Kakhet'i "in payment for the blood of King Simon." Finally an agreement was concluded whereby King T'eimuraz ceded some villages to Rostom (see Karst, *Corpus Juris Ibero-Caucasici*,

2. The princes and dukes are divided into three classes. Those ranking as grandees (*didebulni*) are assessed at 1,536 tomans (equivalent
to 15,360 rubles silver). The same sum is stipulated for an archbishop of the rank of metropolitan. Only six noblemen are entitled to
rank in this highest category: the dukes of the Aragvi and the
K'sani; the heads of the clans of Amilakhori, Orbeliani, and Tsitsishvili; and the *melik* or lord lieutenant of Somkhet'i (the southern
province of K'art'li, bordering on Armenia). Princes of the second
class, and also subordinate members of clans headed by grandees of
the first class, together with bishops, are assessed at 768 tomans.
The third class of princes, as well as archimandrites of the church,
are rated at 384 tomans.

3. The lesser nobility or squirearchy (*aznaurni*) are likewise divided
into three categories. The highest of these is assessed at 192 tomans,
which is also the blood-money of an abbot; the next, with the foremost members of the merchant guild, at 96 tomans; the third class
of aznaur or squire and the second grade of merchant or burgher, at
48 tomans.

4. In the lower categories are included the *msakhurni* (retainers or
vassal-lieges of the royal family or aristocracy), as well as the third
grade of merchants, both at 24 tomans. At the bottom come peasants
and small tradesmen at 12 tomans. The lower grades of clergy are
assimilated into the last-mentioned groups.

A more rough and ready system has prevailed until quite recent
times among the Georgian mountain clans. For example, a Svan
noble's blood equaled that of two commoners. Among the T'ushians
the distinction was made on a religious basis, a Christian being worth
two Moslems, their wergilds 60 and 30 cows respectively.[54]

From the mediaeval laws of Europe, one can adduce innumerable
parallels to the Georgian scale of wergild rates. For the sake of
brevity, we may content ourselves with recalling the provisions of
the most ancient Russian code, the *Russkaia Pravda,* which prescribes
80 grivna as blood-money for a prince's man and 40 for other classes

---

III, 488–89). In spite of the obvious political motivation in this case, it shows that
wergild could in fact be exacted for the blood of a king, but only if slain by
order of another king.

[54] A. Grigolia, *Custom and Justice in the Caucasus,* p. 146.

of society, and with the later code of King Stephen of Hungary (1514), which orders 50 cattle as blood payment for a noble, 10 for a soldier, and 5 for a villein.

One may ask what Wakhtang's wergild rates amounted to in money values of the time. We have seen, for example, that a *didebuli* or prince magnate was assessed at 1,536 tomans. In terms of the exchange rates of the early eighteenth century, this was roughly equivalent to 15,360 rubles silver, no doubt a substantial fortune when living was cheap and money relatively scarce. The purchasing power of money may be judged from a document of 1707; there, it is learned that in Georgia a sheep cost 2 abazi (i.e., a twenty fifth of a toman, or 40 copecks silver), a cow 6 abazi, and a load of wine 10 abazi.[55] Thus the wergild of a prince magnate was equivalent to the price of 38,400 sheep, 12,800 cattle, or 7,680 loads of wine. At this level, therefore, the prospect of paying wergild must have been a real deterrent to potential troublemakers. It is to be noted that failing payment of the full sum in cash, the offender's jewels, flocks, and serfs were to be accepted as wergild payments. There can have been few private fortunes in Georgia at that time which could bear so substantial a loss without involving their owner in serious financial embarrassment or utter ruin.

The wergild rates enumerated in Wakhtang's code do not apply to all homicides. When a warrior was slain in battle, or a man killed another in self-defense, or dispatched his wife's or servant girl's paramour, then no wergild was due. In certain instances (involving violence between husband and wife) the ecclesiastical court would institute criminal proceedings either instead of or in addition to the imposition of wergild. Moreover, if a peasant or a member of the squirearchy killed a person of higher standing, he would have to pay one and a half times the basic rate, and probably suffer some criminal penalty as well. Bandits who murdered their victims were liable for a triple assessment, or they might be sentenced and executed by the criminal court.

Besides homicide, almost every form of injury or insult had its official scale of compensation. For seduction of a wife, the corespond-

[55] Petition of the catholicos of Mtskhet'a, published by Karst, in *Corpus Juris Ibero-Caucasici*, II, 271.

ent would pay the whole or half the wergild to the husband, according to whether the latter sued for divorce. If, however, the guilty party abducted the wife to sell her into slavery to the Turks—an outrage only too common at this period—then triple wergild was required. A judicial decision of the time of King Erekle II confirms that kidnaping was an offence punishable by imposition of wergild in favor of the victim.[56] There are also authentic court decisions condemning seducers of servant girls to pay wergild to the girls' masters, in default of which the offender was forced to become a serf of the plaintiff.[57] Full wergild was payable for injury involving loss of both eyes, both feet, or both hands, while loss of one of them was compensated at a third. For wounds there was an elaborate ritual of calculation based on the number of barleycorns which would fit into the scar.[58] This latter method of reckoning has remained current among the Georgian mountain clans almost until the present day.[59]

An important section of Wakhtang's code deals with theft. In general, the thief was to restore to the owner seven times the value of the article stolen. Light is cast on the social structure of Georgia by the provision that a nobleman or squire was entitled to the entire sevenfold compensation, whereas a serf received only two sevenths, the rest going to his feudal lord.[60]

It would be a mistake to conclude, as have some writers, that the Georgian legal code excluded the barbarous penalties which were almost universally applied in other countries during the seventeenth and eighteenth centuries. Though scarcely ever mentioned in Wakhtang's code itself, corporal punishment, mutilation, and execution were certainly featured in the Georgian penal system. Deserters from

[56] P'urtseladze, *Gruzinskie krest'ianskie gramoty,* p. 23 (a document of 1769).

[57] P'urtseladze, *Gruzinskie krest'ianskie gramoty,* pp. 8, 42 (documents of 1708 and 1783).

[58] For judgments of Georgian courts based on these provisions, see "Étude sur les Chartes," published as an appendix to M.-F. Brosset, *Histoire de la Géorgie,* Vol. II, Part 2, Addition XVI. Note that the Anglo-Saxon laws of England also contain a tariff for injuries short of death (Pollock and Maitland, *History of English Law before the Time of Edward I* [Cambridge, 1895], I, 23); so do the *Russkaia Pravda* and the old Welsh codes (Lea, *Superstition and Force,* p. 17).

[59] A. Grigolia, *Custom and Justice in the Caucasus,* p. 151.

[60] Karst, *Corpus Juris Ibero-Caucasici,* I, 189.

the royal army, for instance, were punished by the loss of a foot, while those who betrayed their lord in time of war suffered the death penalty. Poisoners were burnt alive. Should a serf strike or insult his lord, he would lose either his hand or his tongue, unless allowed to pay the appropriate amount of blood-money. According to Prince Wakhusht, the eighteenth-century Georgian authority, the punishment for sacrilege was death or blinding, following conviction by the ordeal of single combat. Habitual robbers were liable to blinding, while petty thieves at the third offence might have their feet amputated. For drawing a sword with violent intent in the royal palace precincts, the hands were cut off.[61] Gruesome mutilations inflicted in seventeenth-century Mingrelia are described by Father Lamberti.[62] Indeed, the right of the Dadian of Mingrelia to inflict mutilation on criminals survived long after the country was placed under Russian suzerainty. The Dadian's criminal jurisdiction was not suspended until after 1840, when it was replaced by the Russian penal code.[63]

The lay jurisdiction of the Georgian kings was effectively supplemented by those of the court of the catholicos patriarchs and the tribunals of the provincial metropolitans who played a prominent part in public affairs. The political and judicial power of the church had, if anything, increased in proportion as the strength of the Georgian monarchy declined from the thirteenth century onwards. The patriarchs represented a unifying influence, a rallying point for the Christian population when it was hard pressed by the Mohammedan powers. They were able, therefore, to make their voices heard in matters of legislation and in the dispensing of justice, even when the kings would command but scant obedience. Feudal lords, however defiant of the royal power, hesitated to expose themselves to the wrath to come. Public opinion was more

---

[61] Wakhusht, *Description géographique de la Géorgie,* p. 19; Vacheishvili, *Narkvevebi k'art'uli samart'lis istoriidan,* p. 91.

[62] Lamberti, "Relation de la Mengrellie," in Thévenot, *Relations de divers voyages,* I, 37.

[63] See the unpublished dispatch of the French consul at Tiflis, Direction Politique, No. 9, March 20, 1843, in the archives of the French Foreign Ministry: "Dépêches Politiques du Consul à Tiflis," pp. 129–32, in Correspondance Politique, Russie (1830–44).

likely to heed the anathema of the patriarch than the edicts of the prince.

These factors explain the increasing intervention of the church in the judicial field in the later period of the monarchy. It is noteworthy that in earlier days the ordinances of the Georgian Church had been virtually confined to matters of morals and church discipline. This may be seen in the early Great Nomocanon of the Georgian Church, translated from the Greek by Arseni of Iqalt'o early in the twelfth century, and in the ordinances of the Church Council of Ruis-Urbnisi of the year 1103.[64] Much wider in scope, however, was the revised Nomocanon of the Georgian Church as drawn up by the general council of the prelates of Western Georgia summoned in the sixteenth century by Catholicos Evdemon of Abasgia and revised by the Patriarch Malak'ia II early in the following century.

The text of this revised Nomocanon was incorporated by King Wakhtang VI in his code of laws. Its introductory paragraph explains the circumstances attending its promulgation. A great famine had overtaken the land; murder, slave-trading, the spoliation of churches, and marital irregularities had become rife. Divine vengeance could be averted only by stringent corrective measures. Among the punishments laid down by the Nomocanon, we may note hanging, prescribed for selling Christians into slavery to the Turks or for sacrilege, as, for example, the pillaging of a shrine. For stealing from a church, mutilation was ordered, while loss of a hand, followed by banishment, was laid down for parricide or fratricide. The relationship between church and royal jurisdiction is brought out in the clauses which provide that those who defied church authority should be treated as guilty of personal insubordination against the king, while anyone guilty of treason against the king should be condemned to death by the church.[65]

It may be instructive to compare this state of affairs with that prevailing in Anglo-Saxon England, where

---

[64] Karst, "Recherches sur l'histoire du droit ecclésiastique Carthvélien," in *Archives d'Histoire du Droit Oriental,* I, 12–22.

[65] Text and translation of the revised Nomocanon in Karst, *Corpus Juris Ibero-Caucasici,* VI, 59–87.

secular and ecclesiastical courts were not separated, and the two jurisdictions were hardly distinguished. The bishop sat in the county court; the church claimed for him a large share in the direction of even secular justice, and the claim was fully allowed by princes who could not be charged with weakness.[66]

In Georgia, while the patriarch's tribunal was distinct and separate from that of the king, the interdependence of the two jurisdictions was a close one. In Wakhtang's code crimes for which settlement in terms of wergild payments was inadequate were repeatedly referred to the judgment of the patriarch. Among such crimes were parricide, fratricide, and the wounding of a husband by his wife. In some cases, murderers already condemned by a lay court to pay blood-money were sent to the church tribunal for imposition of penalties according to canon law.[67] Witchcraft and its suppression, as might be expected, were the special province of the church courts. In 1788, for example, we find the patriarch of Georgia ordering that special measures be taken against "sorcerers, enchanters, diviners and fortune-tellers." Such persons were liable to fines payable to the church, or, in bad cases, to mutilation or death by stoning.[68] In addition, the church tribunals regularly exercised jurisdiction over clerics accused of criminal offenses. This is vividly illustrated by a royal order of the year 1798, directing priests accused of assault and "the cracking of pates" to be punished by their archbishop.[69]

In describing Wakhtang's legislative work, attention has been focused so far on the criminal side. But the prince regent's laws are equally important for their provisions in matters of civil law, reflecting Wakhtang's outstanding grasp of administrative detail in everyday affairs. This attention to detail emerges in the care devoted to setting forth tables of weights and measures, specifying rates of interest payable on loans, regulating dowries and inheritances, regulating the duties and reciprocal relationships between the nobility and the peasantry, framing rules governing land tenure and

[66] Pollock and Maitland, *History of English Law,* I, 16–17.

[67] See, for example, a case of 1803, arising from a murder committed in Imeret'i, cited in P'urtseladze, *Gruzinskie krest'ianskie gramoty,* p. 110.

[68] Karst, *Corpus Juris Ibero-Caucasici,* II, 131–32.

[69] P'urtseladze, *Gruzinskie krest'ianskie gramoty,* pp. 69–72. This order relates specifically to the district of K'isiq in Kakhet'i.

irrigation, and in general providing for the equitable solution of the many problems affecting the interests of citizen and peasant. Wakhtang's civil code is further supplemented by an important manual of administrative procedure drafted under his supervision, and promulgated in the year 1706 under the title Dasturlamali.[70] Besides defining the duties and fees of the various officials, the Dasturlamali describes how taxes are assessed and collected, with the amounts due from each class of society. Another interesting section sets forth the rules governing the fishing rights in the rivers of Georgia. Other paragraphs contain instructions on conducting royal funerals, and other court ceremonials.[71]

Wakhtang's code owes its historical importance less to any novel reforms contained in it than to its value as a summary of the traditions, institutions, and beliefs of the Georgian people. Wakhtang's laws were so much in accord with the spirit of the Georgian nation that many of them survived the Russian annexation of 1801. Though criminal offences were thereafter tried according to Russian law, Emperor Alexander I decreed that civil cases should continue to be settled according to Wakhtang's code.[72] In 1828, a Russian translation of Wakhtang's laws was privately printed by the senate at St. Petersburg for the guidance of officials in the Transcaucasian provinces.[73] Little by little, however, Wakhtang's code was superseded by Russian law, though in mountain districts of Georgia it is to this day revered as a sacred book.[74]

[70] From the Arabic and Persian *Dastur al-'amal* (regulations). The Georgian text of the Dasturlamali was published as edited by P. Umikashvili (Tiflis, 1886). It indicates many analogies between the Georgian administrative system and that of Safavid Iran (Minorsky, ed., *Tadhkirat al-Muluk*, p. 205). It also incorporates a number of edicts issued by earlier Georgian monarchs. For a discussion of the sources of the Dasturlamali, see Lort'k'ip'anidze, *Nizhniaia Kartliia*, I, 33–37.

[71] For convenient summaries of the Dasturlamali, see M.-F. Brosset, *Histoire de la Géorgie*, Introduction, pp. CIII–CIX; Karst, *Corpus Juris Ibero-Caucasici*, II, 323–25.

[72] Manifesto of September 12, 1801: *Polnoe Sobranie Zakonov* (Complete Collection of Laws of the Russian Empire), Vol. XXVI, No. 20,007.

[73] Holldack, *Zwei Grundsteine*, p. 105. This private edition was superseded by the complete Russian version edited by Frenkel and Bak'radze. It should be noted that the latter is the only printed edition containing all the Armenian, Byzantine, and other codes collected by Wakhtang's commission; Karst's *Corpus Juris Ibero-Caucasici* includes the indigenous, specifically Georgian laws only.

[74] There exists, nevertheless, a tradition that Wakhtang despaired of the possibility

From the foregoing survey of Georgian laws and political institutions, certain conclusions may be drawn about the machinery of government in Georgia during the seventeenth and early eighteenth centuries.

Of fundamental importance was the division of the country into Turkish and Persian spheres of influence. This division, combined with the jealous particularism of each of the three Bagratid royal houses of K'art'li, Kakhet'i, and Imeret'i, prevented national reunification. The pretensions of the dukes also tended to undermine royal authority in both Eastern and Western Georgia. Since the kings could no longer dispose freely of fiefs, the Georgian feudal system decayed, though feudal institutions lived on, sometimes in fossilized form, to provide the basic political structure of Georgia.

Each of the three Bagratid sovereign houses claimed it ruled by divine right, as lineal descendants of Solomon and David of Israel. In fact, the kings of K'art'li and Kakhet'i ruled under the aegis of the Persian shahs, and the king of Imeret'i, though in theory reigning in his own right, depended in reality on the grace and favor of the sultan of Turkey. The Bagratid rulers of K'art'li enjoyed a distinct advantage over their royal rivals, to whom they were senior, by possession of the former metropolis of united Georgia, Tiflis, which commanded important trade routes, and by their favored position as viceroys of the Persian shah.

Justice and civil administration were largely patriarchal in character, often dispensed by the king in person. The royal officers of state were mainly hereditary, their dignities and titles remaining in one family for generations. Representative institutions as we understand them did not exist on a national scale, though municipal affairs, and those of the more remote tribes and clans, were directed in part by elected provosts, elders, and headmen. The provincial administration was entrusted wherever possible to deputy governors chosen by the king, but large areas enjoyed autonomy under hereditary dukes.

---

of legal reform in Georgia, and to such an extent as to write in the margin of his code: "Although I have composed this book of laws, justice has never been done in Georgia, nor ever will be" (Holldack, *Zwei Grundsteine,* p. 92; Haxthausen, *Transkaukasia,* II, 195).

The Georgian criminal code, as we have observed, rested largely on two principles: the ordeal for determining guilt or innocence and the imposition of blood-money or wergild fines in cases of murder, violence, or other personal tort. The ordeal is witness to the general survival of a somewhat naive religious faith, while the wergild system is characteristic of societies where deeds of violence are common and are not considered morally reprehensible in themselves. Both ordeal and wergild were of great antiquity in Georgia, the former clearly traceable to the era of Iranian domination in pre-Christian times. Their persistence in Georgia until the eighteenth century must be regarded as a symptom of retarded political evolution. At the same time, we may discern in the Georgian wergild principle, with its emphasis on the right of the individual victim or his dependents to compensation for wrong suffered, a philosophy of law not without merit. At any rate, the system compares favorably with the savage and senseless penalties inflicted at that time in countries reputed socially and politically more advanced than Georgia. It is true that mutilation and the death penalty were not unknown in Georgia, but the country at least remained free of the shadows of the dungeon and the galleys, the rack, the wheel, and the knout, which were such grim features of life in Europe during the seventeenth and eighteenth centuries.

3

Social and Economic Conditions during the Mukhranian Period

THE preceding discussion of Wakhtang's code of laws, in which the relative status of the various classes of society is laid down with almost mathematical precision, gives an impression of the social structure of seventeenth–eighteenth century Georgia. But documents of this kind can do little more than provide the bare outline of the picture. To know what life was really like in Georgia at this time, we must refer to the eyewitness accounts of contemporary travelers, and to personal memoirs and documents.

Fortunately, these are exceptionally rich for our period. Europeans in Constantinople, for instance, were much interested in events and conditions on Turkey's Caucasian border, and eagerly interrogated Georgian visitors to the Turkish court. A number of French and Italian missionaries were stationed in both Western and Eastern Georgia. Particular mention must be made of that vivid writer, Father Arcangelo Lamberti, and also of the outstanding missionary doctor and artist Father Cristoforo Castelli, who worked for twenty-six years in Georgia during the first half of the seventeenth century. Castelli has left seven volumes of sketches and notes, including 1,176 drawings of Georgian scenes, costumes and historical personages.[1] In addition, Russian envoys visited Georgia on a number of

---

[1] The complete manuscript collection of Castelli is preserved at the Communal Library in Palermo, while selections from his drawings are published in Tamarati, *L'Église géorgienne des origines jusqu'à nos jours,* and in Allen, *History of the Georgian People.*

occasions, and left valuable accounts of their experiences and observations.[2] Another visitor was the Orthodox Patriarch Macarius of Antioch, who traveled through Georgia on his way to the general ecclesiastical council which deposed the Russian Patriarch Nikon in 1666. Macarius's description of Georgia was written originally in Arabic. A high place among seventeenth-century travelers must be accorded to the French jeweler and merchant Jean Chardin, later Sir John Chardin, whose description of Georgia and Persia is well known to oriental scholars. Chardin had some disagreeable experiences on the Black Sea and in Georgia, where he traveled in daily terror of being shipwrecked, robbed, or assassinated on account of his valuable wares, so that his account of the country, especially of Mingrelia, is somewhat lurid, and has to be taken with the proverbial grain of salt. Important also is the account of the French botanist Pitton de Tournefort, who toured Transcaucasia in search of rare plants, and collected much general information on the state of the country.

By way of introduction, it is worth recalling that the picturesque accounts of life in Mingrelia given by the Italian missionary Lamberti and by Chardin are strikingly anticipated in the *Turkish Letters* of Busbecq, ambassador of the Holy Roman Empire in Constantinople. This work has apparently not previously been quoted in Georgian historical literature. Busbecq, describing the visit to the Ottoman capital about 1560 of the ruling prince or Dadian of Mingrelia, calls him "a man of dignified mien and huge stature, but, according to all reports, of a low grade of civilization," who "arrived with a large and ragged retinue, in poor and worn-out clothing." [3] Through the arrival of this embassy, Busbecq was able to collect information about Western Georgia, the Colchis of the ancients.

The whole district in which the Colchians live is rich in produce of every kind, which grows practically without cultivation, except wheat

[2] These are summarized in English in Allen, *History of the Georgian People*, pp. 343–49.

[3] In his "Relation de la Mingrellie," Father Lamberti says that the Mingrelians purposely pretended to be extremely poor and destitute so that the Turks might not be tempted to invade and annex their country. (Lamberti's "Relation" is in Thévenot, *Relations de divers voyages*, Vol. I.)

and barley, which, it is supposed, would also abound if a little trouble was taken. The inhabitants, however, prefer to be idle. Millet is sown in a slovenly manner and comes up in the greatest abundance, its yield being so plentiful that one crop suffices for two years. To this they have become accustomed and eat of it in abundance, and desire no better corn.[4] They produce plenty of quite tolerable wine from vines planted at the foot of the very tall trees. These vines, spreading among the branches over which they are trained, are productive for a long period. Of wax and honey they have abundance from the wild bees that produce them in the woods; the only trouble is to find out their haunts. The woods also provide plenty of game, being full of pheasants and partridges. A proof of the fertility of the soil is provided by the melons, which not only have an excellent flavour but often grow to a length of three feet.

After noting that trade was conducted mainly by barter, and that life in Mingrelia was generally carefree and easygoing, Busbecq described the universal cult of St. George, the patron saint of Georgia.

When they enter a church, the presence of images of the Virgin Mother, St. Peter, St. Paul, and the other saints has but little interest for them; but there is always one picture for which they look, that of St. George on horseback, and before this they prostrate themselves in adoration and imprint kisses all over it, not omitting even the horse's hoofs. St. George, they declare, was a man of might, a famous warrior, who often in single combat fought with the Evil Spirit on equal terms and was victorious, or at least left the field unbeaten.[5]

Apart from Busbecq's vivid description and a few scattered observations by Russian and German travelers, material for the social

[4] Even today, this millet is made into a kind of paste called *gomi*, which in Mingrelia is cooked and eaten instead of bread. The Russian envoys Elchin and Zakhar'ev, who were in Mingrelia in 1639–40, have left an account of a communal feast at which the guests squatted beside wooden planks set on the ground, while the cook carried round the *gomi* and chopped large chunks off newly slaughtered carcasses to pop into the cauldron. (Likhachev, *Puteshestviya Russkikh poslov*, pp. 224–25.)

[5] E. S. Forster, tr. and ed., *The Turkish Letters of Ogier Ghiselin de Busbecq*, pp. 126–32. In the seventeenth century, Russian envoys were scandalized at pagan elements in the cult of St. George. On the night before the saint's festival a village soothsayer was shut up in a church with an icon of St. George, and on the following day uttered prophecies in the saint's name concerning the harvest, or on who was going to die during the following year, etc. (Likhachev, *Puteshestviya Russkikh poslov*, p. 219.)

history of Georgia in the sixteenth century is somewhat sparse. When we approach the mid-seventeenth century, on the other hand, we are confronted by an almost bewildering abundance of information, so that it is possible to reconstruct a fairly coherent picture of the life and condition of the various classes of Georgian society.

Strong adherence to Georgian national customs and traditions was combined in the way of life of the royal courts and leading aristocratic families with many elements imported both from Europe of the Renaissance and from the neighboring courts of Turkey and Persia. This is clearly brought out in the drawings of the Italian missionary Castelli. We see portraits of noblemen with flowing locks, wearing plumed hats and richly embroidered doublets; a king wearing a long mantle and bearing the scepter and other insignia of royalty; a prince on horseback in chain armor with plumed helmet, a round shield and long spear, looking like a mediaeval knight; a party of courtiers at a feast, sitting round a table spread with a cloth, the ladies with pointed bonnets, and a lap dog looking up expectantly from the floor, the whole scene reminiscent of some illustration for Boccaccio. According to Chardin, the consort of the prince or Dadian of Mingrelia used to wear robes of gold brocade, a headdress set with precious stones, and a coquettish veil. Her face was made up with cosmetics, and she was amenable to entertaining visitors of the male sex.[6]

In Castelli's drawings, we also see unmistakable evidence of Persiàn and Turkish influences. King T'eimuraz I of Kakhet'i is shown wearing a turban surmounted by an aigrette, like a Persian grandee, while other figures in Castelli's album wear costumes of Turkish fashion. Turkish influence was especially prominent in the province of Samtskhe in southwestern Georgia, since the mid-sixteenth century under direct Ottoman rule. The local aristocracy was obliged to adopt Turkish titles. Instead of the Georgian titles of *t'avadi, mt'avari,* and *aznauri,* a patriotic chronicler noted with disgust, one now heard of nothing but *pashas, beyis, alay-beyis,* and *aghas.*[7] In Eastern Georgia, now under the suzerainty of the shahs,

---

[6] Chardin, *Voyages en Perse,* II, 24.

[7] Wakhusht, "Histoires particulières . . . du Samtzkhé," in M.-F. Brosset, tr. and ed., *Histoire de la Géorgie,* II, Part 1, 231.

Persian influence was naturally strong. A royal marriage feast which Chardin attended at Tiflis in 1672 was served in the Persian manner, with the guests sitting cross-legged on carpets. Chardin also noted that the houses of the nobility were built according to the Persian style of architecture.[8]

In the Western Georgian kingdom of Imeret'i, the reign of Alexander III (1639–60) was a swan song before the era of civil war which destroyed the court's old magnificence. Foreign ambassadors of the time describe Alexander's apparel as of sable and velvet, with a caftan of watered silk stitched with gold thread, and give accounts of splendid feasts given at the royal palace in K'ut'ais.[9] One of Castelli's drawings shows a banquet with court musicians performing on a balcony in the palace dining hall.

While the court of K'ut'ais was rapidly declining during the latter half of the seventeenth century, that of Tiflis was gaining luster under the prosperous administration of the Mukhranian viceroys. The palace had large apartments opening onto spacious gardens and onto the River Kura, as well as fine aviaries, kennels, and falconries. In front of the palace was a square which could accommodate a thousand horses. In addition, the king of K'art'li had a summerhouse and garden at the outskirts of the city.[10] A royal wedding feast at which Chardin was present was attended by more than a hundred guests. It took place under a marquee erected on the palace balcony, whose floor was covered with rich carpets. Lighting was provided by gold and silver torches. Prominent in the menu were several kinds of pilau, rice dishes delicately served after the Persian style. Libations of excellent local wine and music played by the court band added to the gaiety of the occasion.[11]

The French botanist Tournefort who saw the palace at Tiflis in 1701 described it as

very ancient and tolerably well laid out, considering what Country it is in. . . . They carried us into a new Hall, which was agreeable enough, though built of nothing but Wood. It has Windows on every side, which

[8] Chardin, *Voyages en Perse,* II, 131, and Plate V.
[9] Allen, *History of the Georgian People,* pp. 348–49.
[10] Chardin, *Voyages en Perse,* II, 160.
[11] *Ibid.,* pp. 184–88.

are glaz'd with great Squares, of blue, yellow, grey, and other colour'd Glasses. . . . The Ceiling consists of Compartments of gilded Leather.[12]

A few years after this, Wakhtang VI erected a new palace in Tiflis, lavishly decorated with mirrors and gilding. "By Heaven," a Georgian contemporary exclaimed, "I have seen none finer, not even in Persia!" [13]

Even apart from official receptions and banquets, the life of the royal family and court of Georgia was not lacking in amenities. In good weather, there was hunting, polo in the hippodrome, as well as mounted archery contests and other trials of skill. These sports are depicted in several of the sketches in Father Castelli's album. The Georgian writer Sekhnia Chkheidze tells us that King Wakhtang VI was especially fond of such exercises. In Mingrelia, too, hunting was so popular that a current proverb, recorded by Father Lamberti, ran to the effect that human happiness consists in having a horse, a good hound, and a fine falcon.[14] In the evening, one could indulge in merrymaking, or the more tranquil pursuits of chess-playing and the cultivation of poetry and literature. The imposition of Persian manners resulted under some of the Mukhranian viceroys in a trend toward segregation of the sexes after the Mohammedan fashion, but this was far from universal. Indeed, Georgian women played a prominent part in the social and intellectual life of seventeenth-century Georgia. We may mention in this connection the talented Georgian poetess Vominisa Beridze, of whom Father Castelli has left us a portrait.

Urban life naturally centered round the court and central administration of the several Georgian kingdoms and principalities. The chief bazaars and markets of the land were to be found in the regional capitals, namely the metropolitan city of Tiflis, and T'elavi in Kakhet'i; in Western Georgia, K'ut'ais and the Mingrelian town of Zugdidi; Akhaltsikhe, residence of the Turco-Georgian pashas of Samtskhe in the southwest. There was also a flourishing Armenian

---

[12] Tournefort, *Voyage into the Levant,* III, 152–53.

[13] Chkheidze, "Chronicle," in M.-F. Brosset, tr., *Histoire de la Géorgie,* II, Part 2, 28.

[14] "Relation de la Mengrellie," in Thévenot, *Relations de divers voyages,* I, 36.

merchant community at Gori, in the Kura valley northwest of Tiflis.

The burgher class in Georgia was made up mainly of Armenians, with a certain proportion of Jews, Greeks, and Persians. As a social group, they stood somewhat outside the feudal hierarchy of Georgia, though in some privileged instances, they might become landowners and own serfs. Their prerogatives were considerable. In criminal cases, a burgher was normally entitled to escape corporal punishment or execution by payment of a fine to the treasury. When the shah or the sultan demanded a tribute of slave girls or boys, the city burghers could buy immunity for their families.

Among the main guilds or corporations of the Tiflis merchants and craftsmen were those of the masons, the carpenters, the butchers, the gardeners, the candlemakers, the grocers and the wine-merchants. They paid an annual tax, known as the *makhta,* to the king, as well as dues in cash and in kind to the municipal authorities. They elected a burgomaster or *k'et'khuda* to uphold their common interests.[15] The more prominent among them could enter state service, since certain posts in the court and municipal administrations were reserved for them, especially posts in the departments of finance, the royal secretariat, and the magistracy. Their social standing may be assessed by the fact that the blood-price of a first-class burgher was equivalent to that of a squire of the second class.[16]

For impressions of town life in Georgia, and particularly in Tiflis, we must again turn to the descriptions left by contemporary travelers. The French merchant-adventurer Tavernier notes that Tiflis "enjoys a fine situation, is pretty large and well built, and a flourishing silk trade is carried on there." [17] Chardin spent a few weeks there, and devotes several pages to describing the city's buildings and commerce. He calls Tiflis one of the finest towns of the Persian empire, with a large and busy bazaar quarter, well maintained, and a number of caravansaries for the accommodation of traveling merchants.

[15] P'urtseladze, *Gruzinskie krest'ianskie gramoty,* p. 5.

[16] See further Karst, *Corpus Juris Ibero-Caucasici,* II, 273–93 ("Taxes, redevances et rentes au profit du Moouravat"), and pp. 404–11 ("Corporations ou guildes"); Ioseliani, *Goroda, sushchestvovavshie i sushchestvuiushchie v Gruzii,* pp. 83–84; Macarius III, *Histoire de la Conversion des Géorgiens.*

[17] Tavernier, *Les six voyages,* I, 447–48.

There were six Georgian Orthodox and eight Armenian Gregorian churches in the city, as well as an establishment of French and Italian Capuchin missionaries, who had made themselves popular through their medical skill. The Mohammedan faith was poorly represented, although the king was nominally a Moslem. Among the principal places of social rendezvous were the famous natural springs of Tiflis, the water of which was very hot and sulphurated. Many people resorted to these baths for health reasons, as well as for cleanliness. The city suburbs contained pleasant gardens and orchards, some with summerhouses.[18]

Some thirty years after Chardin, in 1701, Tournefort found Tiflis "a pretty large town, and very populous; the houses are low, dark, and for the most part built of mud and bricks; and even these are superior to the houses in the rest of the province." The city was situated, notes the same observer, "upon the declivity of a hill, which is quite bare, in a pretty narrow valley, five days journey from the Caspian, and six from the Black Sea, tho' the Caravans reckon it double the way." The citadel was in a sorry crumbling condition. In front of it was an open square, used for sport and exercise, which made a handsome and spacious market place, where the best wares of the country could be bought. The Armenians were the largest group in the city population, which totaled about twenty thousand, the rest being Georgians, Persians, and Tatars.[19]

The Mukhranian monarchs were well aware of the advantage to be derived from fostering commerce, and Tiflis was certainly the most important commercial center of Georgia. King Wakhtang V (1658–76), anxious for European trading establishments to open branches in Georgia, assured the French merchant Chardin that he was prevented from entering into negotiations with the French East India Company only through fear of incurring the displeasure of the shah of Persia. Wakhtang was particularly eager to make his capital a depot for transit trade between Europe and the East Indies via Tiflis and the Black Sea, thus diverting this trade from the Baghdad-Aleppo and Tabriz-Erzerum routes.[20] Wakhtang V's grandson,

---

[18] Chardin, *Voyages en Perse,* II, 155–64.
[19] Tournefort, *Voyage into the Levant,* III, 144–53.
[20] Chardin, *Voyages en Perse,* II, 194–95.

Wakhtang VI, also sought to enter into trade relations with France, but his efforts were thwarted by the collapse of the Safavi empire in 1722.

Eastern Georgia carried on a substantial export business in local commodities. Furs were sent into Persia and Turkey. Georgian silk, as well as that of Ganja and Shamakhi in the neighboring Persian province of Shirvan, was bought up by Armenian traders and shipped off to Europe via Smyrna. A large quantity of dyestuffs was produced in Georgia, particularly madder, two thousand camel loads of which were annually transported to Diarbekir and other Turkish textile centers, as well as to India. Among other local manufactures were gunpowder and linseed oil. Frequent caravans left Tiflis for Erzerum in Turkey and Tabriz and Isfahan in Persia.[21]

The capital of the kings of Imeret'i at K'ut'ais in Western Georgia was in a declining state as a result of civil war and invasion, and in 1672 it contained only about two hundred houses and was without fortifications. The seat of the Turco-Georgian pashas ruling over southwestern Georgia, the town of Akhaltsikhe, was larger and better preserved. Indeed, after Erzerum and Trebizond, it was the most important Turkish city in Eastern Anatolia, with four hundred houses, mostly of wood, a formidable citadel, several churches and mosques, and a caravansary. The population was made up of Turks, Armenians, Georgians, Greeks, and Jews.[22]

In Western Georgia commercial enterprise suffered much from the ravages of civil wars. These had a most detrimental effect on industry and trade, which the energetic and unscrupulous Prince-Regnant Levan Dadian of Mingrelia (1605–57) had fostered in the early seventeenth century.[23] After Levan's death, the country went to ruin. In the 1660s, the Patriarch Macarius of Antioch found Western Georgian commercial enterprise in the most stagnant condition. The raising of silkworms had been largely abandoned, despite excellent climatic conditions. A certain amount of linen was still made from locally grown flax, but much of this went to pay the

---

[21] Tournefort, *Voyage into the Levant*, III, 153–57.
[22] Chardin, *Voyages en Perse*, II, 95, 108.
[23] Lamberti, "Relation de la Mengrellie," in Thévenot, *Relations de divers voyages*, I, 34, 44.

tribute demanded by the sultan of Turkey. Hemp, garlic, onions, and tobacco were found growing wild, but insecurity combined with native insouciance hindered any attempt to market these commodities on a commercial scale.[24]

The lack of commercial enterprise in Western Georgia had to be compensated for by the activities of Turkish and Levantine traders, who made trips round the Black Sea coast of Georgia, bartering cheap European manufactured goods for the products of the country. From Abkhazia, they took furs, deer and tiger skins, spun flax, boxwood, wax, and honey, as well as captives to be sold into slavery.[25] From Mingrelia they shipped silk, flax, linen, boxwood, oxhides, sable and beaver skins, wax and honey, as well as some iron from local mines.[26] Conditions of trade were not very well regulated. Chardin landed on the Black Sea coast, and was astonished to see "a dozen shabby wretches, scantily clad, bow and arrow in hand, frightening to behold." These, he was told, were the local customs officers.[27] Their uncouthness, along with extortion and robbery by brigands and local authorities alike, must have served as a deterrent to foreign trading houses who might otherwise have been tempted to set up agencies in Georgia's Black Sea ports.

We may now turn to the largest section of the population, the peasantry, with their lords, the country nobility and the gentry. We have had occasion in an earlier chapter to outline briefly the feudal system as evolved in Georgia by the twelfth–thirteenth centuries, in the great heroic days of the united monarchy. The Georgian word for feudalism is *patronqmoba,* i.e., lord and vassalship—the relationship linking the *patroni* or master with the *qma* or liege. It is essential to remember that in this earlier epoch, the term *qma* was far from being invariably synonymous with that of "serf," as was true later. Under Queen T'amar, in the thirteenth century, the greatest nobles of the land were proud to be called "the good *qmani,* the favoured of the *patroni,*" that is to say, good and faithful subjects

---

[24] Macarius III, *Histoire de la Conversion des Géorgiens;* Chardin, *Voyages en Perse,* I, 252.

[25] Chardin, *Voyages en Perse,* I, 120, and II, 18.

[26] Chardin, *Voyages en Perse,* I, 146; Tavernier, *Les six voyages,* I, 449; report of the Russian envoy Elchin in Likhachev, *Puteshestviya Russkikh poslov,* pp. 212, 224.

[27] Chardin, *Voyages en Perse,* II, 4.

of the sovereign.[28] Indeed, the word *qma* is often used in the classics of Georgian mediaeval literature in the sense of a young man, a champion, a valiant knight.[29] The *patroni* was at the same time lord, guardian, or owner-proprietor, according to context, while the *qma* was essentially a man under the protection of another, or owing obedience to another. This hierarchy extended through all classes of society, and the king himself was thought of as holding his realm by the Grace of God.

In general terms, we are justified in applying to Georgia during the Golden Age of the monarchy most of the principles of feudal society as understood by Western historians. Among these principles were

the relation of vassal and lord; the principle that every holder of land is a tenant and not an owner, until the highest rank is reached, sometimes even the conception rules in that rank; that the tenure by which a thing of value is held is one of honourable service, not intended to be economic, but moral and political in character; the principle of mutual obligations of loyalty, protection and service binding together all the ranks of this society from the highest to the lowest; and the principle of contract between lord and tenant, as determining all rights, controlling their modification, and forming the foundation of all law.[30]

Or again, "Its [feudalism's] sentimental inspiration was extremely powerful. Personal devotion, loyalty, the vassal's spirit of sacrifice, the suzerain's patronage, were the deep and lasting foundations of this organisation . . ."[31]

Tenure of domains in early mediaeval Georgia until about the thirteenth century was dependent on the sovereign's grace and favor, and took the form of personal or, more rarely, hereditary grants of fiefs, bestowed on officers of state or duke-viceroys of provinces. This tenure, theoretically at least, was dependent upon the fulfillment of a tacit contract of loyal service. The same tacit con-

---

[28] Allen, *History of the Georgian People*, p. 250.

[29] As in the epic *The Man in the Panther's Skin*, by Shot'a Rust'aveli. See further the examples given in Chubinov, *Gruzino-Russkii slovar'*, col. 1380. Various uses of the word *qma* are discussed further by Nat'adze in *Materialy po Istorii Gruzii i Kavkaza*, Part V, p. 355.

[30] G. B. Adams, "Feudalism," in *Encyclopaedia Britannica* (14th ed.).

[31] Petit-Dutaillis, *Feudal Monarchy in France and England*, p. 1.

tract governed the status of the important class of peasant-vassals who attached themselves voluntarily to the estate of a squire or prince, under stipulated conditions, often including the right to depart at will.[32] Common to all grades in the Georgian feudal hierarchy was the obligation to appear on the field of battle at the behest of lord or king.

Throughout the later middle ages, from the thirteenth century onwards to the period under review, we can detect a gradual decay in the feudal principle which had been the mainspring of the public life of the united Georgian kingdom. Above all, it was foreign domination which prevented the normal historical evolution of Georgian society. It was the deliberate policy of the Mongol overlords who dominated the country from the reign of Queen Rusudan (1223–45) on to sap and undermine the foundations of loyal service on which the Georgian monarchy rested. Thus in 1266, we find the Mongol ruler of Persia, the Il-Khan Abagha, encouraging the grand constable of Samtskhe (southwestern Georgia) to set himself up as an independent potentate under the direct protection of the Mongols.[33]

That incident was an ominous augury of later events. After the death of King Alexander (1412–43), last monarch of united Georgia, and the fall of Constantinople to the Turks in 1453, Georgia's situation rapidly deteriorated. Local dukes and princelings revolted with impunity against central authority. As trade routes and communications with Europe were cut, economic decline weakened the power of the kings. As we have seen, the country was by now divided into no less than three small kingdoms and four more or less autonomous principalities. As in Western Europe after the decay of the Carolingian empire, "anarchy had produced the system of lordship," [34] and centrifugal forces within the feudal system became dominant. Indeed, the political structure of Georgia from the fifteenth century on is referred to in Georgian sources as t'avadoba, which means literally "the rule of princes."

[32] Berdzenishvili, Javakhishvili, and Janashia, *Istoriia Gruzii,* p. 187. These peasant-yeomen are known variously as *nebieri* (i.e., voluntary), *siglosani* (having a charter), or *t'avdadserili* (self-inscribed).

[33] *Ibid.,* pp. 269–70.

[34] Petit-Dutaillis, *Feudal Monarchy in France and England,* p. 1.

Symptomatic of this trend toward disintegration in the later days of the Georgian monarchy is the fact that grants of fiefs and benefices (*shedsqaleba*) by the sovereign ceased to be the basis of land tenure. The hereditary principle became dominant among the dukes, the princes, and the squirearchy alike; each sat in his castle or manor and did much as he pleased. The situation was summed up by the eighteenth century Georgian annalists who wrote: "No longer were either dukes or princes liable to be replaced [i.e., by the king]: they all became hereditary proprietors of their vales and domains and provinces and places; to whomsoever a patrimony was granted, it was given in perpetuity, and all became strong, magnates, dukes and princes." [35] Certain provincial dynasts, such as the *atabags* of Samtskhe and the Dadians of Mingrelia, even arrogated to themselves the prerogative of striking their own coins.

Consequently, in the later years of the Georgian kingdom, each principality (*sat'avado*) existed as a more or less separate political and economic unit within its specific territorial boundaries. The prince (*t'avadi*) with his immediate family and retainers would occupy the family seat, while other members of the princely house or clan (cousins, brothers, nephews, etc.) would occupy residences elsewhere within the territorial limits of the duchy or principality. The prince governed all the general affairs of the *sat'avado*, and represented the interests of the principality as a whole when dealing with the king, with other princes, or even, as often happened, with foreign powers. Each member of the princely family had his own private property in lands and serfs (*sakut'ari, sat'avist'avo*); but each had a share in the use and profits of the common family demesne (*sakhaso*), which comprised such properties as plough lands, pastures, forests, orchards, vineyards, serfs, herds, dairies, dye works, wine presses, mills, toll houses, fortresses, monasteries, the family cemetery, and so forth. Portions of the princely demesne or *sakhaso*

---

[35] Egnatashvili, *Akhali K'art'lis tskhovreba,* p. 46. A similar trend is noted in Persia following the Mongol invasions: "A striking feature of the Mongol period is the great increase which appears to have taken place in the size of private estates and private fortunes" (Lambton, *Landlord and Peasant in Persia,* p. 96). Again, in Persia under the Safavis, "at first drafts were made on the revenue for the military leaders, then the land itself was assigned, and finally it became, or tended to become, by usurpation, *de facto* private property" (*ibid.,* p. 105).

might from time to time be detached as the apanage (*saup'lisdsulo*) of a younger son of the ruling prince, constituting a more or less self-contained demesne on its own.

As time went on, the administration of the principalities came to reproduce in miniature the main features of the royal government. The lands were administered by the *mouravi,* or steward, with his deputy, the *natsvali,* or bailiff; in the villages, authority was exercised by the *mamasakhlisi* or headman. At the prince's court, one would find such officials as the *sakhlt'khutsesi* or chamberlain; the *bok'ault'khutsesi* or chief executive officer (originally, in Mongol times, the *bukavul* had been a military official in charge, among other things, of the payment of the army and the distribution of booty); the *eshikaghasi,* or master of ceremonies; the *meghvinet'-ukhutsesi,* or wine master; the *mejinibet'ukhutsesi,* or stable master; the *mdivani,* or secretary; and the *naziri,* or overseer.

Very often, these officials were recruited from the *aznaurs* or squires who held estates on the prince's domains. An *aznaur,* be it noted, enjoyed personal liberty, including that of leaving his suzerain; but in this case, his estate reverted to the overlord. The domain of an *aznaur* was not a freehold possession, and he had no right to sell it without his overlord's permission.

In Georgia, as in Russia, the demoralizing effect of Mongol occupation hastened the transition from feudalism to serfdom. With the balance of power tilted in favor of the great nobles, the status of the peasantry inevitably deteriorated. Georgian historians agree that it was in the thirteenth century that the peasantry of Georgia became, generally speaking, bound irrevocably as serfs or villeins to their master's lands. In relations between lord and peasant, proprietorship took the place of protection and mutual service. Symptomatic of the trend was the modification suffered by the word *qma:* formerly applied to knights-liege and servants of the state, it is scarcely used in the seventeenth and eighteenth centuries otherwise than in the sense of bond-serf. The former basis of Georgian society, often termed *patronqmoba* or lord-vassal relationship, is replaced by the principle of *batonqmoba,* which may best be rendered as "proprietor-serf relationship."

It would, however, be a mistake to confuse serfdom as it existed in Georgia with utter and unrelieved slavery. As in Western Europe, so under the Georgian monarchy, the status of the serfs or villeins was largely governed by the custom of the manor, which tended to harden into a local law defining the extent of a peasant's obligations to his lord. A peasant who was bought (*nasqidi*) was technically the absolute property of his master, except that the master could not, at least in theory, inflict mutilation or capital punishment on the peasant; in the course of a generation or two, however, the descendants of such a peasant might well have become *mkvidri* or hereditary vassal-serfs. Peasants belonging to this category were both debarred from leaving their land and insured against being arbitrarily expelled by their lords. Once this status had been established, the villein tenement would normally pass undivided from father to son, in return for feudal dues and customary services.

In discussing the different categories of serf, a distinction must be drawn between peasants belonging directly to the king, to members of the royal family, or to prince-magnates owning large hereditary domains, and those belonging to the church or to squires (*aznaurs*) who themselves stood in feudal relationship to the king or to some prince-magnate. The former category was termed *sakhaso* peasantry, from the Arabic-Persian *khass,* meaning "special, select, for royal use, or whatever the king enjoys as his private property." [36] Serfs of small private proprietors were called *memamuleebis qmebi,* or peasants belonging to private estates. For statistical and taxation purposes, serfs were classified as *mosaure* or *gamomgebi,* i.e., those with land, liable for poll tax (*mali*), quitrent, and so forth, and *bogano* or *euli,* who were without land, and formed a kind of agricultural proletariat. We also have to take account of two privileged classes of peasant, the *t'arkhani,* enjoying exemption from some or all taxes and personal servitude, and the *khizani,* who were free peasants renting land from proprietors on agreed terms.[37]

---

[36] For elucidation of this term and its use in Transcaucasia under the Mongols of Persia in the fourteenth century, see Barthold, "Die persische Inschrift an der Mauer der Manūčehr-Moschee zu Ani," Hinz, tr. and ed., in *Zeitschrift der Deutschen Morgenländischen Gesellschaft,* 101, 259–60; see also Nat'adze, in *Materialy po Istorii Gruzii i Kavkaza,* V (1937), 326–28; Lambton, *Landlord and Peasant in Persia,* p. 431.

[37] Lort'k'ip'anidze, *Nizhniaia Kartliia,* I, 85–92, giving Russian and Georgian texts;

Country priests were usually in a condition of feudal dependence on their local squire, and were numbered for practical purposes among his serfs and retainers.[38] The Georgian poet Akaki Tseret'eli cites in this connection a Georgian proverb: "Honor is not paid to the domestic chaplain," adding that this was because he was thought of as part of the household staff.[39]

We may attach a certain political significance to the fact that the term *sakhaso* was applied in seventeenth- and eighteenth-century Georgia not only to crown peasants, but also to those belonging personally to the great magnates. As used in Persia, whence it came into Georgian official terminology, the word *khass* (Georgian *khasi*) was restricted to the private domains of the crown. That peasants belonging to the great feudal domains of the Georgian prince-magnates, as well as those belonging to the king, were now referred to as *sakhaso,* shows that the king was now reduced to the status of *primus inter pares* among the Georgian feudal magnates. In fact, historians agree that in the seventeenth and eighteenth centuries, it was customary for Georgian kings on their accession to confirm feudal magnates in their domains, but that the sovereign had no right to interfere in the internal administration of those domains.[40]

It is not surprising that there was rivalry between the kings and the great nobles for control of the *sakhaso* peasantry. The king's personal peasant-vassals formed the only body of manpower on whom the crown could rely implicitly when dealing with rebellious nobles. Under a strong monarch, the king's own *sakhaso* peasants naturally tended to increase in number, as a result of successful expropriation from disloyal or ineffectual landowners. In 1788, for example, King Erekle II managed to dispossess the powerful duke of the K'sani, and turned all the duke's serfs into crown peasants. In view of the *sakhaso* peasantry's important political role, the monarchy did its best to conciliate this class by preferential treat-

---

Karst, *Corpus Juris Ibero-Caucasici,* III, 72–77; P'urtseladze, *Gruzinskie krest'ianskie gramoty,* p. III; Gvritishvili, *P'eodaluri Sak'art'velos,* pp. 196–208.

[38] M.-F. Brosset, *Histoire de la Géorgie,* Introduction, p. CXV.

[39] Tseret'eli, *Perezhitoe,* p. 47.

[40] Nat'adze, "Krest'iane 'Sakhaso' v vostochnoi Gruzii v kontse XVIII stoletiia," in *Materialy po Istorii Gruzii i Kavkaza,* V (1937), 328.

ment. In the case just referred to, Erekle II promised the K'sani peasants his perpetual good will, and invited them to send a deputation to discuss any grievances. We later find the Crown Prince Giorgi intervening on behalf of one of these K'sani crown peasants and warning the local bailiff not to ill-treat him.[41]

Some impression of the distribution of the principal categories of peasant in the central provinces of Georgia is given by a contemporary statistical survey of that part of K'art'li known as *medsinave drosha*, i.e., the "forward banner," the area from which the vanguard of the royal army was recruited in time of war. This region was situated to the south of Tiflis, and comprised the districts of Somkhit'i and Sabarat'ashvilo. The survey was drawn up in 1721 by Prince Wakhusht and the royal scribe Givi T'umanishvili. This area contained most of the personal domains of the K'art'lian royal family.

According to the data furnished by this survey, the region in 1721 contained 5,848 peasant hearths, made up of 4,638 hearths of *gamomgebi*, or landed peasants, liable for the supply of 5,749 soldiers for the vanguard of the royal army, and 1,210 hearths of *bogano* or landless peasants, liable to furnish only 461 soldiers. Six hundred and forty-eight peasant families are listed as removed, that is to say, migrated into other districts, kidnapped by raiders, or sold into slavery. Forty-nine families are listed as having died out. It is also worth noting that the area numbered 129 squires without serfs, forming a déclassé category of small-holders.[42]

By far the most substantial landowners in the area were the royal house of K'art'li and the Orbeliani-Qap'lanishvili family. The Orbelianis possessed over one thousand peasant hearths. Their serfs were outnumbered only by those of all the members of the royal family combined, viz: [43]

---

[41] *Ibid.*, pp. 329–30.

[42] The survey from which we are quoting is printed in Lort'k'ip'anidze, *Nizhniaia Kartliia*, I, 85–209, with commentary in Georgian and Russian.

[43] These figures are subject to caution, being based on a collation of two variants of the statistical survey of the year 1721. The totals given by Nat'adze in *Materialy po Istorii Gruzii i Kavkaza*, V (1937), 343, have been verified as far as possible by reference to those in Lort'k'ip'anidze, *Nizhniaia Kartliia*, I, 93–178.

Members of the Royal Family	Hearths
The King (Wakhtang VI)	554
The Queen	393
The King's daughter-in-law	28
Prince Simon	116
Prince Wakhusht	60
Prince Bak'ar	173
Total	1324

Next in importance in the "forward banner" come the Amilakhori family, with 117 hearths. No other princely family could muster more than a few dozen peasant hearths in this region. Most of the remaining peasant families were distributed in groups of a score or less among various squires and monasteries. We may conclude from these data that the royal family and the Orbeliani-Qap'lanishvilis between them dominated this region. The clash of interests which this situation might have been expected to produce was avoided by the Orbeliani family's exceptional loyalty to the Georgian crown during this period.

Another of the relatively few areas of Georgia for which we have statistical data for our period is the semiautonomous domain of the Princes Amilakhori, situated in K'art'li along the river Liakhvi. This was an important grain-producing area of Eastern Georgia. During the Mukhranian period, the head of the Amilakhori family was hereditary commander in chief of the K'art'lian royal army. At the end of the seventeenth century, the Amilakhori domains numbered just over 900 peasant hearths, of which 400 were *sakhaso* (belonging personally to Prince Amilakhori) and 501 were attached to estates of squires or church foundations. Of 44 minor proprietors who were vassals of Prince Amilakhori, 26 possessed 10 or fewer hearths. The most substantial of these 44 minor landowners was the bishop of Samt'avisi, with 51 hearths.

From these figures, we may estimate that the head of the Amilakhori family could put into the field over a thousand men, nearly half of them his personal serfs.[44] This helps to explain the prominent

[44] Nat'adze, in *Materialy po Istorii Gruzii i Kavkaza*, V (1937), 334, puts the figure as high as 2,000, which seems rather too large.

role which the Amilakhoris played in Georgian politics throughout the seventeenth and eighteenth centuries, until the family was ultimately disgraced for its part in a plot against King Erekle II. Fully cognizant of the threat presented by the existence of such self-contained princely domains within the Georgian kingdom, Erekle took stern measures to break up the Amilakhori estates. By the end of the eighteenth century, we find the Amilakhori lands much diminished, and parceled up into small and separated areas.[45]

So much for the limited material available to us on the relative distribution of the peasant population of seventeenth–eighteenth century Georgia among the several classes of proprietor. We may now inquire what the physical and social conditions of the life of the Georgian peasantry were like at this period. What were the accepted norms governing the relationship between lord and serf? While drawing fully on the impressions of foreign travelers, we shall try to correct their often sweeping assertions by reference to charters and administrative documents edited by such scholars as Brosset, T'aqaishvili, and Karst.

Some foreign observers give a lurid and clearly overdrawn picture of feudal tyranny in Georgia. "The nobles," says Chardin of Eastern Georgia,

exercise over their subjects a more than tyrannical power. It is even worse than in Colchis [i.e., Mingrelia]. They make their peasants work for months on end, and as much as they require, without giving them pay or food. They have right over the property, the liberty, and the life of their vassals. They take their children and sell them, or keep them as slaves.[46]

Tournefort embroiders on Chardin's strictures, adding that the peasants' masters "stand over them with sticks, to force them to work."[47]

These allegations must, of course, be viewed with a sense of

---

[45] Nat'adze, in *Materialy po Istorii Gruzii i Kavkaza*, V (1937), 336, quoting documents in the Tiflis archives. For the history of the Amilakhori or Amilakhvari family, an important source is Karbelashvili, "Amilakhvart'a sagvareulos istoriuli gujrebi," in *Dzveli Sak'art'velo*, II, 101–38. See further the relevant sections in Gvritishvili, *P'eodaluri Sak'art'velos*, pp. 109–20 and 170–72.

[46] Chardin, *Voyages en Perse*, II, 131.

[47] Tournefort, *Voyage into the Levant*, III, 151.

proportion, as a chance visitor will always tend to be forcefully struck by cases of violence or scandal. In reaching an estimate of Georgian rural life under the later monarchy we must thus beware of accepting unchecked the generalizations of even the best-informed foreign travelers. Though, by the seventeenth century, hereditary proprietorship of estates had replaced the principle of tenure of fiefs in return for loyal service to the crown, and the class of free peasant vassals or *t'arkhani* had declined in importance, this did not mean that all idea of mutual obligation between lord and vassal was dead. Such obligations were often established either by solemn charter or by hallowed custom. An instance of a serf's rights being guaranteed by a legal deed is recorded under the year 1778: a certain Ghviniashvili declares himself to have entered voluntarily into serfdom under the Mourav K'aikhosro and his sons. "You are good," said Ghviniashvili, "I will be faithful; do me no injustice." The charter is countersigned by five witnesses. Again, in 1672, a peasant voluntarily declared himself a serf of Qorghanashvili in return for food and protection. If later he should manage to buy himself free, he promised to leave Qorghanashvili one of his sons in his stead.[48] Other cases show that such voluntary subjection by peasants, and even by members of the squirearchy, into vassalage, was not uncommon. Such a condition, if safeguarded by charter, was often preferable to poverty or insecurity in a freer social status.[49] Also extant are documents showing that temporary serfdom, pending repayment of a debt, was at this period a recognized institution,[50] as well as diplomas recording the liberation of serfs in exchange for cash or payment in kind.[51] Sometimes provision was made for a serf to be liberated on his master's death.[52] Social custom prevented

---

[48] P'urtseladze, *Gruzinskie krest'ianskie gramoty*, p. 6. This recalls instances in Western European feudal custom where the unprovided-for son of a small freeman might declare himself a *villanus sponte sua*, or villein of his own accord, and thus acquire land to give himself a livelihood in return for the assumption of the burdens incidental to villeinage. See A. L. Poole, *From Domesday Book to Magna Carta, 1087–1216* (Oxford, 1951), p. 44.

[49] Karst, *Corpus Juris Ibero-Caucasici*, III, 19.

[50] See a document of 1670, published by T'aqaishvili in *Sak'art'velos sidzveleni*, Vol. III, Charter No. 580, Karst, tr., *Corpus Juris Ibero-Caucasici*, III, 19–20.

[51] Karst, *Corpus Juris Ibero-Caucasici*, III, 21–24.

[52] M.-F. Brosset, *Histoire de la Géorgie*, Introduction, p. LXXXII.

the arbitrary transfer of a serf settled on the land to the lord's domestic service; that was reserved as punishment.

Travelers' reports of the period contain highly colored accounts of landowners selling their serfs into slavery to the Turks. There can be no doubt that this was a great abuse of the time. The king of K'art'li was sometimes obliged to send consignments of boys and girls for the shah's service, but it was in Western Georgia that the shameful trade was most rife. Tavernier even relates the amusing story of a Mingrelian ambassador at Constantinople in the seventeenth century who arrived with a retinue of two hundred followers whom he sold off little by little to pay his expenses until only his private secretary and two valets were left.[53]

Especially forcible were the strictures of the patriarch of Antioch, Macarius, who was in Georgia during the 1660s. Not only, says the patriarch, did the Abkhaz, the Circassians, the Svans, the Laz, and other frontier peoples carry off the population in their raids, but the landed proprietors had no scruples about selling their serfs for profit. Many Georgians regarded this traffic as no more blameworthy than any other form of trade, and ladies thought nothing of exchanging a few peasants for new dresses. Bishops and priests taken prisoner in civil wars were sold in this way. Certain bishops themselves were not above sending handsome boys and girls in their diocese to Turkish seraglios. A Mingrelian bishop, whom Macarius excommunicated, had sold sixty persons to the Turks in one year. Another had forcibly separated a married couple with four children, selling the children into slavery. Cases of people disposing thus of wives, brothers, or sisters were not unknown. Mothers were even driven to kill their offspring, rather than see them surrendered to the Turks.[54]

Despite such scandals as these, there were certainly many landowners who faithfully defended their serfs against oppression and upheld the patriarchal traditions of the Georgian way of life. Other-

[53] Tavernier, *Les six voyages,* I, 450.

[54] Macarius III, *Histoire de la Conversion des Géorgiens.* See Krachkovskii, "Opisanie puteshestviia Makariia Antiokhiiskogo," in *Sovetskoe Vostokovedenie,* VI, 185–98. There is a special chapter on the slave trade in Allen, *History of the Georgian People.* For the punishment of individuals found guilty of engaging in this traffic, see M.-F. Brosset, *Histoire de la Géorgie,* Introduction, pp. LXXXIII–LXXXIV.

wise it would be hard to explain the popular opposition met by the Russian authorities early in the nineteenth century when they tried to exile or dispossess members of the Georgian nobility and royal family. The attachment of the peasant to his lord, and the lord's defense of the interests of his vassals, are factors with which we have to reckon even in the darkest days of the Georgian monarchy. We should bear in mind the words of a French consular official, in 1835, after the Russian annexation: "If slavery is a state contrary to nature, and in opposition to modern ideas, in Georgia at least it is fortunately mitigated by the humane character of the masters, who in general treat their men with extreme mildness." [55]

The positive aspects of the feudal system in later days are well set forth by the great Georgian lyric poet Akaki Tseret'eli (1840–1915), who writes in his autobiography:

The relationships which had been introduced long ago in connection with the system of serfdom had entered into the people's very marrow and were treated as law, the breaking of which was deemed a sin. In our country, in contrast to other lands, the feudal relationship was conditional and limited. Serfs knew what their obligations were, masters, what they could require of their serfs, and both sides carried out their duties meticulously. Not all serfs were taxed the same amount of quitrent. Some peasant families paid less, some more; certain ones, having paid off their quitrent, received manumission. For instance, the quitrent of one of our peasants was equivalent to half an egg. This peasant used to arrive in the courtyard at the beginning of Shrovetide, would cook his egg in the kitchen, peel off the shell, cut the egg into two equal halves with a horse hair, and hand one half to his lord as his quitrent. This half-egg quitrent so burdened the peasant that he more than once begged his lord: "Let me off the quitrent, and I will bring you a cow."

But his master retorted: "The quitrent was fixed by our forefathers. I will not cancel it for the sake of a cow, or everyone will say that I was motived by greed. . . . But if you show your devotion in some other way, perhaps I will remove this quitrent. . . ."

One of the peasants had to provide ten *koka* of wine a year.[56] In a season when the grape harvest was bad, the master ordered him to bring

---

[55] Archives of the French Ministry of Foreign Affairs, Correspondence Commerciale, Tiflis, II, 109 (Dispatch No. 29 of Consul Ratti-Menton, dated August 30, 1835).

[56] The *koka* is a Georgian liquid measure, varying from district to district, and equivalent to from 1½ to 6 Russian *vedro,* or about 30 to 100 bottles.

ten *koka* of water in wineskins and pour it into the wine storage jars.

"By God's will, the vines have not produced any crop," said the master. "The peasant has labored no less than in past years. We cannot demand from him what he does not possess. But water flows past his very door, so I have had him bring some water at least, so that he should not think that I have completely let him off his quitrent. I do not ask any more from him than he has owed me from our grandfathers' times, but what is owed I will not give up. So it was commanded by our ancestors, and this testament we should pass on to our children."

The peasants themselves firmly insisted on the precise fulfillment of mutual obligations—they were ready to die rather than pay anything extra.

The village of T'avasa was as famous for its pigs as Shrosha for its cocks, Ratcha for its calves, and Argvet'i for its sheep. The peasants of T'avasa were obliged to present at the courtyard every year after Christmas, towards Shrovetide, one, year-old pig per household. According to their custom, each peasant used to cut off the right leg from the carcass he had brought and take it home. This was called, "bringing back your good luck." [57]

Akaki Tseret'eli was born in 1840, so that his personal experience did not extend earlier than the period of Russian occupation. But what he says about the extreme conservatism of the Georgian peasant and his master makes it clear that the customs described have their roots in earlier centuries, and are fully applicable to the period with which we are concerned.

Not every Georgian peasant was as privileged as those on the Tseret'eli estate. Among the various dues and services which might be required of him were working a stipulated number of days on the lord's private land, helping to build the lord's house or barns, handing over a share of the harvest or of his flocks and herds, offering hospitality to the lord's guests and their retinues, gathering and delivering firewood, and providing food for the lord's table for weddings and church festivals. We should also note that serfs were debarred from selling property or incurring debts without their master's permission, [58] though this applied only to such transactions

---

[57] Tseret'eli, *Perezhitoe*, pp. 47–49.

[58] Karst, *Corpus Juris Ibero-Caucasici*, III, 74–76; Brosset, *Histoire de la Géorgie*, Introduction, p. CLXIV; P'urtseladze, *Gruzinskie krest'ianskie gramoty*, p. 11.

as the selling or leasing of houses, fields, and so on, and not to the marketing of farm or garden produce.

Particularly interesting is the picture of feudal life in the province of Mingrelia by Father Lamberti. He describes how the nobles had retainers or equerries whose duties were to serve them in their castles and follow them into battle.[59] The Mingrelian peasantry provided their lords with firewood, carried their baggage when traveling, and followed them on foot to battle. They supplied annually one cow per household, and a cartload of millet, bread, wine, and poultry. The peasant was expected to entertain his lord whenever he deigned to pay the peasant a visit, and also any visitors whom the lord might wish to receive. Lamberti adds that the feudal lords of Mingrelia possessed power of life and death over their serfs and inherited the property of any peasant family on their domains should the family die out.[60]

Of taxes in cash, the principal were the *bash-mali* (the name derives from Turco-Persian fiscal terminology and means poll tax) and the *makhta,* a fixed due levied annually on each household. There were additional levies such as the *sat'at'ro* and *saqeeno* taxes, which originally were earmarked for tribute to the Mongols and the shahs of Persia.

Brosset has collected more than a hundred different terms from charters and official documents specifying various forms of taxes and feudal dues,[61] and a further selection is supplied by the important collection of charters recently published by Professor Berdzenish-vili.[62] The picture is further complicated by the exemptions enjoyed by estates belonging to the church or by individual peasant families as a reward for loyal service to the king or to their lord.

Besides regular taxes and dues, foreign invaders who occupied the

---

[59] Further details on the duties and status of these retainers, known as *msakhurebi* (i.e., those rendering service) or *azatebi* (freemen) are given by P'urtseladze, in *Gruzinskie krest'ianskie gramoty,* p. 106.

[60] Lamberti, "Relation de la Mengrellie," in Thévenot, *Relations de divers voyages,* I, 34.

[61] M.-F. Brosset, *Histoire de la Géorgie,* Introduction, pp. CLXIV–CLXXVI. Details of taxes paid specifically by peasants living in the Aragvi valley are given by Natadze, in *Materialy po Istorii Gruzii i Kavkaza,* V (1937), 351–54.

[62] Berdzenishvili, *Dokumentebi Sak'art'velos,* Vols. I and II: *Batonqmuri urt'iert'-oba.*

country from time to time seldom failed to extort special contributions. The most rapacious of these conquerors was Nadir Shah of Persia, whose demands drove the Georgians to desperation and in 1747 almost provoked a general insurrection. Nadir's exactions took the form of a special poll tax, levies on the merchants and on landed property, and the compulsory supply of corn and forage to the Persian army at artificially low prices.[63]

As a result of this multiplicity of taxes, we might expect the seventeenth-century Georgian peasant to be wretchedly poverty-stricken. This does not seem to have been the case. Even the most critical foreign travelers comment on the fertility of the country. In 1672, Chardin found the province of Samtskhe, in southwestern Georgia, abounding in honey, corn, wine, fruit, pigs, and cattle. He lodged with peasants and was provided with poultry, eggs, and vegetables, as well as with wine, fruit, and bread. Approaching Tiflis, Chardin noted that the land was productive and provisions abundant and cheap. Excellent apples and pears could be had and plenty of meat and game.[64] Thirty years later, Tournefort arrived in Georgia from Turkey, and was impressed by it as a fine country, with "a great many pretty considerable villages." He was pleased with his reception at the hands of the country folk, who "come and present you with all manner of provisions, bread, wine, fowls, hogs, lambs, sheep." He contrasted the Georgians' smiling countenances with the "serious fellows that survey you gravely from head to foot" in Turkey. The honest Georgian countrymen gave Tournefort a hen "as fat as a turkey" for a necklace worth six farthings, and "a great measure of wine for bracelets of eighteen deniers." The same traveler speaks highly of the orchards and cornfields he passed on his travels in Georgia.[65]

---

[63] Chronicles of Sekhnia Chkhcidze and Papuna Orbeliani, summarized in M.-F. Brosset, *Histoire de la Géorgie*, Introduction, pp. CLXIII–CLXIV; also in Karst, *Corpus Juris Ibero-Caucasici*, III, 26–28.

[64] Chardin, *Voyages en Perse*, II, 92–94, 127–28.

[65] Tournefort, *Voyage into the Levant*, III, 137–42. The Mingrelian peasants in the western region of Georgia seem to have been less well off at this period; the Russian envoy Elchin comments on the amount of "nakedness" he saw, adding that in Mingrelia "everyone lives in the woods, and where there are no woods, there are no people either." (Likhachev, *Puteshestviya Russkikh poslov*, pp. 224–25.)

We may safely say, therefore, that the lot of the Georgian peasant in the seventeenth and eighteenth centuries, if not always enviable, had its favorable side. The peasant was usually settled on a plot of land under the protection of either king, prince, or squire, to whom his obligations were regulated by ancient custom, if not by written charter. It is true that most categories of peasants could be bought or sold, together, in principle, with the estates on which they lived, or else to be settled on other land. Political and social insecurity, however, often weighed heavy on the serf. In Western Georgia, the slave trade with Turkey was assuming scandalous proportions, in spite of the efforts of the more enlightened princes and clergy to stamp it out. In Eastern Georgia, raids by the Lezghian tribesmen of Daghestan resulted in frequent kidnaping. But these abuses arose as much from the enfeebled and precarious state of the Georgian monarchy as from any inherent vice in the national character or social system.

From this survey of the various classes of the laity, we may pass on to consider the spiritual role and economic position of the Georgian clergy.

It has already been noted that the Georgian church was founded in the fourth century, and after being for a time dependent on the Orthodox Patriarchate of Antioch, subsequently became autocephalous, with its own elected catholicos-patriarch. Unlike the Armenian Gregorian church, the Georgians remained within the Eastern Orthodox communion. During the troubled period under the Mongol yoke, a separate patriarchate was set up in Western Georgia, the head of which assumed the title of Catholicos of Abkhazet'i or Abasgia.

What, it may be asked, did the Georgian church contribute to the country's national life during the seventeenth and eighteenth centuries? Some writers, including such eminent scholars as M.-F. Brosset and Mr. W. E. D. Allen, minimize the Church's constructive role. Stress is laid on its failure to "concern itself with the country's material well-being," "contributing as little as possible to production, and regularly to an enormous consumption," [66] or on the seventeenth-

[66] M.-F. Brosset, *Histoire de la Géorgie,* Introduction, p. CIX. Allen, *History of the Georgian People,* p. 272.

century Georgian clergy's "ignorance, drunkenness, immorality and levity." Color is lent such adverse judgments by the censorious reports of Russian priests attached to the various embassies sent by the tsars to Georgia during the period. These clerics, obsessed with ritualistic minutiae, were quick to seize on any deviation from the Orthodox liturgy as performed in Russia.[67] When we recall that the Russian Church itself was at this point rent by the Nikonian schism, we may feel that these Russian priests would have shown greater discretion had they refrained from intolerant criticism of Georgian Church ritual.

We also have to discount much of the censure directed by Roman Catholic missionaries against the Georgian clergy and their conduct of church services. It must be remembered that these missionaries had come to Georgia with the object of converting the people from their traditional Orthodox creed to the Roman confession. Typical of the Roman Catholic missionaries' highly colored accounts of the abuses of the Georgian church is the report of Father Zampi, published by Chardin in his *Travels,* dealing at length with the spiritual shortcomings of the Mingrelians and their clergy.[68] It is interesting to find, however, that the seventeenth-century French biblical scholar and critic, Richard Simon, defends the Georgians against Father Zampi's accusations of impiety and error.[69] In any case, a declaration of faith drawn up by the Georgian bishops in 1672, and transmitted by this same Father Zampi to the French government, contains

[67] Amusing instances of this attitude occur in the report of the Russian envoys to Mingrelia in 1639–40. The Russian priest Paul Zakhar'ev got into an argument with a Mingrelian archimandrite about "how the Lord created heaven and earth, and then who were the descendants of Adam, and who begat whom. Then they reached a point where the archimandrite started claiming that Elias lived before Enoch. But Paul the Priest began asserting, 'Enoch certainly lived before the Flood, whereas Elias lived after the Flood, in fact many years later on.' So then they started quarreling and could not reach any agreement; finally they stopped talking altogether." Sometimes one feels that the Georgians had the best of the argument, as when the Russians enquired about which manifestation of the Virgin Mary a certain monastery was dedicated to, and were told by the Georgians that there was only one Virgin Mary. (Likhachev, *Puteshestviya Russkikh poslov,* pp. 209, 214.)

[68] Chardin, *Voyages en Perse,* I, 152–248. See also Lamberti, "Relation de la Mengrellie," in Thévenot, *Relations de divers voyages,* I, 40–43.

[69] Simon, *Critical History of the Religions and Customs of the Eastern Nations,* pp. 64–74, "Of the Belief and Customs of the Georgians."

nothing to support any charge of heresy or lapse from the fundamental tenets of the Christian faith.[70]

This is not to deny that the Georgian church was subject to abuses. But many of these were equally prevalent in Western Europe. For instance, the Patriarch Macarius comments on the fact that bishops were sometimes appointed from among scions of the Georgian nobility when still children, a custom to which countless parallels could be found in the ecclesiastical history of France during the same period. Again, Macarius justifiably criticizes certain Georgian bishops for their mercenary attitude, one of them having refused to consecrate a new church because the parishioners were too poor to pay his fee. Here again, it would not be difficult to adduce similar cases from the annals of churches far more prosperous than that of Georgia. Even Macarius pays frequent tribute to the Georgians' religious zeal, relating, for instance, how the principal chieftain of the Svans, a Georgian mountain clan nominally ministered to by two absentee bishops, came with large numbers of his followers to be baptized.[71]

Among the special difficulties hindering the work of the Georgian Church which one must take into account were the efforts made by the Turks and Persians to wean the Georgians from Christianity to Islam. After the Turkish occupation of Georgia's southwestern provinces in the sixteenth century, the Ottoman authorities pursued a campaign against Georgian religion and nationality. Mosques sprang up everywhere, and churches fell into ruin.[72] In Eastern Georgia, the area in the Persian sphere of influence, many of the principal churches and monasteries were laid waste by the ruthless Shah 'Abbas I early in the seventeenth century. Later, however, the Mukhranian viceroys of K'art'li, though officially supposed to be Mohammedans, favored the Georgian Church, and protected it from oppression by the Persian overlords. In particular, Shahnavaz I (otherwise known as Wakhtang V) and his pious consort, Queen

[70] Full text in Tamarati, *L'Église géorgienne*, pp. 140–41.

[71] Macarius III, *Histoire de la Conversion des Géorgiens*.

[72] Wakhusht, "Histoires particulières . . . du Samtzkhé," M.-F. Brosset, tr. and ed., *Histoire de la Géorgie*, II, Part 1, 231.

Mariam, did everything in their power to help the Georgian Catholicos Domenti II in his efforts to reform the Georgian Church.[73]
Equally active was King Wakhtang VI, during his regency from
1703 to 1711. He restored the Sion Cathedral at Tiflis, and richly
adorned the Cathedral of the Living Pillar at Mtskhet'a.[74] Wakhtang VI's introduction of printing into Georgia in 1709 resulted in
greatly increased diffusion of the Holy Scriptures.

Nothing would be farther from the truth than to conceive of
Georgian Church dignitaries as idle parasites. We have already
shown that they exercised extensive judicial functions, usefully
supplementing the work of the royal courts. As in Europe, the patriarchal court's special domain included such matters as sacrilege,
witchcraft, marital relations, and moral transgressions. The patriarch
and the bishops were also responsible for checking the traffic in
slaves for the harems of Persia and Turkey. This duty they carried
out with varying zeal and efficiency. They also played an active
political role. One cannot read the Georgian annals without constantly noting cases where the advice of the patriarch was sought
on important questions of war and peace. In western Georgia during the 1660s, the archbishop of Gelat'i played a prominent role in
the sinister court intrigues and civil wars of the time.[75] Ecclesiastics
often acted as ambassadors to Russia, Western Europe, or even the
Mohammedan powers. Prominent among these envoys was Nicephorus Irbakhi-Choloqashvili, a monk of the Order of St. Basil,
who undertook an important mission to Rome in 1626, on behalf of
King T'eimuraz I of Kakhet'i.[76] It was another monk, Sulkhan-Saba
Orbeliani, who went on an embassy to France and Rome in 1713
to enlist support for King Wakhtang VI. After the Turkish invasion
of 1723 the Catholicos Domenti III went to Constantinople to intercede with the sultan of Turkey on behalf of the Georgian people.[77]

[73] Wakhusht, "Histoires particulières du Karthli," in M.-F. Brosset, tr. and ed.,
Histoire de la Géorgie, II, Part 1, 79.
[74] Chkheidze, "Chronicle," in M.-F. Brosset, tr., *Histoire de la Géorgie,* II, Part
2, 28.
[75] Chardin, *Voyages en Perse,* II, 52.
[76] Tamarati, *L'Église géorgienne,* pp. 501-15.
[77] Wakhusht, "Histoires particulières du Karthli," in M.-F. Brosset, tr. and ed.,

Bishops regularly accompanied the Georgian army into battle at the head of their vassals and serfs. A characteristic anecdote is related of a seventeenth-century Georgian prelate on the battlefield, who was asked whether he would officiate that day at the communion service. Replying that he saw no reason to give up either his military or his church duties, the bishop added: "It is for the religion and faith of Christ that the battle is to be fought this day, and not simply for me. Therefore I desire one thing only, and that is to shed my blood while wielding my sword at your head." [78] In the province of Mingrelia, the bishops used to follow their prince into battle "with helmets on their heads and scimitars at their sides." [79] As most wars fought by the Georgians were against the Mohammedan powers, the participation of the Georgian clergy gave them something of the atmosphere of a religious crusade.

The patriarchs of Georgia enjoyed, by virtue of royal charters, the right to appoint their own general to command the squires and peasant-vassals of the church. The king's military officers had no authority over them.[80]

The very extensive domains of the Georgian Church were being augmented constantly by gifts and pious benefactions. A fifteenth-century royal charter includes a long list of villages belonging to the Patriarchal See of Mtskhet'a, from which it can be computed that the patriarch then owned over 2,500 peasant hearths.[81] This does not take into account the separate domains of the many bishoprics and abbeys situated throughout Eastern and Western Georgia. What is more, the church estates occupied a privileged status, with many exemptions from taxes and impositions. For instance, they were often excused from "offerings of bread, wine, animals for

Histoire de la Géorgie, II, Part 1, 125–26; Shay, *The Ottoman Empire from 1720 to 1734*, p. 121. Extracts from an epic poem, *Kat'alikoz-Bak'ariani*, by Iese Tlashadze, containing details of Domenti's mission, are given by E. T'aqaishvili in *Sbornik Materialov dlia Opisaniia Mestnostei i Plemen Kavkaza*, XXXIX (Tiflis, 1908), 236–40.

[78] Wakhusht, *Description géographique de la Géorgie*, pp. 50–51.

[79] Father Jean de Luca, in Thévenot, *Relations de divers voyages curieux*, I (Paris, 1696), 23.

[80] Charter No. 405 of Mtskhet'a, cited by M.-F. Brosset, in *Histoire de la Géorgie*, Introduction, p. CX; P'urtseladze, *Gruzinskie krest'ianskie gramoty*, pp. 21–22.

[81] M.-F. Brosset, *Histoire de la Géorgie*, Introduction, pp. CXV–CXXV.

slaughtering, straw, barley, billeting, capitation tax, provision of fire-wood," etc.[82]

The Church in Georgia was the principal agent of education. Within the limitations imposed by adverse political conditions, it acquitted itself conscientiously of its task. It would of course be foolish to pretend that the Georgian Church schools attached to the principal monasteries were now in anything like the flourishing state attained in the Golden Age of the twelfth and thirteenth centuries. As is well known, during these and earlier centuries, Georgian monasteries on Mount Athos, at Jerusalem, on Mount Sinai, and elsewhere in the Near East transmitted to their homeland many of the finest works of early Christian literature, as well as important original works in the field of theology and Church history. The work of these monasteries had been emulated within Georgia at the academy founded at Gelat'i near K'ut'ais by King David the Builder early in the twelfth century.

This tradition was kept alive even in the darkest days of the later monarchy. In the seventeenth and eighteenth centuries, the principal monuments of Georgian ecclesiastical literature were copied afresh by the monks. Their diligence may be appreciated by reference to the catalogues of the great collections of Georgian manuscripts in libraries at Tiflis, Moscow, Leningrad, Oxford, Paris, and the Vatican. Even during the decline of the Georgian kingdom, the level of literacy remained high. This is shown by the mass of historical writings, private letters, poems, and business and administrative documents, which often displayed a high standard of calligraphy, emanating from seventeenth–eighteenth century Georgia. This must be credited largely to the church schools and seminaries.

Tribute must also be paid to the achievements of the Catholic missions active in Georgia during this period. Links between the Georgian monarchy and the Vatican had been created at the time of the Crusades. In 1329 a Roman Catholic bishopric was established in Tiflis, though the ravages of the Mongols and other obstacles resulted in its abandonment.[83] During the seventeenth cen-

---

[82] See extracts from numerous documents in M.-F. Brosset, *Histoire de la Géorgie*, Introduction, pp. CXLIX–CLVII.

[83] Tamarati, *L'Église géorgienne*, pp. 440–50.

tury, increasing French influence at the Ottoman and Persian courts made it possible to resume Catholic missionary work in Georgia. The Theatine Order sent a group of missionaries, including several physicians, to Western Georgia in 1626. This mission made great headway until civil war and lack of funds eventually forced its withdrawal about 1700. The Theatines were excellent observers and left important accounts of Georgian life. The talented artist, Father Cristoforo Castelli, whose drawings are such an important source for Georgian social history, belonged to this order.

In Eastern Georgia, the Capuchins had a mission house at Tiflis for nearly two centuries, from 1661 until they were expelled by the Russian authorities in 1845. The Georgian rulers valued them for their medical and general intellectual ability, and also for the link they provided between Georgia and Christian Europe. Indeed, several of the Mukhranian princes showed distinct Catholic sympathies. In 1687 we find King Giorgi XI of K'art'li writing to Pope Innocent XI acknowledging his spiritual suzerainty, congratulating him on the victories of the Christian powers over the Grand Turk, and regretting that his relations with the shah of Persia prevented him from joining a general crusade against Islam.[84] Even more pronounced were the Roman Catholic leanings of Giorgi's nephew K'aikhosro, also known by the Persian title of Khusrau-Khan. According to an unpublished document in the French Foreign Office archives,

Khosro Khan publicly confessed the Catholic faith, having three European priests always with him: a French Discalced Carmelite named Father Basil of Paris, and two Italian Capuchins called Father Reginaldo and Father Ambrose of Milan. He attended three Masses regularly every day, and gave generously to charity, even presenting a thousand crowns each to the missions at Tiflis, Tabriz, Ganja, Gori, Isfahan, and Shiraz. In short, he was a prince of exemplary piety and devotion.[85]

Even the hierarchy of the Georgian Orthodox Church was affected by this trend. The brother of Prince K'aikhosro, the catholicos-patriarch of Georgia, Domenti III, toyed with the idea of becoming in secret a Roman Catholic Uniat. His application was forwarded

---

[84] Text of Giorgi XI's letter in Tamarati, *L'Église géorgienne*, pp. 574-75.

[85] Archives of the French Ministry of Foreign Affairs, Correspondance Politique, Perse, VI, 267. See also *Chronicle of the Carmelites*, I, 569-70.

to Rome, but rejected by the Sacred Congregation on the grounds that regulations did not admit of secret conversions.[86] Domenti's nephew, who later became the Georgian Catholicos Antoni I, was also sympathetic toward Roman Catholicism. This fact was exploited by his enemies and rivals with the result that Antoni was temporarily exiled in 1755 and spent some years as an archbishop in Russia.

Without impugning the sincerity of the Mukhranian princes, it must be conceded that the favor they showed to the Roman Catholic Church was not exclusively religious in origin. At a time when European influence in the Levant was rapidly increasing, the Georgians saw in the Pope, the Holy Roman emperor, and the king of France valuable allies in their struggle with the Mohammedan powers. What is more, the missionaries were often men of diplomatic acumen and personal charm. Coming from the great cultural centers of France and Italy, they were in their modest way the bearers of the Renaissance heritage. The sober Chardin, in fact, was shocked at a banquet in Tiflis to hear the head of the local Capuchin mission performing on the spinet. After playing a version of the *Te Deum* and the *Magnificat,* he further scandalized Chardin by performing a selection of Spanish and Italian operatic arias.[87] It was at the Catholic mission in Tiflis that the great Georgian historian and geographer, Prince Wakhusht, received most of his formal education and insight into historical method. In addition to their general culture, many of the missionaries were trained physicians, a rare and valued qualification in the primitive and unsanitary conditions of the time.[88]

These successes of the Roman Catholic missionaries did not fail to stir up jealousy on the part of both the Georgian Orthodox and the Armenian Gregorian clergy. As a result of the existence of an important Armenian element in the towns of Tiflis and Gori, where Catholic missions were situated, the jealous reaction of the Armenian clergy was particularly virulent there. They instigated several dis-

[86] *Chronicle of the Carmelites,* I, 569.

[87] Chardin, *Voyages en Perse,* II, 188–89.

[88] In his "Relation de la Mengrellie," Father Lamberti gives a list of diseases prevalent in Georgia.

graceful incidents of mob violence against the Catholics, which led the Pope and the king of France to intercede with the Persian court in the missionaries' behalf.[89]

Such outbreaks of religious fanaticism were an exception to the general rule of religious toleration which prevailed in Georgia. As early as the twelfth century, one may find Moslem historians paying tribute to the tolerance of the Christian kings of Georgia.[90] This tradition persisted in spite of the ravages the country had to endure from invading Turks and Persians. It is worth noting that it was the Armenians, themselves a privileged religious minority, and not the Georgians, who instituted the persecutions against the Catholic missions. The substantial Moslem minority in Georgia, which included a large proportion of the Tiflis artisans and the nomadic Tatar tribes in the southern provinces, were free to carry on their communal life and to worship according to Mohammedan rites. There were two mosques in seventeenth-century Tiflis where the Persians and Tatars were free to worship, though it is true that fear of scandalizing the Christian population prevented the Muezzins from climbing to the minarets to call the Faithful to prayer.[91]

The history of the time affords numerous examples of this religious tolerance. For instance, there is a document of the year 1667 in which the Armenian Catholicos Jacob of Echmiadzin praises the grace and favor shown to the Armenians by the late King Rostom of Georgia, himself a Moslem. As a token of friendship, Rostom had granted to the Patriarchal See of Echmiadzin the village of Nakhiduri in the province of Borchalo.[92] We have already seen how this same Mohammedan King Rostom conciliated his Christian fellow-countrymen by restoring the principal Georgian churches. Thus one finds a Georgian Moslem ruler subordinating religious zeal to constructive statecraft, and taking pains to conciliate both the Georgian Orthodox and the Armenian Gregorian communities by acts of

[89] Tamarati, *L'Église géorgienne,* pp. 605–23; *Chronicle of the Carmelites,* I, 522–23; Archives of the French Ministry of Foreign Affairs, Correspondance Politique, Perse, III, 19.

[90] Allen, *History of the Georgian People,* p. 333.

[91] Tournefort, *Voyage into the Levant,* III, 160.

[92] P'urtseladze, *Gruzinskie krest'ianskie gramoty,* p. 95.

largesse. The same policy was followed by Rostom's successors. To win his throne Erekle I (1688–1703), originally a member of the Georgian Orthodox church, was circumcised and professed Islam. But he was far from bigoted. "He went to the mosque," says Tournefort, "and came to Mass too at the Church of the Capuchins, where he would drink his Holiness's [i.e., the Pope's] health." [93]

Such broadmindedness should not lead one to overlook the many instances of heroism shown by Georgian Christians in the profession of their faith. Most famous of the Georgian martyrs of the seventeenth century was Queen K'et'evan, mother of King T'eimuraz I of Kakhet'i. The queen was held as hostage at the Persian court for the good behavior of the rebellious T'eimuraz. But T'eimuraz persisted in defying Shah 'Abbas of Persia. The shah offered K'et'evan every inducement to become a Moslem, even proposing to make her his wife. Enraged by her disdainful refusal, he ordered her to be tortured to death. The sentence was executed at Shiraz in 1624, with every refinement of cruelty.[94] Her martyrdom is regularly commemorated by the Georgian church to this day.

From this survey of Georgian society during the rule of the Mukhranian viceroys it may be concluded that Georgia's political and social evolution was artificially hampered by the division of the country into Turkish and Persian zones of influence, by constant struggles against invaders, and by internecine feuds between the different kingdoms and principalities. Economic decline and general impoverishment, especially in Western Georgia, led to such flagrant abuses as the slave trade.

It should, further, be borne in mind that the rule of the Georgian kings and sovereign princes was largely patriarchal in character, the idea of representative government virtually unknown. Feudal institutions persisted from much earlier times, though in modified form. The principles of vassalage and loyal service to the crown as the basis of land tenure had been replaced largely by the system of hereditary proprietorship founded on serfdom. This system was

[93] Tournefort, *Voyage into the Levant*, III, 147.

[94] Avalov, "T'eimuraz I and his Poem, 'The Martyrdom of Queen K'et'evan,'" in *Georgica*, Vol. I, Nos. 4–5.

accepted and taken for granted by all sections of the community. In defense of their pretensions, feudal magnates were often led to open defiance of their king, to the detriment of law and order.

Religion played a prominent part in the national life. The Georgian church did much to preserve national consciousness in spite of political division. Tolerance was the rule. Georgian Orthodox, Armenian Gregorian, Roman Catholic, and Persian and Tatar Mohammedan communities had their recognized rights and privileges and lived together in general harmony, marred only occasionally by isolated outbreaks of mob violence.

The existence of tyrannical landlords and corrupt prelates can no more be denied in seventeenth-century Georgia than it can in respect of countries of Western Europe during the same period. But the negative features of Georgian life should not blind us to its better aspects. In the Mukhranian viceroys, Georgia was fortunate in finding a dynasty which, for a few brief decades, contributed greatly to healing the country's wounds and rebuilding its national life. That they could not achieve even more than they did was, as will be seen, less their own fault than the result of Georgia's entanglement in a web of Great Power rivalry quite outside their control.

4

Political History of the Mukhranian Period, 1658-1703

THE political and diplomatic history of Georgia during the rule of the Mukhranian viceroys in Tiflis is highly complex. Internally, the various Georgian dynasts had to contend with factional strife instigated by the great nobles, as well as with their own mutual rivalries and animosities. These causes of tension were adroitly utilized by the Turks and Persians, who followed a policy of "divide and rule" in the Caucasus. The premature intervention of the Russian court on a number of occasions merely served to exacerbate Christian Georgia's relations with the Mohammedan powers and to encourage the Georgians in a mistaken reliance on what they imagined to be sure protection in times of trouble. That the Mukhranians, to a great extent at least, triumphed over these difficulties and secured for Eastern Georgia several decades of relative peace and prosperity is a tribute to their powers of constructive statecraft. Though the story of these decades, with their complicated intrigues, may sometimes be a tedious one, an attempt will be made to establish at least a firm outline of fact for the political history of the period.

The first of the Georgian kings of the house of the Mukhranian Bagratids to rule in Tiflis as viceroy of the shah was Shahnavaz I, known in the Georgian annals as King Wakhtang V. He succeeded his adoptive father, King Rostom, on the latter's death in 1658. According to contemporary testimony, Shahnavaz was a man of imposing presence, a good horseman and general, skillful in negotiation and courtly in manner.[1]

His abilities were soon put to the test. On his accession large areas of Georgia were seething with unrest. The Persian governor of Kakhet'i, Selim Khan, who was supposed to act in consultation with Rostom, had taken advantage of the latter's last illness to embark on a policy of repression against the local populace. Selim encouraged Tatar tribesmen to profane the Christian churches, thus provoking the duke of the Aragvi to rise in revolt. The Persians suffered a crushing defeat. But the duke now overreached himself by repudiating his allegiance to the new king, Shahnavaz. Ruthless measures seemed called for, and Shahnavaz soon afterwards had the duke assassinated, and confiscated a large portion of his estates.

Though peace was now restored in Eastern Georgia, the situation in Imeret'i to the west was far from satisfactory. The kingdom of Imeret'i had for a number of years been in the throes of civil war. The energetic prince or Dadian of Mingrelia, Levan II (1605–57), had refused to acknowledge Alexander III of Imeret'i as his overlord, and aspired to displace him from his throne.[2] Both rulers sought Russian support in their cause. Envoys from Moscow visited Mingrelia in 1639–40, though without achieving any positive results. In response to an appeal from King Alexander of Imeret'i, another embassy arrived at K'ut'ais in 1651, with instructions to take Alexander under the protection of Tsar Alexis Mikhailovich in return for an oath of fealty to the Russian crown.[3]

The Russians were still too far removed from Transcaucasia to afford either side anything more than moral support so that their intervention had little effect on the course of events. Levan Dadian continued to wage war against King Alexander, whose brother Mamuka was captured and murdered by Levan. But on Levan's

---

[1] Peyssonnel, *Essai sur les troubles,* pp. 43–44; "Notice sur une histoire en vers du roi Chah-Nawaz Ier, par Phechang," in M.-F. Brosset, *Histoire de la Géorgie,* Vol. II, Part 1, Addition VIII.

[2] See Lamberti, "Relation de la Mengrellie," pp. 33, 39.

[3] Solov'ev, *Istoriia Rossii,* III, 546–61; Allen, *History of the Georgian People,* pp. 344–49; Polievktov, *Evropeiskie puteshestvenniki XIII–XVIII vv. po Kavkazu* (Tiflis, 1935), pp. 36–39, 42–44, 67–71; Polievktov, *Posol'stvo stol'nika Tolochanova.*

death in 1657, Alexander invaded Mingrelia and installed his own nominee, Wamiq, as prince-Dadian. For a short time the authority of the crown of Imeret'i was reestablished throughout Western Georgia. But in 1660, Alexander himself died, and the court of K'ut'ais again became the scene of intestine rivalry and intrigue. King Alexander had been twice married: by his first wife, he had had a son named Bagrat, though his second consort, Darejan, the daughter of King T'eimuraz of Kakhet'i, was childless. The legitimate heir, Bagrat, was accordingly crowned king. But he had reckoned without his stepmother, Darejan, who had no intention of giving up her power. She suggested to Bagrat that he should now marry her. On the king's refusal, he was seized by a gang of Darejan's supporters who put his eyes out. The queen-dowager now seized power, married an insignificant lord named Wakhtang Tchutchunashvili, and had him crowned king.

This marriage did not commend itself to Darejan's aristocratic partisans who enlisted Turkish and Mingrelian aid and restored Bagrat to the throne. Darejan was exiled to Akhaltsikhe, in Turkish Georgia.

These events had been closely watched by the Eastern Georgian court in Tiflis. King Shahnavaz, who had now subdued the rising in Kakhet'i, realized that the internal dissensions in Western Georgia provided an excellent opportunity for an attempt to reunify the whole of Georgia under one crown. By appealing to Shahnavaz for help, Darejan's hard-pressed faction now gave him the pretext he needed. He managed to obtain the shah of Persia's permission, and in 1661 marched on K'ut'ais with his son Archil and the army of K'art'li.

After a successful campaign in Western Georgia, Shahnavaz had his fourteen-year-old son Archil crowned king of Imeret'i. But the reunification of Georgia under the house of Mukhran was short-lived. The local nobility of Western Georgia resented having a king from the Eastern royal house of K'art'li. The sultan of Turkey strongly objected to what the Ottoman government justly considered a Persian-inspired incursion into the Turkish zone of influence. A Turkish ultimatum was soon received in Isfahan, threatening a declaration of war if Shahnavaz maintained his son on the throne of Western Georgia. Shahnavaz was forced to recall Archil from K'ut'ais in 1663 and to restore the rightful king, Bagrat.

The political stability of Western Georgia could not so readily be reestablished. In 1668 the pasha of Akhaltsikhe marched on K'ut'ais, replaced Darejan on the throne, and carried off many of the inhabitants into slavery. But Darejan and her husband did not long survive to benefit from this fresh usurpation. Different accounts are given of the manner of their deaths. According to the Georgian historian Prince Wakhusht, certain of the nobles of Imeret'i persuaded Darejan's favorite to kill her. The favorite, according to this version, murdered her with a spear as she was doing her hair, while other conspirators dispatched her husband Wakhtang in the square outside. The French traveler Chardin relates, on the other hand, that the favorite lured Darejan to his apartment where she was stabbed to death. Following Chardin, Darejan's husband was held until the arrival of the blind Bagrat, the legitimate monarch, who had his hand guided as he stabbed the usurper repeatedly, exclaiming, "Traitor, you had my eyes put out; I shall tear out your heart!" [4]

We now revert to events in Eastern Georgia. The Turks' violent reaction to Shahnavaz's attempt to reunify Western with Eastern Georgia under the Mukhranian dynasty made it clear to the king that his objective could not be permanently reached at this juncture. Shahnavaz therefore abandoned this project in favor of a more limited one, namely the reunification of the two East Georgian kingdoms, Kakhet'i and K'art'li. If Archil could be set on the throne of Kakhet'i while Shahnavaz continued to rule over K'art'li, then at least all Eastern Georgia would be reunited. To gain the shah's consent, Archil was prevailed upon, much against his will, to become a nominal convert to Islam, assuming the title of Shah-Nazar-Khan.

Unfortunately Archil had to contend again in Kakhet'i, as in Imeret'i, with the claims of the legitimate local royal house. The

---

[4] This account has been abridged from Wakhusht, "Histoires particulières . . . de l'Iméreth," in M.-F. Brosset, tr. and ed., *Histoire de la Géorgie*, II, Part 1, 276-83, and Chardin, *Voyages en Perse*, II, 45-59.

representative of the Bagratids of Kakhet'i, Nicholas (known in Georgia as Erekle), was a grandson of the veteran King T'eimuraz, who had recently died in Persia. Born in 1643, Erekle had been taken to Russia when King Rostom of K'art'li defeated T'eimuraz on the field of battle in 1648. Many of the Kakhs remained loyal to Erekle and refused to obey Archil. Erekle was recalled from Moscow by his supporters. In 1664 a pitched battle took place between the rival kings of Kakhet'i, in which Erekle was worsted and obliged to flee to Russia, where he won a distinguished position at the court of Alexis Mikhailovich.[5]

For a time the two kingdoms of Eastern Georgia were virtually united under Shahnavaz and his son. This brought undoubted benefit to the interests of Georgia. Making the city of T'elavi his residence, in place of Gremi which was ruined by the Persians, Archil set out to restore Kakhet'i to its ancient prosperity. He won renown for his justice and administrative ability. However, the promising situation was of short duration, as a result mainly of the ill will of the Persian grand vazir, Shaykh 'Ali Khan. This influential minister harbored a grudge against Shahnavaz who had refused him his daughter in marriage. The grand vazir sought to avenge this slight by turning the new shah of Persia, Sulayman,[6] against the Georgian royal family whom he represented as disloyal to Persian interests. To further his designs, the grand vazir invited the prince of Kakhet'i, Erekle, to return to Persia from Moscow. Simultaneously, the Turkish pasha of Akhaltsikhe was persuaded to invite Archil to make another bid for the throne of Imeret'i. Archil, who detested the Persians and their religion, readily fell into the trap. In 1675 he abruptly left Kakhet'i and went over to the Turks.[7]

Archil's father, King Shahnavaz, was now placed in a position of

[5] Wakhusht, "Histoires particulières . . . du Cakheth," in M.-F. Brosset, tr. and ed., *Histoire de la Géorgie,* II, Part 1, 176. Nicholas (Erekle) featured prominently at the wedding of Alexis Mikhailovich to Natalia Naryshkin, and stood in high favor with the Russian royal family. See Tatishvili, *Gruziny v Moskve,* Part I: "Tsarevich Nikolai."

[6] Sulayman succeeded Shah 'Abbas II in 1666.

[7] Wakhusht, "Histoires particulières . . . du Cakheth," in M.-F. Brosset, tr. and ed., *Histoire de la Géorgie,* II, Part 1, 177; Peyssonnel, *Essai sur les troubles,* pp. 45–47; M.-F. Brosset, *Perepiska . . . Gruzinskikh Tsarei,* p. LXVII; Chardin, *Voyages en Perse,* X, 39–42, 215–19.

the utmost delicacy vis-à-vis the shah of Persia, who naturally resented Archil's desertion to the Turks and suspected Shahnavaz of complicity. The grand vazir, who had engineered the whole affair, was able to represent the entire Georgian royal family as unreliable and hostile to Persian interests. Shah Sulayman summoned his viceroy, King Shahnavaz, to Isfahan to give an account of his conduct. In 1676, Shahnavaz set out for the Persian capital, leaving his second son Giorgi as regent in Tiflis. On the way, he was taken ill, and died near Kazvin. His body was buried at the Persian holy city of Qum.[8]

So ended the eighteen year reign of the first of the Mukhranian viceroys. Shahnavaz must be given credit for furthering the commercial and agricultural recovery of Eastern Georgia. His statesmanlike attempt at the reunification of all three Georgian kingdoms under the same dynasty failed, as a result both of the particularism of the landed aristocracy and of the inevitable hostility of the Persian and Ottoman governments. In spite of this failure, Shahnavaz must be numbered among the most able rulers of Georgia during the later period of the monarchy. His personal prestige and the brilliance of his court made him a respected figure throughout Persia and Transcaucasia.

In the normal course of events, Shahnavaz's successor and heir should have been his eldest son, Archil. But Archil had forfeited his claims by his ill-considered act of going over to the Turks. The throne now passed to his brother Giorgi. Both Archil and Giorgi were destined to have careers both brilliant and erratic. Both were fated to die far distant from their homeland, one in Moscow, the other in Afghanistan, on the very frontiers of India. To trace these two princes' lives and careers to their end, we must leave the domestic politics of the Tiflis court, and range far afield into the wider spheres of Russian and Persian imperial policies.

After Archil had gone over to the Turkish frontier authorities at Akhaltsikhe, he was soon reestablished in K'ut'ais with the aid of the local pasha. But both Archil and the pasha had reckoned without the intervention of the Ottoman court at Constantinople. The

---

[8] Wakhusht, "Histoires particulières du Karthli," in M.-F. Brosset, tr. and ed., *Histoire de la Géorgie,* II, Part 1, 81.

sultan was furious at Archil's reappearance in the Turkish zone of influence. Orders were given for the pasha's execution, and Archil only reigned for one year before the Turks expelled him in 1679, and again the rightful king, the blind Bagrat, was replaced on the throne.

After roaming about the mountain fastnesses of the Caucasus for some time, Archil decided to take refuge in Russia. The court of Moscow, though aware of his value as a source of embarrassment to the Turks, granted him a grudging welcome. He was made to reside in the frontier settlement of Terki and not invited to the capital until 1686.[9] But the life of an émigré did not suit Archil, and his energetic and restless temperament was little suited to retirement. Encouraged by his brother Giorgi, king of K'art'li, Archil recrossed the Caucasus range in 1689 and succeeded in regaining the throne of Imeret'i. The next few years were spent in guerrilla warfare against the Turks and the leader of the local aristocracy, Prince Abashidze. By this time Western Georgia was in a state of anarchy. In the words of Prince Wakhusht, "One saw nothing but perfidy, slave trading, raids, pillage and wickedness, not only among the nobility but even among the common people." Eventually Archil gave up hope of reestablishing himself permanently in this troubled kingdom and crossed the mountains once more into Russia, where he was to pass the rest of his life.[10]

The British naval officer and engineer John Perry, who met King Archil soon after his final return to Russia, described him as "a tall well-looked gentleman," and added,

Whether in Complaisance or no, I cannot tell; but he wore a beard like the Russes. . . . And when he came to Mosco he was receiv'd with great kindness by the Czar, and had the revenue of several Villages appointed to him, to subsist with his followers.

Perry goes on to give details of preparations made by Peter to send an expeditionary force to restore Archil to the throne of Imeret'i.

[9] An interesting account of Archil's reception on his first arrival in Russia is given by Tumanskii, in *Sobranie raznykh zapisok o zhizni Petra Velikogo,* V, 302–22. See also M.-F. Brosset, "Notice sur les divers séjours du roi Artchil en Russie," in *Histoire de la Géorgie,* Vol. II, Part 2.

[10] Wakhusht, "Histoires particulières . . . de l'Iméreth," in M.-F. Brosset, tr. and ed., *Histoire de la Géorgie,* II, Part 1, 294–99.

These came to nothing on account of the Russian defeat at the battle of Narva and the subsequent revolt of the Don Cossacks.[11]

The disaster inflicted by the Swedes on the Russian army at Narva in 1700, in addition to frustrating Archil's hopes of regaining his throne, also brought tragedy into his family life. Archil's son, Prince Alexander Archilovich, had been brought up at the Russian court on terms of great intimacy with the young Peter the Great. Alexander accompanied his sovereign to Western Europe on the Great Embassy of 1697. At The Hague and Utrecht he studied modern artillery technique. In London, contemporary observers mention that he shared a bedroom with Peter. On returning to Russia, Alexander Archilovich was appointed head of the Pushkarskii Prikaz or Artillery Department, and made general of ordnance (*Feldzeugmeister*) of the Russian army.[12]

In this capacity, Alexander took part in the famous battle of Narva in November, 1700, where he, with many other Russian generals, was taken prisoner by the Swedes under Charles XII.[13] A neglected passage in Voltaire's *Histoire de Charles XII* gives important details on Alexander's capture:

Among the prisoners taken at the battle of Narva was one who presented an outstanding example of the vicissitudes of fate: he was the elder son and heir apparent to the Georgian crown; he was called the czarafis Artfchelou. . . . His father, Mittelleski,[14] czar and lord of the most beautiful part of the lands situated between the Ararat mountains and the eastern end of the Black Sea, had been expelled from his kingdom by his own subjects in 1688, and had elected to throw himself on the mercy of the emperor of Muscovy rather than have recourse to the sultan of Turkey. The son of this king, who was nineteen years of age, wished to follow Peter the Great in his expedition against the Swedes and was captured in the fray by some Finnish soldiers who had already stripped him and were about to murder him. Count Renschild snatched him from their hands, had clothes given him, and presented him to his master. Charles sent him to Stockholm, where this unfortunate prince died some years

[11] Perry, *State of Russia under the Present Czar,* pp. 97-98.

[12] Bogoslovskii, *Petr I,* II (Moscow, 1941), 159, 275-76, 301, and IV (Moscow, 1948), 271 (citing throughout the *Pis'ma i Bumagi Petra Velikogo*).

[13] Solov'ev, *Istoriia Rossii,* III, 1247.

[14] For "czarafis Artfchelou" read "Tsarevich Alexander Archilovich," and for "Mittelleski," "Imeretinskii."

later.[15] As he watched him depart, the king could not refrain from making a natural comment out loud in front of his officers on the strange destiny of an Asiatic prince, born at the foot of the Caucasus mountains, who was going to live in captivity in icy Sweden: "It is, said he, as if I were one day to be a prisoner among the Crimean Tartars." These words made no impression at the time; but afterwards people remembered them only too well, when the course of events had turned them into a prediction.[16]

To try to secure Alexander's release, King Archil begged the Austrian court to intercede at Stockholm. The Austrian ambassador at the Swedish capital received instructions from the Austrian chancellor, Prince Kaunitz, to negotiate Alexander's release, but was unable to bring the matter to a successful outcome.[17] In 1706, after his son had been six years in captivity, Archil addressed a personal appeal to Charles XII, imploring him to restore Alexander in exchange for a number of Swedish officer prisoners.[18] The necessary arrangements, however, were made too late, and it was not until 1710 that Alexander was allowed to leave Stockholm. But he was then a sick man and died at Riga before being reunited with his family. Alexander's death was a bitter blow to his father. Archil did not long survive his son. In 1713 he too died, and was buried in the Donskoi Monastery at Moscow.

Neither Archil nor his son Alexander fulfilled their brilliant promise. The careers of both father and son were brought to an untimely end, but they were men of courage, who were highly thought of by their contemporaries. To quote an eighteenth-century writer,

Archil had excellent qualities: nature had endowed him with intrepid bravery and such exceptional strength that he could behead a bull with his sword, holding it in one hand. He loved the pursuit of letters, worked constantly to educate himself, and had a mind adorned with every

[15] By way of correction of Voltaire's otherwise excellent account it should be noted that Alexander was twenty-seven, not nineteen years of age in 1700, and that he died at Riga, not Stockholm.

[16] Voltaire, *Histoire de Charles XII,* livre II. The allusion is, of course, to Charles XII's enforced residence in the Ottoman dominions after the battle of Poltava.

[17] See the dispatch dated Vienna, August 27, 1704, cited by Tchqonia, "Gorkis olk'shi aghmochenili k'art'uli sidzveleni," in *Literaturuli dziebani,* IV, 271–72.

[18] The text of this letter is printed by M.-F. Brosset, "Notice sur une lettre géorgienne du roi Artchil à Charles XII," in *Mélanges Asiatiques,* II, 213–17.

branch of knowledge that could be acquired in lands so stripped of resources. He was good-natured, but so quick-tempered that nothing could restrain him in moments of anger. But as his lively temper was combined with a good heart, he always began with irascibility and finished by kindness. Good fortune was the only thing he lacked in order to be a great prince.[19]

Our study of Archil's eventful career has taken us far from Georgia—to Moscow and even to the battlefield of Narva and to the Swedish capital of Stockholm. The career of Archil's younger brother Giorgi, on the other hand, ran its course for a time within Georgia itself, but then switched to Persia, and finally ended among the fierce Afghan tribesmen of Qandahar on the Indian border.

To appreciate the course of events which led to Giorgi's being appointed commander in chief of the armies of the shah of Persia, it must be recalled that the Persian government had since the time of Shah 'Abbas I (1587–1629) made it a deliberate policy to employ mercenary troops from Georgia and other minority areas. These mercenaries formed a picked corps, under their own commander, called the *qullar-aghasi,* who was usually a Georgian prince. The shahs appreciated the Georgians' energy and ability, and were all the more anxious to attract them to their service as this prevented the more ambitious Georgians from becoming involved in movements of resistance in their homeland. The shahs could also use the Georgians to crush the pretensions of the Persian provincial khans and tribal leaders on whose vacillating loyalty the Safavi dynasty had previously been obliged to depend.[20]

There are a number of testimonies as to the size and fighting qualities of the Georgian contingent in the armies of Shah 'Abbas the Great. In 1619, Pietro della Valle wrote that "the strength of the Persian army consists today in the Georgian soldiers, who form its greater and best portion." [21] Sir Thomas Herbert, who was in

---

[19] Peyssonnel, *Essai sur les troubles,* pp. 48–49. On Archil and his descendants, see also M.-F. Brosset's important monograph, "Nouvelles recherches sur l'historien Wakhoucht, sur le roi Artchil et sa famille, et sur divers personnages géorgiens enterrés à Moscou," in *Mélanges Asiatiques,* Vol. III.

[20] Chardin, *Voyages en Perse,* VI, 15–18. Further details are given in the present writer's article, "Georgia and the Fall of the Safavi Dynasty," in *Bulletin of the School of Oriental and African Studies,* XIV, 523–39.

[21] P. della Valle, *Voyages dans la Turquie* (Rouen, 1745), IV, 69.

Shiraz in 1627, commented that, "For comeliness of body, height of spirit, and faithfulness in trust [the Georgians] are of that repute, especially with the Persian, that many of them are employed in places of command, especially against their turbulent adversary the Turk." [22] At various times during the seventeenth century, the size of the Georgian cavalry corps in the Persian army is given as ranging between eight and forty thousand, though the latter figure is probably too high.[23] A sidelight on the Georgians' military reputation is provided by the fact that a French missionary and explorer who had to travel in Persia in disguise chose to wear Georgian dress, since this "inspired awe all over Persia." [24]

In civil dignities, also, many Georgians attained high rank. We have seen how King Rostom of Georgia was a former prefect of Isfahan, the Persian capital. Georgians were appointed to the governorship of the key fortress of Erivan in Persian Armenia. Georgians also monopolized such strategic offices as that of hereditary grand porter of the royal harem. Many of the shahs, princes of the blood, and prominent grandees had Georgian wives, some of whom were of the Georgian royal family, others, captives taken during the Persian campaigns against Georgia in 1614–16.

The French missionary Father Sanson, who was in Persia between 1683 and 1691, commented that

the policy of the Shah is admirable with regard to the Georgians, who might cause him a lot of trouble if they were united among themselves. He knows how to keep them divided by self-interest. He promotes all the great nobles in such an advantageous manner that they forget their fatherland and their religion to attach themselves to him. The greatest posts of the empire are today in their hands, and those who do not hold any of these have their places at the royal table and emoluments from the Treasury.[25]

With regard to religion, the Georgians were obliged to become nominal Mohammedans on entering Persian service. That they were far from pious converts to Islam is attested by an Italian traveler of

[22] Herbert, *Some Yeares Travels into Africa and Asia*, p. 155.

[23] Sources quoted in Lang, "Georgia and the Fall of the Safavi Dynasty," in *Bulletin of the School of Oriental and African Studies*, XIV, 525.

[24] Avril, *Voyage en divers états d'Europe et d'Asie*, p. 60.

[25] Sanson, *Voyage de Perse*, pp. 176–77.

the period who met a party of Persian soldiers from Georgia "having suffered themselves to be circumciz'd only to follow their master's fortune, never regarding to pray after the Mahometan fashion, and cursing that false prophet." [26]

It is against this background that the chequered career of King Giorgi XI of K'art'li, son and successor of Shahnavaz, must be surveyed. It has been recorded earlier how the grand vazir of Persia had inflamed the shah's suspicion and hostility toward the Georgian royal house. When King Shahnavaz fell ill and died in 1676 on the way to Isfahan to justify his conduct, it seemed to the Persians an excellent opportunity to stir up civil war in Georgia, and, later, to bring the country under more direct Persian control. The Persians intended to use as a puppet the rival claimant to the Georgian throne, Prince Erekle (Nicholas) of Kakhet'i. Erekle, however, ruined his chances by refusing to become a Mohammedan and by producing a letter from the tsar of Russia, Fedor Alekseevich, in which it was claimed that the Georgians were vassals of Russia and that the Persians had no right to interfere with them. [27] Threats of a rebellion in Georgia put an end to the wavering of the shah and his advisers, and it was decided that Giorgi be appointed to succeed his father as viceroy at Tiflis. Having agreed to become a Mohammedan, Giorgi was in 1678 confirmed in this dignity.

The effective reign of Giorgi XI in K'art'li lasted only a decade, from 1678 to 1688, and was marked by increasingly strained relations with the Persian government. Giorgi still had to contend with the intrigues of the Persian grand vazir, a master of the art of machination. The situation was made worse by the oppressive policies of the Persian military governors at Tabriz and in the neighboring Georgian kingdom of Kakhet'i. Discrimination against the local Christian population in favor of the Moslem Tatars and Lezghis led to widespread dissatisfaction. In 1688, Giorgi received an appeal from the people of Kakhet'i to help them drive out the Persian governor. He consented to do so, but the coup failed. [28]

[26] Gemelli-Careri, *Voyage round the World,* in Churchill, *Collection of Voyages and Travels,* IV, 119–20.

[27] M.-F. Brosset, *Perepiska . . . Gruzinskikh Tsarei,* p. LXVI.

[28] Wakhusht, "Histoires particulières . . . du Cakheth," in M.-F. Brosset, tr. and ed., *Histoire de la Géorgie,* II, Part 1, 178.

The shah of Persia decided that Giorgi must be dethroned and replaced by his rival, Prince Erekle of Kakhet'i. The latter, after thirteen years residence at the Persian capital, had now become more amenable on the subject of religion and had agreed to become Mohammedan. With a Persian army corps, Erekle advanced on Tiflis. Giorgi fled to Western Georgia, where he made common cause with his brother Archil, still struggling to establish himself on the throne of Imeret'i.[29]

Occupied mainly with skirmishes against the displaced but by no means resigned Giorgi, the reign of Erekle in Tiflis offers little of interest to the historian. It was not until 1696 that Giorgi admitted defeat and came to Isfahan to offer his submission to the new Persian shah, Sultan Husayn. By this time unfavorable reports of Erekle's administration had reached the Persian government. It seems that Erekle, who had been brought up in Russia and Persia, lacked knowledge of Georgian national customs. A vacillating ruler, addicted to strong drink, though capable at times of being both brave and philanthropic, he never really achieved a firm grasp of Georgia's political problems, or made himself popular with his subjects.[30]

As the Persian court now began to lose confidence in Erekle, it soon learned to value the talents of his rival, Giorgi. Since the great martial era of 'Abbas the Great, the central administration had gradually been sinking into a supine condition. By 1700 its grip on the outlying provinces was far from secure. Especially menacing was the situation in Afghanistan, on the Indian frontier. In that region, the key fortress of Qandahar itself was threatened, and claims for its restitution to India were being pressed by the Mogul emperor at Delhi. The local Persian garrison was constantly in difficulty with the Afghan tribesmen of the surrounding country. Nearer home, the Baluchis were becoming restive and raiding with impunity the provinces of Kerman and Yazd.[31]

[29] Wakhusht, "Histoires particulières du Karthli," in M.-F. Brosset, tr. and ed., *Histoire de la Géorgie,* II, Part 1, 86-87; M.-F. Brosset, in *Mélanges Asiatiques,* II, 231-32.

[30] "Extraits de l'histoire de Pharsadan Giorgidjanidze," in M.-F. Brosset, ed., *Histoire de la Géorgie,* II, Part 1, 572.

[31] Wakhusht, "Histoires particulières du Karthli," in M.-F. Brosset, tr. and ed.,

As none of the Persian generals were equal to the task of restoring order in the Eastern marches of Iran, Shah Sultan Husayn appointed Giorgi, the deposed king of K'art'li (known in Persia as Gurjin Khan), to be governor general of Kirman. His brother Levan was placed in command of a detachment of Georgian troops, with which he inflicted heavy losses on the Baluchi raiders. In the course of the year 1700, the two brothers cleared most of the eastern provinces of marauding tribesmen. In recompense, the shah made Levan chief justice of Iran and Levan's son K'aikhosro (or Khusrau-Khan) prefect of Isfahan.[32]

Further to the east, however, the situation at Qandahar continued to deteriorate. The Persian governor was blockaded in the citadel. The only hope was to send Giorgi with a special expeditionary force to relieve the Persian garrison. To overcome Giorgi's reluctance to undertake this arduous and thankless mission, he was given the title of commander in chief of the Persian army, and restored to the rank of viceroy of Georgia. Giorgi's nephew Wakhtang, later King Wakhtang VI, was sent to take charge of the administration of Georgia during his uncle's absence on campaign. Meanwhile, Giorgi set out for Afghanistan with a reinforcement of four thousand Georgian cavalry.

There exists in the archives of the French Ministry of Foreign Affairs an unpublished account of this ill-fated Qandahar expedition, written by an Armenian Catholic from Georgia, named Joseph Abisalamian, who was secretary to the French consul in Isfahan.[33] According to this well-informed source,

The insatiable rapacity of the Persian governors who were in command at Qandahar up to the accession of Shah Sultan Husayn rendered their rule so detestable to the local inhabitants that at the turn of the century they plotted sedition and insurrection, going so far as to expel the

---

Histoire de la Géorgie, II, Part 1, 97–98; La Mamye Clairac, *Histoire de Perse depuis le commencement de ce Siècle,* Vol. I, Bk. 1; Krusinski, *Revolutions of Persia,* I, 143–44; Hanway, *Revolutions of Persia,* I, 26–27.

[32] Chkheidze, in M.-F. Brosset, tr., *Histoire de la Géorgie,* II, Part 2, 16–23.

[33] "Mémoire sur la dernière guerre civile de Perse," dated January 31, 1723, in the archives of the French Foreign Ministry, Correspondance Politique, Perse, VI, 262–78. The writer would like to repeat here his thanks to the Librarian and to the Director of Archives at the Quai d'Orsay for kind assistance in his research.

Persian garrison of Qandahar. In this conjuncture the Shah, desiring to reduce the rebels to submission and punish the ringleaders, cast his eyes on Gurjin Khan, otherwise known as Shahnavaz, Georgian by birth, as brave a soldier as he was an able general. He directed him to quit his governorship of the province of Kirman, and to proceed as Viceroy to Qandahar with an army of 20,000 Persians and 4,000 Georgians. The Afghans, awed by the despatch of a new Governor, whose courage and severity were only too well known to them, far from opposing his entry into the kingdom, immediately opened the gates of Qandahar to him. Gurjin Khan punished the culprits with rigour, and executed the ringleaders. After installing an adequate Persian garrison in the place, he disbanded the rest of the army, retaining only the light cavalry force of 4,000 Georgians which he had brought with him.

With regard to Mir Vays, who was the principal chief of the rebellion, Gurjin Khan contented himself with sending him in chains to Isfahan, and writing to the Shah at the same time that he ought to get rid of him, as being an ill-intentioned person, a restless and intriguing spirit, capable eventually of dealing some fatal blow to the monarchy. The General furthermore allowed his soldiers to exercise all kinds of outrages and insults on the population, so that one cannot recall without a shudder all that the Afghans had to suffer at the hands of the Georgians: fathers and mothers were no longer masters of their daughters and sons, nor husbands of their wives, merchants of their property and money, nor were the inhabitants even sure of their lives.[34]

A contemporary Turkish report further alleges that Giorgi exacted increased dues from local tribal nomads for the right of pasturage, and that taxes were generally raised.[35] Such measures naturally made the Georgians unpopular among both the tribesmen and the Qandahar townspeople.

The Afghan rebel leader Mir Vays, whom Giorgi had sent to Isfahan, was possessed of sufficient powers of cunning and persuasion to absolve himself of the charges leveled against him, and even to make Giorgi suspect in the eyes of the shah and his ministers.

[34] This account of the Armenian scribe Joseph served, with Joseph's oral reminiscences, as a source for La Mamye Clairac, Hanway and Petros di Sargis Gilanents. See Lang, "Georgia and the Fall of the Safavi Dynasty," in *Bulletin of the School of Oriental and African Studies,* XIV, 528.

[35] "Traduction d'un Mémoire Turc sur l'origine de la Révolution arrivée en Perse," in the archives of the French Foreign Ministry, Correspondance Politique, Perse, VI, 254.

This was not difficult as there existed a strong anti-Georgian faction at the Persian court, where the Georgians' recent successes had aroused jealousy and resentment among high officials. In addition, Mir Vays secured his position by procuring a decree from the heads of the Mohammedan hierarchy in Mecca, authorizing him to declare a holy war against the infidel Georgians who were oppressing the True Believers of Qandahar. Feigning submission to the shah, Mir Vays was sent back to Qandahar where he pretended to be reconciled with the Georgian occupation authorities but was only waiting for a chance to strike.[36]

Giorgi's intelligence service must have been far from efficient, for he remained ignorant of the Afghans' plot. Disaster finally overtook the Georgian force on Ash Wednesday, 1709. Profiting by the absence of a detachment commanded by Giorgi's nephew Prince Alexander, who had gone to restore order in an outlying district, Mir Vays invited Giorgi and his retinue to a feast in his camp to celebrate the restoration of good relations between the Georgians and the Afghans.

In the words of the Turkish report already cited,

The Georgian commander, who had accepted the invitation, proceeded in pomp and splendor with a numerous cortege to the camp of Mir Vays, which was only two or three leagues from the city. Mir Vays received him with all imaginable respect and honor. He gave him the best of everything; everyone tucked up their sleeves and hastened to serve him; they all vied with one another to pay him respect. Finally, so that nothing might be forgotten to complete the entertainment of their guests, the principal Afghan chiefs invited and conducted to their tents the noblemen who had accompanied the governor. A splendid feast was served up, and after the customary libations, the great cup was circulated. The governor and his suite soon had their heads heavy with the fumes of wine, and their affairs rapidly took an evil turn. Each Afghan strangled his guest, and with blows of sword and club they awoke the death rattle in the throats of those whom intoxication had given over to slumber. In a moment, all had become food for the cutting sword.

The narrative of the Armenian scribe Joseph Abisalamian also describes these events in detail, and adds that Giorgi sprang up at

[36] La Mamye Clairac, *Histoire de Perse*, I, 31–34, 43–46.

the first sound of the massacre, and defended himself with desperate courage against some fifty Afghans, commanded by Mir Vays in person, eight of whom he felled to the ground. Finally he died, pierced through and through by Afghan spears. The Afghans easily overcame the city garrison of Qandahar, and Mir Vays was acclaimed a national hero.[37]

When the news of this disaster finally reached Isfahan, it filled the Persian court with consternation. The feeble and superstitious Shah Sultan Husayn was in despair, until it occurred to him to send Giorgi's nephew, K'aikhosro, to avenge his fallen countrymen. K'aikhosro was given his uncle's former title of viceroy of Georgia and the command of a fresh expeditionary force of some 30,000 Persians and 1,200 Georgians.

This second Georgian expedition was ill-fated from the start. The anti-Georgian faction at the Persian court, headed by the new grand vazir, Fath-'Ali Khan Daghistani, had established links with the rebel Mir Vays. A Persian steward assigned to K'aikhosro's household was in league with the Afghans, while part of the funds assigned for paying K'aikhosro's troops was misappropriated.

At first, however, things went comparatively well. K'aikhosro brushed aside Afghan resistance at the approaches to Qandahar, and laid siege to the city, and the inhabitants sent to sue for terms of capitulation. The Georgian general, overconfident of success, insisted on unconditional surrender, which provoked the besieged to desperate resistance. "In the meantime," relates the Armenian scribe Joseph,

Mir Vays was daily reinforcing his army and ravaging the country round about to deprive the enemy of means of subsistence and force them to raise the siege for lack of victuals and fodder. This scheme succeeded perfectly, for the Persians, discouraged by the length of the siege and shortage of supplies, began to desert in such numbers that finally the army was reduced to two thirds of its original effective. In these circumstances, the General was advised by his followers to retire, but this was no longer possible. Mir Vays, who had brought sixteen thousand recruits into the city, gave battle to the Persians, who immediately took to flight without paying any attention to the pressing commands of their

[37] Other versions of the disaster are cited in Lang, "Georgia and the Fall of the Safavi Dynasty," in *Bulletin of the School of Oriental and African Studies*, XIV, 532.

General, who vainly tried to hold them back. Ashamed to survive so ignominious an event, he hurled himself headlong into the main force of his foes at the head of two hundred Georgians, which was all that he had with him. He accomplished prodigies of valour and intrepidity until at last, succumbing to violence, his head was smitten with an iron-headed mace.[38]

Out of the whole Perso-Georgian army, only seven hundred men escaped. Not only did the catastrophes at Qandahar spell ruin for the feeble Safavi regime; they deprived Georgia of the flower of her generals and manpower at a time when she could least afford to spare them. This drain on her resources exposed Georgia still more to the raids of Lezghian marauders from Daghestan, and in the long run it gravely hampered the attempts of King Erekle II to set up a durable Transcaucasian state later in the eighteenth century.

From this account of the chequered careers of the early Mukhranian kings, it becomes clear that the political future of Georgia could not be worked out on her home ground or without reference to the great powers dominating the Caucasian isthmus. As yet, the supremacy of Turkey and Persia in Transcaucasia was unchallenged. In trying to reunite the two halves of Georgia comprising Ottoman and Persian spheres of influence King Shahnavaz was merely battering his head against a stone wall. Neither Persia nor Turkey wanted to embark on a general war, and it was inconceivable that the sultan would cede the Black Sea provinces of Georgia to Persia or that Persia would tamely submit to having Tiflis come under Turkish control. Shahnavaz found himself stalemated. National reunification was foredoomed to failure so long as the Mohammedan powers were in a position to maintain the status quo to the south of the Caucasian range.

In their dealings with Russia during the late seventeenth century, the Georgian princes showed blind and touching optimism. It does not seem to have occurred to them that the Russians had other preoccupations in their dealings with Persia and Turkey than to

---

[38] Archives of the French Foreign Ministry, Correspondance Politique, Perse, VI, 268–69. Father J. T. Krusinski records that the Afghans were so impressed by the bravery of the Georgians that they used to say that though Persians were but women compared with Afghans, the Afghans were but women compared with the Georgians (*Revolutions of Persia*, I, 198).

rescue the Georgians from their difficulties, or that Russia's own internal stresses and the bitter wars with Sweden might make effective aid impossible. Entrenched round the northern shores of the Caspian Sea, and having extensive commercial interests in Shirvan, Azerbaijan, and Gilan, it did not yet suit Russia to come into the open in defense of Christian minorities in the Persian shah's dominions. Nor did the court of Moscow wish to lose entirely its contact with what might be a useful "fifth column" in that area. For the moment, therefore, the tsars did little more than receive the Georgian princes' oaths of allegiance, intercede in a half-hearted way with the shahs of Persia on their behalf, and provide them with a haven in times of trouble. At the same time, the Russians sedulously kept alive the image of an all-powerful Orthodox state waiting only for an opportunity to extend its beneficent power over Christians groaning under the Mohammedan yoke.

5

Political History of the Mukhranian Period, 1703-1723

W E now pick up the thread of Georgian history at the point where King Giorgi XI, after some years in disgrace, was re-appointed viceroy of K'art'li by the shah in 1703 in return for undertaking the reconquest of Qandahar. Giorgi's nephew Wakhtang was commissioned to administer Georgia for him during his absence in distant Afghanistan.

The regency of Wakhtang, which lasted from 1703 until 1711, brought about a renaissance in Georgian national life. The Persian government, which relied on the Georgian army to extricate it from its difficulties, refrained from undue interference at Tiflis. Wakhtang, still a young man of twenty-eight, took advantage of this to embark on the far-seeing measures of reform and reconstruction which entitle him to rank as one of the outstanding Georgian statesmen of the modern period. His legal code has already been examined in some detail. The digging of canals to irrigate large areas of wasteland and bring them back into cultivation may be mentioned as one of his constructive projects. He devoted great care to the restoration of Georgia's principal cathedrals.

Wakhtang maintained Georgian national prestige in the face of the Persian occupying authorities. On one occasion when the soldiers of the Persian garrison in Tiflis mutinied against him, Wakhtang simply cowed them into submission. He also reasserted the royal authority in outlying areas of Georgia, undertaking in 1711 a punitive expedition against the mountain Ossetes and obliging them to pay tribute. Operations against the Lezghian raiders from the hills of Daghestan were less successful; they were hindered by the weakness of Wakhtang's neighbor, the new king of Kakhet'i, David II, also known by the Persian title of Iman-Quli-Khan. David suffered a serious defeat at the hands of the Lezghis in 1706, as a result of which their raids into Eastern Georgia became daily more intolerable.[1]

In Western Georgia, the political situation continued to deteriorate throughout this period. The sultans of Turkey through their representatives, the Turco-Georgian pashas of Akhaltsikhe, continued to foment civil wars there. The Turkish frontier authorities intensified their campaign against Georgian religion and national sentiment. Mosques were built to replace Christian churches. The Theatine Catholic mission to Imeret'i and Mingrelia, which had exerted a most beneficial influence throughout the seventeenth century, had to be withdrawn owing to lack of support.

As a result of these adverse factors, the history of Imeret'i and Mingrelia during the early eighteenth century is characterized by anarchy. One monarch, King Simon, was shot dead in the night outside his bedroom. His assassin, Prince Mamia Gurieli, enjoyed the spoils of power for one brief year before being displaced by the feudal magnate Giorgi Abashidze. A Turkish invasion in 1703 threatened Western Georgia with decimation, and but for the death of Sultan Mustafa, the country would have been completely devastated. Prince Abashidze was replaced in 1707 by the legitimate heir to the throne of Imeret'i, the Bagratid King Giorgi V. The reign of this vicious and miserly monarch offers to the historian little but acts of bloodshed and disorder, accompanied by a serious growth in the slave trade with Turkey. He was murdered in 1720.[2]

Such then was the situation in the various provinces of Georgia during Wakhtang's regency from 1703 to 1711. As a result of the regent's personal ability, in combination with the internal weakness

[1] Wakhusht, "Histoires particulières du Karthli," and "Histoires particulières . . . du Cakheth," in M.-F. Brosset, tr. and ed., *Histoire de la Géorgie,* II, Part 1, 108–9 and 182–83; Peyssonnel, *Essai sur les troubles,* p. 60.

[2] Wakhusht, "Histoires particulières . . . de l'Iméreth," in M.-F. Brosset, tr. and ed., *Histoire de la Géorgie,* II, Part 1, 306–13.

of the other Georgian principalities, the kingdom of K'art'li and the Tiflis court played the leading role in Georgia's political and cultural life. When the news of King K'aikhosro's death in Afghanistan in 1711 reached Georgia, Wakhtang was acclaimed his successor. It seemed that Eastern Georgia would continue to enjoy the era of "calm and contentment" which had been inaugurated during Wakhtang's regency.[3]

These hopes were doomed to disappointment. Wakhtang was now summoned to Isfahan to receive his investiture from the shah. It was not long before the bigoted Shah Sultan Husayn and his entourage made it clear that he could not be confirmed in his kingdom without renouncing the Christian faith. In August, 1712, one of the French Capuchin missionaries at the Persian capital wrote to the French ambassador at Constantinople:

The Prince of Georgia . . . has arrived at Isfahan over a month ago. After the death of his brother, generalissimo of the Persian army, the Shah has summoned him to induce him to embrace Islam. He has already made several assaults on his constancy, which this prince has so far resisted with great firmness. He told me in two or three interviews when I have had the honour to see him that he would sooner be cut to pieces than abandon his religion; but the Georgian nation not being over firm in matters of religion, it is to be feared that this Prince, seeing himself deprived of his estates, may let himself slide like his grandfather, father, uncle and two of his brothers before him. He appears however to be quite determined to renounce his domains sooner than his faith.[4]

In this predicament, it seemed that Wakhtang's only hope of release lay in the intervention of the French court, with which Persia had lately entered into diplomatic relations with a view to negotiating a trade convention.[5] Wakhtang therefore sent to Versailles and to the Pope a personal mission comprising his uncle and tutor, Prince Sulkhan-Saba Orbeliani, who was a Georgian Uniat monk of the order of St. Basil, and a French missionary, the Abbé Richard.

This mission reached Paris in March, 1714. Sulkhan-Saba drew up a memorandum outlining the advantages which would result both

[3] Chkheidze, "Chronicle," in Brosset, tr., Histoire de la Géorgie, II, Part 2, 28.

[4] Father Pierre d'Issoudun to the Comte des Alleurs, in the archives of the French Foreign Ministry, Correspondance Politique, Perse, III, 19.

[5] See Herbette, Une Ambassade persane sous Louis XIV.

to French interests and to the Catholic faith if the shah could be persuaded to let Wakhtang return to Tiflis without abandoning his
Christian faith. Stress was laid on the existence of a practicable trade
route from Constantinople via Tiflis into Persia, bypassing the Turkish port of Trebizond. (Wakhtang did undertake to open up this
route on his release and to grant French merchants special privileges
and franchises.)[6]

At an audience granted by Louis XIV to Sulkhan-Saba at Versailles,
the Georgian envoy presented a personal letter from his sovereign
thanking Louis for his messages of encouragement and promising to
further French interests in Georgia as soon as he could regain possession of his kingdom. Added Wakhtang,

> Although we have fallen into the hands of the Infidels who have
> deceived our predecessors, and are abandoned here in a foreign land,
> like the Israelites were for the sins of their fathers, nevertheless my sons
> and brothers, who govern my domains in my absence, will execute
> punctually and zealously all that we shall ordain for the service of
> Your Majesty.[7]

The French court at first lent a favorable ear to Sulkhan-Saba's
petition, and the question of interceding for Wakhtang and opening
a trade route through Georgia was referred to the Ministry of Foreign
Affairs.[8] Unfortunately, a Persian ambassador extraordinary, sent to
execute the Franco-Persian commercial treaty of 1708, was at this
point reported to have arrived in Constantinople on his way to France.
This news had the most adverse effect on Georgian interests. It was
realized at Versailles that the success of the forthcoming talks, affecting French interests over a good deal more of the Middle East than
Georgia alone, would be jeopardized if the shah of Persia learned
that the French government was in direct contact with Wakhtang,
a vassal of the shah. French official circles now conveniently concluded that Wakhtang's fate was, after all, an internal matter to be
fought out by the Georgians and the Persians. It was promised that

---

[6] Archives of the French Foreign Ministry, Correspondance Politique, Perse, III,
93–94; M.-F. Brosset, "Documents originaux sur les relations diplomatiques de la
Géorgie avec la France," *Nouveau Journal Asiatique,* IX (1832), 342–44, 347–51.

[7] Full text in Lang, "Georgian Relations with France during the reign of Wakhtang VI," *Journal of the Royal Asiatic Society,* October, 1950, p. 120.

[8] *Ibid.,* p. 121.

when a French consulate was established in Isfahan, the consul would doubtless extend to the Georgians what support he properly could.[9] With such vague assurances, Sulkhan-Saba had to rest content.

The other principal object of Sulkhan-Saba's embassy was to arrange for the sending of more French Catholic missionaries to Georgia. The French government advised him to apply to the Pope direct. Armed with letters of recommendation to Rome, Sulkhan-Saba arrived there in July, 1714, after having been granted a farewell audience by Louis XIV.

As Sulkhan-Saba was himself a convert to Roman Catholicism, the Pope certainly entertained hopes of making considerable conversions among the Georgian Orthodox through his intermediacy. The Pope received the Georgian envoy with cordiality, presenting him with the skull of St. Clement and a crystal crucifix in which was set a fragment of the True Cross.[10] Though Sulkhan-Saba aroused the hostility of the prefect of the Capuchins by suggesting that the new missionaries for Georgia should be drawn from the Lazarist and Jesuit orders, a letter was sent to France with instructions for the latter's recruitment and dispatch to Georgia. Then Sulkhan-Saba paid a visit to the grand duke of Tuscany. From Florence he proceeded to Leghorn and embarked for Constantinople, hoping that the missionaries would follow shortly.

The French government by this time had its hands full with the Persian ambassador, who had arrived at the end of 1714 and created endless trouble by his eccentric conduct and exorbitant pretensions. Intervention with him on Wakhtang's behalf was out of the question. Finally the death of Louis XIV in 1715 and the resulting changes in the direction of French foreign policy put an end to any hope of French support for the Georgian cause. In 1716, Sulkhan-Saba returned sorrowfully to Georgia, accompanied by only two Capuchins and one Jesuit missionary.

While Sulkhan-Saba Orbeliani was in Europe, Wakhtang's own position had grown even more untenable. Finding him unshakable

[9] Archives of the French Foreign Ministry, Correspondance Politique, Perse, III, 179–80.

[10] Archives of the French Foreign Ministry, Correspondance Politique, Perse, III, 201; Tamarati, *L'Église géorgienne,* pp. 600–605.

in his resolve to remain a Christian, the shah sent Wakhtang's rene-gade brother Iese ('Ali-Quli-Khan) to Tiflis as viceroy in his stead. When Iese arrived in K'art'li in October, 1714, opposition manifested itself at once, with many princes of the blood and prominent nobles retiring to the hills rather than submit to the usurper.[11] Plague broke out in Tiflis, and the Lezghian marauders became ever more trouble-some. Instead of attending to administration, Iese spent his time carousing and writing to the shah to denounce his brother Wakh-tang.[12]

By 1716, when Sulkhan-Saba returned from his unsuccessful Euro-pean mission, the shah was as tired of Iese's inefficient rule in Georgia as Wakhtang was of being a virtual prisoner in Persia. Seeing no other hope of regaining his kingdom, Wakhtang at last became a Moslem, assuming the title of Husayn-Quli-Khan. He was appointed generalissimo of Iran, and his son Bak'ar was nominated regent of Georgia until Wakhtang's own return there.

At heart, Wakhtang remained a Christian, and of this he assured the Russian ambassador Artemii Volynskii who visited Isfahan in 1717. The assurance was of particular interest to this envoy of Peter the Great, as the objects of his mission included spying out the land with a view to ultimate invasion by Russia. Besides discovering the anti-Mohammedan sentiments of the Persian generalissimo, Volyn-skii was able to satisfy himself of the generally precarious condition of the Safavi empire. So eager were members of Wakhtang's entou-rage to see the Russian tsar invade Persia that Volynskii had to re-strain them from compromising both themselves and the tsar by premature action.[13]

Eventually, in 1719, Wakhtang was allowed to return to Georgia to subdue the Lezghis. By this time, the Persian monarchy was show-ing still more ominous signs of disintegration. The situation in Af-ghanistan had further deteriorated, the rebel Mir Vays having set up an independent regime there; in the Persian Gulf, the sultan of

[11] Archives of the French Foreign Ministry, "Nouvelles de Géorgie," March, 1715, in Correspondance Politique, Perse, IV, 46–47.

[12] Wakhusht, *Histoires particulières du Karthli,* in M.-F. Brosset, tr. and ed., *Histoire de la Géorgie,* II, Part I, 112.

[13] Lebedev, "Posol'stvo Artemiia Volynskogo v Persiiu," in *Izvestiia Akad. Nauk SSSR,* V, 535–37; Solov'ev, *Istoriia Rossii,* IV, 665–66.

Muscat seized the port of Bahrein. The Persian ministers, to quote a contemporary source,

by reason of vain personal objects and hypocrisy . . . veiled their eyes to what was expedient for the state. Every time that any one of them wished to move, each of the others would make an excuse and prevent anything from being done. They postponed their departure and occupied themselves with pleasure, . . . practising the selling of offices and receiving bribes.[14]

Wakhtang was greeted with enthusiasm by nobility and people alike on his arrival in Tiflis in August, 1719. His formal accession was celebrated by a ceremony in which quantities of coins were poured over his shoulders—a ritual preserved from ancient times. In the spring of 1720, his army killed enough Lezghian tribesmen to send 400 heads as a trophy to the shah.[15]

To follow up this success, Wakhtang established a blockade against the Lezghian villagers of the Jaro-Belakan district. In the winter of 1720–21, many of these were cut off from their winter quarters and perished from starvation and cold. All seemed to portend speedy and complete victory when Wakhtang received a peremptory order from the shah to cease hostilities forthwith. So enraged was he by this message that he drew his sword in the presence of the shah's courier, and swore never to use it again in the service of the Safavi dynasty. The Georgian army retired from its positions, and the Lezghis, to use the phrase of a Georgian chronicler, were as pleased as the king was angry to think that they were escaping the lion's claws.[16]

The reason for this abrupt change in Persian military policy was that a palace revolution had occurred involving the fall of the grand vazir. As one of the deposed grand vazir's daughters was married to a brother of Wakhtang, the new party in power feared reprisals from the Georgians and decided to force Wakhtang to disband his army. It also appears that the Persians had learned of Wakhtang's pro-Russian sympathies, and wished to prevent him from assisting Peter the Great with the latter's designs on Transcaucasia.

[14] Lockhart, *Nadir Shah*, pp. 3–6.

[15] Dispatch of the French consul Padéry, in the archives of the French Foreign Ministry, Correspondance Politique, Perse, V, p. 271.

[16] Chkheidze, "Chronicle," in M.-F. Brosset, tr., *Histoire de la Géorgie*, II, Part 2, 35; Krusinski, *Tragica Vertentis belli Persici Historia*, pp. 147–49.

The consequences of the shah's order to Wakhtang could not have been more disastrous. Now that the Georgians were disarmed, the Lezghian mountaineers broke into open revolt, swooped down from their fastnesses, and sacked the great trading center of Shamakhi. Russian traders there lost property estimated variously at from 472,000 to 4,000,000 roubles. This spoliation gave Peter the Great an excellent excuse to open hostilities against the Lezghians' nominal suzerain, the shah of Persia.[17]

It was doubly unlucky for the shah that the Shamakhi outrage occurred in August, 1721, just as Peter was about to sign the Treaty of Nystad with Sweden. This treaty ended the great Northern War, which had monopolized Russia's military energies for over twenty years. An excursion to the subtropical shores of the Caspian was a pleasing prospect after years of campaigning round the frosty Baltic. Nor did the Persian adventure promise to be very arduous. In 1717 the Russian ambassador Volynskii had reported:

In my humble opinion God is leading this empire to its ruin. . . . As a result of the weakness here, we can begin a war with Persia without any apprehension, for with a small detachment, let alone a complete army, a great part of the country could be annexed to Russia.

Volynskii had since been appointed governor of Astrakhan, with orders to keep in touch with Russian sympathizers in Persia and prepare the way for military intervention. The Georgian and Armenian minorities in the shah's dominions proved eager to cooperate. The Armenians, who played a great role in the Persian silk trade with Europe, were regularly in contact with the Russian authorities in Astrakhan. They did not fail to stress the advantages which Russia could derive from possession of the great silk-producing provinces of Gilan, Mazanderan, and Shirvan on the Caspian shores.[18]

[17] See the eyewitness accounts of the Jesuit missionary Father Bachoud in *Lettres Édifiantes et Curieuses: Mémoires du Levant*, IV (Paris, 1780), 113–24; and of the Catholicos Esaï Hasan-Dchalaliants, in Brosset, *Collection d'historiens arméniens*, II (1876), 210, 229. The incorrect date of 1712 given for the sack of Shamakhi in Butkov, *Materialy*, I, 3–9, is due to the accidental transposition of the final digits of the date in the original manifesto of Peter the Great declaring war on Persia. This error is repeated in most Russian historical works dealing with this period.

[18] Solov'ev, *Istoriia Rossii*, IV, 665–66 *et seq.*; Lebedev, "Posol'stvo Artemiia Volynskogo," in *Izvestiia Akad. Nauk SSSR*, V, 535; Ezov, *Snosheniia Petra Velikogo s armianskim narodom*; Arutiunian, "Bor'ba armianskogo i azerbaidzhanskogo

As soon as the Swedish treaty was safely signed, Peter and his energetic representative Volynskii concentrated their attention on the
Persian project. A message was sent to King Wakhtang in Tiflis, an-
nouncing the forthcoming Russian campaign. Wakhtang responded
in November, 1721, by sending an agent to Russian headquarters
with plans for joint Russo-Georgian military operations and details
of routes for the Russian army to follow.[19] Meanwhile, Peter sent an
official to the Persian court, ostensibly to demand reparations for the
damage suffered by Russian merchants in the sack of Shamakhi, but
in reality to report on the situation in Persia with a view to the military intervention.

At this point, the harassed Shah Sultan Husayn was in no position
to afford satisfaction, however willing he might have been to do so.
The Safavi dynasty was by now on the very verge of collapse. Early in
1722, Mir Mahmud, son and successor of the Afghan leader Mir Vays,
had profited by the confusion in the Persian capital to advance on
Isfahan with a cavalry force some twenty thousand strong. He encountered virtually no opposition and by March was in sight of the
shah's capital.

The decisive engagement between the Persian and Afghan armies
was fought out on March 8, 1722, at Gulnabad, a few miles to the
east of Isfahan. The new grand vazir advised a postponement of the
conflict, alleging the unprepared state of the city's defenses. The commander of the king's bodyguard, Rostom, brother of King Wakhtang
of Georgia, protested against this policy of caution, exclaiming, so
it is reported: "This is no time to debate, but to fight; it would be an
eternal shame to so numerous an army, in which is the flower of the
nobility of the empire, to be afraid of appearing before a gang of
robbers and rebel herdsmen." [20] Without awaiting further orders,
Rostom launched his squadrons against the Afghan left wing.

It seemed at first that the Persians, with the Georgian cavalry

---

narodov v 20-kh godakh XVIII veka za prisoedinenie k Rossii," in *Uchenye Zapiski
Instituta Vostokovedeniia,* IV, 108–38 (an article marred by bias, but containing
copious references to primary sources).

[19] M.-F. Brosset, *Perepiska . . . Gruzinskikh Tsarei,* p. 138; Solov'ev, *Istoriia
Rossii,* IV, 703.

[20] La Mamye Clairac, *Histoire de Perse,* I, 238; Hanway, *Revolutions of Persia,*
I, 106.

guards, would carry the day. But some of the irregular troops captured the Afghan baggage train, and turned aside to loot it; this gave Mir Mahmud a chance to regroup his forces and return to the offensive. The Afghans surrounded Prince Rostom's Georgian cavalry corps, which fought with desperate courage until completely wiped out, its commander falling on the battlefield.[21] The contemporary Persian historian Mohammed Muhsin pays tribute to the Georgians' valor at the battle of Gulnabad, and writes in his *Cream of the Histories* that "if the other leaders had not acted as cowards, and if they had supported the Commander of the Bodyguard, they would have driven the Afghans off the field, but by the decree of fate . . . it happened that there was a major defeat." [22]

The victorious Afghans now laid siege to Isfahan. The Persian shah's first impulse was to send for help from Wakhtang in Georgia. But the viceroy adhered to his decision never to march to the relief of the Safavi dynasty. In vain did the shah appoint Wakhtang's son Bak'ar commander of the bodyguard, in succession to the slain Prince Rostom of Georgia. Bak'ar remained loyal to Persia, and made a gesture of marching on Isfahan in May, 1722, but he was recalled by his father before he had passed the Armenian frontier.[23]

There can be little doubt that the Georgian king's refusal to relieve Isfahan was the immediate cause of the shah's downfall. An Armenian observer records that "the Afghans specially feared the Georgians, whose strength they had experienced on previous occasions," [24] while Father Krusinski even considers that Mahmud would have faced a mutiny in his army if the Georgians had been reported on their way. The same view was expressed by the French consul in Isfahan, who wrote in June, 1722, to his government from the beleaguered Persian capital:

[21] Gilanents, "Dnevnik osady Ispagani Afganami," in *Zapiski Imp. Akademii Nauk,* XVII, Appendix No. 3, 5–6; Reports of the French Consul at Isfahan, Gardanne, and the Armenian Secretary Joseph Abisalamian, in the archives of the French Foreign Ministry, Correspondance Politique, Perse, VI, 148–49, 277–78.

[22] This extract from Mohammed Muhsin was kindly supplied to me by Dr. L. Lockhart from the manuscript in the Cambridge University Library.

[23] Chkheidze, "Chronicle," in M.-F. Brosset, tr., *Histoire de la Géorgie,* II, Part 2, 36.

[24] Gilanents, "Dnevnik osady Ispagani Afganami," in *Zapiski Imp. Akademii Nauk,* XVII, Appendix No. 3, 31.

People assert that the Prince of Georgia . . . is sending his son here at the head of 12,000 Georgians. That, My Lord, is the real way to restore the affairs of this kingdom and oblige Mahmud to retire, for otherwise he would run great risks against the Georgian troops.[25]

Soon all these hopes were dispelled. Wakhtang's defection from the Persian cause became known, and the Persian Crown Prince Tahmasp escaped from Isfahan to set up temporary headquarters in the provinces. Exhausted by famine, the city surrendered in October. Shah Sultan Husayn abdicated in favor of Mir Mahmud.

By this time, the Russian invasion of the Caspian and Transcaucasian regions was in full swing. While Peter the Great occupied Derbent, Wakhtang of Georgia advanced on the town of Ganja with the object of effecting a junction with the Russian forces, which were expected to advance from the Caspian up the Kura valley to Tiflis. Unforeseen obstacles brought this plan to nought. The Russians were faced with a Turkish declaration of war, and had suffered a naval disaster in the Caspian. These and other political difficulties caused the emperor to leave Derbent and return abruptly to St. Petersburg.[26]

Wakhtang now found himself between two fires. On the one hand, an Ottoman army was massing to the southwest of Tiflis to overrun the prostrate Persian empire's western provinces. On the other, the Persian crown prince, naturally indignant at Wakhtang's desertion of the Persian cause, conferred the Georgian throne on an archenemy of Wakhtang, King Constantine of Kakhet'i. Constantine was also appointed governor of the key Persian frontier citadel of Erivan.[27]

Events now moved rapidly to a climax. Constantine launched a series of attacks on Tiflis, forcing Wakhtang to evacuate the city in May, 1723. Simultaneously the Turks under Ibrahim Pasha marched on the Georgian capital, which capitulated in June without a fight. The Turks found a willing collaborator in Wakhtang's reprobate

---

[25] Archives of the French Foreign Ministry, Correspondance Politique, Perse, VI, 184.

[26] For the political and military repercussions of Peter's campaign, see Solov'ev, *Istoriia Rossii*, IV, 678, 696; Sumner, *Peter the Great and the Emergence of Russia*, p. 178; Shay, *The Ottoman Empire from 1720 to 1734*, pp. 94–106.

[27] Gilanents, "Dnevnik osady Ispagani Afganami," in *Zapiski Imp. Akademii Nauk*, XVII, Appendix No. 3, 32.

brother Iese. Having already sampled the Christian and Shi'a Moslem faiths, Iese now turned Sunni to suit the Turks, and governed in Tiflis under the title of Mustafa Pasha.[28]

For a few months, Wakhtang and Constantine forgot their differences, and carried on guerrilla warfare together against the Turks and their allies, the Lezghis of Daghestan. Wakhtang was still buoyed up by hopes of reinforcements from Russia. But by the middle of 1724 his situation had become desperate. "The Georgians are laughing at me," he wrote. "While Peter plans to succor Paul, Paul is being skinned." [29]

The Russians were not prepared to risk a war with Turkey in order to save the Georgians. By the terms of the Russo-Turkish agreement, negotiated largely through the good offices of the French ambassador at Constantinople, Bonnac, and signed in July, 1724, Peter recognized Turkey's conquest of Georgia in exchange for Turkish recognition of Russian annexations on the Caspian.[30] The governor of Astrakhan was instructed to offer Wakhtang sanctuary in Russia. In August, 1724, the Georgian king crossed the Caucasus with Queen Rusudan, his sons Bak'ar and Wakhusht, and a suite 1,200 strong, including many members of the nobility and clergy.[31]

Wakhtang's policy had been founded on a mistaken evaluation of the Near Eastern balance of power. He failed to appreciate that Russia was not yet ready to conquer the whole area. Nor did he see that the collapse of the Persian empire, which he himself did so much to accelerate, would be bound to result in a move by the Turks to fill the resulting political vacuum. As it was, the delicately poised scales of power in Transcaucasia were thrown abruptly out of balance, and

---

[28] For details of these events, see Brosset, *Histoire de la Géorgie,* Vol. II, Part 1, Addition VII; Butkov, *Materialy dlia novoi istorii Kavkaza,* Vol. I, Chapters 4–9; Allen, *History of the Georgian People,* pp. 181–87; Chkheidze, "Chronicle," in M.-F. Brosset, tr., *Histoire de la Géorgie,* II, Part 2, 35–39; Archives of the French Foreign Ministry, Correspondance Politique, Perse, VI, 364–66.

[29] M.-F. Brosset, "Notice historique sur . . . Wakhtang VI," in *Bulletin Historico-Philologique,* III (St. Petersburg, 1847), 341.

[30] Butkov, *Materialy,* I, 58–62; Comte de Saint-Priest, *Mémoires sur l'Ambassade de France en Turquie* (Paris, 1877), pp. 121–23; Shay, *The Ottoman Empire from 1720 to 1734,* pp. 115–19.

[31] M.-F. Brosset, "Notice historique sur . . . Wakhtang VI," in *Bulletin Historico-Philologique,* III, 356.

Wakhtang now found himself swept away in the resulting turmoil.

Before Wakhtang could reach the Russian capital, Peter the Great died in February, 1725. The Russians remained in possession of Persia's Caspian provinces, including Baku and Gilan. But the advisers of Catherine I had less zest for oriental adventures than had the great emperor. Wakhtang and his followers were adequately provided for, but his attempts to interest the Russian government in plans for re-conquering Georgia were coldly received. Indeed, Wakhtang was reminded somewhat sharply when he complained of having been misled by the late tsar that he was equally to blame for having failed to join the Russian army at the crucial moment, and for having be-come involved instead in personal feuds with local rulers.[32]

While Tiflis was thus in the hands of the Turks, the Afghan usurper Mahmud was terrorizing Persia. In a massacre carried out by the Afghans after the fall of Isfahan, a number of young Persian and Georgian princes were turned loose into the open country and hunted down like wild beasts by the Afghan cavalry.[33] These scenes of horror were accompanied by a remarkable act of courage on the part of a certain Georgian woman, recorded in a French consular report on the year 1724. In the words of this document,

It was then that one saw and admired the bravery of a young Georgian heroine; what she did against the Afghans seems to deserve inclusion in this narrative. This magnanimous woman, learning that her husband had been slain by the enemy at the taking of the bridge and citadel of Isfahan . . . , resolved to go and avenge his death in the very blood of those who had killed him. Accordingly, confiding to her brother her property and the upbringing of her two little children, she disguised her sex, armed herself well, and without being put off by the harshness of the season or the length of a journey of almost four hundred leagues, she proceeded immediately to Isfahan, and arrived there when Mahmud was making his second entry. Scarcely had she set eyes on the Afghans and the place where her husband had been killed, when the desire for vengeance increased more and more in her heart. Without waiting any longer, weary though she was from the fatigues of her journey, she cast herself impetuously, sword in hand, on a body of Afghans, and killed more than twenty of them before she could be seized. Hearing of this

[32] M.-F. Brosset, *Perepiska . . . Gruzinskikh Tsarei,* pp. LXXIX–LXXX.
[33] La Mamye Clairac, *Histoire de Perse,* II, 61–62.

woman's deed, Mahmud had her put in prison, only intending to punish her a little and send her away afterwards, but the Afghans, so they say, did away with her in prison.[34]

The Russians never recognized the Afghan regime in Persia, but continued to side rather with the Safavi crown prince, Tahmasp. Continual Turkish encroachments on the Russian sphere of influence in Persia made it necessary to encourage the revival of the Persian monarchy, without which the Turks would become a real menace to Russia's position in the Caspian. To buttress the Persians against both the Afghans and the Turks, King Wakhtang of Georgia was sent to Resht in 1726 to establish relations with Tahmasp and to organize a Russo-Persian campaign against the Turks. These negotiations proved indecisive, and Wakhtang was soon recalled.[35]

It was not until 1732 that a Russo-Persian convention was signed at Resht. This treaty provided that Wakhtang be restored to the throne of K'art'li as soon as the Turks could be expelled from Tiflis.[36] But the rise of Nadir, the great Persian military adventurer, soon made this agreement obsolete. By 1734, Nadir had reconquered virtually all Persia's western provinces, after having exterminated the Afghan invaders, and was in a position to dispense with Russian aid. Nadir made a gesture of inviting Wakhtang and his son Bak'ar to his headquarters, but they not unreasonably suspected a trap, and declined the honor.[37] Wakhtang spent the last years of his life at Astrakhan, where he died in 1737.

In the words of a recent appreciation,

As a man Wakhtangi was the most pleasing of all the gifted house of Mukhrani. Gentle and studious, of a mind devout and equable, he was yet a gallant soldier, a fine horseman, a courtier of grace and wit. But he was rash and sentimental, without judgment or dexterity, or the peculiar *flair* which jealous men call luck.[38]

[34] "Relation de ce qui s'est passé dans la dernière guerre de Perse," by Monsieur Lemaire, French Consul at Tripoli, Syria, dated April 9, 1726, in the archives of the French Foreign Ministry, Correspondance Politique, Perse, VII, 29–30.

[35] "Protokoly Verkhovnogo Tainogo Soveta," in the *Sbornik* of the Imperial Russian Historical Society, Vols. LV, LVI, LXIII, LXXIX (St. Petersburg, 1886–91); M.-F. Brosset, *Perepiska . . . Gruzinskikh Tsarei,* pp. LXXXI–LXXXIII.

[36] Butkov, *Materialy,* I, 113.

[37] M.-F. Brosset, *Perepiska . . . Gruzinskikh Tsarei,* pp. LXXXVI–LXXXVII.

[38] Allen, *History of the Georgian People,* p. 186.

The epitaph on his tomb is a succinct account of his career and achievement:

I, the least of my brothers, Wakhtang by name,

In four years restored the shrines of Mtskhet'a and Urbnisi, rebuilding their domes,

In Tiflis, I repaired the fabric of the Sion Cathedral,

For myself I built a palace of mirrors to enjoy pleasant merriment within.

I brought in a printing press from Wallachia, multiplying the ink of books.

I carried the stream of K'tsia to Khunan and irrigated the fields on the far side,

Joining the Mashaveri canal to the lake, I introduced all kinds of fish into its waters.

I hunted over the hills and slew deer and wolves.

I wrote a book of laws, so that the judges should have no cause for dispute,

Also a commentary on *The Man in the Panther's Skin;* but to other writings I lay no claim.

The knights of my entourage were renowned for their courtly manners.

Finally the world took from me my riches and royal lineage.[39]

As an epilogue to this account of Wakhtang VI's career, one must not omit a description of the far-reaching effects on Russo-Georgian relations of his emigration to Russia in 1724. There has been frequent occasion to mention the activities of Georgian princes at the Russian court from the mid-seventeenth century onwards. Under Tsar Alexis, Prince Nicholas of Kakhet'i stood in high favor in the Kremlin, while Archil's son Alexander, the first general of artillery of the Russian army, had been a bosom companion of the young Peter the Great.

This older generation of Georgian émigrés in Russia soon began to die out. King Archil was buried in 1713, three years after his son Alexander. By their passing, an English observer commented, "the pleasing prospect which the Czar had in view of making a conquest of Georgia when he should have had opportunity for it, or at least of settling a colony there, . . . seems now to be wholly lost." [40]

---

[39] Translated from the text given by M. Janashvili, in his article "Sak'art'velos deda-k'alak'i Tp'ilisi," in *Krebuli,* VI, 65.

[40] Perry, *State of Russia under the Present Czar,* p. 98.

The arrival of Wakhtang in Russia in 1724, with his huge suite, including many distinguished nobles and ecclesiastics, opened a new phase in Russo-Georgian relations. Peter the Great had originally envisaged a rapid reconquest of Georgia with the help of these Georgian émigré forces, leading up to Wakhtang's restoration. Since events made this impossible, Peter's successors gave Wakhtang and his followers grants of money and lands in Russia. In the principal Georgian colony at Moscow, the Georgians had three churches of their own. King Archil had earlier set up a Georgian printing press there on which the first complete Georgian Bible was printed in 1743. There were also Georgian communities at St. Petersburg and Astrakhan, as well as in the Ukraine, around Nizhnii Novgorod, and at Kizliar' in the North Caucasian steppe. Many of these exiled Georgians took Russian brides.

Georgian links with Russia were further strengthened by the encouragement given the emigrés to take up careers in the Russian army and administration. Wakhtang's son Bak'ar, who died in 1750, was a lieutenant general under the Empresses Anne and Elizabeth. One of Wakhtang's nephews, Cyril, rose to become a Russian senator. A great-nephew of Wakhtang, General Peter Bagration, was the illustrious hero of the Napoleonic Wars who fell at the Battle of Borodino in 1812. A number of Georgians fought in the Russian army during the Seven Years' War. Suvorov's disciple, General Tsitsianov, later governor general of Georgia under Alexander I, was descended from a Georgian prince, Tsitsishvili, in Wakhtang's suite. We also find a number of Georgians working in the Russian Foreign Ministry, especially in the Near Eastern section. Among these was Lashkarev, one of Catherine the Great's advisers on Turkish affairs. Eminent also in the Georgian exiled community was Wakhtang's natural son Wakhusht, the pioneer historian and geographer of Georgia.[41]

[41] Among the source material on the eighteenth-century Georgian colony in Russia, see M.-F. Brosset, "Nouvelles recherches sur l'historien Wakhoucht," in *Mélanges Asiatiques*, III, and the same author's "Monographie géorgienne de Moscou," in *Bulletin Scientifique de l'Académie des Sciences*, IV, 279–302. There is useful material in the symposium *Letopis' Gruzii*, Esadze, ed., and in the introduction to the latest (1941) edition of Prince Wakhusht's geographical description of Georgia, Lomouri and Berdzenishvili, eds. On the Georgian colony in the Ukraine, see

The presence of these Georgian communities in eighteenth-century Russia certainly affected the Russian attitude toward Georgia. The Russian government learned to value the Georgians' bravery and enterprise and to take an added interest in the small Christian kingdom isolated from Europe and at grips with the Mohammedan powers. The existence of a Georgian colony in Russia facilitated contact between the two countries. On the other hand, it may be doubted whether the growth of a Russianized Georgian official cadre served the national interests of Georgia as much as it did those of Russia. Often we find prominent Georgians in the Russian service anxious to further the tsar's cause, even at the expense of their home country. This was particularly true later in the eighteenth century when the reunited kingdom of Eastern Georgia was ruled by Erekle II of the Bagratids of Kakhet'i. The Mukhranian exiled princes in Russia and their partisans regarded him as a usurper, and tried to prejudice the Russian government against him. Their intrigues were not without effect on the Russian decision to abolish the Georgian monarchy in 1801. One must conclude that while the presence of the Georgian exiles in Russia contributed to closer relations between the two peoples, it did not always favor Georgian national interests in the long run.

Kosarik, *David Guramishvili.* On the Georgians living near Nizhnii Novgorod, see Tchqonia, "Gorkis olk'shi aghmochenili k'art'uli sidzveleni," in *Literaturuli dziebani,* IV. On the Georgian community at Kizliar' and their treatment by the Russian government, see "Nakaz ot zhivushchikh v Kizliare Gruzin (1767)," in *Materialy Ekaterininskoi zakonodatel'noi komissii* (Materials of the Empress Catherine's Legislative Commission), published in the *Sbornik* of the Imp. Russian Historical Society, CXXXIV (St. Petersburg, 1911), 221-31. Petitions and decrees relating to the employment and remuneration of the Georgian royal family and its dependents are printed in the "Protokoly Verkhovnogo Tainogo Soveta" (Protocols of the Supreme Privy Council) for 1726-30, published in the *Sbornik* of the Imp. Russian Historical Society, Vols. LV, LVI, LXIII, LXXIX, LXXXIV, CI (St. Petersburg, 1886-98), and in the "Bumagi Kabineta Ministrov Imperatritsy Anny Ioannovny" (Papers of the Ministerial Cabinet of Empress Anna Ioannovna) for 1731-40, in the same series, Vols. CVIII, CXI, CXIV, CXVII, CXX, CXXIV, CXXVI, CXXXVIII, CXLVI (Iuriev, 1900-1915).

6

Culture during the Mukhranian Period

THE Golden Age of Georgian literature was attained during the reign of Queen T'amar in the late twelfth and early thirteenth centuries. At the summit of Georgian literary achievement stand Shot'a Rust'aveli's epic, *The Man in the Panther's Skin,* and the noble odes of Chakhrukhadze and Shavt'eli, which glorify the sovereigns of Georgia's heroic era.[1]

The Mongol yoke, which weighed heavy on the land in the thirteenth and fourteenth centuries, and the subsequent disintegration of the kingdom had an adverse effect on Georgian literature. Scarcely any original works of merit have survived from this period, though the poetic gifts of the Georgian people were kept alive through their folksongs. We also have to record the growth of a cycle of imaginative and fantastic verse romances, modeled on the Persian national epic of Firdawsi, the *Shah-Nameh* or *Book of Kings.* Principal among these is the *Rostomiani,* embodying the exploits of the Persian national hero Rustam. Other Persian poetic works adapted by later mediaeval Georgian bards are Nizami's *Khusrau wa Shirin* (in Georgian, *Khosrov-Shiriniani*), and Jami's *Yusuf wa Zulaikha.*

The two main trends in the Georgian poetic tradition—the national tradition of Shot'a Rust'aveli and his imitators, on the one hand, and the foreign influence of exotic Persian romance, on the other—are

[1] For bibliography, see Karst, *Littérature géorgienne chrétienne,* pp. 122–37; Shanidze, *Dzveli k'art'uli ena da literatura,* pp. 82–116; Baramidze, Radiani, and Zhghenti, *Istoriia gruzinskoi literatury,* pp. 29–45.

blended in the work of the first great figure of the Georgian renaissance of the seventeenth century, King T'eimuraz I (1589–1663).
This is the same King T'eimuraz of Kakhet'i whose name has been
mentioned in the political history of Georgia in connection with the
struggle against the Persian Shah 'Abbas I. T'eimuraz, brought up
at the court of Isfahan, had a perfect command of the Persian language. At the same time, the atrocities committed by the Persians
against his native country roused him to fanatical patriotism. The
keynote of his poetry is an elegiac melancholy, turning often to bitter lament, as in his ode on the martyrdom of his mother, Queen
K'et'evan, tortured to death in 1624 by order of the shah.[2] Among
T'eimuraz's many adaptations and original compositions, the most
successful are, perhaps, his wistful *Dialogue between Spring and
Autumn,* the epicurean *Discourse of Wine and Lips,* and the charming poem of the *Rose and the Nightingale,* or *Vard-bulbuliani.*[3]
After a lifetime spent in heroic, if sometimes quixotic, campaigning
against the Persians and their partisans in Georgia, T'eimuraz ultimately surrendered to his rival, King Shahnavaz of K'art'li. He was
sent to the Persian court, and thence to exile at Astarabad on the
Caspian Sea, where he died in 1663.

Another great poet of seventeenth-century Georgia was also of
royal lineage, and played a comparable role in the history of his
time. This was King Archil (1647–1713), son of Shahnavaz (Wakhtang V) of Georgia. As has been recorded, he reigned at various
times in both Imeret'i (Western Georgia) and Kakhet'i, and ended
his career in exile at Moscow.

Archil's poetic technique represents a reaction against the Persianized style of King T'eimuraz. Indeed, one of Archil's most important works is an imaginary poetic dialogue between T'eimuraz
and the national bard Rust'aveli, in which Archil reproaches T'eimuraz for the artificial mannerisms of his style, as well as for having set
himself above the sublime Rust'aveli. Archil further advocates a
move toward poetic "reality," based on a true reflection in poetry of

---

[2] See Avalov, "T'eimuraz I and His Poem, 'The Martyrdom of Queen K'et'evan,'"
in *Georgica,* Vol. I, Nos. 4–5 (1937).

[3] Shanidze, *Dzveli k'art'uli ena da literatura,* pp. 117–35; Baramidze, *Narkvevebi
k'art'uli literaturis istoriidan,* II, 114–62.

the national life and customs of Georgia. This poetic dialogue forms part of Archil's great composite work, the *Archiliani,* or the *Lay of Archil,* which also contains odes and poems based on episodes of Georgian history. Particularly interesting is the poem *On the Battle of Marabda,* which describes the Georgian military disaster of 1624, when King T'eimuraz and the Grand Constable Saakadze were defeated by the Persians. Of both poetic and documentary value is Archil's essay in verse, *The Manners of Georgia,* which gives an impression of the outlook and way of life of an educated Georgian of the seventeenth century. Emphasis is laid on such virtues as piety, fidelity, foresight, and prudence. The work has a distinct didactic tendency. It sets forth the ideal curriculum for the education of a Georgian aristocrat, who is supposed to master the sciences of arithmetic, jurisprudence, theology, geography, foreign languages, and elegant handwriting. Of more intimate inspiration are Archil's lyrics, which have a quality of genuine poetic feeling.[4]

A friend and contemporary of Archil was Joseph Saakadze, bishop of Tiflis (d. 1688), who composed an epic saga dealing with the life of his celebrated relative, the Grand Constable Giorgi Saakadze. The title of this poem, which was composed about 1670, is *Did-Mouraviani,* or *The Lay of the Grand Constable.* It gives a dramatic account of the history of early seventeenth-century Georgia. The narrative centers on the turbulent and controversial personality of Giorgi Saakadze, who at different stages of his career served and betrayed the Georgian king and the Persian shah, only to be executed finally by order of the sultan of Turkey. In spite of certain rhetorical embellishments and a tendency to gloss over the hero's less creditable actions, this poem is an important historical document as well as a fine example of Georgian patriotic verse.[5]

The line of royal poets is continued by the great reformer Wakhtang VI. While in exile in Persia from 1712 until 1719, he occupied his leisure hours by translating from Persian into Georgian the famous collection of oriental fables called *Kalilah wa Dimnah.* His

[4] See the edition of King Archil's complete works by Baramidze and Berdzenishvili, *Archiliani.*

[5] Ioseb Tp'ileli, *Did-Mouraviani,* Leonidze, ed.; Russian translation by G. Tsagareli.

translation was revised and completed by the eminent Georgian man of letters, Sulkhan-Saba Orbeliani.[6]

A faithful follower of Wakhtang VI, who joined his sovereign in exile in Russia, was David Guramishvili (1705–92). His great cycle of poems, the *Davit'iani,* was composed near Mirgorod in the Ukraine where the Russian government granted him an estate. The most important of the poems in this cycle, entitled *The Woes of Georgia,* contains a vivid panorama of Georgian history. Particularly effective is the description of the fall of the Mukhranian dynasty and Wakhtang VI's departure for Russia, as Guramishvili was an eyewitness of many of the events described. The poem also has a strong autobiographical element, as when Guramishvili tells how he was captured by Lezghian brigands and carried off into the mountains. Guramishvili turned his back on the artificial style of earlier Georgian lyric poets and cultivated a directness of idiom new in Georgian verse. In this, the inspiration of Russian and Ukrainian popular poetry has been detected. Guramishvili's rustic vein is well brought out in the charming idyll, *Katsvia the Shepherd.* While steeped in the classical tradition of Rust'aveli, Guramishvili initiated the somber and romantic poetry of nature which was to find its culmination in the work of the great bard of the Georgian highlands, Vazha P'shavela (1861–1915).[7]

The age of Wakhtang VI saw the evolution of modern Georgian prose literature. The pioneer in this field was Sulkhan-Saba Orbeliani (1658–1726). Sulkhan belonged to one of the great princely families of Eastern Georgia. He gained the reputation of being the most learned man of his country and age, and was appointed tutor to the future King Wakhtang VI. In 1698, he became a monk of the Order of St. Basil, under the name of Saba. This order had strong Uniat affiliations at this period, and Sulkhan-Saba, who was on close terms with

[6] Published by I. Tchqonia, *K'ilila da Damana* (Tiflis, 1886). For a survey of Wakhtang's poetic writings, see Tchqonia, "Vakhtang VI t'khzulebat'a p'ragmentebi," in *Literaturuli dziebani,* VI.

[7] On Guramishvili, see Baramidze, *Narvevebi k'art'uli literaturis istoriidan,* II, 276–347; Kosarik, *David Guramishvili;* S. Chikovani, *Pesn' o Davide Guramishvili* (Moscow, 1946). A new edition of Guramishvili's poetic works, under the title of *Davit'iani,* was published at Tiflis in 1955 by A. Baramidze and a committee of scholars.

the Catholic missionaries at Tiflis, himself ultimately became a Roman Catholic. As has been noted in the historical narrative, Sulkhan-Saba undertook an embassy to Rome and to Versailles on behalf of his sovereign, Wakhtang VI. He has left an interesting account of his journeys in Europe, one of the earliest examples of Georgian travel literature.[8] In 1724, Sulkhan-Saba accompanied his monarch into exile in Russia; there he died two years later.

Sulkhan-Saba Orbeliani's most durable contribution to Georgian literature is his *Dsigni sibrdzne-sitsruisa,* which may be rendered as *The Book of Wisdom and Lies.* The work is constructed within the imaginary framework of a dispute between a group of personages including Leon, the enlightened tutor of a king's son, and Ruk'a, an embittered eunuch of the royal court. The discussion ranges over a wide field, and is continually punctuated by illustrative tales and fables. Many of these tales are derived from the common fund of Near Eastern traditional stories which has given us such famous collections as the *Thousand and One Nights,* the Persian *Sandbad-Nameh,* and the Armenian fables of Vardan. The scene changes from tale to tale. One story takes us to Aleppo, another to Baghdad, a third to India, a fourth to Constantinople. We also have echoes of the author's trip to Europe, with references to the French court and to Italian artists. Again, much of the material is taken from the rich fund of Georgian folklore, which helps to explain the popularity of the book in Georgia, where it occupies much the same place as do the fables of La Fontaine in France and those of Krylov in Russia. *The Book of Wisdom and Lies* is also notable for its comments on education, including recommendations for sport and physical exercises. In political ideology, Sulkhan-Saba shows himself to be a partisan of enlightened absolutism, while condemning the abuses characteristic of oriental despotism.[9]

[8] Edited by Iordanishvili, under the title *Mogzauroba Evropashi;* see also extracts in A. A. Tsagareli, *Kniga Mudrosti i Lzhi,* pp. 211–16. A manuscript copy of the travel diary of Sulkhan-Saba Orbeliani is in the Wardrop collection in the Bodleian Library, Oxford.

[9] There are several Georgian editions, including that by G. Leonidze (1928, reprinted 1938); Russian versions by A. A. Tsagareli, *Kniga Mudrosti i Lzhi,* and Gogoberidze (more correctly, Ghoghoberidze), *O Mudrosti Vymysla;* English by Wardrop, *The Book of Wisdom and Lies;* German by Tseret'eli, *Die Weisheit der*

Sulkhan-Saba Orbeliani is also renowned as one of the pioneers of Georgian lexicography. The compilation of his dictionary of the Georgian language, sometimes known as *Sitqvis-kona,* or *Bouquet of Words,* occupied many years of his life. It circulated in manuscript copies, many finely illuminated, throughout the eighteenth century. Some of these copies have a supplement containing Turco-Tatar wordlists with Georgian equivalents. In the main body of the work the definitions are all in Georgian. The esteem in which this dictionary was held may be judged from a letter addressed to its compiler by King Giorgi XI of K'art'li when on campaign in Afghanistan in 1707 as Persian commander in chief. "You had sent hither the Lexicon," wrote Giorgi. "It gave me pleasure, in truth, such pleasure. . . . If you will have it copied out for me in a good clear hand and sent to me again, it will be well." [10] Sulkhan-Saba's dictionary remains a primary source for the study of classical Georgian, and has been twice edited and published in modern times.[11]

It has already been stated that King Wakhtang VI, the outstanding Georgian administrator and legislator, was a disciple of Sulkhan-Saba Orbeliani. During his regency, between 1703 and 1711, he supervised the reediting of the Georgian annals, known under the collective title of *K'art'lis tskhovreba,* or the *Life of Georgia.* These annals, as modern scholarship has long since shown, existed in more or less connected form long before Wakhtang's time. The most ancient manuscript preserved, the so-called Queen Anne codex, dates from between 1479 and 1495. The narrative breaks off, however, early in the fourteenth century, doubtless as a result of the chaotic conditions prevailing in Georgia during the later Mongol period. To bring the annals up to date and incorporate other histori-

---

Lüge. See further Shanidze, *Dzveli k'art'uli ena da literatura,* pp. 162–76; Baramidze, *Narkvevebi k'art'uli literaturis istoriidan,* II, 247–75.

[10] *Sak'art'velos sidzveleni,* T'aqaishvili, ed., II, 223.

[11] First ed. by R. Erist'avi (Tiflis, 1884), second ed. by I. Qip'shidze and A. Shanidze (Tiflis, 1928). Mr. W. E. D. Allen has shown me a fine eighteenth-century manuscript copy in his possession, with illuminated initial letters, copied by Ioane Laradze for the judge and man of letters, Mzetchabuk Orbeliani. (Detailed description in Sotheby's *Catalogue of Fine Oriental Manuscripts,* London, January 28, 1952, pp. 8–9.)

cal source material which had come to light during the intervening period, Wakhtang summoned together a commission of scholars. One of the members, the monk Egnatashvili, was to compose a continuation of the annals, bringing the account of Georgia's history up to the end of the seventeenth century. Among the historical sources incorporated by Wakhtang's advisers into the main body of the annals was the Life of Peter the Iberian, a fifth-century Georgian bishop of Maiuma near Gaza in Palestine and one of the most remarkable figures of the Monophysite church.[12]

Wakhtang's historical work was worthily continued by his natural son Prince Wakhusht (c.1695–1772), who followed his father into exile and lived for many years in Moscow. Wakhusht had been partly educated by the Roman Catholic missionaries in Tiflis, who grounded him in the classics and gave him an insight into scholarly techniques, as understood in the eighteenth century. Wakhusht's work, based on original sources and personal observations, marks a great advance in the study of the history, geography, and national customs of Georgia. He composed an epitome of the history of the ancient period, based on his father's redaction of the Georgian annals (*K'art'lis tskhovreba,* or *Life of Georgia*). Wakhusht's epitome of the older annals is less valuable than his own original work, namely, the histories of each of the several Georgian kingdoms and principalities into which the united realm was split in the mid-fifteenth century.[13] This treatise, based on authentic documents now largely extinct, remains the indispensable authority for the history of the later mediaeval period, from the fifteenth to the eighteenth centuries. It is true that Wakhusht sometimes shows traces of bias against historical personages who came into conflict with his own branch of the Geor-

---

[12] The best critical study of the sources of the Georgian Annals is by Professor C. Toumanoff, "Medieval Georgian Historical Literature," in *Traditio,* Vol. I (New York, 1943); see also the same author's "The Oldest Manuscript of the Georgian Annals," in *Traditio,* Vol. V (1947). Since the various studies by Javakhishvili, the most complete analysis in Georgian of the Annals is that by K. Grigolia in his monograph, *Akhali K'art'lis tskhovreba,* which treats specifically the changes introduced into the chronicles by Wakhtang as well as those brought by later redactors.

[13] "Histoires particulières du Karthli, du Cakheth, du Samtzkhé et de l'Iméreth," in M.-F. Brosset, tr. and ed., *Histoire de la Géorgie,* Vol. II, Part 1.

gian royal family, and that recent research has upset some of his dates and genealogies, but on the whole Wakhusht is a remarkably accurate and fair-minded historian.

Also of the highest value is Wakhusht's geographical description of Georgia, *Aghdsera samep'osa Sak'art'velosa*. The introduction to this treatise contains important data on the social structure, religious beliefs, military organization, and manners and laws of ancient Georgia. Wakhusht's geographical knowledge is remarkable for its richness and precision, and the literary elegance with which it is conveyed to the reader is notable. Interspersed with exact particulars of every town, village, and river of any size are picturesque details on local products and customs. The documentary value of his book is enhanced by an atlas of over twenty maps, some of which are reproduced in the first edition of Wakhusht's *Geography,* published posthumously in 1842.[14]

The historical work of Wakhtang and his son Wakhusht was usefully supplemented and kept up to date by several contemporary chroniclers who noted the events of the day. Prominent among these was P'arsadan Giorgijanidze, an Armenian from Gori in Georgia. P'arsadan used the Georgian language to write an account of Georgian and Persian history to the opening of the eighteenth century. He occupied high posts at the Persian court, and was often employed on confidential matters affecting Georgia, so that he was exceptionally well informed. His chronicle gives a clear idea of Perso-Georgian relations during the period and shows how prominently the Georgians figured in the Persian administrative service.[15] We should also mention the excellent Sekhnia Chkheidze, who had an adventurous career in the Georgian army and public service under Kings Giorgi XI and Wakhtang VI. His chronicle is lucid and reliable.[16]

With this renaissance of Georgian letters during the seventeenth century, there arose an increased demand for fine manuscripts of the

---

[14] *Description géographique de la Géorgie,* Brosset, tr. and ed. M. Janashvili published a Russian translation and a reedition of the Georgian text (both at Tiflis, 1904), but without the important maps. There is a more recent (1941) edition by Lomouri and Berdzenishvili, but also without the maps.

[15] Extracts from P'arsadan's history are translated by M.-F. Brosset, in *Histoire de la Géorgie,* Vol. II, Part 1; the Georgian text was edited by S. Kakabadze.

[16] Tr. by M.-F. Brosset, in *Histoire de la Géorgie,* Vol. II, Part 2.

classics of Georgian literature. The art of the calligraphist and the miniaturist was brought to a new pitch of elegance. This revival was aided by increased cultural contacts with the brilliant decorative artists of Persia. Nor were these contacts confined to borrowings or imitations on the part of the Georgians. We find Georgian artists in the employ of the shahs, playing an important part in the artistic life of Safavid Persia. The seventeenth-century Persian chronicler, Iskander Munshi, writes of one of these Georgian miniaturists working in Persia,

Siawush Beg the Georgian attained great success. An incomparable artist, he wielded a most delicate brush and was a great master of elegant work. No master could compete with him in the art of sketching with the pen, or depicting hills. His drawings of groups of figures were above reproach.[17]

Siawush Beg had a number of disciples who won renown in Persian and Turkish court circles. Another Georgian artist, 'Ali-Quli Jabadari, worked for Shah 'Abbas II in the second half of the seventeenth century. Of special interest is one painting by Jabadari showing a reception at the shah's court, with the titles of the grandees in attendance inscribed in Georgian characters.[18]

It is natural to find Georgian scribes and miniaturists looking to Persia for their inspiration. Illustrations for manuscripts of the Persian national epic, Firdawsi's *Shah-Nameh* or *Book of Kings,* were often imitated. While religious painting and art generally remained within the Byzantine tradition, illustrations for works of poetry and fiction took on an increasingly Persianized, exotic air. This is reflected in the fine seventeenth-century manuscripts of *The Man in the Panther's Skin* by Rust'aveli. One important illuminated manuscript of this epic, with twenty-one miniatures, was recently acquired by the Bodleian Library, Oxford, from the Sir Bernard Eckstein library, and has been described in an article by Mr. Basil Gray.[19] Other illus-

[17] Quoted in Berdzenishvili, Javakhishvili, and Janashia, *Istoriia Gruzii,* p. 382, where Siawush Beg's beautiful miniature painting of a falcon is reproduced in color.

[18] Reproduced in Berdzenishvili, Javakhishvili, and Janashia, *Istoriia Gruzii,* p. 383. See further Amiranashvili, *Istoriia gruzinskogo iskusstva,* I, 280–84, with references to earlier literature.

[19] B. Gray, "The Man in the Panther Skin," in *The Bodleian Library Record,* III, No. 32 (Oxford, 1951).

trated Rust'aveli manuscripts, in Georgian collections are described in a special chapter of Amiranashvili's survey of Georgian art.[20] Also worth noting in this connection are the attractive and highly Persianized miniatures illustrating a manuscript of King Wakhtang VI's Georgian version of *Kalilah wa Dimnah,* now in the Oriental Institute of the Soviet Academy of Sciences.[21]

In Western Georgia, as one would expect, the Persian influence was less pronounced. A seventeenth-century manuscript of Rust'-aveli's epic, copied in 1646 for the Prince-Regnant Levan Dadiani of Mingrelia, has a number of curious miniatures which follow Ottoman Turkish and Georgian national styles. The costumes in particular reflect the mixture between Georgian traditional, Turkish, and Western European elements characteristic of the period. These miniatures are also of interest for their quaint attempt to convey perspective.[22]

In Georgia, as earlier in Europe, the art of the calligraphist and the illustrator was soon to meet with competition from the printer and the engraver. The introduction of printing into Georgia was due to the initiative of the reformer King Wakhtang VI, whose regency, we have seen, was a decade of constructive activity in every sphere. Not the least of Wakhtang's achievements was the setting up of the first printing press at Tiflis in 1709.

Before tracing the early history of printing in Georgia proper, we must go back some eighty years, to survey the activities of a group of Italian and Georgian missionaries working in Rome during the early and mid-seventeenth century. As a result of the establishment of Catholic Theatine and Capuchin missions in Georgia, the need for manuals of the language as well as for devotional texts was felt at the headquarters of the Congregatio de Propaganda Fide in Rome. A chance to provide for this need occurred in 1626, when the Georgian Prince-Monk Nicephorus Irubak'idze or Irbakhi-Choloqashvili, an envoy of King T'eimuraz I of Kakhet'i, arrived in Rome on a diplomatic mission. Nicephorus collaborated with Italian scholars to

[20] *Istoriia gruzinskogo iskusstva,* Vol. I, pp. 281–87, Pl. 188.

[21] *Ibid.,* Pl. 186.

[22] See the reproductions in S. Kakabadze's edition of *The Man in the Panther's Skin* (Tiflis, 1927), and also Amiranashvili, *Istoriia gruzinskogo iskusstva,* Vol. I, p. 285 and Pl. 189.

produce an extensive Georgian-Italian vocabulary, as well as a brief collection of prayers in colloquial Georgian. The results of these joint labors were the following publications, the first printed books in Georgian:

Dittionario Giorgiano e Italiano, composto da Stefano Paolini con l'aiuto del M.R.P.D. Niceforo Irbachi Giorgiano, Monaco di S. Basilio. Ad uso de' Missionarii della Sagra Congregatione de Propaganda Fide. In Roma, Nella Stampa della Sagra Congr. de Propag. Fide. CID D CXXIX (1629).

This dictionary contains over three thousand words. Like the other early Georgian books published in Rome, it is printed in large, clear type of the *mkhedruli* or civil alphabet.

Alphabetum Ibericum, sive Georgianum, cum Oratione Dominicali, Salutatione Angelica, Symbolo Fidei, Praeceptis Decalogi, Ecclesiae Sacramentis, et Operibus Misericordiae, Latina, et Iberica lingua compositis, et Charactere Georgiano impressis: Accesserunt Litaniae B.V. eisdem lingua, et characteribus Ibericis. Romae, Typis Sac. Congr. de Propag. Fide, MDCXXIX.

These two works, though containing inaccuracies unavoidable at this embryonic stage of Georgian studies in Europe, are for their time of great merit. They played an important role in acquainting European linguists with the Georgian tongue, which had hitherto been completely inaccessible to Western scholarship.

The pioneer work of Paolini and Nicephorus was continued by the missionary F.-M. Maggio, who published the first systematic Georgian grammer under the title:

Syntagmatôn Linguarum Orientalium quae in Georgiae Regionibus audiuntur. Liber Primus, complectens Georgianae, seu Ibericae vulgaris linguae Institutiones Grammaticas. Liber Secundus, complectens Arabum et Turcarum orthographiam ac Turcicae linguae Institutiones. Authore D. Francisco-Maria Maggio, Clerico Regulari, Panormitano. Romae, Ex Typographia Sacrae Congregationis de Propaganda Fide. MDCXLIII.

A second printing of this book appeared in 1670. Several other Georgian texts, of a theological character, were published in Rome during the eighteenth century.[23]

[23] For further particulars of these early Italian editions, see *K'art'uli dsigni (Das*

After Rome, the next pioneer center for the printing of texts in Georgian was Moscow. There the initiative was taken by the exiled King Archil. A personal friend of Archil, the geographer and historian Nicholas Witzen, who had served as Dutch resident in Russia, had a fount of Georgian type cut in Amsterdam. With this, Archil printed the first edition of the Georgian version of the *Psalms of David* at the Synodal printing press at Moscow in 1705. This is the first Georgian printed book to employ the *khutsuri* or ecclesiastical alphabet.[24]

By the beginning of the eighteenth century, a good start had been made in printing books in the Georgian language. The disadvantage was that till now these had been appearing far from Georgia itself, namely in Rome and Moscow. Difficulties of transportation and distribution meant that these editions could not circulate freely within Georgia. Although the art of the skilled copyist had reached a new peak of excellence in seventeenth-century Georgia, the production of manuscript copies of sacred texts and the classics of Georgian literature could never keep up with the demand.

This lack was keenly felt by Wakhtang VI. With the help of the eminent Georgian cleric Anthim the Iberian (d. 1716), archbishop of Wallachia and one of the outstanding figures in the history of the Rumanian Church, Wakhtang set about installing a printing plant in Tiflis itself. Anthim, it should be noted, was himself a master printer and engraver of the first order and a noted pioneer in Rumanian printing as well as in the provision of sacred literature for the Christian communities of Syria and the Levant. It was one of Anthim's disciples, the master printer Mihaĭ Iṣtvanoviċ, known in Georgia as Mikhail Step'aneshvili, who came to Tiflis to open the first press there, under Wakhtang's auspices.[25]

Wakhtang took a very personal and direct part in the work of the Georgian printing house, contributing prefaces to several of Mikhail's

---

georgische Buch), Kiknadze, ed., I, 1–5, 42–44; Karst, *Littérature géorgienne chrétienne*, p. 96.

[24] Described with facsimiles in Kiknadze, ed., *K'art'uli dsigni*, pp. viii, 5.

[25] G. P'eradze, "Georgian Influences on the Cultures of the Balkan Peoples," in *Georgica*, Nos. 2–3 (London, 1936), pp. 14–15; Berdzenishvili, Javakhishvili, and Janashia, *Istoriia Gruzii*, p. 390; Bianu and Hodoș, *Bibliografia Românéscă Veche*, I, 483–84, 543–48.

editions. Some of these also have lifelike engraved portrait frontis-pieces depicting Wakhtang. Other illustrations and decorative motifs include the arms of the Georgian royal family, as well as various ornamental vignettes.

The following list includes all known works printed on Mikhail Step'aneshvili's press under Wakhtang's auspices in Tiflis before the Turkish invasion of 1723 put a stop to its activities: [26]

Four Gospels in Georgian, 1709

Psalms of David, 1709; 2d edition, 1711; 3d edition, 1712; 4th edition, 1716

Book of Liturgies, 1710

Prayer-Book, 1710; 2d edition, 1717

Book of Hours, 1710 (two printings); 2d edition, 1717; 3d edition, revised by Nicholas, bishop of Ruisi, 1722

Germanos the Monk, Manual on How the Teacher Should Instruct His Pupil, 1711

Shot'a Rust'aveli, Vep'khis tqaosani (The Man in the Panther's Skin), 1712

The *editio princeps* of the Georgian national epic, this work has a commentary written by Wakhtang VI himself, attempting to explain the religious and mystical significance of the poem. This edition is extremely rare, since many copies were later burnt by church author-ities during subsequent reigns under the pretense that the poem was profane and ungodly.

Missal, 1713, translated from the Greek by Cyprian, bishop of Samt'-avisi

Book of Church Ritual, 1719–20

Paraklitoni, 1720 [the *Parakletike,* a liturgical book of the Orthodox Church].

The Book of the Knowledge of Creation, 1721, a Persian astronomi-cal treatise, including a section on astrolabes, translated into Geor-gian by King Wakhtang VI in collaboration with the Persian scholar Mirza Abduriza Tavrizeli (i.e., Mirza 'Abd al-Riza Tab-rizi). This work is taken from the scientific treatises by Ulugh

[26] The list is based on the descriptions compiled by the National Book Centre or Dsignis Palata of the Georgian SSR, and published in Kiknadze, ed., *K'art'uli dsigni,* Nos. 5–24.

Beg (1393–1449), grandson of Tamerlane and ruler of Samarkand. Portions of the Bible, comprising the Prophets and the Gospels of Matthew, Mark, and Luke, n.d. [probably between 1709–22].

The printing of this edition of the Bible was interrupted by the Turkish invasion of 1723. The text breaks off shortly before the end of the Gospel according to St. Luke.

With this unfinished publication of the Georgian Bible, the work of Wakhtang VI's Tiflis press came to an abrupt end. After arriving in Russia in 1724, Wakhtang and his sons set about restoring the Georgian printing house at Moscow in which the exiled King Archil had printed the first edition of the Psalms in 1705. Wakhtang's sons Bak'ar and Wakhusht were especially active in reorganizing Archil's old press, for which new type was cut at St. Petersburg by the Georgian master printer Christopher Guramishvili.[27] The latter also produced a Russo-Georgian alphabet book, with texts of prayers in Georgian and Latin and notes in German, which was published by the Imperial Academy of Sciences in 1736–37.[28]

The list of Georgian books printed at Moscow under the auspices of the Georgian royal family in exile during this period is as follows: [29]

Psalms of David, 2d Moscow edition, 1737

Zatiki (Book of Hymns Sung from Easter to Whitsun), 1738

The Testament of Basil the Macedonian (i.e., the Byzantine Emperor Basil I, 867–86), 1739, translated from the Russian version by Prince Alexander, son of King Archil of Georgia, general of artillery of the Russian army

Feofan Prokopovich, Manual of Education for Children, 1739, translated from the original Russian by Gabriel Chkheidze, and edited by the Archimandrite Germanos

Holy Gospels, 1739

Triodion, 1741

This book is especially interesting as it contains references in the preface and conclusion to the infant Tsar Ioann Antonovich. All but one of the few surviving copies of this work have these compromising

[27] Kiknadze, ed., K'art'uli dsigni, p. ix.

[28] Ibid., quoting Bulich, Ocherki istorii iazykoznaniia v Rossii, I (St. Petersburg, 1904), 475–79.

[29] Kiknadze, ed., K'art'uli dsigni, Nos. 25–30, 33–37.

references torn out, as is the case with most books issued in Russia
during Ioann's brief and ill-starred reign.

Holy Bible, 1743

The first complete edition of the Georgian Bible, with text based
mainly on the Georgian Athonite redaction, though some passages
were newly translated from the Slavonic; this fine folio volume of
over a thousand pages bears the crest of the Bagrations on the title
page and has prefaces by the Princes Bakʻar and Wakhusht.

Book of Hours, 1743

St. John Damascene, The Exact Exposition of the Orthodox Faith,
    translated from the Greek by Arseni of Iqaltʻo, 1744

This work by St. John of Damascus is the classic treatise of Christian doctrine, the *Ekdosis akribes*. The Georgian translator Arseni
was prominent in the intellectual life of early twelfth-century Georgia.

Stefan Iavorskii, The Rock of Faith, n.d. [probably c.1737–44], trans-
    lated into Georgian by Prince Wakhusht

The printing of this Georgian version of Iavorskii's theological
treatise, *Kamen' very,* was never completed; the printed part breaks
off abruptly before the end.

Collection of Prayers, translated from the Russian, n.d. [probably
    c.1737–44]

The foregoing shows that by mid-eighteenth century, Georgian
books had been printed and produced in four main centers: Rome,
Moscow, Tiflis, and St. Petersburg. Throughout, biblical and liturgical texts predominate. At the same time, the revival of Georgian
national literature is reflected in the appearance of the first edition
of Rustʻaveli's epic poem, *The Man in the Panther's Skin.* We also
note the diffusion of scientific and educational works in the shape of
Wakhtang's translation of a Persian astronomical treatise, as well as
a Georgian version of Prokopovich's manual of elementary education.
From a bibliographical standpoint, all these early Georgian books
are great rarities. In some cases only one or two copies have been
traced.

While the period reviewed above represents the pioneer and his-
torically most significant phase of Georgian printing, it may be convenient to add here a brief continuation, to bring the outline of the

story up to the time of the Russian annexation in 1801. In Georgia itself publishing was resumed after the Turkish and Persian occupations had ended following the murder of the Persian despot Nadir Shah in 1747. Under the auspices of Kings T'eimuraz II and Erekle II, the Tiflis press inaugurated by Wakhtang VI was restored and resumed operation in 1749. During the second half of the eighteenth century it produced chiefly theological works. During the same period, the Moscow Georgian press also published a few more liturgical texts before lack of funds forced it to close down in 1768. At Mozdok in North Caucasia, the Georgian Archimandrite Gaioz T'aqaishvili opened a small printing press in 1796 under Russian auspices. Gaioz published several grammatical and pedagogical works, mainly of his own authorship, as well as the first book ever printed in Ossetic, an important Iranian language of the Central Caucasus. Finally, a printing house was established for the first time at the capital of Western Georgia, K'ut'ais, by King Solomon II in 1800. A number of sacred texts were printed there in the early years of the nineteenth century. As a result of the unsettled conditions preceding the Russian annexation of Imeret'i in 1810, this press had to be moved from K'ut'ais into the country for safety; there it functioned until 1817.

In general, Russian occupation at first had a most discouraging effect on the production of books in Georgia, as the country was kept under martial law with rigid censorship. With the 1830s, however, the situation became somewhat easier, and from that time on the publication of books in Georgian has continued in an ever-increasing spate, both at Tiflis and in the main provincial centers.[30]

Architecture in Georgia during this period offers little of outstanding originality. A feature of seventeenth- and eighteenth-century building technique is the greatly increased use of brick, for both churches and public buildings. But in design and layout churches continued to follow the traditional patterns which had come to fruition in the Golden Age of the Georgian mediaeval kingdom. The dominant feature of the traditional design persisted—namely the cone-shaped, pointed cupola, supported on an octagonal or cylin-

[30] The best short survey of printing in Georgia is by Karitchashvili, *K'art'uli dsignis betchdvis istoria.*

drical dome resembling a huge drum. This design gives a highly distinctive and conspicuous effect, and is also characteristic of Armenian Church architecture, though with certain modifications. Compared with Georgian churches of earlier periods, those of the seventeenth century may often be distinguished by a tendency of their domes to become taller and more slender.

Many Georgian churches, including those constructed in earlier periods, are decorated with mural paintings and frescoes by seventeenth- and eighteenth-century artists. Among the subjects depicted are scenes from the Bible, lives of saints and martyrs, and local princes and pious benefactors. Sometimes these paintings are stylized after the Byzantine manner, but often they give precious clues that help us reconstruct Georgian costume and manners of the time. Many portraits of Georgian historical personages, for instance, exist solely as part of a church fresco.[31] The same applies to many of the magnificent icons and other examples of the gold- and silversmith's art dating from the seventeenth and eighteenth centuries. Here, beside finely molded images of St. George, St. Saba, and other popular saints, we often find kneeling effigies of Georgian kings, princes, and bishops of the time.[32]

In short, the period from the accession of King Rostom in 1632 until the fall of Wakhtang VI in 1723 marked a rebirth of Georgian cultural life. It was a period rich in poetry and belles-lettres. Historical, and geographical studies, and even astronomy and chemistry,[33] flourished. The arts of the penman and the printer were in strong demand, and manuscripts and books multiplied. Churches were restored and new ones built according to the classic patterns of Georgian mediaeval architecture. In ecclesiastical art and letters, the Byzantine tradition was kept alive, while secular painting and literature owed much to Persian styles evolving under the enlightened patronage of the Safavi shahs. These influences were blended with

[31] See the references to specialist literature in Amiranashvili, *Istoriia gruzinskogo iskusstva*, I, 265–75, and the section on Transcaucasia in D. R. Buxton, *Russian Mediaeval Architecture* (Cambridge, 1934).

[32] Amiranashvili, *Istoriia gruzinskogo iskusstva*, Vol. I, Pls. 190–200.

[33] On Wakhtang VI and his studies in astronomy and chemistry, in which he was assisted by the Roman Catholic missionaries in Tiflis, see K. Grigolia, *Akhali K'art'lis tskhovreba*, pp. 331–39.

native, original inspiration into a distinctive Georgian artistic style. It is true that this period of reawakening can scarcely bear comparison with the achievements of the Golden Age of David the Builder and Queen T'amar. It was, however, a real renaissance, the Silver Age of Georgian civilization.

7

Georgia under Turkish and Persian Rule
1723-1747

THE dramatic collapse of the empire of the Persian Safavi shahs in
1722 had produced a political vacuum in that area. This vacuum
was very soon filled by three rival powers—Turkey, Russia, and Afghanistan—each suspicious and hostile toward the others. While the
heir-apparent of the legitimate Persian royal line maintained himself
precariously in the provinces, the Turks held Tiflis, Erivan, Tabriz,
and the other cities of Georgia, Armenia, and Western Iran, the Russians occupied the Caspian littoral, and the Afghans ruled over the
central and eastern regions from the Persian capital of Isfahan.

In Georgia, the local people did not submit to Turkish domination
without active discontent and sporadic resistance. At Tiflis, King
Wakhtang VI's brother, the adaptable debauchee Iese, became a
puppet ruler for the Turks, characteristically adopting the Ottoman
title of Mustafa Pasha. In the eastern marches of Kakhet'i, the Georgian Bagratid King Constantine retained control of the more inaccessible areas.

Their hold over Eastern Georgia enabled the Turks to reinforce
their grip on Western Georgia as well. In 1723, they occupied the
key Black Sea port of P'ot'i, and established bases in other coastal
areas of Mingrelia. The West Georgian monarch, King Alexander
V of Imeret'i, had been harassed by his turbulent vassals, and encouraged the Turks to break down their resistance. With this in
view, Alexander supported the Ottoman army against the Mingre-

lians and the Abkhaz. But in 1733, the Abkhaz won a complete victory over the Turks, and almost wiped out their army—a success popularly attributed to the divine intervention of St. George, the national patron saint of Georgia.[1]

On the death of the renegade Iese in 1727, the Ottoman governor general of Tiflis, himself of Georgian descent, suspended the K'art'-lian monarchy completely. He divided up the country among the feudal grandees. These he kept in order by stirring up their mutual rivalries and by elevating creatures of his own to posts of authority.[2]

If the Turks hoped to integrate Eastern Georgia permanently into the Ottoman Empire, they were doomed to disappointment. It was not long before their position in Persia was seriously threatened by the spectacular feats of the Persian military leader Nadir. Posing as champion of the legitimate Persian royal line, Nadir rallied the nation to his standard, and by 1729 had reoccupied Isfahan and Teheran and exterminated the Afghan invaders. In this he was encouraged by the Russians, who were finding the garrisoning of the Caspian provinces an onerous responsibility. The unsettled state of the country had greatly interfered with Russo-Persian trade, and the Russian court soon came to desire the restoration of a peaceful and united Iran.[3]

When in 1730 Nadir attacked the Turks and recaptured Tabriz, the Russians gave him encouragement and military aid. The Ottoman position in western Persia was seriously shaken. The Georgians began to throw off their allegiance to the Turkish authorities. King Constantine of Kakhet'i made the mistake of showing his hand too soon and of antagonizing the Turks before the time was ripe for their final expulsion. In December, 1732, the Turks lured Constantine to a rendezvous where he was treacherously shot down. In the ensuing massacre, the Turks murdered the Archbishop of Alaverdi and wiped out the assembled army of Kakhet'i.[4]

---

[1] Wakhusht, "Histoires particulières . . . de l'Iméreth," in M.-F. Brosset, tr. and ed., *Histoire de la Géorgie,* II, Part 1, 315–17.

[2] Wakhusht, "Histoires particulières du Karthli," in M.-F. Brosset, tr. and ed., *Histoire de la Géorgie,* II, Part 1, 127.

[3] Manstein, *Memoirs of Russia,* pp. 58–59.

[4] Wakhusht, "Histoires particulières . . . du Cakheth," in M.-F. Brosset, tr. and ed., *Histoire de la Géorgie,* II, Part 1, 192; Chkheidze, "Chronicle," in M.-F. Brosset,

The Turks hoped to find Constantine's brother T'eimuraz more docile toward their views, and granted him the kingdom of Kakhet'i. This nomination marks an important step in the emergence of the Bagratids of Kakhet'i, to which family Constantine and T'eimuraz belonged, as the ruling house over all Eastern Georgia. T'eimuraz was married to Princess T'amar, daughter of King Wakhtang VI of K'art'li. Thus the son and heir of this union, the future King Erekle II, born in 1720, was a grandson of the last reigning sovereign of the Mukhranian line and united in himself the two royal houses of K'art'li and Kakhet'i.[5] This fact was of decisive importance when the time came to rally the whole country in a campaign for national liberation.

If the Ottoman authorities counted on using T'eimuraz as a puppet, they made a miscalculation. T'eimuraz was a prince of unusual tenacity and patriotism. He and his son Erekle were only waiting for the signal to head a general movement to drive the Turks from Eastern Georgia. The time came in 1734 when Nadir and the Persians launched a general assault on the Turkish occupation zone of Transcaucasia. Occupying the great silk town of Shamakhi without difficulty, Nadir also forced the Russians to give up their occupation zone, including the ports of Baku and Derbent.[6]

The following spring Nadir marched on Georgia. He was joined by several of the Georgian leaders, including King T'eimuraz, who welcomed the Persians as liberators. The powerful nobleman Prince Givi Amilakhori drove the Turks from Gori, while Tiflis surrendered to the Perso-Georgian forces in August, 1735.[7]

It was not long before the Georgians came to rue their ready welcome to Nadir and his bloodthirsty hordes. After a triumphal entry into Tiflis in October, 1735, Nadir sent forces to cow the autonomous Georgian dukes. Churches were profaned and women and children

---

tr., *Histoire de la Géorgie*, II, Part 2, 46; M.-F. Brosset, *Perepiska . . . Gruzinskikh Tsarei*, p. LXXXIV; Peyssonnel, *Essai sur les troubles*, pp. 68–69. The entry in the *Perepiska* confirms that Constantine's murder occurred in 1732, as stated by Chkheidze, and not in 1729, as given by Wakhusht.

[5] See the genealogical tables in M.-F. Brosset, *Histoire de la Géorgie*, Vol. II, Part 1, Addition IX.

[6] Lockhart, *Nadir Shah*, pp. 83–84.

[7] Peyssonnel, *Essai sur les troubles*, p. 71; Allen, *History of the Georgian People*, pp. 189–90.

massacred. Five thousand of the local inhabitants were carried off into slavery. The ill-disciplined soldiery devastated the country. Whole villages were deported to remote and desolate regions of eastern Persia.[8]

In spite of these outrages against the population, Nadir, like so many of the Persian shahs before him, did not fail to make use of the Georgians' warrior abilities. In so doing he was also actuated by the desire to keep the ablest of the Georgian military leaders under his personal supervision. In Nadir's campaigns in India between 1737 and 1740, he was loyally supported by a Georgian contingent under the future King Erekle II. Erekle's courage and resourcefulness won the shah's highest commendation.[9]

On returning from India and from the subsequent expedition to Turkestan, Nadir Shah set about subduing Daghestan and the whole Eastern Caucasus. In 1741, he reached Ghazi-Ghumuq in the heart of Daghestan, and was contemplating an attack on Avaria when the lateness of the season compelled him to retreat to Derbent. For nearly two years Nadir remained on the borders of Daghestan, striving fruitlessly to bring the defiant tribes under his domination.

The Persian dictator was now suffering from megalomania verging on insanity. At one point he threatened to invade Russia, boasting that the hand that had humbled the Grand Mogul of Delhi had only to be waved toward the north to bring the Court of St. Petersburg to heel.[10] Events soon showed the folly of Nadir's Caucasian adventure. Wrote the British merchants in Persia,

it is reported that in an attempt against the Lazgees and some other of those Northern People, he has lost to the number of sixty thousand men. . . . The opposition the Lazgees have made against Nadir Shaw [sic] (they having twice defeated him) has greatly frustrated his designs against the Turks. . . . He is now [i.e., in February, 1742] froze up in his Winter Quarters near Deerbent, and as soon as the weather breaks

[8] Chkheidze, "Chronicle," in M.-F. Brosset, tr., *Histoire de la Géorgie,* II, Part 2, 49–50; Wakhusht, "Histoires particulières du Karthli," in M.-F. Brosset, tr. and ed., *Histoire de la Géorgie,* II, Part 1, 132.

[9] Kherkheulidze, "Vie du roi Eréclé II," in M.-F. Brosset, tr. and ed., *Histoire de la Géorgie,* II, 207, and letters of King Erekle II in the same volume, Addition XII.

[10] See the Russian envoy Kalushkin's report in S. M. Solov'ev, *Istoriia Rossii v tsarstvovanie Imp. Elisavety Petrovny* (2d ed.; Moscow, 1879), I, 102.

up, he intends to go again against the Lazgees, as in case of a war with the Turks, they would be too powerful an enemy to leave behind him.[11]

A few months after this was written, threats of a Turkish invasion of Persia forced Nadir to leave the Caucasus forever and hurry southwards with the sorry remnants of his army. He had proved the truth of the Persian proverb, "If any Persian king is a fool, let him march against the Lezghis." [12]

During this disastrous campaign, Georgia had borne the full brunt of Nadir's frustrated wrath. Threatened with famine in his encampment on the bleak Caspian shore, the shah had sent his agents into K'art'li to extort contributions in cash and kind from the inhabitants. Complains the annalist:

Children, animals, everything was taxed. Gardens, buildings of all kinds, ruins, mills, all were assessed at so high a rate that it was absolutely impossible to pay it. When the Turks were masters of the land for a time, they also demanded a *miri* or tax, but never had the rulers of Persia made a census of K'art'li. We must blame our sins for this misfortune. Meanwhile, many of the inhabitants emigrated, the country was exceedingly depopulated: each one with his own hands uprooted his trees and devastated his vineyards and gardens. All those who remained continued to hope for a prince of the legitimate line.

As a result of these extortions there was a bread famine. Persian quartermasters beat peasants to death in attempts to force them to reveal their stocks.[13]

As a result of this oppression, Duke Shanshe of the K'sani headed a mass uprising against Nadir's tyranny. This formidable feudal magnate allied himself with Nadir's adversaries, the Lezghis, and presented a constant threat to the Persian army's left flank. Shanshe harbored a pretender to the Persian throne, who lay claim to royal Safavi descent. It took a Persian force of 12,000 men to crush this revolt.[14]

[11] India Office Factory Records, Persia, Vol. XV: Reports from Gombroon and Basra (hitherto unpublished).

[12] Lockhart, *Nadir Shah*, pp. 197–211; Butkov, *Materialy dlia novoi istorii Kavkaza*, I, 211–28.

[13] Papuna Orbeliani, "Chronicle," in M.-F. Brosset, tr. and ed., *Histoire de la Géorgie*, II, Part 2, 57–59.

[14] Papuna Orbeliani, "Chronicle," in M.-F. Brosset, tr. and ed., *Histoire de la*

In 1743, Nadir embarked on another campaign against the sultan of Turkey. This was the signal for fresh disorders in Georgia. This time the rebellion was headed by Prince Givi Amilakhori, whom Nadir had earlier made his viceroy in Georgia. In addition to disgust with Nadir's tyranny, Givi's rising was inspired by the intention of restoring the deposed Mukhranian dynasty to the K'art'lian throne. Givi got in touch with Wakhtang VI's son Bak'ar, at this time in Astrakhan, and offered to restore him to the throne if he would return from Russia. This move naturally alienated the claimants to the Georgian throne on the spot, namely T'eimuraz II and his son Erekle of Kakhet'i, whose ambitions would have been shattered by the return of Bak'ar. T'eimuraz and Erekle therefore rallied to Nadir's cause against Givi. Although Givi received help from a Turkish expeditionary force, he was no match for T'eimuraz and Erekle, and was forced to surrender in 1745.[15]

As a reward for their loyal services, Nadir granted the kingdom of K'art'li to T'eimuraz and that of Kakhet'i to Erekle. In 1745, for the first time in over a century, a king of K'art'li was crowned with traditional pomp at the Georgian Patriarchal Cathedral of the Living Pillar in Mtskhet'a. The contemporary annalist Papuna Orbeliani has noted many interesting features of the ceremony, which had fallen into disuse since the invasions of Shah 'Abbas the Great and was now revived and performed by the Catholicos-Patriarch Antoni I, who had succeeded in 1744 to the primacy of the Georgian Church.

On the day before the coronation, the army of K'art'li assembled in Tiflis under its four standards. The first banner was entrusted to Prince K'aikhosro Orbeliani, the second to Constantine, prince of Mukhran, the third to Prince Dimitri Amilakhori, and the fourth remained under the king's direct command. As the army moved from Tiflis toward the Patriarchal Cathedral at Mtskhet'a, it was joined by contingents from the duchies of the K'sani and the Aragvi, who were ranged 'neath the banner of the prince of Mukhran. Arriving before the cathedral, the king passed the night in prayer and

---

Géorgie, II, Part 2, 58–61; Archives of the French Foreign Ministry, Correspondance Politique, Perse, VII, 192–93: "Nouvelles de Perse," dated October 23, 1741.

[15] Papuna Orbeliani, "Chronicle," in M.-F. Brosset, tr. and ed., *Histoire de la Géorgie*, II, Part 2, 79–98; Butkov, *Materialy*, I, 228–30; Peyssonnel, *Essai sur les troubles*, p. 79.

vigil. The next morning, the procession moved from the royal encampment toward the cathedral. In front marched military bands, followed by the picked cavalry corps bearing the standard of the commander in chief. Then came King T'eimuraz himself, surrounded and supported by the principal court dignitaries. The royal armor-bearers and the bulk of the army brought up the rear.

To the sound of hymns, the procession was met at the cathedral porch by the catholicos and clergy, who escorted the king to a double throne set up in the center of the cathedral, on which both king and catholicos sat. At the appropriate moment, the king went forward to the high altar to be anointed and crowned, and receive into his hands the scepter and orb. After this, the commander in chief girded him with the royal sword. Salvoes of artillery greeted the monarch's departure from the cathedral. The proceedings concluded with banquets and popular merrymaking.[16]

The Persian despot Nadir's gratitude toward Kings T'eimuraz and Erekle of Georgia did not prevent him from bleeding the country white with demands for money and stores to be expended on his ceaseless campaigns. All over the Persian empire the story was the same. From Armenia a Catholic missionary wrote,

After having killed all men of position, put out the eyes of those who saw well and sold their families to the soldiers, after having taken away from the community all their ploughing animals and removed all the grain for the army, he has turned to harass the people and fleece them with impossible taxes, which leave them as naked as worms.[17]

In 1746, Nadir Shah imposed a tribute of 300,000 tomans on Georgia. This sum, equivalent to 3 million silver rubles or some £750,000 sterling at the exchange rates of the time,[18] far exceeded the land's resources. On receiving the news, the Georgians prepared to evacuate Tiflis and offered armed resistance to the shah's officers. King T'eimuraz resolved to proceed in person to the shah's court to plead for his people, and, if necessary, give his life for their cause.[19]

---

[16] Papuna Orbeliani, "Chronicle," in M.-F. Brosset, tr. and ed., *Histoire de la Géorgie*, II, Part 2, 101–5.

[17] *Chronicle of the Carmelites in Persia*, I, 630.

[18] See Rabino, *Coins, Medals and Seals*, Table IV: "Values of Iranian Coins in Foreign Currencies."

[19] Papuna Orbeliani, "Chronicle," in M.-F. Brosset, tr. and ed., *Histoire de la Géorgie*, II, Part 2, 114–18.

Before T'eimuraz had time to reach Nadir's encampment, the shah was assassinated in June, 1747, by a group of his own officers, whom Nadir had planned to execute. Nadir's nephew 'Ali Quli Khan was already in rebellion, and now assumed power under the title of 'Adil Shah. On the arrival of the Georgian monarch, he was received with favor and distinction by the new shah, who was married to one of T'eimuraz's daughters and anxious to foster his Georgian connections. 'Adil Shah invited his father-in-law, T'eimuraz, to remain for a time to assist him in establishing authority over Persia.[20]

Thus ended a bleak quarter century in the history of Eastern Georgia. The country had to bear the burden first of Turkish, then of Persian military rule. For a number of years, the monarchy was suspended and the people bullied by foreign governors. But the dictatorship of Nadir Shah finally proved too much even for his own countrymen to bear. The murder of the despot was to be a turning point in the revival of the national Bagratid monarchy in Georgia.

[20] *Ibid.*, pp. 118–25; Lockhart, *Nadir Shah*, pp. 259–64.

8

The Struggle for National Independence
1747-1762

IN the chaotic conditions prevailing throughout Persia after the murder of Nadir Shah, it seemed at first that Nadir's nephew 'Adil Shah would emerge as the new sovereign. This would have been advantageous to Georgian interests, in view of the influence which King T'eimuraz was able to exert on the new shah through his daughter K'et'evan, 'Adil's favorite wife. As commander of the Persian royal guard, the shah appointed the Georgian nobleman Givi Amilakhori, whose rebellion had given Nadir so much trouble. Altogether, 'Adil Shah had about a thousand Georgians in his service.[1]

As events turned out, 'Adil's reign was a brief one. He proved unequal to the task of reestablishing order in Persia, and succumbed in 1748 to a revolt headed by his brother Ibrahim. Disorders also broke out in Georgia. The Persian usurper Ibrahim was hostile to the Georgian royal family, and encouraged a rebellion against T'eimuraz and Erekle which was headed by a scion of the rival Mukhranian dynasty. The latter, a son of the renegade Iese named Archil, managed to occupy the citadel of Tiflis in 1748. Nothing daunted, the resourceful Erekle wheeled up a huge cannon weighing a ton, left in Georgia by Nadir Shah, and calculated, according to eyewitnesses, to inspire terror in Archil's untrained levies. When Erekle had fired four shots from this alarming piece of artillery which shook the

[1] Butkov, *Materialy*, I, 234-35.

whole city with its din, the garrison became panic-stricken and Erekle was able to launch a successful attack on the Georgian capital.[2]

After Erekle had reoccupied Tiflis in July, 1748, his prestige was at its height. Many of the provincial rulers of Persia looked to him as the arbiter of the Iranian monarchy. "Without the submission of K'art'li and Kakhet'i," says a contemporary,

that of Azerbaijan could not be counted on. Everyone had their eyes fixed on King Erekle. The khans said to him: "The side you take, we also will support." He was feared furthermore for his warlike exploits, and the Shah respected him.[3]

It was not long before Shah Sultan Ibrahim, as Ibrahim styled himself, succumbed in his turn to Nadir's grandson Shahrukh. The latter set up his court in Meshed and attempted to secure Georgian support by appointing King T'eimuraz his viceroy in Azerbaijan and central Persia. Soon afterwards, Shahrukh was himself deposed and blinded—partly, so it appears, owing to the unseemly conduct of his Georgian favorite, whose name was Rasul Beg and who scandalized the pious Moslems of Meshed by making free with the harem of his master.[4]

Persia was again rapidly lapsing into anarchy. As the chronicler expressed it, "Obscure men seized upon provinces and towns at will, and did not cease from attacking one another and laying waste the lands of the vanquished." In 1749, one of the assassins of Nadir Shah, Mohammed Khan Qajar, attacked the khan of Erivan in Armenia, who was an ally of the Georgians. T'eimuraz and Erekle marched against the invader, who was completely defeated, leaving nearly two thousand dead on the battlefield. The khan of Erivan agreed to pay tribute to the Georgian crown, an

[2] Papuna Orbeliani, "Chronicle," in M.-F. Brosset, tr. and ed., *Histoire de la Géorgie,* II, Part 2, 130-33; Kherkheulidze, "Vie du roi Eréclé II," in M.-F. Brosset, tr. and ed., *Histoire de la Géorgie,* II, Part 2, 210; M.-F. Brosset, *Histoire de la Géorgie,* II, Part 2, 230.

[3] Papuna Orbeliani, "Chronicle," in M.-F. Brosset, tr. and ed., *Histoire de la Géorgie,* II, Part 2, 138-39.

[4] Archives of the French Foreign Ministry, Correspondance Politique, Perse, VII, No. 81.

arrangement which continued in force until the invasion of Agha Mohammed Shah in 1795.[5]

The building up of Georgian political power in Transcaucasia continued in the following year of 1750 with the defeat of Panah-Khan, a Tatar chieftain who was ravaging Shirvan and the country of the Qarabagh Armenians. Qarabagh and the khanate of Ganja were taken under Georgian protection in return for an annual subsidy to the Georgian exchequer.[6]

The fortunes of war fluctuated during the next year, 1751. In a battle against the khan of Shekki and the Lezghis of Daghestan, the Georgians were beaten with heavy loss of life. This disaster was redeemed later in the year in a great victory over the Afghan chieftain Azat Khan, which gave the Georgians temporary possession of all the country north of the River Araxes.[7]

The Georgian victory over Azat Khan was followed by campaigns and skirmishes against several other Persian and Caucasian chieftains, which it would be tedious to follow in detail here.[8] Of wider interest are the international repercussions of the Georgians' feats of arms. It was at the Turkish capital of Constantinople that these aroused the keenest attention. Foreign diplomats accredited to the Sublime Porte sent home colorful and sometimes misleading reports of Erekle's prowess. It was said, for example, that the Russians had sent to Georgia a prince of the royal blood of the Safavis, and that Erekle would head a movement to set him on the Persian throne. More reliable reports stated that the Ottoman government hoped that Erekle's progress would prove a source of weakness and division for the Persian empire, and that it was resisting the

[5] M.-F. Brosset, *Histoire de la Géorgie,* II, Part 2, 231; Papuna Orbeliani, "Chronicle," in M.-F. Brosset, tr. and ed., *Histoire de la Géorgie,* II, Part 2, 144–46.

[6] Butkov, *Materialy,* I, 238, 385–86; Allen, *History of the Georgian People,* p. 197.

[7] Peyssonnel, *Essai sur les troubles,* pp. 123–25. These battles are commemorated by the Georgian annalists, and also by patriotic bards. See the poems "Erekle mep'e da Dat'una Bostashvili" and "Azat-Khani da Erekle" in *Khalkhuri poezia,* Gomiashvili and Gvetadze, eds., pp. 347–48, 264–66.

[8] See Papuna Orbeliani, "Chronicle," in M.-F. Brosset, tr. and ed., *Histoire de la Géorgie,* II, Part 2, 172–73; Butkov, *Materialy,* I, 240; Peyssonnel, *Essai sur les troubles,* pp. 144–48; Archives of the French Ministry of Foreign Affairs, Correspondance Politique, Perse, VII: "Traduction d'une lettre italienne écrite par un Missionaire de Géorgie" (1753).

demands of Turkish public opinion for intervention in favor of the Persians and Afghans against the Georgians. According to the French ambassador,

The Sultan observes with pleasure the number of rival claimants to the Persian throne. He regards with indifference the manoeuvres and intrigues of Russia which, he knows with certainty, is encouraging, supporting and trying to establish in Persia Prince Heraclius of Georgia. The Russians and Germans announce here that he is winning great successes every day. The Turks say that he is completely worsted. Each speaks as his views and interests dictate.[9]

It now seems clear that the aid given to Erekle by the Russians was negligible at this point in his career. Indeed, since the Empress Anne had handed back Derbent and Baku to Nadir Shah in 1735, the Russian government had shown very little inclination to intervene in Persian and Caucasian affairs, preferring to leave the warlike Persian dictator to deal massive blows against Turkish territory in Asia. Fear of arousing Nadir's jealousy helps to explain why the Russians declined to stage a Caucasian diversion against the Turks during the war of 1735–39, despite the eagerness of King Alexander V of Imeret'i, who sent Archbishop Timothy of K'ut'ais on a special mission to St. Petersburg.[10] The murder of Nadir Shah in 1747 and the consequent chaos in Persia might have tempted the Russians to fish in these troubled waters had it not been for the Empress Elizabeth's preoccupation with European affairs. From the peace of Aix-la-Chapelle in 1748 until the outbreak of the Seven Years War in 1756, the European courts were uneasily jostling for position in preparation for the major conflict which now loomed as inevitable on the horizon. This was no time for hazardous sideshows in the Caucasus. For the time being, Russia's interests were best served by the maintenance of the Near Eastern status quo.

These considerations may help to explain the fact that when the Georgian Metropolitan Athanasius arrived in St. Petersburg from Tiflis in 1752 with a request for Russian military support against

[9] Archives of the French Ministry of Foreign Affairs, Correspondance Politique, Perse, VII: "Mémoire pour servir d'instruction au Sieur Simon" (1752).

[10] Wakhusht, "Histoires particulières . . . de l'Iméreth," in M.-F. Brosset, tr. and ed., *Histoire de la Géorgie,* II, Part 1, 318–21; M.-F. Brosset, *Perepiska . . . Gruzinskikh Tsarei,* p. XC; *Istoriia S.S.S.R.,* Grekov, Bakhrushin, and Lebedev, eds., I, 594.

Georgia's Mohammedan neighbors, his petition was rejected.[11] At the same time, Russian diplomacy did its utmost to placate the Turks and prevent Ottoman intervention in Persian and Georgian affairs. In April, 1752, the Russian representative in Constantinople, Obrezkov, was instructed to "hint to the Turkish ministers that the Porte should leave the Persians to settle their own affairs, since owing to the Persians' weakness, they can present no danger to Turkey's frontiers." Obrezkov was to

repeat to the Turkish ministers that we [i.e., the Russians] have not so far been giving any aid to the Georgians, that this little nation does not merit the attention of so mighty a power as the Porte, and that there is no point in the Porte's becoming irritated against it.

Obrezkov replied that although the Turks would never believe that the Georgians were not receiving secret Russian aid, this did not matter greatly. The sultan was aware that Erekle's victories had been greatly magnified by rumor, and had no intention of departing from his neutral policy.[12]

This Russian policy of nonintervention in Georgia is further reflected in a communiqué inserted in the Russian official organ *Sanktpeterburgskie Vedomosti* (St. Petersburg News) of November 23, 1753. "From various foreign newspapers," the announcement states,

it has been noticed here that their writers continue to fill the public ear with false news about the progress of the Georgian Prince Irakli, ascribing to him prodigious deeds of valour, and many notable successes in the Persian empire, even including the conquest of the capital city of Isfahan. They allege that he has even made public speeches to the populace there, and then add far-reaching and quite disjointed political speculations, involving conclusions fraught with future peril, particularly to the Ottoman Porte. . . . It has therefore been deemed necessary to communicate a brief summary of the genuine and reliable reports which have been received here from time to time.

The communiqué proceeds to give a factual narrative of military events in Georgia between 1750 and 1753, without minimizing the heavy losses suffered by the Georgians. In conclusion, the announcement reproduces verbatim a sentence in a letter from King T'eimuraz

---

[11] Butkov, *Materialy,* I, 240.

[12] Solov'ev, *Istoriia Rossii v tsarstvovanie Imp. Elisavety Petrovny,* III (2d ed.; Moscow, 1881), 176–77.

of Georgia to the Russian commandant at Kizliar': "The land of Georgia, surrounded by enemies on all sides, is in a state of great devastation." [13]

By this time, the Turks' neutrality combined with Russia's policy of nonintervention in Perso-Georgian affairs had produced a slackening of tension in diplomatic circles at Constantinople. In February, 1753, the French ambassador at the Sublime Porte wrote to his government that

Erigler Khan,[14] prince of Georgia and son of Temiras Khan, who has handed over the government to him, at present occupies a good part of the provinces situated between the north and west of Persia. But his successes and projects are far from being as great as public report has led one to suppose. It is natural that developments in those areas, being on the frontier, should have attracted greater notice among neighbouring states and made more noise in the world, since they have been all the more easily spread about by travellers' reports and missionaries' letters. For all that, these events are of no greater importance than the other disorders which have occurred in the interior of Persia.

The Georgians, the French ambassador continued, were not in league with the Russian government. In fact, Erekle entertained a natural distrust of Russia as the family of the former King Wakhtang VI was still resident there and presented a threat to the security of the new dynasty in Georgia. "It is highly possible," added the French ambassador,

that the opinion of the participation of the Russians in Georgian affairs may have been adroitly spread by them and their supporters to give color to this universal influence which they affect, notably with regard to the Greeks, who entertain gigantic notions of this new Georgian power.[15]

Far from embarking on the conquest of Persia, the Georgians were only too happy during this year, 1753, to come to an agreement with the most powerful of the pretenders to the Persian throne, the

[13] Butkov, *Materialy,* I, Appendix N.

[14] Erigler Khan, Irakli, and Heraclius are of course simply variants of the name Erekle, which is the Georgian form of the Greek Herakles (Hercules).

[15] Archives of the French Foreign Ministry, Correspondance Politique, Perse, Vol. VII, No. 81: "État présent des affaires de Perse" (1753).

Afghan military leader Azat Khan. A convention was reached, providing that the Persians and Afghans should refrain from military operations to the north of the River Araxes. King T'eimuraz of Georgia gave Azat Khan one of his nieces in marriage, and sent a contingent of the Georgian army under Prince Zaal Orbeliani to enter Azat's service. This force, some four thousand strong, played a prominent part in events in Persia during the next few years. Finally, when Azat Khan was overcome in 1756 by his rival, Mohammed Hasan Khan Qajar, Prince Zaal Orbeliani fled to Baghdad with only a dozen Georgian survivors.[16]

The rival candidates to the Persian monarchy had by now fought themselves to a state of exhaustion. In 1760, Mohammed Hasan Khan was himself defeated and killed by a new Persian leader, Kerim Khan Zend, who soon afterwards put to flight the once formidable Azat Khan. Azat hoped to find refuge in the mountain fastnesses of Daghestan, but King Erekle of Georgia intercepted him on the way. The Georgians were able to secure Kerim Khan's good will by surrendering the Afghan leader captive to him. By this adroit handling of the situation in Persia, T'eimuraz and Erekle were thus able to secure their southern frontier and to obtain the Persian regent Kerim Khan's recognition of Georgian suzerainty over the Persian khanates north of the River Araxes.[17]

In spite of Georgia's enhanced international prestige, the country was still plagued without respite by the marauding incursions of the Lezghian tribesmen of Daghestan. An Armenian who lived through these troubled times recorded that in 1755,

[16] Papuna Orbeliani, "Chronicle," in M.-F. Brosset, tr. and ed., *Histoire de la Géorgie,* II, Part 2, 177–78. A letter from the Roman Catholic bishop of Babylon, written from Baghdad to the French government, gives interesting details of the distinguished reception accorded to Prince Orbeliani by the Turkish authorities there. The local pasha clad him in a robe of ermine, sent him a valuable steed, superbly caparisoned, and a present of 3,000 piastres in cash. Prince Orbeliani had an interview with the Catholic bishop, whom he informed that the king of Georgia had supported Azat Khan solely from motives of expediency. The Georgians were in reality delighted at Azat Khan's defeat, which was accompanied by the death of ten or twelve thousand Afghans. See Archives of the French Foreign Ministry, Correspondance Politique, Perse, Vol. VII, No. 104.

[17] Butkov, *Materialy,* I, 246; Kherkheulidze, "Vie du roi Eréclé II," in M.-F. Brosset, tr. and ed., *Histoire de la Géorgie,* II, Part 2, 218.

the Lesgians made incessant incursions into Georgia, plundering and
laying waste the country, which at the same time was afflicted by so
severe a famine that the people were obliged to subsist on grass like the
cattle, or on anything else they could find; and at last the inhabitants
were reduced to such extremity, that parents, stifling the emotions of
natural affection, cast from them their own offspring.[18]

Sometimes, as in the invasion of Kakhet'i by Nursal Beg in
1754, the Lezghis would assemble in force and lay siege to some
town or village in Georgia. When the Georgian army showed itself
capable of defeating them in open warfare, the Lezghis would assemble in compact and mobile bands. Avoiding contact with Erekle's
main forces, they would steal in groups of a few dozen at a time
to unguarded hamlets, robbing the peasants and carrying them off
into slavery. Quite often, these gangs would pass right across
K'art'li into Western Georgia, and wreak havoc in Imeret'i. On
other occasions, they ventured as far as the gardens surrounding
Tiflis. In 1758, Constantine, prince of Mukhran, a nobleman of royal
blood, was murdered by one of these raiding parties. Churches had
to be fortified to serve as refuges for the villagers.

Needless to say, this state of affairs resulted in a decline in agriculture and commerce. Merchants and their caravans were prevented from passing between the trading cities with the result that
essential commodities were in short supply. The consequent rise in
the cost of living caused much distress.

In spite of suspicions that the Russian government intended to
restore the former Mukhranian dynasty to the Georgian throne,
King T'eimuraz decided to appeal once more to St. Petersburg for
help. By now, toward the year 1760, this veteran campaigner felt
that his fighting days were over. Relegated more and more to the

---

[18] *Memoirs of the Life of Artemi, of Wagarschapat, near Mount Ararat,* p. 8. While
much of this work bears the stamp of authenticity, it has been proved by later research that its author, an Armenian in Russian official service, was a highly dubious
character. In the Caucasus he bore the name of Khachikiants, at Astrakhan he took
the alias of Ivanov, and in Moscow, styled himself Artemii Bogdanov Araratskii. For
further details on this writer, see the review by Marr in *Zapiski Vostochnogo
Otdeleniia Imp. Arkheologicheskogo Obshchestva,* IX (1896), 311–13, of the Armenian pamphlet, *The Fraud of Arutiun of Ararat Unmasked* (Baku, 1894).

background by his ambitious son King Erekle II, T'eimuraz determined to render at least one more service to his country by undertaking a personal mission to the Empress Elizabeth Petrovna.

On his arrival at the Russian capital, the empress accorded T'eimuraz a most honorable reception. While he conducted negotiations with the Russian ministers during the summer of 1761, the Georgian monarch was lavishly feted at court. Unfortunately for T'eimuraz's plans, Russia was at this time fully preoccupied with the conduct of the Seven Years War. It was not long since the famous Russian occupation of Berlin; Elizabeth's army had suffered heavy casualties in the struggle against the military genius of Frederick the Great; the empress's advisers were unable to recommend any departure from that time-honored principle of Russian strategy—namely, to avoid military commitments in Asia when embroiled in war with the Western European powers.

In these circumstances, King T'eimuraz's request for military assistance against the Lezghian tribes of Daghestan, though received with sympathy, was politely shelved. His more ambitious suggestion that a Russo-Georgian army should proceed to the Persian capital of Isfahan, there to preside at the election of a shah subservient to Russian interests, was also found unacceptable. Such action would certainly have aroused hostility on the part of the Turks, whose neutrality was necessary to Russia for the time being.

The Empress Elizabeth died in December, 1761. When preparing to set out on his return journey to Georgia, King T'eimuraz felt his own strength waning, and he too died in Russia in January, 1762. His body is interred at Astrakhan, near that of his father-in-law, King Wakhtang VI of K'art'li.[19]

The struggle of Kings T'eimuraz and Erekle for the national integrity and independence of Eastern Georgia is paralleled in Western Georgia by the rise of King Solomon I, known as the Great, of Imeret'i. Solomon's worthless and incapable father, King Alexander V, had died after a reign of thirty-two years in 1752.[20]

[19] M.-F. Brosset, *Histoire de la Géorgie*, II, Part 2, 236; Berdzenishvili, Javakhishvili, and Janashia, *Istoriia Gruzii*, p. 409.

[20] His death was attributed to divine retribution for an act of sacrilege of which Alexander had been guilty. See M.-F. Brosset, *Histoire de la Géorgie*, II, Part 1, 406.

His death was followed by a widespread rebellion by prominent feudal grandees, headed by Rostom, duke of Ratcha, and his ally, Prince Levan Abashidze. Solomon soon found himself expelled from his kingdom, and took refuge with the Turkish pasha in Akhaltsikhe, but, assisted by a Turkish contingent, he just as soon regained his throne. To strengthen his position, Solomon then allied himself to the Dadian or prince-regnant of Mingrelia, his most formidable potential rival, by marrying the Dadian's sister. He also took steps to conciliate the influential Prince-Regnant Mamia of Guria.

One of Solomon's first acts was to prohibit the slave trade with Turkey. The Turkish frontier authorities were indignant at this threat to their livelihood and issued an ultimatum demanding resumption of the trade. In 1757, the Turks, with the followers of Duke Rostom and Prince Abashidze, invaded Solomon's dominions. At the battle of Khresili, not far from K'ut'ais, Solomon and the royalist party of Imeret'i were victorious. Prince Levan Abashidze was slain, and the king was able to confiscate a large part of the family's vast domains.[21]

Solomon saw clearly that Georgia's great weakness was lack of unity, not only within the Western Georgian kingdom, but also as between the two ancient thrones of Tiflis and K'ut'ais. To cement friendly relations with the royal house of K'art'li and Kakhet'i, Solomon went in 1758 to a conference with Kings T'eimuraz and Erekle at Gori. A treaty was signed among the three monarchs, providing for mutual assistance in the event of war.

In spite of continued hostilities on the part of the Turks, who instigated the khan of Avaria in Daghestan to ravage Solomon's dominions, the young ruler continued to hold his own. In 1759 a council of the leading ecclesiastical and lay dignitaries of Western Georgia assembled at K'ut'ais. They signed a convention swearing to resist Ottoman demands for resumption of the slave trade, and to uphold Solomon in his fight for national independence. Among those present were the Princes-Regnant Katsia Dadian of Mingrelia

[21] Papuna Orbeliani, "Chronicle," in M.-F. Brosset, tr. and ed., *Histoire de la Géorgie*, II, Part 2, 201; Berdzenishvili, Javakhishvili, and Janashia, *Istoriia Gruzii*, pp. 415–18, where a portrait of King Solomon is reproduced.

and Mamia Gurieli. On adhering to this convention, these semi-autonomous rulers recognized Solomon's authority as supreme lord of Western Georgia.[22]

By the year 1762, when the dauntless King T'eimuraz died in Russia, great strides had thus been made toward the reestablishment of the authority and prestige of the crown in both Eastern and Western Georgia. In the east, the two kingdoms of K'art'li and Kakhet'i, united for practical purposes under Erekle and his father T'eimuraz, had emerged triumphant but ravaged from a decade of patriotic war. Georgian arms were feared and respected throughout Persia. Several of the khanates of Armenia and Azerbaijan were paying tribute to the court of Tiflis. Only the Lezghis of Daghestan remained, by their mobility and inaccessibility, a constant source of danger. In Western Georgia, King Solomon of Imeret'i, now an ally of the Eastern Georgian monarchy, had at last achieved some measure of unity. The slave trade with Turkey was outlawed, at least in theory, and the right of the Ottoman Empire to interfere in the affairs of Imeret'i could be successfully challenged for the first time in over a century.

[22] Berzhe, and others, eds., *Akty sobrannye Kavkaz. Arkh. Kom.*, I, 56–57; Berdzenishvili, Javakhishvili, and Janashia, *Istoriia Gruzii*, p. 419.

9

Toward a Russian Orientation
1762-1783

THE accession of Erekle II to the united throne of K'art'lo-Kakhet'i in 1762 meant that Eastern Georgia, for the first time in three hundred years, was formally fused into a single political entity. This development, essential for the continued existence of an independent Georgia, was not achieved without difficulty. In spite of Erekle's popular prestige, the K'art'lian nobility still had hopes of seeing the Mukhranian dynasty restored, and the "Patara Kakhi," or "Little Kakhet'ian," as Erekle was affectionately nicknamed, could not count on the aristocracy's undivided loyalty. In 1765 a plot was devised to give the throne to Paata, an illegitimate son of Wakhtang VI and a man of learning and culture, who had been living for some time quite inoffensively at Tiflis. The conspirators were apprehended and punished by death or mutilation. Paata paid with his life for the comparatively passive part which he had played in the affair.[1] The following year, Paata's nephew Alexander, son of Prince Bak'ar and a grandson of Wakhtang VI, left the Russian army to join Kerim Khan, regent of Persia, to seek to stir up trouble for Erekle from that quarter.[2]

Erekle's monarchy was essentially a personal creation. The king was in effect his own prime minister, chief justice, and commander

[1] Berdzenishvili, Javakhishvili, and Janashia, *Istoriia Gruzii,* p. 412; David Batonishvili, "Shedegi Kakhet'is tskhovrebisa," in *K'art'lis tskhovreba,* Chubinov and Brosset, eds., II, 506.

[2] Butkov, *Materialy dlia novoi istorii Kavkaza,* III, 108.

in chief. The functionaries who held these titular, often hereditary, offices were, as was also not unusual in the enlightened despotisms of eighteenth-century Europe, little more than the executive agents of the sovereign. To facilitate the transaction of public business, departments of internal affairs, finance, and war were established in Tiflis, all under the king's personal supervision. In affairs of importance the monarch could summon an advisory council or *divan,* either in the form of the small group of officials in his personal entourage or else in that of the Great Council of State, which included the princes of the blood, the catholicos, the leaders of the royal banners (*sadrosho*), and other dignitaries.[3]

In the provinces, Erekle's policy involved the absorption of the hereditary *erist'avates* or dukedoms of the K'sani and the Aragvi, and the diminishing of the autonomy of other powerful feudal domains. The *erist'avate* of the Aragvi had been abolished in 1743, but that of the K'sani survived until 1777. The *erist'avis* were replaced by *mouravs,* or prefects, selected from among the king's family and retainers.[4]

With regard to foreign relations, it is interesting to note that the first European power to make overtures to Erekle after his succession to the reunited throne of K'art'lo-Kakhet'i was not Russia but France. The dispatches of the French representatives at St. Petersburg contain details on an abortive project to win over Erekle, erroneously believed to control most of Persia, to French interests and turn him against Russia. France thus hoped to create difficulties for Russia in the Near East and so to weaken her hand in the all-important Polish question.

The scheme was mooted in September, 1763, by the French chargé d'affaires in St. Petersburg, Bérenger, and approved by the Duc de Praslin, then at the head of the French Foreign Ministry. It was proposed that as intermediary between Bérenger and Erekle a French priest, Father Ange, who was often in Tiflis on missionary work, be

[3] Berdzenishvili, Javakhishvili, and Janashia, *Istoriia Gruzii,* pp. 428–30; T'aqaishvili, ed., *Sak'art'velos sidzveleni,* Vol. I, Charter No. 191; Report of Captain Iazykov (1770) in A. A. Tsagareli, *Gramoty,* I, 184–87.

[4] "Zapiska ob Eristovstvakh Aragvskom i Ksanskom" (Memorandum on the Duchies of the Aragvi and the K'sani), in A. A. Tsagareli, *Gramoty,* I, 37–38; *Materialy dlia istorii Gruzii i Kavkaza,* V, 416.

employed. Writing to his court in December, 1763, Bérenger outlined his scheme as follows:

I am waiting for news from Moscow to see whether Your Grace's commands arrived in time to initiate a correspondence with Prince Heraclius. The motives, My Lord, which led me to take the liberty to suggest it, arise from my conviction that more than one power must take steps to divert Russia from European affairs by creating as many difficulties as possible on her Asiatic frontiers. She holds under her suzerainty nations filled with courage who sigh for liberty, and who would certainly free themselves if the science of war were less unknown to them. I have been assured that Prince Heraclius has not forgiven Russia for the refusal which his father Theimouraz met with two years ago when he came to solicit support, and that it would be easy to embitter him by arousing suspicion about the unexpected death of that old man in this country. The Georgian princes whom I have known in Moscow are very discontented with being detained there. One of them has confided to me his grievances against this government for the wrongs it has done him, and shown me several letters written by the Popes to his ancestors who made known their desire to adopt Catholicism. It appeared to me, My Lord, that in case of need it would be possible to take advantage of these circumstances. . . . If Russia does not destroy herself by internal convulsions, I consider it essential to overlook nothing in order to prevent the abuse of the power which a more reasonable administration might easily attain for her.[5]

It does not appear that Father Ange's projected intrigue had any results; perhaps Catherine's intelligence service got wind of it. At any rate, nothing further is heard of Father Ange in the French envoys' reports. But this attempt to make Erekle into an anti-Russian catspaw of French foreign policy is not without significance, particularly as it shows the prestige enjoyed by the Georgian king in Western Europe. It is also interesting as the first attempt to establish relations between France and Georgia since Sulkhan-Saba Orbeliani's mission to Versailles in the reign of Louis XIV.

The attitude of Great Britain toward Russia's relations with Trans-

    [5] "Correspondance diplomatique des représentants de France à la Cour de l'Impératrice Catherine II," Vol. I (1762–65), in Sbornik Imp. Russkogo Istoricheskogo Obshchestva, CXL (St. Petersburg, 1912), 677. Other dispatches dealing with this subject are printed on pp. 234, 261–62, 298, 676.

caucasia was very different. The British government as yet saw no reason to check Russian expansion in the Near East, where it was France and not Russia that threatened British interests. A number of British politicians supported the plan of Joseph Emin (Emin Osipov) to liberate Armenia from the Moslem yoke with Russian and Georgian aid and to revive the Armenian monarchy. Emin was in Georgia during the 1760s, but failing to arouse Erekle's enthusiasm for his project, he eventually abandoned it, and retired to India.[6]

In Western Georgia, the position of King Solomon of Imeret'i deteriorated markedly in the course of the 1760s. Abandoned by his vassals, the erist'av of Ratcha, the Dadian of Mingrelia and the prince of Guria, Solomon was driven out of his capital by the Turks into the woods and hills, whence he waged a guerrilla war with the invaders. A cousin of Solomon, T'eimuraz, occupied the throne of K'ut'ais.[7]

Rather than agree to the Turkish conditions for his restoration, which involved payment of an annual tribute in slaves, Solomon addressed himself in 1766 to the Russian government through the commandant at Kizliar', General Potapov, asking for asylum in Russia if his position remained untenable. In addition, he sought Erekle's mediation between himself and the Ottoman government. At the same time, Obrezkov, the Russian resident at Istanbul, reported that the Turks were tired of their ineffectual efforts to subjugate Imeret'i, and would be only too glad of an excuse to come to terms.[8]

The newspapers of the time published wildly exaggerated accounts of Solomon's struggle with the Turks, in which he was commonly confused with Erekle. In June, 1766, for example, the Marquis de Bausset wrote from St. Petersburg to the Duc de Choiseul that Erekle was reported as having taken Akhaltsikhe, though Count Panin had assured the marquis that Erekle had nothing to do with the fighting in Imeret'i:

[6] Emin's *Life and Adventures*, written by himself, were published in London in 1792, and reprinted in India in 1918. His impressions of Georgia are reproduced in Allen, *History of the Georgian People*, pp. 196–206.

[7] Butkov, *Materialy*, I, 276.

[8] A. A. Tsagareli, *Gramoty*, I, 1–3.

I thought nevertheless that I perceived in Monsieur Panin's tone and in his eagerness to counter this rumor how greatly Russia is afraid of causing umbrage to the Porte and rousing it from its lethargy. . . . It is very probable that all the variations they are circulating at St. Petersburg about the story of Prince Heraclius are aimed at distracting public attention from the plausible suspicions which are entertained, namely, that the rebellion of the Georgians, subject or otherwise to that prince, is fomented by Russia.[9]

At this juncture, Bausset's suspicions were unfounded. Deeply committed in Poland, the Russian government had not the slightest desire to provoke Turkey by interference in Transcaucasia. In 1767, General Potapov was told to dissuade Solomon from coming to Russia and encourage him to make his peace with the Porte. Meanwhile, however, Solomon had sent off the Metropolitan Maxim of K'ut'ais on an embassy to St. Petersburg. In September, 1768, when Maxim was on his way over the Caucasus range, Turkey declared war on Russia. This emergency immediately altered the relationship between Russia and the Georgian states. Georgia was now drawn into the larger orbit of international hostilities in the Near East.

The Turkish declaration of war was largely the outcome of French intrigue. After the Seven Years War the European powers came to grips on the shores of the Bosphorus, as well as in Poland. To counter Catherine's designs on Poland, and restore France's waning prestige by discomfiting Russia, Choiseul had instructed the French ambassador at Istanbul, Vergennes, to do his utmost to goad the Turkish government into a declaration of war. Vergennes' task was made easier by Turkish resentment at Russia's Polish policy and her extension of influence into the Ukraine and North Caucasia, together with the construction of the fort of Mozdok and increasing Russian activity among the Circassians.[10]

The British government, it is worth noting, was perfectly willing for Russia to gratify her ambitions in this area. The attitude of George III's ministers is summed up in a dispatch of 1769 from the Earl of Rochford to Lord Cathcart at St. Petersburg:

[9] *Sbornik Imp. Russkogo Istoricheskogo Obshchestva*, CXLI, 93, 97, 111. Wild rumors were also current that Erekle had been to Germany and served with Frederick the Great.

[10] For the background to these developments, see Solov'ev, *Istoriia Rossii*, Part VI;

Great Britain, naturally connected by a commerce equally advantageous to both nations, considering Russia as the Power most able, and most willing to form a counter-balance to the formidable league of the House of Bourbon, removed by her situation from every occasion of rivalship, can never take alarm at the progress of the Empress's arms any otherwise than as it may be prejudicial to Russia herself, or to the general tranquillity of Europe by awaking the apprehensions, or giving play to the ambition and malignity of other Powers very differently disposed towards her.[11]

The rupture between Turkey and Russia in 1768 was thus a triumph for Catherine's enemies, and notably for France. But the empress, though taken by surprise, was not slow in showing that Russia was more than capable of holding her own. While her main armies prepared for operations on the Crimean and Bessarabian fronts, and her navy was fitted out for its famous voyage to the eastern Mediterranean, Catherine decided to stage a military diversion on Turkey's Caucasian frontier. The commander of the North Caucasian Line was instructed to speed the Imeret'ian envoy, Archbishop Maxim, on his way to the capital: "The arrival of this Metropolitan is exceedingly opportune and timely, and it only remains to make use of the dispositions of his sovereign toward the Turks, which dispositions are so much in accordance with the aims of this Court." Efforts were to be made to persuade Erekle to join forces with Solomon in an offensive against the Turks.[12]

The Transcaucasian project was sound enough in itself, but its execution was vitiated from the start by Catherine's choice of commanding general. It so happened that in 1769 Count Gottlieb Heinrich von Todtleben, a German adventurer who had fought in the Russian army during the Seven Years War, and had been sentenced to death for treasonable communications with Prussia but reprieved, now applied to the empress for asylum in Russia. His debts and general notoriety prevented him from staying in Germany. Frederick the Great warned Catherine not to trust Todtleben, terming him

Sorel, *La question d'Orient au XVIIIme siècle;* Driault, *La question d'Orient;* Butkov, *Materialy,* I, 273-74.

[11] *Sbornik Imp. Russkogo Istoricheskogo Obshchestva,* XII, 482. The assistance given by England to the Russian navy in its Aegean expedition is well known.

[12] A. A. Tsagareli, *Gramoty,* I, 19-22.

"a wretch capable of every infamy, who could ruin the conduct of a campaign unless treated with the most vigilant precaution." [13] The empress, however, mindful of her own German origins, was disposed to be indulgent toward her repentant compatriot. Despite the opposition of Count Zakhar Chernyshev, vice president of the College of War, Todtleben was taken back into the Russian army and assigned to the Caucasian front, where it was thought that he could do the least damage.[14]

An officer, Prince Gregory Khvabulov, had meanwhile been sent to reconnoiter the Transcaucasian military situation. Khvabulov, who was of Georgian descent, was enthusiastically received by Solomon, who was now in a stronger position, having defeated and captured Duke Rostom by a ruse.[15] Erekle also promised cooperation, and the two kings held a conference at Tiflis in May, 1769, at which joint action against Turkey was decided upon, with the proviso that five Russian regiments be sent and Georgia's interests safeguarded in the ultimate Russo-Turkish peace settlement. Erekle wrote to the Russian foreign minister, Count Panin, confirming his readiness to declare war on the Porte, provided that K'art'lo-Kakhet'i be protected against subsequent reprisals on the part of the Ottoman Empire.[16] So eager were the Georgians to commence operations, indeed, that a raiding party attacked some villages in Javakhet'i, on the Turkish border, and carried off quantities of booty.[17]

Count Todtleben showed himself no less impetuous. In August, 1769, he set off from Mozdok with a company of Hussars, a detachment of Cossacks, and a couple of small cannon. He passed through

[13] Frederick the Great to the Comte de Solms, April 19, 1769, in *Sbornik Imp. Russkogo Istoricheskogo Obshchestva*, XXXVII, 224–25.

[14] A. A. Tsagareli, *Gramoty*, I, vi–viii; Lang, "Count Todtleben's Expedition," in *Bulletin of the School of Oriental and African Studies*, XIII, 883, 901. The French Chargé d'Affaires, Sabatier de Cabres, reported: "Monsieur de Todtleben . . . is regarded here as a restless and dangerous spirit, and they have been very glad to get rid of him." (*Sbornik Imp. Russkogo Istoricheskogo Obshchestva*, CXLIII, 20.)

[15] Rostom and his sons were blinded. It is related that Solomon desired to spare the youngest, a child of three, but his henchman Papuna Tseret'eli burnt the boy's eyes out over a furnace. These details were related to me orally from the local tradition of the province by Dr. Givi Kobakhidze, himself a native of Ratcha.

[16] A. A. Tsagareli, *Gramoty*, I, 59.

[17] See Khvabulov's report and letters from Solomon and Erekle to General Potapov in A. A. Tsagareli, *Gramoty*, I, 420–39; also Butkov, *Materialy*, I, 277–79, 455–58.

Kabarda and Ossetia, reaching the Dariel Pass without incident, and arrived at the frontier village of Step'an-dsminda early in September. The force was joined en route by Archbishop Maxim and Prince Mouravov, a liaison officer of Georgian descent. Shortly afterwards Todtleben was reinforced by three hundred infantry and dragoons under Major Remennikov, bringing his total strength up to about five hundred men.[18]

Erekle and his suite came from Tiflis to greet the Russian commander at the village of Khoda. The king advised Todtleben to let his troops winter in K'art'li until the time was ripe for the spring campaign, but the general replied that his instructions obliged him to head for Imeret'i without delay and to try to capture some of the Turks' fortified points before the end of the season.[19] Erekle was disappointed at the small size of the Russian force and wrote to St. Petersburg asking that at least fifteen regiments be dispatched. Only thus could any decisive victory be won over the Ottoman forces in eastern Anatolia at the same time that Georgia's eastern frontier was safeguarded against the Lezghis.[20] This request did not coincide with the views of the Russian government, which needed every available soldier for the European front. Count Panin told Todtleben and Mouravov to do their best to unite Solomon and Erekle and to make the greatest possible use of Georgia's own military resources, using the Russian detachment as an auxiliary reserve.[21]

Todtleben had by now arrived in Imeret'i. His meeting with King Solomon has been described by Captain de Grailly de Foix, Todtleben's French aide-de-camp:

[18] Lang, "Count Todtleben's Expedition," in *Bulletin of the School of Oriental and African Studies*, XIII, 884–85.

[19] The interview is described by a French officer with Todtleben, Captain Charles de Grailly de Foix, in *ibid.*, pp. 885–87, and by Prince Mouravov in A. A. Tsagareli, *Gramoty*, I, 61–63.

[20] The reception of Erekle's envoys at the Russian court is amusingly described by the French chargé d'affaires, Sabatier de Cabres, who was scandalized at their being treated on the same footing as the ambassadors of the European powers. "L'Ambassadeur d'Angleterre," he reported, "se confond en courbettes avec ces Géorgiens. . . ." (Dispatch of December 8, 1769 in *Sbornik Imp. Russkogo Istoricheskogo Obshchestva*, CXLIII, 69).

[21] A. A. Tsagareli, *Gramoty*, I, 82–89, 444–47.

The poor appearance of this prince, his dress, his suite gave us an impression of him that agreed with that which Erekle had already given us. Solomon did not possess any town. Wandering in the woods with about fifteen hundred men, he established his headquarters in one place for only a fortnight at a time for fear of being surprized by the Turks. Mistrusting even his own subjects, he was more like a brigand chief than a sovereign prince. He was about forty years old, and his character was fairly similar to that of Count Todtleben. They made all kinds of protestations of friendship to one another at first, but did not trust each other. The Count was saying, I can see that there is nothing to be done in this country, as Solomon is incapable of backing me up. Solomon was saying the same thing, This man is coming to assist me: What can he do with his little cannons and five hundred men? [22]

Solomon would have liked to recapture his own capital, K'ut'ais, but Todtleben learned that there was a Turkish garrison in the near-by fort of Shorapani, which he resolved to assault. The garrison consisted of only twenty-three janissaries, but the natural strength of the fortress, lack of victuals, and the news of a skirmishing attack by the Dadian of Mingrelia on the western borders of Imeret'i seriously hampered operations. Solomon left to repel the Dadian and collect provisions. Todtleben abruptly retired into K'art'li, without waiting to notify the Imeret'ians, and took up winter quarters at Tskhinvali.[23]

Having abandoned Solomon, Todtleben now proceeded to quarrel with Erekle. He tried to kidnap envoys sent by the pasha of Akhaltsikhe to induce Erekle to betray the Russians. Erekle had already rejected their proposals, and was naturally indignant at Todtleben's violation of the immunity of diplomatic envoys. Furthermore, the Russian troops were ravaging the property of Georgian villagers. "Our Cossacks," relates Captain de Grailly,

according to their wont, were pillaging everywhere they could, especially oxen and horses. Complaints were made to the Count, who failed to carry out justice. Our Cossacks became all the bolder, and the other soldiers more or less imitated their example. We were living in Georgia as in a conquered land.

[22] Lang, "Count Todtleben's Expedition," in *Bulletin of the School of Oriental and African Studies,* XIII, 888.
[23] *Ibid.,* p. 889.

Nor could Erekle have been agreeably impressed by the rude and peremptory tone adopted by Todtleben in his dealings with the Georgian court. On one occasion, the general invited David Erist'avi, one of the principal nobles, to join him in a surprise attack on Akhaltsikhe. The king knew nothing of this until informed by David, all of which provoked an angry scene between Erekle and Todtleben's aide-de-camp.[24] Within the Russian camp, disputes occurred between Todtleben and his officers of Georgian origin, whom the general accused of siding with Erekle against Russian interests. Matters were made worse by the general's ignorance of both Russian and Georgian, leading to frequent misunderstandings.

The arrival of Russian reinforcements, consisting of four pieces of artillery and four hundred men, improved the situation somewhat. Erekle's pride was mollified by the receipt of a personal rescript from the empress, with the insignia of the order of St. Andrew.[25]

Early in the spring of 1770, the Russian troops left their winter quarters at Tskhinvali and advanced to Suram. Erekle for his part decreed a levy of the royal army under its banners, which were to assemble near Suram in the middle of March. The Georgian army, a contemporary relates, was organized as follows:

K'art'li and Kakhet'i are divided into seven banners. The first is that of Erekle, which is the most considerable. He assembles beneath it all the men fit for service from the domains in his personal possession. The second is that of the Patriarch: he collects all the peasants belonging to the churches and monasteries. Erekle appoints a chief for them. The third is that of the Prince Erist'avi who assembles the peasants from his lands, including those from the town of Akhalgori which belongs to him. The fourth is that of Prince Amilakhori, who owns the town of Gori. The fifth is that of Prince Tsitsianov [Tsitsishvili], son-in-law of Prince Erekle. The estates of the latter are in Kakhet'i. The sixth is that of Prince Orbeliani, also in Kakhet'i, while the seventh is under Prince Machabeli. The lands of this prince used once to appertain to Imeret'i, but he has removed himself from this jurisdiction and placed himself under Erekle's protection. He has furthermore gained some victories over the Kubanians and won the right to have a banner. These banners are made in the form of small standards; those who are entitled

[24] Ibid., pp. 892–93.
[25] A. A. Tsagareli, Gramoty, I, 444.

to possess one are petty sovereigns. They have the right of life and death in their estates, although they are entirely dependent on Erekle. They cannot declare war and assemble troops without his permission, and as soon as he orders them to muster, they are compelled to obey. Erekle decides any disputes that arise between them. When the head of one of these families happens to die, the succession is divided in equal portions between all the heirs, but they recognize a head to whom the banner belongs. The family of Prince Amilakhori has multiplied greatly, and the present holder of the banner is no richer than the others.

Erekle orders these lords to collect a certain number of troops, which he fixes according to the need of the moment and the number of vassals they possess. He directs them to proceed on such and such a day to a given place, with victuals and forage for a month. After this time has elapsed, Erekle has to provide them with subsistence in order to continue the projected campaign, otherwise they are free to retire, unless the promise of booty, which always belongs to them, induces them to continue. Those who possess horses form the cavalry. They obey their lord when marching under his banner, and the lord obeys Erekle, who disposes the troops at will. So if the head of a banner is unable to command his men, which rarely occurs, they substitute a commander nominated by Erekle.[26]

Another report of the period says of Erekle's military resources:

The Georgian army is renowned in this area for its courage, and the king even more for his qualities as a cavalier and commander. He can put into the field fifteen thousand infantry and cavalry (leaving part of them to protect his country from the Lezghis), and in case of need, even more; he carries four cannon with the army. Everyone here can shoot and possesses a gun, and is always ready for combat. . . . Fine infantry and light cavalry could be formed from the Georgians, for they are excellent shots, can move lightly equipped, and require no food besides bread.[27]

The Georgian and Russian troops had not long been encamped at Suram before fresh trouble broke out. The plan of campaign was to march on Akhaltsikhe, taking the fort of Adsquri on the way, but Todtleben made exorbitant demands on Erekle's commissariat and declined to move before large quantities of food and forage were made available. In vain Erekle represented that it would be

[26] Narrative of Captain de Grailly, in Lang, "Count Todtleben's Expedition," in *Bulletin of the School of Oriental and African Studies,* XIII, 894–95.

[27] Report of Captain Iazykov (1770) in A. A. Tsagareli, *Gramoty,* I, 184–86.

better to attack the Turks forthwith and live off their country. Such methods went against the general's German parade-ground training. Matters were made worse by an abortive mutiny, organized by Colonel N. N. Choglokov, an irresponsible hothead who attempted to make capital out of the fact that he was related to the late Empress Elizabeth Petrovna. The plot was discovered in time, but Todtleben suspected Erekle and the liaison officer Mouravov of playing a part in it.

Erekle grew tired of waiting for Todtleben to move, and set out for Adsquri with his own forces. The Russian commander reluctantly marched out in his wake, and proceeded on April 17, 1770, to bombard Adsquri, a fortress of great strength on the right bank of the River Kura. His four small cannon had no effect. Hearing that seven thousand Turks and Lezghis were advancing from Akhaltsikhe, Todtleben suddenly raised the siege and hastened back in full retreat to K'art'li. Erekle was left to face the enemy alone. "I can clearly perceive," the king bitterly remarked, "why the Count is betraying me. He hopes that I shall succumb in this engagement, and when I am no more, he will be the master in Georgia." [28]

A pitched battle between the Turkish and Georgian armies took place on April 20 at Aspindza, a village on the east bank of the Kura, some two hours' ride from Akhaltsikhe and twenty versts from Adsquri. Dividing his army, now reduced to about three thousand men, into three parts, Erekle confided the first to his son-in-law Prince Tsitsishvili, whom he stationed on the left flank in a wood close to the bridge over the Kura. The second corps under Giorgi Batonishvili was stationed three versts to the right of the bridge, while the king's own troops occupied the center, some four versts back from the river. The Turks advancing from Akhaltsikhe failed to see Tsitsishvili's detachment lying in ambush, and passed over the bridge to attack Erekle. When they had come to grips with the king's force, the Georgian right wing came up in support, while Tsitsishvili fell on the Turks guarding the bridge and destroyed it. As a result of these skillful tactics, the Ottoman army found itself

[28] A. A. Tsagareli, *Gramoty*, I, 452–58; Lang, "Count Todtleben's Expedition," in *Bulletin of the School of Oriental and African Studies*, XIII, 895–96.

caught between Erekle's now triumphant soldiers and the fast
flowing river, into which many hundreds flung themselves and were
drowned. The Georgian losses amounted to only twenty-five killed
while the Turks were almost annihilated, leaving a number of high-
ranking officers on the field of battle.[29]

Indignant at Todtleben's desertion, Erekle now seriously considered siding with the malcontents in the Russian corps to remove
him forcibly from his command.[30] Todtleben for his part made no
secret of his intention to depose Erekle and send him into exile in
Russia, together with any of the Georgian nobility who opposed
his plans, and then to annex Georgia to the Russian crown. A stream
of recrimination from both sides flowed into St. Petersburg.[31]

Catherine was deeply concerned at this unfortunate turn in a
project by which she set great store. In January, 1770, she had
written to Voltaire in sanguine tones:

The Georgians have indeed taken up arms against the Turks. . . .
Heraclius, the most powerful of their princes, is a man of intelligence and
courage. He previously helped the famous Nadir Shah to conquer India.
My troops have crossed the Caucasus this autumn and joined forces
with the Georgians.[32]

The empress was rather piqued than otherwise at the news that
Erekle had won a battle without Russian participation. She and
Count Panin in their letters to Erekle sought to justify Todtleben's
conduct of affairs. The king alone was blamed for the deterioration
in Russo-Georgian relations, and there was no word of appreciation
for Erekle's notable success in the joint cause. A Guards officer,

[29] Report of Prince Mouravov, in A. A. Tsagareli, *Gramoty,* I, 106–8; narrative
of Captain de Grailly, in Lang, "Count Todtleben's Expedition," in *Bulletin of the
School of Oriental and African Studies,* XIII, 896–97; Gogebashvili, "Battle of
Aspindza," in *Georgica,* I, Nos. 4–5, 297–302; Kherkheulidze, "Tskhovreba mep'is
Irakli meorisa," in Chubinov and Brosset, eds., *K'art'lis tskhovreba,* II, 491–92.

[30] Lang, "Count Todtleben's Expedition," in *Bulletin of the School of Oriental
and African Studies,* XIII, 897.

[31] A. A. Tsagareli, *Gramoty,* I, xv, 225–26. The Austrian envoy at St. Petersburg,
Seddeler, reported to Prince Kaunitz that Todtleben had cast the gravest aspersions
on Erekle: "I have had occasion to see a report from this General in which he
portrays that Prince in the most loathsome colours" (Dispatch of September 21,
1770, in *Sbornik Imp. Russkogo Istoricheskogo Obshchestva,* CIX, 468).

[32] *Sbornik Imp. Russkogo Istoricheskogo Obshchestva,* X, 402.

Captain Nikolai Iazykov, was sent to report on the state of affairs in Georgia and to attempt to effect a reconciliation.[33]

Todtleben sought to make up for his previous fiascos by another sally into Imeret'i. Solomon had already managed to take Shorapani, where the garrison had been panic-stricken by Erekle's victory at Aspindza. Todtleben arrived in time to take the citadel of Baghdadi on July 2, whence he advanced with Solomon to K'ut'ais, which the Imeret'ians were already blockading. Without telling Todtleben, the king agreed to let the Turks evacuate the town on the night of August 5; as a result the place was taken without opposition the following day. Todtleben had looked forward to a more resounding success and accused Solomon of treachery. Relations between them became exacerbated.[34]

Erekle for his part continued to harry the borderlands of Samtskhe, with such effectiveness that the inhabitants abandoned their villages and blockaded themselves in the castles of Akhalk'alak'i, Khert'visi, and Adsquri. The mountaineers of T'ushet'i valiantly routed four thousand Lezghis from Daghestan who invaded their domains at the instigation of the Turks. In accordance with their custom, they sent several hundred of the noses of the slain, neatly threaded on string, as a trophy to Erekle.[35]

The regent of Persia, Kerim Khan, wrote to Erekle at this point, urging him to cease cooperating with the Russians. Captain Iazykov, the Russian emissary, persuaded the king to reply to Kerim Khan stressing the opportunity presented by the present Russo-Turkish war for Persia to win back the provinces lost to Turkey since the time of Nadir Shah.[36] For the time being, however, the cautious regent maintained his neutrality.

[33] A. A. Tsagareli, *Gramoty*, I, 132–41. Iazykov's instructions contained provisions for cowing what the Russian Foreign Ministry delicately termed, "the Georgians' barbarous minds."

[34] Butkov, *Materialy*, I, 282–84; Lang, "Count Todtleben's Expedition," in *Bulletin of the School of Oriental and African Studies*, XIII, 898.

[35] Report of Prince Mouravov, August 28, 1770, in A. A. Tsagareli, *Gramoty*, I, 158–59.

[36] *Ibid.*, pp. 174–75; Russian translations of the letters between Erekle and Kerim Khan are published by Tsintsadze in *Materialy po Istorii Gruzii i Kavkaza*, XXXII (Tiflis, 1955), 140–46.

Iazykov's attempts to reconcile Todtleben with Erekle and Solomon remained fruitless. The general joined forces with the Dadian of Mingrelia, nominal vassal but inveterate enemy of the king of Imeret'i, and went off to the Black Sea coast in an attempt to capture P'ot'i from the Turks.

Wrote Captain Iazykov to Count Panin,

I will relate to Your Excellency, sincerely and without prejudice, as a true son of the Fatherland, in what mood I found Count Todtleben, all factors considered. His idea is to operate alone against the enemy, thinking thereby to win vain glory for himself. Many of his men have perished before K'ut'ais and now before P'ot'i, and all in vain. . . . From the enclosed letters addressed by him to me, Your Excellency will see that he neither wishes to be reconciled with King Erekle and Solomon, nor have anything to do with them. . . . By civility you can do anything you will with the people of this country, but rudeness and harsh treatment repel them. I expected in the circumstances that I should have trouble in winning over King Erekle; instead of this the king is in all things obliging and completely devoted to our Empress.[37]

In another dispatch Iazykov reported:

Count Todtleben publicly insults both kings and refers to them like common soldiers, all of which reaches them through spies. Although they are not men of enlightenment, nevertheless they are set on maintaining the dignity of their royal title. The Count is universally detested by the people here, and it seems to me that nothing but harm can result if the Count remains here for the next campaign.[38]

Even before these reports reached the empress, she had decided on Todtleben's recall. "I think," she wrote to Panin on December 19, 1770, "that he is more capable of ruining our plans in Georgia than bringing them to fruition. I feel we had better nominate somebody else."[39]

The new choice was Major General A. N. Sukhotin, an officer with more experience in naval than land operations. He arrived in Georgia in April, 1771, to find the Russian corps in the most wretched state, "naked, without horses, and almost without arms." In defiance of Erekle's advice, Sukhotin marched to resume the

---

[37] Report of December, 1770, in A. A. Tsagareli, *Gramoty*, I, 175–76.
[38] *Ibid.*, pp. 181–82.
[39] *Sbornik Imp. Russkogo Istoricheskogo Obshchestva*, X, 441.

siege of P'ot'i, where he and a thousand of his men promptly fell ill of marsh fever in the summer heat of that pestilential region. By October, the general was petitioning the empress for his recall.[40]

As in the previous year, it was Erekle who bore the brunt of the active fighting in 1771. In October he seized and razed to the ground the fortress of Khert'visi in T'rialet'i. His operations were a source of acute embarrassment to the Ottoman high command, for their efforts to recruit soldiers from eastern Anatolia for the Balkan front were thwarted by the need for maintaining adequate forces to restrain the Georgians. The local Turkish commanders, alarmed by Erekle's energy and exaggerated reports of Russian strength, sent urgent appeals to Constantinople, which met with no response. The *seraskier* of Kars had no more than six hundred men at his disposal. From this it can be deduced that Erekle had done more than his share of campaigning, and that it was only Russian incompetence which prevented the allies from achieving some more decisive advantage.[41]

To justify his conduct in the eyes of the Russian court, as well as to petition that K'art'lo-Kakhet'i be taken under permanent Russian suzerainty, Erekle dispatched in December, 1771, a personal embassy comprised of his son, Prince Levan and the Catholicos of Georgia, Antoni. Among the conditions proposed by Erekle were the permanent stationing of four thousand Russian troops in Georgia, the confirmation of Erekle and his heirs upon the throne of K'art'lo-Kakhet'i, the maintenance of the autocephalous Patriarchal See of Mtskhet'a, the granting of a concession to Russia to exploit Georgia's mineral resources, and the launching of an immediate offensive to win back the pashalik of Akhaltsikhe for the Georgian crown.[42]

The embassy reached Astrakhan early in 1772, but was detained there for several months pending instructions from St. Petersburg. Reaching the capital in 1773, the envoys found the Russian government too much preoccupied with terminating the war against Turkey and quelling the revolt of Pugachev to pay attention to

---

[40] A. A. Tsagareli, *Gramoty,* I, 484–85.

[41] Kherkheulidze, "Tskhovreba mep'is Irakli meorisa," Chubinov and Brosset, eds., *K'art'lis Tskhovreba,* II, 492–93; A. A. Tsagareli, *Gramoty,* I, 302, 319–25, 407, 487.

[42] A. A. Tsagareli, *Gramoty,* I, 329–32.

Erekle's project. Though received with high favor, Levan and the catholicos were sent home in 1774 bearing a polite but firm refusal. The government promised, however, that Georgia would be protected by the forthcoming treaty with the Porte.[43]

Long before the embassy reached Tiflis on its return journey, Russian commitments in Transcaucasia had been drastically curtailed. Sukhotin had achieved nothing. Prospects of uniting Erekle, Solomon, and the Dadian for a joint offensive seemed faint. Transport and supplies continued to present acute difficulties. It was decided to recall the Russian auxiliary corps altogether and leave the Georgians to their own devices. Captain L'vov was left as chargé d'affaires to try to stir them to further efforts.[44]

The recall of the Russian force naturally caused consternation among the Georgians, who feared the vengeance of the Turks and Lezghis. Erekle wrote in vain to the empress, imploring her to alter her decision: "The retreat of Your Majesty's troops from here has plunged us into the deepest sorrow, and we have thereby fallen into the same grievous and intolerable situation as when the soul is parted from the body." [45] The king did not remain inactive. Despite the Russian military failure, he had seen the superiority of regular armies on the European model and was convinced of the need for reorganization of the Georgian feudal levies. In 1774 a system of compulsory part-time service known as *morige* was introduced; the king set an example by serving for one month every year. The king's principal assistant in this scheme was Prince Levan, whose enthusiasm and courage were proverbial.[46]

Abandoned by Russia, Erekle and Solomon reached a formal agreement in 1773, providing for a defensive and offensive alliance against the Turks and Lezghis.[47] On the strength of this, the forces

---

[43] *Ibid.*, pp. 394–97, 400–401.

[44] Lang, "Count Todtleben's Expedition," in *Bulletin of the School of Oriental and African Studies*, XIII, 899.

[45] A. A. Tsagareli, *Gramoty*, I, 328, 356.

[46] Butkov, *Materialy*, I, 287–88. Erekle's ordinance establishing the *morige* is published by E. T'aqaishvili, in *Sak'art'velos sidzveleni*, I, Part 1 (1920), 177–89.

[47] Text in A. A. Tsagareli, *Gramoty*, I, 378–80. This entente had long been hampered by the intrigues of Erekle's consort, Darejan, cousin of Solomon's unruly vassal, the Mingrelian Dadian.

of Imeret'i and K'art'lo-Kakhet'i united in the autumn of that year to the total of some ten thousand, together with a thousand Ossete and Ingush auxiliaries and six small cannon. This army invaded Javakhet'i in mid-October and besieged Akhalk'alak'i. Little Turkish opposition was encountered. The larger part of the army was sent to roam through the province and ravage the land at will while the two kings blockaded the town. The country was laid waste as far as Kars and Ardahan. Solomon falling ill and the army sated with booty, the siege of Akhalk'alak'i was raised at the end of the month, and the Georgians returned home triumphant.[48]

In the meantime the khan of Avaria, Nursal Beg, had taken advantage of Erekle's absence to make a surprise attack on the Kakhet'ian province of K'isiq. He was decisively repulsed by the local forces under their courageous *mourav*, Prince Revaz Andronika-shvili.[49] Nursal was killed shortly afterwards while attacking Shamakhi. His son Omar, also a determined foe of Georgia, succeeded him.[50]

An attempt by the pasha of Akhaltsikhe to avenge himself on Solomon for his part in the raid on Javakhet'i was thwarted in 1774, with the Turkish invaders cut off and almost exterminated.[51]

In view of the impending peace settlement, it was decided at St. Petersburg to adopt a policy of appeasement toward Turkey. The Russian chargé d'affaires, Captain I. L. L'vov, was recalled later in 1774, much to Erekle's disgust. The king expressed his disappointment in a letter to Count Panin, in which he described the dangers to which the country had been exposed by acceding to the empress's wishes and breaking with the Porte. "And therefore the Turks, opening wide their jaws, like snakes, surround us, the Persians like savage lions are observing us, and the Lezghis are sharpening their teeth against us like hungry wolves." [52]

The Treaty of Küchük-Kainarji, signed on July 10, 1774, brought to an end Catherine the Great's first Russo-Turkish War. This

[48] Kherkheulidze, "Tskhovreba mep'is Irakli meorisa," in Chubinov and Brosset, eds., *K'art'lis Tskhovreba*, p. 493.

[49] Butkov, *Materialy*, I, 289.

[50] *Ibid.*, II, 17.

[51] Report of Captain L'vov, February 28, 1774, in A. A. Tsagareli, *Gramoty*, I, 401–3.

[52] *Ibid.*, p. 408.

treaty marks a new stage in Russian penetration of the Near East. The adroitness of the Russian negotiators resulted in the virtual recognition of Russia's right to intervene at any time in defense of the Christian minorities in the Ottoman Empire.[53] The interests of Georgia are dealt with in Article XXIII as follows:

The fortresses situated in a part of Georgia and Mingrelia, such as Bogdadgick, Kutatis and Scheherban, which were conquered by Russian arms, shall be regarded by Russia as belonging to those in whose possession they were in former times, so that if formerly or since a long time ago these towns have been under the effective dominion of the Sublime Porte, they shall be recognized as belonging to it; and after copies of the present Treaty have been exchanged, the Russian troops shall evacuate the above-mentioned provinces of Georgia and Mingrelia within the agreed time limit; the Sublime Porte for its part undertakes in accordance with the provisions of Article I to grant a general amnesty to all persons in these countries who may have caused it offense in any manner whatsoever in the course of the present war. It renounces solemnly and for all time any claim to tributes of boys and girls and every other species of imposition. It undertakes to recognize as its subjects only those members of these nations who have belonged to it from ancient times; to quit and give back all the castles and fortified places which have been under the domination of the Georgians and Mingrelians to their own control and administration, as well as not to oppress in any way the exercise of religion, or the monasteries and churches, and not to prevent the reconstruction of those which are ruined or the building of new ones; and these peoples shall not be oppressed by the governor of Tschildir [i.e., the pasha of Akhaltsikhe] and other chiefs and officers by exactions stripping them of their possessions. But since the above-mentioned peoples are subject to the Sublime Porte, Russia shall not in future intervene in any way in their affairs, nor molest them.

Article XXV includes the provision that all Georgians, as well as other Christians taken prisoner by the Turks during the war, should immediately be set at liberty without ransom or restriction.[54]

In spite of the ambiguity of Article XXIII, due no doubt to the negotiators' ignorance of the details of the Georgian situation, these stipulations were not unfavorable to Georgia. The main mistake was

[53] Sorel, *La question d'Orient au XVIIIme siècle*, pp. 288–89.

[54] Martens, *Recueil de Traités . . . des Puissances et États de l'Europe*, II, 311–17. Russian text in A. A. Tsagareli, *Gramoty*, I, 413.

to concede that Georgia in general ("Gruziia") was subject to Turkey when only Imeret'i (Western Georgia) was meant. If Erekle owed allegiance to anyone (which was more than doubtful), it was to Persia rather than to Turkey. Russia's undertaking to withdraw her troops from Georgia was meaningless, since they had left two years previously. At the beginning of Article XXIII, Baghdadi, K'ut'ais, and Shorapani are apparently ceded to Turkey, whereas later in the paragraph, the Turks undertake to return all the Georgians' and Mingrelians' fortified places to them. The vagueness of these provisions naturally led to trouble on the spot, Solomon repelling Turkish attempts to reoccupy K'ut'ais by force of arms.[55] With regard to the provisions on the Porte's renunciation of the tribute of slaves, and its undertaking to refrain from persecuting Christians, these could not be enforced effectually, since there were no Russian consuls in the area. Nevertheless, it was something for two of the main objects of Solomon's struggle to receive this official recognition.

Erekle, who had contributed most to the campaign, received least reward. Subjected to heavy expense in supplying transport and provisions to the Russian corps, he was thwarted of his hoped-for territorial gains in Samtskhe. Furthermore, his delicately balanced alliances and cordial relations with the Mohammedan khans of Azerbaijan were fatally compromised.

From the Russian standpoint, the campaign was not an unqualified failure. The Turks had been effectively harassed, in spite of the Russian commanders' incompetence; and much-needed Turkish reinforcements had been diverted from the European front; but Russian losses had also been heavy, amounting to three thousand men and half a million rubles.[56]

Erekle continued to show a touching faith in the might and good will of Russia. When General de Medem occupied Derbent in 1775 to avenge the murder of Professor Gmelin by the chief of the Qaraqaitaq tribe, Erekle urged him to advance along the Kura valley into K'art'li. On De Medem's request for guidance, the empress

---

[55] Butkov, *Materialy*, I, 336.

[56] Lang, "Count Todtleben's Expedition," in *Bulletin of the School of Oriental and African Studies*, XIII, 899.

commented that Erekle was still trying to further his private ambitions with Russian resources, as had become clear to her during the occupation of Georgia, and did not merit any consideration. If Erekle persisted, De Medem was to tell him that his project was quite impossible, and that he should use his own troops to make any conquests after which he might hanker.[57]

As has been noted, K'art'lo-Kakhet'i was not specifically named in the Küchük-Kainarji peace settlement. The sultan deemed it expedient to make a separate peace with Erekle, and addressed a letter to the Persian regent Kerim Khan to complain that Persia had let loose a Georgian lion against the Ottoman Empire. He asked the regent to use his good offices to pacify Erekle. Kerim Khan had himself been meditating on an invasion of Georgia, but was highly gratified by this message, which appealed to his vanity. While letting it be known privately that he was far from displeased at the damage Erekle had done to Ottoman interests, Kerim consented to mediate. The sultan sent an envoy to Tiflis bearing rich presents, and a peace settlement was easily agreed upon.[58]

It now remained for Erekle to restore his authority over the Mohammedan khans of Azerbaijan and Shirvan and to put a stop to the Lezghi raids. His second son, Levan, was a pillar of strength in these enterprises, until he was assassinated in 1781. Expeditions were undertaken in 1779 and 1780 to bring Erivan and Ganja more fully under Georgian control, and the districts were thoroughly pillaged.[59] So considerable was Erekle's renown at this period that even the khans of Khoi and Nakhchevan, of Tabriz and Urmia used to send him presents from time to time in order to secure his good will.[60]

Persia's traditional ambition to subjugate Georgia was now once more reviving at the court of Kerim at Shiraz. In spite of the outwardly friendly relations between Erekle and the regent, concern could not fail to be felt in Persia over Erekle's pro-Russian orienta-

[57] A. A. Tsagareli, *Gramoty*, II, Part 2, 266–67; Butkov, *Materialy*, II, 26.

[58] Butkov, *Materialy*, I, 289; Kherkheulidze, "Tskhovreba mep'is Irakli meorisa," in Chubinov and Brosset, eds., *K'art'lis tskhovreba*, II, 494–96.

[59] Butkov, *Materialy*, II, 73–75. An account of Georgian excesses in the raid on Erivan is given in the *Memoirs of the Life of Artemi*, pp. 36–40.

[60] Butkov, *Materialy*, I, 337.

tion and his grip on the northwestern khanates. The presence at Shiraz of the Mukhranian pretender to the K'art'lian throne, Prince Alexander, grandson of Wakhtang VI, gave the Persians the excuse they needed. It could if necessary be represented, in fact, that they were bound to help restore him to the throne of his fathers by the provisions of the Russo-Persian Treaties of Resht (1732) and Ganja (1735), in which Wakhtang's rights had been guaranteed by Nadir Shah. Alexander, for his part, assured Kerim Khan that he would gladly place Georgia under Persian suzerainty once he was established there. Counting on the affection of many of the K'art'lian nobility for the Mukhranian line, the Persians urged the chief of the Qaraqaitaq to assemble the tribesmen of Daghestan for an invasion of Georgia. These negotiations were for the time being cut short by the death of Kerim in 1779.[61]

The death of the sage regent plunged Persia once more into anarchy. Rival military and tribal magnates carried on civil war, which resulted in a temporary effacement of Persia in the arena of international affairs. As usual, various pretenders to the throne came forward and found support among rival khans. At Tiflis, a young man claiming to be descended from Nadir Shah found refuge in 1780 with Erekle, who seems for a time to have believed his story and to have planned to intervene in Persia in his support. It transpired that he was an impostor, and he died soon afterwards in mysterious circumstances.[62]

By this time Catherine the Great had consolidated her gains from the first Russo-Turkish War, and was meditating about fresh enterprises in the Near East. In 1780 occurred the celebrated interview between her and the Austrian Emperor Joseph II at Moghilev, followed by discussions at St. Petersburg, resulting in a project for partitioning the Ottoman Empire. Vergennes, formerly French ambassador at Istanbul and now in charge of the French Foreign Ministry, intervened in opposition to these plans, which would have destroyed France's privileged status in the Levant and turned the balance of power in Europe against her. Although Joseph offered

---

[61] Butkov, *Materialy*, II, 114–15; Berzhe and others, eds., *Akty sobrannye Kavkaz.*, I, 91.

[62] Butkov, *Materialy*, II, 75–77.

Egypt as an inducement for French consent, Vergennes remained adamant, and his stand, combined with the opposition of Frederick the Great, deterred Joseph from his part in the scheme.[63]

Nothing daunted by Austria's defection, Catherine and Potemkin continued their policy of infiltration in the Kuban and Crimean areas, so effectively that in 1783 these regions were annexed to the Russian crown.[64] This action was naturally resented by France, whose policy, as summed up by Vergennes, was directed toward "preventing the alarming revolution menacing the Ottoman Empire." The Turks for their part would have declared war on Russia at this juncture but for French mediation designed to save them from probable military disaster.[65]

In Persia also Russia pursued a bolder policy after the death of Kerim Khan. In 1780, Count Voinovich appeared off Astarabad, on the southeastern shore of the Caspian, with a Russian flotilla. He sought to induce the local ruler, Agha Mohammed Khan Qajar, to cede to him the town of Ashraf for a Russian trading colony. Agha Mohammed granted him another site on which to settle, but in the following year he conceived suspicions of Russian military preparations in the area and imprisoned Voinovich and his staff. Agha Mohammed soon thought better of his action and released the Russians, but this incident marked the beginning of the enmity between Russia and the founder of the Qajar dynasty in Persia, an enmity which was to have important repercussions for Georgia.[66]

Erekle was aware of increasing European interest in the affairs of the Levant and Transcaucasia, and now sought to renew Georgia's former relations with Western Europe. His principal agents and advisers were the Roman Catholic missionaries at Tiflis and Dr. J. Reineggs, a German adventurer who enjoyed confidence in Georgia because of his medical skill and political acumen. Father Dominic of

---

[63] See Salomon, *Politique orientale de Vergennes;* Driault, *La question d'Orient,* p. 56; T. G. Djuvara, *Cent projets de partage de la Turquie (1281–1913),* (Paris, 1914), pp. 278–305.

[64] See Dubrovin, *Prisoedinenie Kryma k Rossii.*

[65] Salomon, *Politique orientale de Vergennes,* pp. 233, 266.

[66] Butkov, *Materialy,* II, 84–99. Unpublished documents of interest relating to Voinovich's expedition are preserved in the archives of the French Foreign Ministry, Mémoires et Documents, Russie, X, 139–92.

Trieste was sent on a mission to Rome and Vienna in 1781, but died on the way. The following year, Erekle sent Father Mavros (Mauro) of Verona on a similar errand, with letters to the Austrian emperor, the king of France and several of the Italian states. The more important of his two letters to Louis XVI was couched in the following terms:

> To the most magnificent, great, and clement Emperor of France:
> Although we are overcome by confusion in addressing this request to you, yet, as we have communicated to you our country's needs and misfortunes in another dispatch, we now make bold to state that our request consists in imploring means to maintain two regiments, to enable us to recruit soldiers and organize them on the European model, so that our foes, hearing of the formation of such a corps, may not dare to undertake any further hostilities against us.
> The king of K'art'li, Kakhet'i, etc. etc.,
>
> EREKLE

To the Austrian emperor, Erekle wrote that in the event of war between him and the Porte, the Georgians would, in return for a subsidy, undertake to create a diversion in Turkey in Asia.[67] The Russian empress and Prince Potemkin, to whom Erekle solicitously reported these *démarches,* were not a little piqued at the idea, however remote, of other European powers intervening in Caucasian affairs.[68]

Among Erekle's many problems at this time was the reappearance of the Mukhranian pretender Alexander. This time the prince was with King Solomon in Imeret'i. The intrigues of Erekle's consort, Darejan, on behalf of her relative the Dadian of Mingrelia, as well as protection granted to dissident members of the royal house of Imeret'i, had led to a worsening of relations between the courts of Tiflis and K'ut'ais. From Imeret'i, Alexander passed into North Caucasia to stir up the Ossetes and Kabardans. In 1782 he was in Daghestan, where he was joined by Prince Alexander Amilakhori,

[67] The letters to Louis XVI are published by Brosset, "Explication de quelques inscriptions géorgiennes," in *Mémoires de l'Académie des Sciences,* IV, 423–28. The appeal to the Austrian Emperor, with a circular to other European sovereigns, is printed in A. A. Tsagareli, *Gramoty,* II, Part 2, 13–16. See also Tamarati, *L'Église géorgienne,* pp. 639–41. Overtures to the British in India were unsuccessful.

[68] A. A. Tsagareli, *Gramoty,* II, Part 2, 31.

an inveterate enemy of Erekle, who had paid with his nose for his part in the abortive conspiracy of 1765. The two princes were promised support by the khan of Derbent and some of the chieftains of Daghestan.[69] This threat prompted Erekle to renew his requests to be taken under Russian protection, especially as his appeals to the courts of Western Europe had not met with any response.

The Russian government was now much more firmly established in the Black Sea and North Caucasian areas than it had been a decade earlier when Erekle had vainly asked for a Russian protectorate. Since then, Potemkin had come to power, a man whose conception of Russia's potential power in the Near East far outstripped the vision of the cautious Panin. To round off Russia's gains in the Crimea and the Kuban, and further her aims in Persia and Armenia, an extension of Russian influence in K'art'lo-Kakhet'i was clearly called for. Potemkin nominated Dr. Reineggs as Russian commissioner in Tiflis and instructed him to make overtures to Erekle, who welcomed Potemkin's proposals with alacrity.[70]

Erekle was encouraged in his plan by Queen Darejan. She had no affection for the legitimate heir to the throne, her stepson Giorgi, but it was important for her to exclude the Mukhranian pretender and insure the succession for the Kakhet'ian line for the sake of her own sons.[71] A solemn treaty with the Russian government seemed to be the best security for the reigning dynasty. Many of the principal nobles were won over to the plan through hopes of Russian subsidies and the guarantee that the Georgian aristocracy would be granted every prerogative of the Russian nobility.

It is interesting to follow the course of the preliminary negotiations, as reflected in the petition sent by Erekle to the Russian court

[69] Butkov, *Materialy,* II, 116–17.

[70] A. A. Tsagareli, *Gramoty,* II, Part 2, 26–28.

[71] Burnashev, *Kartina Gruzii,* pp. 18–19. Compare the impressions of General Paul Potemkin, who visited Georgia in 1784: "Queen Darejan (Daria) Giorgievna did not exert any influence on affairs of state during the first years of her marriage. But when the princes, her sons, began to grow up, and her daughters were married to prominent grandees, she began three or four years ago to take part in all affairs and participate in councils of state. She has now become so powerful that everything is done by her authority, and Erekle himself places unbounded confidence in her. She has a severe countenance. She was then about forty-five years old" (Butkov, *Materialy,* II, 156). She was born in 1738.

and in the memorandum drafted by the empress and Count Bezborodko in consultation with Potemkin.[72] Erekle's principal demands were that four thousand Russian troops be dispatched for the
reconquest of Samtskhe; that he himself and his line be confirmed
in the possession of K'art'lo-Kakhet'i; that the autocephalous patriarchate of Mtskhet'a be maintained; and that a subsidy for his army
be granted. In return, the king promised to make good the expenses
incurred by Russian troops employed in winning back Samtskhe
from the Turks, to send hostages from the royal family to St. Petersburg, to pay Russia half the profits from mines opened up with
Russian help, to collect and send to Russia an annual levy of seventy
copecks on each family, as well as tribute in kind, and to furnish
conscripts to the Russian army.

The empress for her part authorized Potemkin to negotiate with
Erekle, and also if possible with Solomon of Imeret'i, on the following basis: The Georgian kings were to be deemed allies enjoying
imperial protection and not subjects of the empire; no levies were to
be made on them for cash; only the proffered tribute in kind was to
be accepted; a subsidy would be granted to the Georgians in time of
war; they were to renounce all diplomatic relations with Austria
and other Christian powers; a permanent understanding was to be
brought about between Erekle and Solomon, the Russian authorities
to be arbiters in case of dispute. Some additional points were suggested by Count Bezborodko, namely, that the Georgian kings
should receive their insignia of investiture from the Russian court;
that the catholicos-patriarch should be given a high rank in the
Russian ecclesiastical hierarchy; that the nobility should be accorded
the rights and privileges of the Russian aristocracy; and that two
battalions of infantry and four cannon should be permanently stationed in Georgia, subject to review in time of war.

Erekle received the draft agreement in April, 1783, and had no
difficulty in acceding to its provisions. A meeting of the Russian and
Georgian plenipotentiaries took place at Georgievsk in July. Russia
was represented by Potemkin's cousin General Paul Potemkin,
Georgia by Ioane Bagration, prince of Mukhran, and Prince Garsevan Tchavtchavadze.

[72] A. A. Tsagareli, *Gramoty*, II, Part 2, 30–31; Butkov, *Materialy*, II, 119–20.

By the Treaty of Georgievsk, signed on July 24, 1783, and ratified in November of the same year, the kingdom of K'art'lo-Kakhet'i was placed under the protection of Russia. Erekle undertook to renounce all dependence upon Persia or any other power; he and his line were solemnly confirmed for the present and the future in possession of all territories under their sway; the kings of Georgia, on succeeding to the throne, would request and receive from St. Petersburg their insignia of investiture; Erekle was to desist from conducting his own diplomatic relations with foreign powers, except with the consent of the Russian authorities; a Georgian minister would be accredited to St. Petersburg, and a Russian resident to Tiflis; the empress and her heirs would undertake to treat Georgia's enemies as those of Russia; there was to be no interference in the internal affairs of Georgia; the catholicos was given the eighth place among the Russian prelates and made a member of the Holy Synod; the Georgian nobility were to have the same prerogatives as the Russian aristocracy; special facilities were to be afforded to Russian traders in Georgia and Georgian merchants in Russia; the treaty was to have permanent validity, any modification was to be made only by mutual consent.

Four separate articles were appended: in the first Erekle undertook to refer any dispute between himself and King Solomon of Imeret'i to imperial arbitration; the second committed the Russian government to maintaining two battalions of infantry and four cannon in Georgia for security purposes; the third provided for concerting measures between the Russian and Georgian military commands in the event of war on the Caucasian front; while the fourth stated that Russia would seek by every available means of arms and diplomacy to restore to Georgia her ancient territories (i.e., the province of Samtskhe, since the sixteenth century in Ottoman hands).[73]

Such, in short, were the main provisions of the treaty of 1783, through which Erekle hoped to lay the foundations for a revival of

[73] The text of the treaty may be referred to in Martens's *Recueil de Traités*, III; *Polnoe Sobranie Zakonov*, Vol. XXI, No. 15835; Avalov, *Prisoedinenie Gruzii k Rossii*, Appendix A. It is also reprinted separately, but with some abridgments, in a brochure entitled: *Traité conclu en 1783 entre Catherine II, impératrice de Russie, et Irakly II, roi de Géorgie, avec une préface de M. Paul Moriaud* (Geneva, 1919).

the national life of K'art'lo-Kakhet'i. Its clauses, as has been noted, contained explicit provisions for maintaining the reigning dynasty on the throne and for safeguarding external security. The only way in which Erekle's authority was restricted was by his renunciation of the right to carry on his own foreign relations, but this should have been more than made up for by the Russian guarantee of protection in the event of war. Subsequent chapters will show how Erekle's just expectations were disappointed.

Western Georgia's political problems also claimed the Russian government's attention. King Solomon of Imeret'i had been complaining that "the Turks are making powerful attacks on us from the shores of the Black Sea; they are seizing our people and turning them to Islam, and subjecting the Christians to great enslavement." The king begged Catherine to take Imeret'i under her suzerainty.[74] The difficulty was, however, that Turkish overlordship in that area had received the sanction of the Küchük-Kainarji treaty, and Russia was not ready to risk an open break with the Porte.[75] However, that same treaty forbade Turkish molestation of Christian peoples in Western Georgia, and it was decided to take up Solomon's case energetically with the Ottoman government, making it clear that the Georgian kings were "rulers in the maintenance of whose persons and domains, and their defense from all injury, Her Imperial Majesty, through identity of faith and constant good will toward those peoples, cannot but be interested." [76] In December, 1782, while the treaty with Erekle was being drafted, instructions were sent to Bulgakov, the Russian ambassador at Istanbul, to invoke Article XXIII of the Küchük-Kainarji treaty and protest against Turkish troop concentrations on the Imeret'ian frontier, lending full support to Solomon as well as to Erekle in any protests they might have occasion to make against Turkish provocations.

The Georgians must now have thought they had found a protector on whom they might rely. Russian power in the Black Sea and Caucasus areas was greater than ever before. Events would show, however, that Potemkin and Catherine had advanced beyond

[74] A. A. Tsagareli, *Gramoty,* II, Part 2, 11–12.
[75] Grigorovich, *Kantsler Kniaz'* . . . *Bezborodko,* I, 469.
[76] A. A. Tsagareli, *Gramoty,* II, Part 2, 24.

the limits which they had the resources to maintain. Russia was connected with Georgia only by the tenuous line of the Dariel Pass. Neither the Black Sea nor the Caspian littoral of Transcaucasia was under her control. It might have been foreseen that when the time came for Russia's advance to be challenged, her position in Georgia would prove highly vulnerable, if not impossible, to maintain. But in 1783, such an event seemed remote both in Tiflis and in St. Petersburg.

10

Social and Economic Problems of Erekle's Reign

IN recounting the events that led up to the signing of the Treaty of Georgievsk, the main emphasis has been laid so far on political and military considerations. But these alone do not account for Erekle's decision to abandon, at least in part, Georgia's hard-won independence in exchange for a Russian protectorate. The fact is that the national revival of Georgia was handicapped as much by long-standing social evils and economic retardedness as by military threats from the outside. But so long as these threats persisted, it was impossible to proceed with the work of reorganization that Erekle knew to be overdue.

A clear, over-all impression of the state of Georgia at this time is given in the report submitted to Count Panin by Captain Iazykov, the officer sent by Catherine in 1770 to settle the disputes between Count Todtleben and the Georgian princes. Iazykov, by no means an unsympathetic observer, was assisted in his inquiry by the Catholicos Antoni, one of the best-informed and most learned Georgians of his time.

The royal government, reported Iazykov, was autocratic, though the people were not altogether amenable to discipline, and did not carry out orders very punctiliously. The princes had members of the gentry (*aznaurni*) under their suzerainty, and had the right to punish them. Although the code of Wakhtang VI was theoretically in force, the magistrates judged according to their whim. The high court was composed of four *mdivanbegis,* or senators, who delivered their verdicts orally. If a litigant was dissatisfied, he appealed to the king. All decrees were personally signed and sealed by the king. But even when they saw his seal, people sometimes avoided carrying out his orders in the hope of evading compliance. Punishments in criminal cases consisted of chopping off the head, stoning alive, slitting the tongue, nose, and ears, or in milder cases beating with sticks on the soles of the feet. The king also imposed in most instances the penalty of confiscation of property, which brought him in no small revenue.

The people of K'art'li and Kakhet'i gave the impression of being poverty-stricken, though the latter were better off than the former. In Kakhet'i each peasant owned a vineyard and made splendid wine. Before the Russian corps entered K'art'li hardly any peasant possessed so much as a hundred copecks in cash. If a villager was seen to have any ready money, the king would take it away, unless the villager's lord managed to seize it first! The peasants and their wives wore their clothes until they were in tatters. The women of the nobility and the Armenian merchant class however dressed neatly and cleanly, and many wore robes of brocade.

The diet of the common people was very sparse. Meat was eaten not more than once a month. Their usual food was boiled beans and bread dipped into soup. Many of the princes too were so poor that they sometimes passed a whole day without eating.

By the great number of ruined buildings it was evident that Georgia had once been a rich and powerful state. The land was everywhere good for cereal crops. Wheat and barley were widely cultivated, but not rye or rice. The peasants could not work far from their dwellings or villages for fear of attack by the Lezghis, who took them prisoner in raids on their fields and pastures and even dragged them from their huts to sell to the Turks. The situation was made worse by intestine feuds and rivalries. Sometimes a village would refuse help to another, or a man to his neighbor, in such emergencies. Cases were known of people calling in the Lezghis to wreak vengeance on personal enemies. As a result, the population of Georgia had been reduced by Lezghian raids by over 50 percent. The raiders tried particularly to capture handsome women, for whom the Turks and Persians were prepared to pay up to 5,000 rubles. They entered the country mainly at harvest time, parties of them remaining through the winter. Iazykov had himself witnessed tragic scenes, fathers and mothers weeping for their children, and children for their parents. The Lezghis had even kidnaped villagers before his very eyes. This had been going on for over a century, and the remains of abandoned towns and villages were visible everywhere.

This state of affairs had a paralyzing effect on the development of industry. Erekle tried to start an iron foundry in Borchalo, but was compelled to close it because of Lezghian raids. There were no factories or industries of any size in Georgia, only a few small mills for the manufacture of fancy linen goods and an arsenal at Tiflis where cannons, mortars and cannon balls were cast, but these were of even worse quality than those manufactured in Turkey. Gunpowder of poor quality was also produced. Lead was imported from Persia and iron from Persia and Turkey, but it could be assumed with confidence that rich mineral deposits existed in the hill districts of K'art'li.

No census of the population was kept. According to Iazykov's estimate, the inhabitants of K'art'li numbered less than 100,000, though Kakhet'i was rather more populous. People had a tendency to emigrate from K'art'li to Kakhet'i.

King Erekle was at this time fifty-two years old, of medium height, with a longish, yellowish face, large eyes, and a small beard. He was nimble both in wit and in horsemanship. Having lived at Nadir Shah's court and accompanied him on his campaigns, Erekle had introduced many Persian manners and customs: he wore rich attire, and wound a sash round his cap in the Persian style; he loved pomp and had his court filled with officials (many of them hereditary and irremovable), whose upkeep imposed a heavy drain on the treasury and a burden on the common people.

On the arrival of the Russian corps in Georgia, the king had tables and chairs made, and ordered sets of tableware and porcelain dishes from Russia. The royal banquets were reorganized after the European style, although the cuisine remained much as before. Iazykov noted that many of the princes had taken to eating with knives, forks, and spoons instead of using their fingers in the Persian fashion, and to sitting at table instead of on carpets.

Erekle was reputed to have an income of 150,000 rubles, although no regular accounts were kept of the royal budget. Quit-rent was collected from the peasants in the form of wheat, cattle, and wine according to the condition of the household, amounting on an average to some 8 bushels of wheat and 10 vedros of wine annually. Officials called *esauls* were sent around to collect these dues, and incidentally to help themselves liberally in the collection. The amount of cash received from the peasantry was negligible in view of the scarcity of ready money throughout the country.

There was a mint at Tiflis, farmed out to an Armenian contractor for 30,000 rubles a year. The municipal customs-house was farmed out for 10,000. The khan of Ganja paid a tribute of 10,000 rubles a year, and the khan of Erivan 30,000, as well as gifts.

In Tiflis, there were said to be 5,000 households. Armenians made up a large proportion of the townsfolk. The city gave the impression of being a populous, bustling place, although 6,000 people had recently died in a plague epidemic.

In the bazaar such oriental wares as brocades, taffeta, printed linens, and so forth were sold, as well as commodities imported from Russia. Each handicraft had its own row in the bazaar. There were many orchards on the outskirts of the city, with grapes, almonds, figs, pomegranates, peaches, plums, apples, and pears growing abundantly. The same fruits grew in Kakhet'i, where silkworms also flourished.

While the Tiflis churches were in a fair state of upkeep, those of the villages and townships were quite decrepit. Although the monasteries owned villages and lands, the revenue from them was collected and eaten up by the abbots and the churches allowed to decay.

The second town in K'art'li, Gori, was situated about eighty versts up the Kura from Tiflis and surrounded by a low and dilapidated stone wall. On the hill was an ancient castle, empty except for a watchman. The town's population had declined markedly in recent years, as was attested by a number of ruined houses. There were a few fine houses but mostly plain huts. The other provincial centers of K'art'li, Dushet'i, Mukhran, Tskhinvali, Suram, and Ananuri, had little forts surrounded by stone walls with embrasures. In every village there were towers in which the country folk locked themselves nightly for fear of the Lezghis.[1]

Iazykov's impressions are supplemented by the observations of the Russian liaison officer Prince Mouravov, himself of Georgian origin, and the French officer Charles de Grailly, who were also in Georgia with Todtleben. Mouravov wrote at the time:

The domains of Erekle, the king of K'art'lo-Kakhet'i, are poor by European standards, and the cost of living is everywhere high. He has many towns and villages ravaged and ruined by the Lezghis, who now make frequent raids on the hamlets and on travelers passing through wooded country, where they kill and kidnap people. Many of the Georgian proprietors are robbed of their estates and peasants, and are still being robbed of them, through the incessant and unprecedented depredations of these Lezghis. Nevertheless, the surviving population of both K'art'li and Kakhet'i is obedient to Erekle, and governors have been set up in the villages and townships. In the little centers of Ananuri and Tskhinvali, through which the force marched, there are Armenians and Jews who carry on trade and sell such wares as are in local use.[2]

Captain de Grailly also was struck by the ravages resulting from the Lezghian raids. Ananuri and Dushet'i, he noted, were very small places. Their surrounding area presented nothing but ruins. The Lezghis frequently came down from their mountain fastnesses, seized anyone who wandered far from the town and sold him to the Turks. Of Mukhran the same officer remarked: "Although the Lezghian Tatars make frequent incursions around this town, its environs are better cultivated because there are more inhabitants, who jump on to their horses at the first alarm given by the Tatars

---

[1] Only the salient points have been extracted from Captain Iazykov's report. The full text is found in A. A. Tsagareli, *Gramoty*, I, 183–96. Some material from this report was communicated by Professor P. S. Pallas to the English writer G. Ellis and incorporated in his *Memoir of a Map of the Countries Comprehended between the Black Sea and the Caspian*. The sources of Erekle's income are here reckoned slightly differently: the total of 150,000 rubles is taken as worth £26,250 sterling, made up of £1,750 from the Tiflis customs, £1,750 from the mint, £7,000 from the khans of Erivan and Ganja, and £15,750 from the hearth-money levied on the peasants. (Ellis, *Memoir*, pp. 49–50.)

[2] A. A. Tsagareli, *Gramoty*, I, 75.

and give chase to them." Captain de Grailly also comments on the limited scope of the business carried on in the Tiflis bazaar: "Caravans often arrive from Persia, and that is about all the commerce that is carried on there."[3] It would seem from this that the trade relations with Russia of which Iazykov speaks had not in 1770 reached substantial dimensions.

The decline in population stressed in these reports is confirmed by statistical data from other sources. These show that the process continued steadily up to the end of the century. In 1770 the population of Tiflis numbered between four and five thousand families, or twenty to twenty-five thousand persons; in 1781–82, 3,498 families; at the beginning of the nineteenth century, following the sack of the city by Agha Mohammed Khan, 2,648 families or 12,658 persons. The chief city of Kakhet'i, T'elavi, had 740 hearths in 1770, but only 388 (comprising 1,258 inhabitants) in 1811. The other main town of Kakhet'i, Sighnaghi, which was strongly fortified, tended to grow in this period, from 100 families in 1770 to 268 in 1811. Among the secondary towns of K'art'li, Gori had 500 families in 1770, only 227 in 1794, but 376 (comprising 1,144 inhabitants) in 1811. Akhalgori had 140 families in 1770 but only 88 in 1781–82. Ananuri numbered 100 hearths in 1770 and 95 (with 308 inhabitants) in 1811.

The total population of K'art'lo-Kakhet'i combined has been estimated for 1770 at 55,290 hearths, or approximately a quarter of a million persons. The urban population was 6,480 families, some 12 percent of the total. At the turn of the century, the total for K'art'lo-Kakhet'i was reckoned at little over 160,000 persons. The urban population had sunk to little over 4,000 hearths.[4]

A modern Georgian writer has drawn up the following tentative estimate of the population of the various Georgian principalities around the year 1800:[5]

[3] Lang, "Count Todtleben's Expedition," in *Bulletin of the School of Oriental and African Studies,* XIII, 887–90.

[4] These figures have been compiled from the article by Uchaneishvili, "K voprosu ob ekonomicheskom," in *Materialy po Istorii Gruzii i Kavkaza,* Part V, p. 378; also from a report entitled "Quelques notions sur la Géorgie," submitted to the Emperor Alexander I in 1811 by an unnamed governor of the Caucasus. A copy of this report is in the archives of the French Foreign Ministry, Mémoires et Documents, Russie, X, 297–310. In 1788, however, Ellis calculated the subjects of Erekle II as numbering over 60,000 families, or 350,000 souls. (Ellis, *Memoir,* pp. 49–50.)

[5] F. Makharadze, *Gruziia v XIX stoletii* (Tiflis, 1933), p. 66.

Eastern Georgia (K'art'lo-Kakhet'i)	168,929
Imeret'i	120,000
Guria	25,000
Mingrelia	100,000
TOTAL	413,929

When one considers that the population of Georgia at the time of the Mongol invasions of the thirteenth century was estimated at around 5,000,000, these figures are eloquent of the decline into which the country had fallen.[6]

Not even in the towns was the population safe from Lezghian attacks. At Gori, for example, church bells or gunshot signals would announce an impending raid. The citadel, one of the strongest fortresses of K'art'li, would be filled at sunset with townsfolk and peasants. The commander of the castle, known as the *tsikhist'avi*, was personally responsible for locking the doors and guarding the keys. The garrison would be posted between the inner and outer fortifications. Fourteen sentries, twelve supplied by the townsfolk and two by the *tsikhist'avi*, stood guard all night. Strict rules and precautions were observed. On one occasion, the king himself was refused admittance when he arrived after sunset.[7]

It is not surprising that commerce in Georgia was stagnant during Erekle's reign. In addition to the raids of Lezghis and other brigands, the exactions of local chieftains, and the poor state of communications, trade was hampered by vexatious internal customs barriers. The prevailing insecurity was such that the eighteenth-century Armenian writer Artemii of Mount Ararat relates how merchants passing from Tabriz to Tiflis went in convoy formation, armed from head to foot. To cite another example, when Erekle sent wagons to fetch salt from Kars, he took care to order the convoy leader to see that the carts went in close formation. The route to Russia through the Dariel Pass was fraught with danger and difficulty. The Ossetes had to be bribed every time to let goods through and the state of the track over the mountains was frequently

---

[6] Allen, *History of the Georgian People*, pp. 284–85. It is not certain whether this figure of 5,000,000 refers to all Georgia, or to K'art'lo-Kakhet'i alone. The decline would be striking enough in either case, even allowing for some exaggeration in the total for the earlier period.

[7] Sumbadze, *Gori*, pp. 15–16.

execrable. This made European goods very expensive (e.g., imported Russian iron cost five times the normal price).[8]

It is hardly surprising that many local merchants sought to liquidate their business concerns and transfer their capital to more secure and profitable trading centers. The wealthier Armenian traders made their headquarters in Moscow or Astrakhan. As a result, many of the Tiflis shopkeepers who remained were stall-holders whose stock on hand did not exceed the value of five rubles. In 1794, Erekle issued an edict, clearly directed against the export of capital, ordering the property of citizens of Tiflis and Gori emigrating to other countries to be confiscated and sold for the benefit of the crown.[9] It could be said with truth that "before the sack of Tiflis by Agha Mohammed Khan [1795], trade there was in the most lamentable condition."[10]

This state of affairs had the important effect of alienating the sympathies of the influential Armenian trading class from the Georgian crown. This was particularly unfortunate at a time when the support of a strong middle class would have provided the only means of building up a centralized state machine on the ruins of Georgian feudalism. Socially underprivileged compared with the landed gentry, and unable to make their business enterprises pay, the Armenians eventually became prepared to reconcile themselves with occupation by any foreign power able to provide law and order. In the 1790s many of the Tiflis Armenians even favored an accommodation with Agha Mohammed Khan of Persia. "All the Armenians except two of us support that reprobate," Joseph Bebutov wrote at the time to Yulon Batonishvili.[11] After the Persian menace had receded the

---

[8] Uchaneishvili, "K voprosu ob ekonomicheskom," in *Materialy po Istorii Gruzii i Kavkaza,* Part V, pp. 384–85.

[9] P'urtseladze, *Gruzinskie krest'ianskie gramoty,* p. 42.

[10] Uchaneishvili, "K voprosu ob ekonomicheskom," in *Materialy po Istorii Gruzii i Kavkaza,* Part V, p. 381.

[11] T'aqaishvili, ed., *Sak'art'velos sidzveleni,* III, Nos. 138–39. The merchants alleged that Erekle was indifferent to their well-being, and intent only on squeezing the last penny out of them in taxes. When the heir-apparent, Giorgi, tried to put a stop to their discontented murmuring, one merchant commented: "He will be no good to us either, he is just interested in eating and drinking. We will go our own way, as we find best." (*Materialy po Istorii Gruzii i Kavkaza,* V, 364.) An interesting petition from the burghers of Gori, complaining against the extortions of the city governor set over them by Erekle, has been published by Meskhia in *Materialy po Istorii Gruzii i Kavkaza,* XXXII (Tiflis, 1955).

Armenians looked to Russia for relief. The favors bestowed on leading Tiflis merchants by the Emperor Paul were a significant factor in smoothing the way to Georgia's final annexation.

Another symptom of Georgia's economic weakness was the reluctance of the rich to lend their money at any but the most prohibitive rates of interest. There being little security for loans made to the king or to feudal potentates, people who had money tended to hide it away. The minimum rate of interest charged in Georgia during the eighteenth century, as shown in contemporary deeds, was 12 percent. In most cases it amounted to 18 or 24 percent, and frequently more.[12] It is hardly necessary to lay stress on the inhibiting result of this on government and private enterprise.

Erekle's attempts to exploit Georgia's resources in precious metals were largely thwarted by political and military insecurity. In 1771–72, Dr. J. A. Güldenstädt, a German scientist in the service of the Russian Academy of Sciences, visited K'art'lo-Kakhet'i and Imeret'i, and discovered rich deposits in the Borchalo district.[13] The Russian chargé d'affaires, Captain L'vov, reported in 1774 that Greek artisans had arrived from Anatolia to open up mines at Akhtala. Lead and silver had already been found there.[14] For a few years, quite substantial operations were carried on. Besides copper and iron, the mines brought in annually silver worth 60,000 rubles and gold worth 3,200.[15] Another source states the annual quantity of silver extracted as 90 poods at first, but says that the mine was soon exhausted.[16]

Much of the revenue from the royal mines had to be spent on buying off the Lezghian chieftains. Erekle took a number of them nominally into his service, paying out over 60,000 rubles a year in wages and presents. This expedient was of doubtful benefit, as bands of them used to come into Tiflis for their pay and commit all kinds of outrages with impunity.[17]

[12] Uchaneishvili, "K voprosu ob ekonomicheskom," in *Materialy po Istorii Gruzii i Kavkaza*, V, 397.

[13] See Güldenstädt, *Reisen durch Russland und im Caucasischen Gebürge*, Vol. I.

[14] A. A. Tsagareli, *Gramoty*, I, 406–7.

[15] Butkov, *Materialy*, I, 337.

[16] Archives of the French Foreign Ministry, Mémoires et Documents, Russie, X, 304.

[17] Butkov, *Materialy*, I, 337.

In 1785, Erekle was deprived of this resource. Omar Khan of Avaria invaded K'art'li with a large Daghestanian army and marched on Akhtala, destroying the mining equipment and murdering or kidnaping the Greek artisans and their families.[18] Although attempts were made to revive the workings, they did not attain their former magnitude. In 1795, Agha Mohammed Khan razed what was left, and little more could be done there until after the Russian occupation.[19]

The effect of the Lezghian raids on the basic industry of Georgia, agriculture, has already been described. Some of the blame for its declining condition must also be laid on the persistence of a mediae-val feudal system, based on serfdom, which inhibited the incentive to work. Some of the criticisms leveled by Radishchev in his *Journey from St. Petersburg to Moscow* (1790) against the system of serfdom in Russia could have been applied equally well to Georgia. Indeed, the episodes from Georgian peasant life in the didactic treatise *Kalmasoba* by Ioane Batonishvili (1768–1830) often recall Radishchev's strictures. Although Erekle strove to humble the great landed proprietors, it was not in order to institute basic reforms; rather, it was to bring their domains into the immediate possession of his family and supporters. In such cases, serfs would pass from dependence on their lord to the status of crown (*sakhaso*) peasantry. It has been said, with some justice, that Erekle only tried to increase his power over the feudal nobility in order himself to be the first among his peers.[20]

On several occasions during Erekle's reign, the peasants rose in revolt against their masters. In 1773, the hill-dwellers of P'shavet'i rebelled against Prince Choloqashvili and took him prisoner. The peasants of Prince T'umanishvili also broke into insurrection. The serfs belonging to Justin, Bishop of Urbnisi, and to the landowner

[18] Butkov, *Materialy,* II, 182.

[19] Berdzenishvili, Javakhishvili, and Janashia, *Istoriia Gruzii,* p. 444. A good historical survey of the mining operations in Borchalo is given by Eichwald, *Reise in den Kaukasus,* II, 449–70. See also "Notice sur la mine d'Allahverdi en Géorgie," in *Nouveau Journal Asiatique,* VI (1830), 75–77.

[20] Natadze, "Krest'iane 'Sakhaso' v vostochnoi," in *Materialy po Istorii Gruzii i Kavkaza,* V, 338. There are also interesting reflections on the Georgian peasant question in the report of 1811 already quoted, "Quelques notions sur la Géorgie," in Archives of the French Foreign Ministry, Mémoires et Documents, Russie, X, 304.

Zumbulidze tried in 1776 to throw off their allegiance. In the following decade there were widespread disturbances throughout Kakhet'i.[21]

In the face of all these difficulties, Erekle's achievements become all the more remarkable. For almost half a century, the driving power and personal prestige of the king overcame or obscured the underlying weaknesses of the social organization of K'art'lo-Kakhet'i. In the face of the depletion of the population, the persistence of a feudal way of life, and the impossibility of attracting or creating sufficient mercantile interests to finance a centralized state machine one can only admire the skill with which Erekle so long maintained his country's independence. "Nervous, brittle and intelligent in his small tumbling world," to use W. E. D. Allen's graphic expression, the king "felt out this way and that for the bricks of some stability." [22] He neglected no chance of enlisting the support of European powers. He ardently desired to attract scientists and technicians from Europe to give his country the benefit of the latest military and industrial techniques. His vigilance in the care of his people knew no bounds. On campaigns, he would sit up most of the night watching for the enemy. In time of peace, his contemporaries record, "he spent most of his time, either in transacting the business of the state, or in religious exercises, and devoted but a few hours to sleep." [23] Another account depicts him as

a man of outstanding intelligence, uncommonly patient, and exceptionally pious. . . . Amazingly active, he watches the whole night through until morning, dispatching himself the affairs of state. He sleeps little; in the afternoon he gives audience to envoys arriving from the Persian ruling Khans and the mountains tribes. He dispenses justice to his subjects, even in trifling contentions. He is expert by experience in the political ways of Asiatic nations, having been for a long time in the close confidence of Nadir Shah during his expedition to India. There is nothing toward which he strives more than the reform of his nation on European lines.[24]

[21] Khachapuridze, *K istorii Gruzii pervoi poloviny*, p. 67.

[22] Allen, *History of the Georgian People*, p. 201.

[23] Report of two German missionaries, G. Grabsch and G. Gruhl, relating to the year 1782, extracted from the "Periodical Accounts relating to the Missions of the Church of the United Brethren," and reprinted in Klaproth, *Travels in the Caucasus and Georgia*, p. 420.

[24] Burnashev, *Kartina Gruzii*, pp. 9–10.

From the 1780s, however, Erekle's control of the situation was progressively weakened by discord within the royal family. The heir to the throne, Giorgi, never a strong character, labored under the hostility of his stepmother, Erekle's third wife, Darejan of Mingrelia. By this marriage Erekle had a numerous and self-assertive progeny, who were by now approaching the full flush of manhood. They found in their mother a more than ready supporter for their demands on their father and their country. Between 1791 and 1794 a series of measures were decreed by Erekle parceling out the land into hereditary domains assigned to members of the royal family, in many cases to the detriment of the old nobility. The heir apparent was given 4,000 hearths, his half-brothers 1,000 each. In addition, Erekle was induced to change the order of succession to the throne, making it from brother to brother in order of seniority. The effect of this would have been to exclude Giorgi's sons David and Ioane in favor of Darejan's eldest son Yulon.[25]

Everything indicates that these measures were thrust on the aged king by his wife and entourage. He realized at the time that an injustice was being done, and intended to remedy it. In a letter to his heir, Giorgi, written in May, 1794, Erekle wrote:

The decree establishing the immovable domains which We granted to your brothers, I was forced to seal; but it was drafted without my consent, and written by a person who had no authority to do it, so that the decree is void and unworthy of credence. Believe, I swear by my father T'eimuraz, believe me and God, that I do not consent to that decree. . . . For no cause or inducement will I destroy your birthright, and I annul that former letter given to your brothers.[26]

But Erekle did not live to repeal these decrees publicly, and they continued in force.

These concessions had a lamentable effect on the internal situation.

The royal princes, placed in possession of a most substantial section of the kingdom . . . at the aristocracy's expense, did not think of subordination to the general good. Each was engaged in strengthening his own

[25] Berdzenishvili, Javakhishvili, and Janashia, *Istoriia Gruzii,* p. 441.
[26] Berzhe and others, eds., *Akty sobrannye Kavkaz.,* I, 297.

party and became virtually autonomous, or else spread pernicious disorder in the kingdom. Authority thus dissipated in so small a realm presented the appearance of anarchy.[27]

Even the Russian government remonstrated with the king on the harmful effects of his compliance. Platon Zubov wrote him a rather pompous homily on the subject, taking as his text the Gospel of Mark, 3. 24: [28]

The division of authority is the weakness of states. The discord and disagreement which always arise from so disastrous a situation are capable of destroying and rendering insignificant the most powerful empires. In such a distracted condition, what can authority achieve when it is weakened by schism and unavoidable disunity? [29]

It was indeed regrettable that Erekle's earlier work of consolidation should finally have dissolved into so futile a system.

If such was the social and economic state of Eastern Georgia, that of the Western principalities was even more critical. The rebellion of Duke Rostom of Ratcha in the 1760s left King Solomon in almost destitute circumstances. The capture of Rostom by ruse and the assimilation of Ratcha to the crown, together with the recapture of K'ut'ais during Todtleben's campaign, somewhat improved Solomon's position, but it remained precarious throughout his reign.

Like the kingdom of K'art'lo-Kakhet'i, Imeret'i was an autocracy tempered by feudal institutions. The chief minister of state was the *sakhlt'-ukhutsesi,* or lord chamberlain, an office customarily held by a member of the Tseret'eli or Abashidze families. Other court dignitaries included the king's scribes, head falconer, huntsman, and wine steward. The army was under the command of the *sardar.* In the time of Solomon II, early in the nineteenth century, the kingdom was divided into twenty-six districts, each under its *mourav* or prefect, of which the principal was the *mourav* of K'ut'ais.

The judicial system in Western Georgia was modeled on the Code of Wakhtang VI of K'art'li. The wergild, or blood-money system,

---

[27] Butkov, *Materialy,* II, 335–36.

[28] *Mark,* 3. 24–25: "And if a kingdom be divided against itself, that kingdom cannot stand. And if a house be divided against itself, that house cannot stand."

[29] Letter of April 30, 1796, in A. A. Tsagareli, *Gramoty,* II, Part 2, 141.

owing to the general poverty of the country, was supplemented by mutilations and capital punishment. The use of ordeals to establish guilt or innocence was common. Murderers and slave traders were burnt alive, or buried in quicklime.[30]

With regard to the economic situation, a report of 1769 stated that Solomon and the other princes of Western Georgia had little or no cash revenue. Quit-rent was collected from the peasants in cattle and agricultural commodities. When called on for military service, each man took his provisions with him. In the absence of a regular commissariat, no military campaign could last much more than three weeks at a time. Solomon seemed to be in the direst financial straits and unable to set up an ordered government for lack of funds. As it was, he was hardly able to support the two hundred retainers he kept about him.[31]

Captain Iazykov noted in 1770 that

the Imeret'ians are in general very poor people. . . . How much Solomon's income amounts to he does not exactly know himself. It can merely be stated that he receives very little. Quit-rent is collected from the peasants in wheat, wine, and cattle, but almost nothing in cash.[32]

In the early years of the nineteenth century, under Solomon II, each family paid the king two marchils (slightly over one silver ruble) per annum in cash.[33] In addition, both the king of Imeret'i and the Dadian of Mingrelia were in the habit of moving their court from village to village and living on the hospitality of their loyal subjects.

Concerning trade, it was stated of the Imeret'ians in 1770 that

before the present war they used to sell honey, butter and cattle to the Turks garrisoning the forts, but now they have no commerce at all,

---

[30] See the article "O tsare Solomone II i byvshem pri nem upravlenii" ("On King Solomon II and the administration of his time"), in *Kavkazskii Kalendar'*, XIV (Tiflis, 1858), 429–35.

[31] Report of Prince Mouravov, in A. A. Tsagareli, *Gramoty*, I, 74. We learn from another source that Solomon's diet consisted of millet paste or *gomi*, roast meat and pressed caviar. Forks and spoons were unknown at his court. Solomon's royal decrees were promulgated on Fridays by a crier who climbed up a tree to read them out. (Ellis, *Memoir*, p. 56.)

[32] A. A. Tsagareli, *Gramoty*, I, 194–96. See the impressions of Captain de Grailly, in Lang, "Count Todtleben's Expedition," in *Bulletin of the School of Oriental and African Studies*, XIII, 888–89.

[33] *Kavkazskii Kalendar'*, XIV, 429.

and the Armenians bring all the goods they need from Kʻartʻli. They use Turkish money, but apart from a dingy-looking coin called a para, I have not seen any.[34]

Little improvement seems to have been effected in the following decades. Soon after 1800, for example, it was reported that in Lechkhumi, an extensive province bordering on Imeretʻi and Mingrelia, trade was centered on a single village,

where a few Armenian and Jewish settlers bought up fox and marten furs from the local people, and carted them to Pʻotʻi, whence they brought salt and cotton goods to sell in Lechkhumi. Commerce was in general so insignificant there that only a few households could subsist by it.[35]

In the year 1809 the total revenue from customs duties in all Imeretʻi was only 20,000 rubles.[36]

The traffic with Turkey in human flesh, to which so many allusions have been made, persisted in spite of Solomon I's energetic attempts to stamp it out (it was particularly rife in Mingrelia and Abkhazia). From these coastal regions ships could transport the victims easily and cheaply to Trebizond and Istanbul. The slave trade persisted in Western Georgia well into the nineteenth century, until the Russians gradually suppressed it. A hitherto unpublished document in the French diplomatic archives may be worth quoting here, as it gives a striking insight into the way the trade was carried on. In this document the French consul at Trebizond who was on a visit to Erzerum in the year 1804 relates in his journal:

On this day a singular incident occurred. We were at dinner when a Turkish merchant from the Abkhaz region brought us two Georgian slaves, a boy eight or nine years old, and a girl of ten or twelve, both of them charming. The girl gave promise of great beauty, and the boy had an intelligent and pleasing face; both of them had blue eyes. We made them sit down at our table, where they ate with the timidity common to all children. These unfortunate children inspired our pity. They knew that they were in a state of slavery, but doubtless failed to understand the full meaning of this word when in hands as barbarous as those of the Turks. I deeply wished to purchase them and thus free them from

[34] Report of Captain Iazykov, in A. A. Tsagareli, *Gramoty*, I, 194-96.
[35] Dubrovin, *Zakavkazʻe ot 1803–1806 goda*, p. 142.
[36] *Kavkazskii Kalendarʻ*, XIV, 429.

servitude, but my salary as Assistant Commissioner did not permit of this expense, thus preventing me from carrying out this charitable deed. It began to get late, and the master called for his servant to take the two children back to their quarters. The girl said as they were about to put her veil on, that she did not want to go, but wished to stay with my son, whose hand she came and kissed. It seems that she liked the look of us, and that an inner voice told her that she would be happy with people like us. The boy kept silent. It was only when their master told them that we would settle the price with him the next day that the girl resigned herself to have her veil put on and departed. Before this, she and the boy wanted to kiss our hands again. These two unhappy playthings of cruel fortune left us, our hearts afflicted with grief at being unable to rescue them from slavery.[37]

In spite of the bleakness of the economic situation in Georgia, the second half of the eighteenth century was marked by a revival of cultural and intellectual life. Erekle was not himself an author or poet as had been Wakhtang VI, but showed himself a zealous protector of the liberal arts and sciences. Catholic missionaries and European travelers and scientists like Reineggs and Güldenstädt were always welcomed at court, and their counsel invited on cultural and educational affairs. All observers agree that Erekle was ever receptive to new ideas and anxious to give his country the benefits of Western civilization.

In the intellectual life of the nation the Georgian Orthodox Church continued to play the leading part. It was fortunate in having as its head through most of Erekle's reign a catholicos-patriarch of the caliber of Antoni I. Antoni had occupied for some years an archbishopric in Russia, and was a man of broad vision and sympathies. His Georgian grammar is a landmark in the study of the language. He was versed in Russian and in the classics. In 1762, he translated into Georgian, F. C. Baumeister's *Elementa philosophiae recentioris* under the title of *Akhali filosofia,* and introduced into Georgia the philosophical system of Christian Wolf. He also made a rendering of the *Categories* of Aristotle.[38]

---

[37] "Journal du voyage à Erzerum et retour à Trébisonde de Pierre Jérôme Dupré, Consul de France à Trébisonde, 1804," in Mémoires et Documents, Perse, I, 218, in the archives of the French Foreign Ministry.

[38] M.-F. Brosset, "Acquisitions de livres géorgiens par le Musée Asiatique," in *Bulletin Scientifique de l'Académie des Sciences,* Vol. V (St. Petersburg, 1839); A. S.

The church had a virtual monopoly of education. Most monasteries had a school attached. At the Gelat'i monastery in Imeret'i were taught philosophy and classical languages and literature. Two ecclesiastical seminaries were opened during this period, at Tiflis (1756) and at T'elavi (1782). The latter flourished under the celebrated pedagogue and man of letters, the Rector David Alek'sisdze. In 1801, Tiflis had five schools with four hundred pupils. The Armenian clergy of the larger towns and the Catholic missionaries also contributed to the spread of education among their flocks.

In the domain of profane literature, poetry and the drama were much cultivated. A court theater functioned at Tiflis from time to time, the repertoire of which included plays on national themes as well as some translated from the Russian, notably the heroic tragedies of Sumarokov. The Armeno-Georgian bard Sayat-Nova spent several years in high favor at the court of Tiflis. He is equally renowned for his lyrics and ballads in Georgian, Armenian, and Azerbaijan Turki. In Georgian, his style is notable for its free rhythm and melodious ease. He invented new and more natural verse forms and broke away from the stilted diction of the latter-day imitators of Rust'aveli. Imeret'i also cherished a bard of national stature in Besarion Gabashvili, known as Besiki, renowned for his tender lyricism and strong patriotic feeling. Gabashvili was also a diplomat, and died on a mission to the Russo-Turkish peace conference at Jassy in 1791.

Increased contact with Russia during Erekle's reign, as well as the activities of the long-established Georgian colony in Moscow, resulted in a quantity of translations of European works into Georgian, usually through the medium of Russian. Among these may be noted Marmontel's *Bélisaire,* translated by the Archimandrite Gaioz T'aqaishvili under the title *Velisariani;* the *Meditations* of Marcus Aurelius; two separate renderings of Fénelon's *Télémaque,* one of which was made from the original French by Saridan Choloqashvili; Florian's historical novel *Numa Pompilius,* from the Russian rendering; Voltaire's *Zadig* and *L'Homme à Quarante Ecus.*[39]

Khakhanov, "Zhizn' i deiatel'nost' Katolikosa Gruzii Antoniia I," in *Letopis' Gruzii,* ed. B. S. Esadze (Tiflis, 1913).

[39] M.-F. Brosset, "Histoire et littérature de la Géorgie," in *Recueil des Actes de l'Académie des Sciences,* pp. 168–69.

It must be understood that scarcely any of these translations were ever printed; they circulated in manuscript form among the Georgian reading public both in the homeland and in Russia.

This awakening of interest in European culture might in more propitious times have heralded a social and economic rebirth. But in the conditions of political insecurity and commercial stagnation to which Georgia was condemned by her geographical situation among the hostile Mohammedan powers, these western influences could do little besides awakening a longing for better things, as well as showing up the contrast between the aspirations of Georgia's educated élite, and the general backwardness of the country's antiquated semi-feudal, semi-patriarchal social system.

11

Erekle's Last Years: A Kingdom in Decline, 1783-1798

THE last fifteen years of Erekle's life were a period of catastrophe and lost illusions. The economic and social factors noted in the preceding chapter were taking their toll of Georgia's material resources, while her strategic position in the arena of Near Eastern power politics made her increasingly vulnerable to attack. The alliance with Russia, on which such hopes were placed, failed to produce the advantages anticipated by either side.

In the year 1783, however, the outlook seemed bright enough. The signing of the Treaty of Georgievsk was celebrated in Tiflis with popular demonstrations of joy. In November, Colonel Burnashev arrived with 1,800 men, including two Jäger battalions and artillery. In the following year, the military road through the Dariel Pass was completed, and the fortress of Vladikavkaz founded. Erekle's rival, Prince Alexander of the Mukhranian Bagratids, and the prince's associate, Alexander Amilakhori, were surrendered to the Russian government by the khan of Derbent, and sent into honorable exile at Smolensk and Viborg respectively.[1]

The arrival of Russian troops alarmed the Turkish frontier pashas, particularly Sulayman of Akhaltsikhe. Sulayman was a descendant of the Georgian *atabags* or grand constables of Samtskhe, and had hitherto tried to maintain friendly relations with Erekle. Indeed, he was meditating taking advantage of the enfeebled state of Turkey

[1] Butkov, *Materialy*, II, 131–33.

to restore the autonomy of Samtskhe and set himself up as a sovereign prince. The Russo-Georgian convention was a blow to his ambition; in it, the empress undertook to assist Erekle to reconquer Georgia's lost territories, and Sulayman could have no doubt that it was his domains that were meant. Accordingly, he sent presents to Omar Khan of Avaria, urging him to invade Georgia from Daghestan. In August, 1785, the khan entered Kakhet'i with 20,000 tribesmen and advanced to within twenty versts of Tiflis. Fearing a pitched battle with the Russian regular troops, the khan marched across K'art'li to Akhalk'alak'i, spreading panic and destruction. Joining forces with Sulayman Pasha, Omar Khan undertook a raid into Imeret'i. The Daghestanians then took up winter quarters at Akhaltsikhe in preparation for fresh hostilities in the spring of 1786.[2]

The Russian protectorate over K'art'lo-Kakhet'i precipitated a diplomatic crisis in Istanbul also. The Ottoman government saw in the return of Russian troops to Tiflis a direct menace to their Anatolian frontier. They were able to cite in support of their objections Article XXIII of the Küchük-Kainarji treaty of 1774, in which Turkish suzerainty over all Georgia had been recognized, when it was certainly intended by the Russian negotiators to include only Mingrelia and Imeret'i. On October 14, 1784, Catherine's minister A. A. Bezborodko wrote to Bulgakov, the Russian ambassador at Istanbul:

Our business consists in correcting the error of the Treaty of Küchük-Kainarji about Georgia, in which that country was completely neglected, and correcting it not indeed on paper, but *de fait*. That land is very important to us; but it would be a pity if war broke out prematurely over it.[3]

Bulgakov wrote back: "How am I to extricate myself from Article XXIII, the end of which is very explicit and bad?"[4]

The Russian ambassador protested repeatedly to the Porte against Sulayman Pasha's provocations against K'art'lo-Kakhet'i. The Ottoman government prevaricated and played for time. They had no

[2] Butkov, *Materialy,* II, 161-62, 177-85.
[3] Grigorovich, *Kantsler Kniaz' . . . Bezborodko,* I, 455.
[4] *Sbornik Imp. Russkogo Istoricheskogo Obshchestva,* XLVII, 134.

desire to remove Sulayman or hamper his useful anti-Russian activities. On the other hand, it was feared that continued hostilities by him might provoke a Russian counterattack on Akhaltsikhe. The French and Austrian envoys at Istanbul, aware of Turkey's military unpreparedness, advised caution. The French Foreign Minister Vergennes urged Catherine to accept France's mediation. In the end, *firmans* were sent to Sulayman enjoining him to desist from molesting Erekle. Omar Khan called off his campaign projected for 1786 and returned to Daghestan, though not before forcing Erekle to pay him an annual tribute of 6,500 rubles in the guise of protection money. In the following year, Erekle and Sulayman concluded a formal truce agreement.[5]

The arrival of the Russian corps in Georgia also had a harmful effect on Erekle's relations with the Moslem khans of Azerbaijan and Shirvan. The delicate system of alliances which Erekle had built up depended on careful exploitation of the khans' mutual rivalries, and was shattered as soon as they were united by common fear of Russia. The Tatars in Erekle's dominions, including the nomads of Shamshadilo and other Moslem minorities, emigrated to Ganja and Shusha. The khans of Erivan and Ganja evaded payment of their tribute, as did the Kurds of the Erivan district. Even the faithful Ibrahim Khan of Shusha, for twenty years an ally of Georgia, began to manifest hostility. Georgian and Armenian merchants were set upon and pillaged in the bazaars of Turkey and Persia, and many of them emigrated to Russia.[6]

Fortunately for Erekle, Persia still had no stable government. Isfahan and the central provinces were in the hands of a nephew of the late Kerim Khan Zend, 'Ali Murad Khan, who was supported by a picked corps of two thousand Georgian mercenaries. 'Ali Murad was anxious to come to terms with Russia and sent an emissary to Potemkin in 1784. At the same time, the Austrian court, through the agency of Count Noli, secured his adherence to a scheme to partition the Ottoman Empire among Russia, Austria, and Persia. In

---

[5] *Sbornik Imp. Russkogo Istoricheskogo Obshchestva,* XLVII, 164–91 (dispatches to and from the Russian Ambassador Bulgakov); Butkov, *Materialy,* II, 185–93; Salomon, *Politique orientale de Vergennes,* p. 266.

[6] Butkov, *Materialy,* II, 177–78, 187; Burnashev, *Kartina Gruzii,* p. 16.

return for international recognition as shah, 'Ali Murad declared his willingness to give up all pretensions to Georgia and to allow Russian troops unhindered access to Azerbaijan and Armenia. Persia would annex Kurdistan, including territories extending to Kirkuk and Bitlis, while Basra was to be attached to the province of Fars.[7]

Russia's occupation of Georgia and her maneuvers at the Persian court did not escape the attention of Vergennes.[8] To thwart Russo-Austrian influence at Isfahan, he dispatched a secret envoy, the Comte de Ferrières-Sauveboeuf.[9] Arriving in Persia in March, 1784, Ferrières-Sauveboeuf entered into relations with 'Ali Murad Khan and assured him of France's desire to counterbalance Russian penetration of the north Persian provinces and to establish trade relations with Persia. Deploring 'Ali Murad's adherence to the scheme for partitioning Turkey, the French envoy pointed out that the Russo-Georgian treaty of 1783 was a direct threat to Persia. In his report to the French court, Ferrières-Sauveboeuf claimed that he had persuaded 'Ali Murad Khan to reestablish friendly relations with the sultan and to refuse help to the Russians.[10] All these intrigues were rendered abortive by the sudden death of 'Ali Murad in February, 1785. The country was once more plunged into civil war, with Isfahan taken and looted by Agha Mohammed Khan.[11]

For Georgia, Ferrières-Sauveboeuf's mission was significant in showing that the Moslem powers were not alone in opposing Russia's protectorate over K'art'lo-Kakhet'i. In accepting Russian suzer-

[7] Butkov, *Materialy*, II, 148; archives of the French Foreign Ministry, Correspondance Politique, Perse, Vol. VIII.

[8] Salomon, *Politique orientale de Vergennes*, pp. 169, 187.

[9] See the interesting record of his missions and adventures in *Mémoires historiques, politiques et géographiques des voyages du Comte de Ferrières-Sauveboeuf*, 2 vols. (Paris, 1790). The first volume (pp. 248–98) contains details on the state of Persia and Georgia.

[10] Archives of the French Foreign Ministry, Correspondance Politique, Perse, VIII, 24–39; Malcolm, *History of Persia* (1829), II, 103.

[11] Butkov, *Materialy*, II, 149–55. The Russian government was fully alive to Ferrières-Sauveboeuf's machinations. Catherine wrote to Bulgakov on November 15, 1785: "The Court of Versailles, following its policy of doing us all possible harm and raising barriers against our enterprises wherever it has an opportunity, sent this emissary into Persia to alienate the various local potentates and the late chief administrator of the realm." (*Sbornik Imp. Russkogo Istoricheskogo Obshchestva*, XLVII, 145.)

DAREJAN, QUEEN CONSORT OF KING EREKLE II

EREKLE II, FIRST KING OF UNITED K'ART'LI
AND KAKHET'I

RUSSO-GEORGIAN TREATY OF 1783

SIGNATURES OF THE RUSSIAN AND GEORGIAN PLENIPOTENTIARIES (LEFT). RATIFICATION BY KING EREKLE II, SHOWING THE GREAT SEAL OF GEORGIA (ABOVE).

ainty Erekle had incurred the animosity of France, the most influential of those Western European states whose interests were
bound up with the maintenance of the status quo in the Near East.
The court of Versailles went so far as to make direct representations
to the Russian government on its policy toward Georgia through
Ségur, the French envoy at St. Petersburg. In an account of a conversation with Prince Potemkin, Ségur reported in 1786 that he had
remonstrated against the dispatch of a Russian detachment over the
Caucasus, "that barrier placed by Nature between the two empires,"
stressing the bad impression this had produced in Istanbul. Potemkin
replied that Russia merely wished to control the Tatars and Lezghis,
and to protect a Christian king, the vassal of Russia. In asking his
superiors for further guidance on the Georgian question Ségur stated
his view that Russia would go to war with Turkey rather than surrender her claims to Georgia, adding the following comments:

In taking Georgia under her protection, the Empress has paid more
heed to her *amour-propre* than to her political judgment. But she should
have foreseen that this step, which adds nothing to her power, would cost
her a great number of men and involve her for an indefinite period in
all the quarrels and wars of the Caucasian peoples. And perhaps from
this point of view her enemies ought to observe with satisfaction, and
at least without disquiet, this new type of conquest which, far from
enriching her, tires, worries, and undermines her, and, as well, exhausts her
man power, who are cut down by the sword and eaten up by the climate.
It is asserted that this Caucasian war costs Russia more than twelve
thousand men a year.[12]

The Russian commandant in Georgia, Colonel Burnashev, was
an officer of ability and intelligence. He did much to efface the disagreeable impression that previous commanders had made, and won
Erekle's confidence. Although only Eastern Georgia was officially
under Russian protection, Burnashev was in close touch with King
Solomon of Imeret'i and exerted some influence on the affairs of
Western Georgia.

In 1784, Solomon died, his health undermined by epilepsy and
strong drink, as well as by the hardships of his valiant career. He

[12] Archives of the French Foreign Ministry, Mémoires et Documents, Russie, X,
112-13. (Dispatch of October 15, 1786.)

left no sons, and his brother Bagrat was mentally defective. The succession therefore presented difficulties.

Two factions emerged. The first adopted the cause of Solomon's nephew David, the son of the late king's deceased brother Archil. David, a lad of twelve, had been brought up at Tiflis, as his mother was a daughter of Erekle and Darejan. Solomon had recognized him as his heir, and he naturally enjoyed Erekle's support.

As soon as Solomon was in his grave, the people rebelled at the prospect of having a boy as their king, many of them demanding the accession of Solomon's first cousin, a prince of twenty-nine, also named David, son of the late king's Uncle Giorgi. The powerful *sardar* or commander in chief, Papuna Tseret'eli, was brother-in-law to this second David and had him proclaimed king. An embassy sent to St. Petersburg to announce the king's accession was cordially received there.[13]

But King David soon began to lose ground. He made the mistake of alienating his most influential partisan, Papuna Tseret'eli, and of failing to establish cordial relations with Erekle at Tiflis.[14] Tseret'eli took the rival candidate, the young David, over to the Turks at Akhaltsikhe, and harassed the new king at every opportunity.[15]

Such was the state of affairs in Eastern and Western Georgia when Catherine the Great's second Russo-Turkish War broke out in August, 1787.[16] The Russian plan of campaign did not include operations on the Caucasian front. Memories of Todtleben's fiasco were fresh enough to inspire doubts as to the wisdom of making Georgia a base for land operations. The difficulty of maintaining the supply route through the Dariel Pass, the chronic shortage of food and fodder in Georgia, and the strain imposed by recent fighting against Shaykh Mansur were additional obstacles. The agreement recently concluded between Erekle and the pasha of Akhaltsikhe

---

[13] Butkov, *Materialy,* II, 136–38.

[14] Butkov, *Materialy,* II, 160–61, 184–85.

[15] David Batonishvili, "Shedegi Kakhet'is tskhovrebisa," in Chubinov and M.-F. Brosset, eds., *K'art'lis tskhovreba,* II, 512.

[16] The Turkish ultimatum was partly instigated by the British government, now suspicious of Russia's Near Eastern projects. For the circumstances of the rupture, see G. Soloveytchik, *Potemkin,* in addition to the papers of Bulgakov, printed in *Sbornik Imp. Russkogo Istoricheskogo Obshchestva,* Vol. XLVII.

promised to secure this front, while it was hoped that withdrawal of Burnashev's force would appease the Persians.[17]

The order to evacuate Georgia reached Colonel Burnashev in September, 1787, just as the Russian and Georgian armies then at Ganja, were preparing for an expedition against the khan of Shusha. Erekle was astounded at the news, expecting that war with Turkey would make Georgia an important Russian base. Moreover, the Treaty of Georgievsk not only contained specific provisions for joint action in the event of war, but also had transferred the conduct of Erekle's foreign relations from Tiflis to St. Petersburg. Now, on the contrary, he was left to his own devices and advised to make his peace with neighboring khans and pashas as best he could. All the satisfaction Erekle could obtain from Potemkin was the promise that K'art'lo-Kakhet'i would not be forgotten in the peace treaty with Turkey, and that several pieces of artillery specially cast for the Georgian army would be made available to him. Russia's retreat from Transcaucasia was completed by the abandonment of Vladikavkaz in 1788.[18]

As it turned out, the Porte had no more desire than the Russians to have another front to contend with, and Sulayman Pasha observed the pact which he had concluded with Erekle. Paradoxically enough, as a Georgian historian has remarked,

during the second Turkish War, although Georgia as a state depending on the Russian Empire was strictly speaking at war with Turkey, the latter did not undertake any hostilities against Erekle. In short, at a time of peace with Turkey, the Russian protectorate failed to safeguard Georgia; and in wartime it was found to be superfluous! [19]

Erekle's attention was much occupied during this period by the succession problem in Imeret'i. The dispute between the two Davids had brought about a state of anarchy. In 1789, the younger David managed to overcome King David Giorgievich, and appealed to Erekle for support.[20] A treaty of alliance was signed at Tiflis in

[17] Avalov, *Prisoedinenie Gruzii k Rossii*, pp. 146–48.

[18] Dubrovin, *Bumagi Kniazia G. A. Potemkina-Tavricheskogo*, pp. 273–75, 283; Butkov, *Materialy*, II, 195.

[19] Avalov, *Prisoedinenie Gruzii k Rossii*, p. 167.

[20] See the report of Count Saltykov, quoted in *Arkhiv Gosudarstvennogo Soveta*, I, Part 2 (St. Petersburg, 1869), 776.

1790 between Erekle, David, son of Archil, and the princes of Mingrelia and Guria, in which Erekle's status as chief and *doyen* of the Georgian potentates was clearly defined. A copy of this agreement was forwarded to the Russian government, doubtless in the hope that this sign of returning concord would produce a favorable impression there.[21] The agreement also resulted in isolating King David Giorgievich from the league of princes. An expedition was sent against him under Erekle's grandson Ioane Batonishvili. In 1792, David, son of Archil, was finally placed on the throne of Imeret'i, taking the title of King Solomon II. The displaced king David Giorgievich died in exile a few years later of smallpox.[22]

The second Russo-Turkish War had now been officially ended by the Treaty of Jassy, signed on December 29, 1791. At the peace conference the affairs of K'art'lo-Kakhet'i had been the subject of lengthy and acrimonious exchanges.[23] The Porte was eventually induced to promise (Article V) that it would "confirm by a fresh *firman* the order previously given, that the Governor of Akhaltsikhe, the frontier commanders and others should henceforth in no wise, either secretly or openly, molest or disturb the lands and peoples under the rule of the King of K'art'li." [24]

The curbing of Sulayman Pasha brought a few years of comparative respite to K'art'lo-Kakhet'i, apart from the usual Lezghian raids. Any feeling of security, however, was fated to be short-lived. One of the dangers from which Erekle had sought protection when the Treaty of Georgievsk was signed, namely, the reemergence of a unified and militant Persia, now became daily more imminent.

Since the death of Kerim Khan in 1779, Agha Mohammed Khan Qajar had employed every weapon of guile and force to wipe out the remnants of the Zend ruling clan. For fifteen years he worked to become undisputed master of Persia. Not until 1794 did the fall of Kerman and the capture and murder of his rival, Lutf-'Ali Khan, bring him near the achievement of his ambition.[25]

[21] A. A. Tsagareli, *Gramoty*, II, Part 2, 67–70. The agreement was negotiated by Erekle's able Chancellor (*msajuli*), Solomon Leonidze.

[22] Full details of these vicissitudes are given in Butkov, *Materialy*, II, 282–86.

[23] Grigorovich, *Kantsler Kniaz'* . . . *Bezborodko*, II, 582–87.

[24] Avalov, *Prisoedinenie Gruzii k Rossii*, p. 168.

[25] Malcolm, *History of Persia* (1829), II, 176–89; David Batonishvili, "Shedegi Kakhet'is tskhovrebisa," in Chubinov and Brosset, eds., *K'art'lis tskhovreba*, II, 514.

While the Qajar eunuch felt himself still insecure, he had gone out of his way to make himself agreeable to Erekle and the Russian authorities, and to efface the impression produced by his seizure of Count Voinovich at Astarabad. He asked Prince Zakhar Tsitsishvili, who was on a visit to Persia in 1786, to assure Erekle of his amicable intentions, and offered to confer on the Georgian crown permanent suzerainty over Azerbaijan if Erekle would secure Russian support for the Qajar cause.[26]

As Agha Mohammed's strength increased, his unfriendly disposition became ever more apparent. In 1791 he was at Tabriz, preparing to subdue Erivan and the Karabagh. Erekle was sufficiently concerned to invoke the Treaty of 1783 and apply for Russian military aid.[27] Catherine was much too preoccupied with the unsettled situation produced in Europe by the French Revolution, and with the impending Second Partition of Poland, to pay any attention to this request. General Gudovich, the commander of the Caucasian Line, was told in May, 1792, that the dispatch of troops to Georgia was not now regarded as expedient, especially in view of the strain imposed on that sector in the recent Turkish campaigns.[28]

In the following year, further reports of Agha Mohammed Khan's enterprises roused the Council of War at St. Petersburg to a semblance of activity. The council came to the conclusion that Agha Mohammed

does not show any amity towards Russia, but is rising to power in Persia by violence, having already seized Isfahan, and is oppressing other khans well disposed towards us. It is therefore necessary to instruct General Gudovich, as the commander of the Imperial territories adjacent to Persia, that if Agha Mohammed Khan shows a genuine intention of attacking the frontiers of King Erekle, he should assure this monarch of the Imperial protection, and make suitable representations to the Khan in question that he [Gudovich] cannot look indifferently on such an undertaking . . . and give the King active assistance as far as may be possible without incurring large expenses and commitments.[29]

[26] Butkov, *Materialy*, II, 301. This offer cost Agha Mohammed little to make, as he possessed no firm authority over Azerbaijan at this time.
[27] A. A. Tsagareli, *Gramoty*, II, Part 2, 70.
[28] Butkov, *Materialy*, II, 334.
[29] A. A. Tsagareli, *Gramoty*, II, Part 2, 80–81.

But making "suitable representations to the Khan in question" was unlikely to quell a determined aggressor like Agha Mohammed. The terms of this rather vague resolution did not encourage Gudovich to dispatch any troops into Georgia.

Erekle decided to send Prince Garsevan Tchavtchavadze, who had already served several years as Georgian minister to Russia, on a new mission to St. Petersburg. In a note presented early in 1795, Tchavtchavadze announced that Agha Mohammed had arrived at Ardebil in Azerbaijan with the intention of reducing Georgia to the same status she had occupied under the Safavis. The minister asked that five or six battalions of infantry be sent without delay.[30] No action was taken to meet this request. In July, Tchavtchavadze returned to the charge, inquiring in pressing terms: "Will the Russian court, in accordance with its obligations under the Treaty, afford us help and protection, or not?"[31]

After the fall of Kerman, even the skeptical Gudovich, who had no high opinion of Persian military prowess, began to have misgivings. While assuring the king that Agha Mohammed would take a long time to invade Transcaucasia, Gudovich at the same time advised him to enter into a defensive alliance with the Moslem khans of that region. In May, 1795, the general applied to St. Petersburg for instructions. "I do not see any immediate threat to Georgia," he wrote,

but if Agha Mohammed Khan of Isfahan does indeed attempt to invade Georgia and begins to take hostile action against Russian traders in Persia, and starts making importunate demands on the Khan of Derbent and the Shamkhal of Tarku to recognize him as Shah, and submit to him the provinces over which they rule—then how am I to act in such circumstances?[32]

On May 28, the Council of State at St. Petersburg recommended that Gudovich be authorized to send troops to reinforce Erekle, but this advice was not acted on for the time being.[33]

During the summer, Agha Mohammed advanced on Ganja, be-

---

[30] Ibid., p. 90.
[31] A. A. Tsagareli, Gramoty, II, Part 2, 272.
[32] Ibid., pp. 88–89.
[33] Arkhiv Gosudarstvennogo Soveta, I, Part 2 (1869), 797–99.

sieged Shusha, and sent a detachment to reduce the khan of Erivan and the Armenian patriarch of Echmiadzin to allegiance. This was an overt challenge to Erekle as Ganja and Erivan had for years stood under the protection of Georgia. Agha Mohammed's plan of operations against Georgia was intercepted and communicated to the commander of the Caucasian Line. Gudovich was still reluctant to be convinced of the strength and the hostile intent of "that loathsome individual," as Erekle termed Agha Mohammed, and continued to send soothing messages to Tiflis, assuring the king that he and Solomon of Imeret'i, in conjunction with the khan of Shusha, should have no trouble in warding off any Persian threat.[34]

From his camp before Shusha, Agha Mohammed summoned Erekle to submit. Still counting on support from the north, the king replied that he acknowledged no paramount sovereign but the Empress Catherine of Russia.[35]

Agha Mohammed then sent messengers to the tribesmen of Daghestan to rouse them against Georgia, and prepared to enter the field in person. He was guided and encouraged in his enterprise by Javat Khan of Ganja and two of the Armenian meliks of Karabagh, inveterate enemies of Ibrahim Khan of Shusha; they offered to show the Persians the way into Georgia.[36] At Ganja the Qajar leader assembled a force of nearly 40,000 men, mostly fast-moving, irregular cavalry.

Erekle was not inactive in the face of the mounting peril. He summoned his grandson, King Solomon II of Imeret'i, who soon arrived with 2,000 men, whom Erekle quartered with his own forces at Krdsanisi on the outskirts of Tiflis. It seems however that the defenders' discipline was not all that could be desired. "The Imeretians," an eyewitness recalls,

as well as the volunteers from Tiflis, were so profusely supplied with wine, that they might have bathed themselves in it if they had pleased;

[34] A. A. Tsagareli, Gramoty, II, Part 2, 100.

[35] Malcolm, History of Persia (1869), II, 190; Manvelishvili, Ruset'i da Sak'art'velo, I, 144.

[36] The names of these meliks were Mejnun (or Mejlum) and Abo. According to the Armenian memoirist Artemii, Mejnun's brother had been murdered by some Georgians on an occasion when he and his followers sought to put themselves under Erekle's protection. (Memoirs of the Life of Artemi, p. 214.)

and the people of the town made this sacrifice with the greater cheerful-
ness, as they confidently expected the victory through their aid; for they
considered them as capital soldiers, and estimated their number at eight
thousand. With this assurance they were frequently heard to exclaim:
Now let Aga Mohamed come as soon as he will—who can resist us? [37]

Erekle's own sons gave him little aid, most of them remaining
idle in the hereditary domains he had assigned to them. The heir-
apparent Giorgi remained in Sighnaghi, under pretense of defending Kakhet'i from the Lezghis. According to the contemporary already quoted,

Heraklios, when he perceived the danger on the part of Mahomed-Khan
approaching, more than once dispatched his commands, as well as urgent
entreaties, to him and to the other Zarewitsches, to send some thousands
of troops without delay to his assistance. The Zarewitsch of Signach had
assembled the reinforcements required by his father, and himself accompanied the troops out of the city; but his people were so obstinate, that
they struck into by-roads and returned home; for they gave themselves
no concern about the defence of their country, but only about getting in
their crops in due time, making their wine, and thus providing for their
own subsistence and that of their families. [38]

On September 10, 1795, the vanguard of Agha Mohammed's force
reached the outskirts of Tiflis. They were immediately set upon by
Erekle's grandson David Batonishvili, whose men fought with the
utmost valor and put the Persians to flight. [39] A few hours later,
Agha Mohammed arrived in person before the capital. The decisive
battle began at dawn on the eleventh on the field of Krdsanisi.
Erekle and Solomon could only muster 1,500 men between them,
not a tenth of the Persian strength. Wakhtang was the only one
of Erekle's sons who took part in the combat. David Batonishvili
was posted on the right wing with the Georgian artillery, together
with the remains of the Imeret'ian contingent; the king, with his
son Wakhtang and Prince Ot'ar Amilakhori, occupied the center;

[37] *Memoirs of the Life of Artemi,* p. 204.

[38] *Ibid.,* pp. 208-9.

[39] Butkov, *Materialy,* II, 338; A. A. Tsagareli, *Gramoty,* II, Part 2, 104; *Memoirs
of the Life of Artemi,* p. 214; T'eimuraz Batonishvili, "Précis des guerres qu'eut à
soutenir le Prince-Royal Dawith," in M.-F. Brosset, *Aperçu général de la langue
géorgienne.*

the left flank was under the command of Prince Ioane of Mukhran; while Ioane Batonishvili, David's brother, commanded the vanguard. A militia of volunteers from the city of Tiflis played a prominent part, as did the brave fighters of K'isiq and mountaineers from P'shavet'i and Khevsuret'i.[40]

All day the battle raged with undiminished ferocity. Agha Mohammed was three times repulsed and forced to throw in fresh reserves. He posted Turcoman horsemen behind the front ranks with orders to kill any who gave way. At one point he exclaimed: "Never do I remember my foes to have fought so valiantly." Finally the Georgians were overcome by sheer weight of numbers. The king, in spite of his seventy-five years, fought like a lion at bay. He refused to acknowledge defeat, and would have been killed or captured if Ioane Batonishvili had not hacked his way to the midst of the melee and forced his grandfather to retire to a place of safety.[41]

The Persian occupation of Tiflis was held up for a few hours by a gallant artillery officer in the citadel who wreaked havoc among the advancing hordes. But the royal army was almost wiped out. The king had only 150 men left with him as he fled his capital. Queen Darejan had already taken refuge in the mountains, accompanied by a large number of Tiflis citizens.[42] The general panic was increased by deserters from the Imeret'ian army, who mercilessly plundered the fugitives.

To quote Sir John Malcolm:

The conquerors entered Teflis: a scene of carnage and rapine ensued pleasing to one who desired to make this city an example for such as dared to contemn his authority. The Mahomedan historian of Aga Mohamed Khan, after describing the barbarous and horrid excesses, observes, "that on this glorious occasion the valiant warriors of Persia gave to the unbelievers of Georgia a specimen of what they were to expect on the day of judgment." It is not easy to calculate the number who

[40] Manvelishvili, *Ruset'i da Sak'art'velo*, I, 145-46.

[41] T'eimuraz Batonishvili, "Précis des guerres qu'eut à soutenir le Prince-Royal Dawith," in M.-F. Brosset, *Aperçu général de la langue géorgienne;* David Batonishvili, "Shedegi Kakhet'is tskhovrebisa," in Chubinov and M.-F. Brosset, eds., *K'art'lis tskhovreba*, II, 514-15.

[42] Butkov, *Materialy*, II, 338-39.

perished. Bigotry inflamed the brutal rage of the soldier. The churches were levelled to the ground; every priest was put to death. Youth and beauty were alone spared for slavery. Fifteen thousand captives were led into bondage; and the army marched back laden with spoil.[43]

Mtskhet'a also was sacked, and a party of Persian marauders reached the village of Lamisqana, but there they were repulsed by Ioane Batonishvili. The invaders' path was everywhere marked by the smoke of burning houses and the stench of putrefying bodies.[44]

The king took refuge with a few faithful retainers at Ananuri on the Dariel highway. "I determined to present myself to him," relates Artemii of Mount Ararat.

I went for this purpose to the ancient Grusian convent, as the only place where I was sure of meeting with him. The convent was not large, and everywhere much decayed. In going over the place, I found under the arch of a ruinous cell, in a corner of the wall of the convent, a person clad in a common sheep-skin, sitting with his face to the wall; and near him stood another very aged man. I asked the latter: "Who is it that is sitting there in the corner?"—"He whom thou there seest," replied he, with a deep sigh, in Armenian, "was once a renowned personage, and his name was celebrated throughout all Asia, even in the time of Tachmas-Kuly-Chan. He was an excellent ruler of his people. He governed them forty years with glory, till age cramped his powers. To prevent discord in his family, he thought it would conduce to the interest of his people to divide his kingdom into several parts: but the good Zar was disappointed in his hopes. A eunuch, formerly belonging to Tachmas-Kuly-Chan, and who was one of the lowest at the time when Heraklios was commander-in-chief of the Persian army, has now triumphed over the impotence of his age. His own children too denied him assistance; they would not save their country, for they were numerous, and each of them thought he was not promoting his own advantage but that of another. . . . The glory of his long life is eclipsed; his capital is laid waste, and the prosperity of his people is converted into misery. Behind this wall the Zar of Grusia hides himself from the eyes of men, forsaken by all, and covered only with a sheep-skin. His courtiers and those who were about his person, his native subjects, whom he cherished in his bosom and supported in abundance, have all deserted him; not one has followed his sovereign but myself, one of the lowest of the Armenians."[45]

[43] History of Persia (1829), II, 191.
[44] Memoirs of the Life of Artemi, pp. 228-29.
[45] Memoirs of the Life of Artemi, pp. 232-34.

Agha Mohammed now wrote again to Erekle, demanding his submission. The king duly informed Gudovich of this overture, adding that only the arrival of Russian troops could save him from surrender. The Qajar leader did not however think it wise to count on continued Russian forbearance in the face of his outrages. A week after the sack of Tiflis, the Persians evacuated Georgia to complete the conquest of Shirvan, and took up winter quarters on the Mughan Steppe north of Ardebil, where Agha Mohammed was formally proclaimed *shahinshah* of Iran.[46]

The sack of Tiflis, although followed by evacuation from Georgia, was as great a triumph for the Qajar cause as it was a blow to Russian prestige in the Near East. The French consul in Baghdad reported that the Turkish frontier pashas of Erzerum, Kars, and Akhaltsikhe, who had previously encouraged Erekle to resist the Persians, now sought in every way to appease the shah.[47] The same observer commented that

certain Persian and Georgian notables at Baghdad, as well as other well-informed persons, seeing that in all these hostilities of the Persians against Georgia, the Russians do not take any overt action, either diplomatic or military, to aid the Georgians, their former allies, think and assume with justification that this is a barbarous policy on the part of the Russian court, that it desires Erekle and Georgia to be crushed by Agha Mohammed Khan, and that it will subsequently deploy its strength to come and retake all Georgia to be retained for ever by the right of conquest.[48]

If the French consul at Baghdad was shocked by the atrocities committed in Georgia, his government viewed them with equanimity. The French Foreign Ministry was not slow to seize the opportunity presented by Agha Mohammed's triumph to add to Russia's discomfiture. As early as 1792, following the policy of Vergennes, Roland had organized a mission consisting of Jean-Guillaume Bruguières and Guillaume-Antoine Olivier, who, under guise of a

[46] A. A. Tsagareli, *Gramoty*, II, Part 2, 107; Malcolm, *History of Persia* (1829), II, 192–93.

[47] "Suite des nouvelles de la Perse," from Consul Rousseau, Baghdad, March 8, 1796, in the archives of the French Foreign Ministry, Correspondance Politique, Perse, VIII, 87–88.

[48] "Notions abrégées sur la Perse," October 15, 1795, in the archives of the French Foreign Ministry, Mémoires et Documents, Perse, I, 147.

scientific exploration of Persia, were to conclude a trade agreement
with Agha Mohammed and assure him of French support against
Russia. The fall of Roland delayed the execution of this project, but
in 1795 the French ambassador at Istanbul was told to issue to
Bruguières and Olivier fresh instructions and to send them on their
way to Teheran. Agha Mohammed was to be urged to consolidate
his hold on Georgia and convinced that once Russia was allowed
to establish herself there, Persia could never be secure.[49]

The Russian government, belatedly enough, was now aware that
Agha Mohammed was a power to be reckoned with. When Tiflis
was on the point of being sacked, orders were finally sent to Gudovich to dispatch a force to Georgia.[50] It is not necessary to ascribe
this delay to willful desire for Erekle's ruin. Revolutionary upheavals
in Europe and the final partitions of Poland had temporarily relegated Georgian affairs to the low-priority category. Gudovich had
minimized Agha Mohammed's strength in his reports. The Persians
enjoyed the benefit of surprise (they were able to advance from
Ganja to Tiflis in five days), while the Russians had to cross the
whole Caucasian range to reach K'art'lo-Kakhet'i. After Gudovich
received his orders early in October, it took two months for two
battalions from the Caucasian Line to traverse the Dariel Pass into
Georgia.[51]

The news of the sack of Tiflis aroused indignation in St. Petersburg. The Council of State authorized Gudovich to initiate reprisals.[52] It was not long before the idea of simple retaliation gave
way to more grandiose plans. The empress and her favorite Platon
Zubov saw an opportunity to revive the projects of Peter the Great

[49] These instructions are set forth by Verninac, French Ambassador at Istanbul,
in memoranda dated 13 nivôse and 7 floréal, An 4 (1795), in the archives of the
French Foreign Ministry, Perse, VIII, 83–84, 93; see also the articles "Bruguières"
and "Olivier" in Michaud, *Biographie Universelle*.

[50] A. A. Tsagareli, *Gramoty*, II, Part 2, 113; Butkov, *Materialy*, II, 343–44.

[51] Butkov, *Materialy*, II, 345.

[52] A. A. Tsagareli, *Gramoty*, II, Part 2, 109–14. For a report on these events addressed by Gudovich to Field-Marshal Rumiantsev-Zadunaiskii on October 15, 1795,
and the latter's reply, containing interesting observations on the situation, see
Sbornik Imp. Russkogo Istoricheskogo Obshchestva, XVI (St. Petersburg, 1875),
pp. 304–8, 318–19.

and Potemkin, annexing Azerbaijan and all Persia's Caspian provinces and thus rivaling the British East India Company by opening up strategic trade routes to India and the rest of the Orient.

The command of the expedition was entrusted to Platon Zubov's brother Valerian. The Russian army set out from Kizliar' in April, 1796, and soon captured Derbent. Later in the summer, Baku, Shamakhi, and Ganja were occupied over weak resistance. Communications were established between the main Russian headquarters and the Georgian court, which had moved to T'elavi in Kakhet'i. Garsevan Tchavtchavadze, Erekle's minister to Russia, was at Zubov's camp. In the autumn, the army crossed the Araxes and took up winter quarters on the Mughan Steppe. Major General Rimsky-Korsakov's detachment marched into Georgia. Plans were drawn up for a Georgian attack on Erivan and a Russian advance on Tabriz and Teheran to be undertaken the following spring. Units of the Russian navy menaced the ports of Resht and Enzeli.[53]

Agha Mohammed did little to hinder the Russian advance. He spent the summer of 1796 in Khorasan, where he deposed and tortured to death the blind ruler Shahrukh, and prepared for an invasion of Turkestan. The French envoys Bruguières and Olivier meanwhile arrived in Teheran and had conversations with the grand vazir, Hajji Ibrahim, in which the following exchange of views on Georgia occurred.

We spoke of the treaty between Prince Heraclius and the Empress. "We know about that," said the Minister. We wished to convey at this point our surprise that the Shah, after seizing Georgia, had immediately evacuated it. With this in view, we told the Minister that since Georgia bordered on Persia, and extended to the Black Sea, if Persia occupied that country and established herself firmly on that sea, she could communicate with greater facility with the European powers, establish ports for her trade, receive commodities and manufactured products from Europe and find an outlet for Gilan silk and other exportable goods. The Minister replied, "We will reconquer Georgia whenever we so desire." But the Russians, we observed to him, in accordance with their treaty obligations, will oppose a fresh invasion of that country. "The

[53] Baddeley, *Russian Conquest of the Caucasus*, pp. 57–60; Malcolm, *History of Persia* (1829), II, 198–99; Butkov, *Materialy*, II, 352–419.

Russians," said the Minister, "will be unable to oppose it, when we appear with all our forces."

When we have convinced them that they ought to have retained Georgia and pursued their conquests into the country of the Imeret'ians and Mingrelians, so as to have some ports on the Black Sea to facilitate trade and political connections with the European powers, we shall depart.[54]

When subsequently describing their attempts to spur the shah on to reoccupy Georgia, Bruguières and Olivier did not disguise their personal aversion to the character and policy of that ruler:

Mohammed Shah has none of the qualities of a great man; he is a brigand without good faith or humanity, who rules only through inspiring fear. . . . The Georgian expedition, which was imagined in Europe to be the result of a systematic plan, was nothing but a robber raid. Finally, this man and his ministers are so lacking in good judgment that they are now trying to make believe that in their present war with the Russians, the latter are the aggressors, as if the sack of Tiflis and the murder of the Russians there were not overt acts of hostility which they are powerless to dissimulate.[55]

In spite of the grand vazir's blustering statements, it was clear that the Persian monarchy was in grave danger. Agha Mohammed returned to Teheran in September, 1796, and summoned a war council to deal with the Russian menace. "My valiant warriors," he announced, "shall be led against them; and, by the blessing of God, we will charge their celebrated lines of infantry and batteries of cannon, and cut them to pieces with our conquering sabres." In actual fact, nothing was further from his thoughts than a pitched battle with the Russians. He confided to his intimates that he counted on checkmating them by guerrilla warfare and a scorched earth policy. Meanwhile he addressed a truculent letter to Erekle, expressing astonishment that the king should have allied himself with bourgeois infidels like the Russians, and warning him that if he

[54] Report of 3 vendémiaire, An 5 (1796), in the archives of the French Foreign Ministry, Correspondance Politique, Perse, VIII, 101-4.

[55] Bruguières and Olivier to General Aubert du Bayer, French Ambassador at Istanbul, from Bagdad, 9 nivôse, An 5 (1796), in the archives of the French Foreign Ministry, Correspondance Politique, Perse, VIII, 128. For further details on this mission, see A. R. Ioannisian, "Frantsuzskoe posol'stvo v Iran v 1796 g." (The French Embassy to Iran in 1796), in Sovetskoe Vostokovedenie (1956), I, 162-72.

persisted, the Persian army would "make a flowing river of the blood of the Russian and Georgian peoples." [56]

What outcome the Russian offensive of 1797 would have had must remain a matter for conjecture, for the death of Catherine the Great in November, 1796, brought the whole scheme to an abrupt end. The Emperor Paul, set on reversing his mother's expansionary policies and humbling her favorites, at once recalled Valerian Zubov's force and restored the Caucasian command in the Northern Line to General Gudovich. It is possible that he was also motivated by a desire to mollify Great Britain, uneasy at any threat to India. K'art'lo-Kakhet'i was evacuated in the summer of 1797, in spite of petitions from the Georgian royal family. The last units left Mukhran in September. [57]

The shah of Persia was jubilant, affecting to attribute the Russian retreat into their "detestable country" to terror of his "most lofty intelligence and most fortunate banners." He again summoned Erekle to submit Georgia to the Persian crown. "If you do not carry out our commands," he added, "you know yourself what will ensue." [58] Receiving no satisfactory answer, Agha Mohammed collected his army and invaded Armenia and the Karabagh, with the intention of deporting the population wholesale as Shah 'Abbas I had done two centuries before. Contemporary observers record that he was now in a state of morbid blood-lust verging on insanity, and would torture to death even the grandees of the realm on any trivial pretext. [59]

Although a small detachment of Russian troops still remained in Georgia prior to the evacuation, the kingdom seemed doomed to suffer the full fury of Agha Mohammed's vengeance. Alexander Batonishvili routed a marauding party of Persians near Erivan, but it is more than doubtful if the shah's onslaught could have been resisted. Agha Mohammed occupied Shusha without resistance at the beginning of June, Ibrahim Khan having fled to Daghestan.

[56] Malcolm, *History of Persia* (1829), II, 200–1; A. A. Tsagareli, *Gramoty*, II, Part 2, 146–47.

[57] Okun', *Istoriia SSSR*, p. 159; Butkov, *Materialy*, II, 422; A. A. Tsagareli, *Gramoty*, II, Part 2, 160–64, 173–74.

[58] A. A. Tsagareli, *Gramoty*, II, Part 2, 165.

[59] Malcolm, *History of Persia* (1829), II, 203.

Three days later, the shah was murdered at night by two of his slaves, one of them a Georgian whom he had condemned to be put to death on the morrow.[60]

The resulting chaos in the Persian camp removed the immediate danger to Georgia from that quarter. Erekle realized, however, that as soon as Agha Mohammed's nephew and heir, Baba Khan, was firmly established in Teheran, he would not fail to revive his uncle's bellicose designs. The Georgian minister to St. Petersburg, Tchavtchavadze, was told to press for a formal assurance that Paul would recognize Russia's obligations under the Treaty of 1783. If not, it would be necessary for Georgia to enter into alliance with the Moslem khans of Transcaucasia, and the Lezghian chieftains of Daghestan.

Repeated efforts by Tchavtchavadze to obtain satisfaction from the College of Foreign Affairs met with no success. In December, 1797, he addressed a petition to the emperor, pointing out the untenable position in which Georgia was placed by the Russian court's equivocation.

I hereby take the humble liberty in accordance with the requests of my Sovereign, to bring these facts to the direct attention of Your Imperial Majesty and to ask with the greatest respect: Does it please you, great and omnipotent Emperor, to preserve that Treaty in its previous validity, and will it please you to grant to my Sovereign, reduced by the obligations of that Treaty to the most straitened circumstances, the help promised therein, or is it at the moment for some reason impossible to do so?

The minister requested that if Russia were unable to provide the troops promised by the Treaty of Georgievsk, Erekle should at least not be debarred from recruiting Circassian cavalry from North Caucasia, as he had been free to do before the consolidation of Russian power there. Since then, the Russian commanders had prevented the Georgian army from employing these valuable auxiliaries.[61]

Meanwhile, Erekle had fallen gravely ill at T'elavi. Bowed down

---

[60] Dubrovin, *Georgii XII*, pp. 45–48. With extraordinary recklessness, the shah allowed these two slaves, when under sentence of death, to perform their usual duties about his person.

[61] A. A. Tsagareli, *Gramoty*, II, Part 2, 177–81.

with age and the disasters of the last years, he felt his death approaching. Sending for the heir-apparent, Giorgi Batonishvili, he entrusted him with the conduct of affairs of state. On January 11, 1798, the king died in his seventy-eighth year; for almost fifty-four years of his life he had reigned in Kakhet'i and for almost thirty-six in Kakhet'i and K'art'li combined. His death was regarded as a calamity for the nation, and his passing was mourned by prince and peasant alike.[62]

[62] Butkov, *Materialy,* II, 439–43.

12

Giorgi XII: Last King
of K'art'lo-Kakhet'i, 1798-1800

IN spite of the Queen Dowager Darejan's desire to see her eldest son, Yulon, on the throne, she proved unable to prevent the accession of her stepson Giorgi. She likewise failed in an attempt to deprive Giorgi's consort, Mariam, of the title of queen of K'art'lo-Kakhet'i. By a well-timed show of force, Giorgi obliged even Darejan's partisans to swear the oath of allegiance to himself as the new king.[1]

The outlook for Erekle's successor was from the outset far from encouraging. Giorgi was a pious and well-meaning man, of peaceable disposition, though subject to outbreaks of bad temper. He was a fairly good administrator and played a prominent part in rebuilding Tiflis after the Persian invasion. But he lacked the qualities needed to cope with the present situation. The corpulence of advancing years prevented Giorgi, a notorious gourmand, from shining as a military leader. This was a grave handicap in a land where the king habitually rode into battle at the head of his troops. At the time of his accession, Giorgi was suffering from chronic dropsy, his days already numbered.

Giorgi's most pressing task was to insure the country's external

[1] Dubrovin, *Georgii XII*, pp. 54–55. It should be noted that Giorgi XII was usually styled Giorgi XIII during his lifetime. The reason for this was that Giorgi XI of K'art'li had ruled twice, first from 1678 until he was expelled by Erekle I of Kakhet'i, then *in absentia* from 1703 to 1709, while he was serving as Persian commander in chief. Modern historians have reverted to the more logical style of Giorgi XII.

security. Tchavtchavadze in St. Petersburg had long been pressing in vain for fulfillment of Russia's treaty obligations and the resumption of the protectorate. For the time being, the Emperor Paul persisted in turning his back on the external commitments incurred by his mother, professing through 1797 a policy of ostentatious nonintervention in both Europe and Asia. The Russian government's negative attitude toward Georgia during this year is therefore to be viewed as part of this transitory phase of isolationism in Paul's foreign policy.

It was impossible at Tiflis to fathom the motives behind the eccentric emperor's indifference, still less to foresee the abrupt changes of face to which Paul was given. Giorgi was faced with the choice of waiting indefinitely for the emperor to change his mind, thereby exposing K'art'lo-Kakhet'i to devastation by Persians and Lezghis, or else of coming to terms with these two. From any standpoint he would have been perfectly justified in taking the latter course. By withdrawing her troops in 1787, failing to send them in time against Agha Mohammed in 1795, and again evacuating Georgia in 1797, Russia had undeniably forfeited any juridical right to demand Georgia's continued adherence to the Treaty of Georgievsk.

Agha Mohammed's nephew and heir, Baba Khan, after overcoming several pretenders to the Persian throne, was ultimately proclaimed ruler of Persia under the title of Fath-'Ali Shah. In June, 1798, he advanced into Azerbaijan to receive the submission of the autonomous khans of northwestern Persia. He also sent a threatening letter to Giorgi demanding his country's submission and the surrender of one of the king's sons as hostage to the Persian court:

If your good fortune does not direct you, and your evil fate prevents you from embarking on this happy course, and you show yourself unpunctual in serving us, then this will become evident—our lofty standard will proceed to your lands and, just as occurred in the time of Agha Mohammed Khan, so now you will be subjected to doubly increased devastation, and Georgia will again be annihilated, and the Georgian people given over to our wrath. You will be wise to accept this gracious counsel of ours, and fulfill our command.[2]

[2] A. A. Tsagareli, *Gramoty,* II, Part 2, 182.

While the king was pondering these threats, his eldest son, David, whom the Russian empress had taken into her service, arrived at Tiflis from St. Petersburg. He was now a major general in the Russian army. David brought news that the emperor now expressed himself as well-disposed toward Georgia, although nothing concrete had as yet been said about Russian military aid.[3] It was decided to play for time. With some difficulty, in view of the depleted condition of the treasury, rich presents were collected to be taken to the shah by a special representative, Prince Giorgi Tsitsishvili. These did not however reach their destination, since Tsitsishvili heard en route of fresh disturbances in Persia and returned home without completing his mission.[4] Giorgi also thought of the expedient of putting himself under Turkish protection, for which purpose he sent Prince Aslan Orbeliani to Akhaltsikhe. He then changed his mind and canceled Orbeliani's instructions, much to the annoyance of the Ottoman authorities.[5] Besides these *démarches,* fresh messages were sent to Tchavtchavadze, as well as to influential officials at St. Petersburg, urging the need for a swift decision on Georgia, failing which the king would be forced to seek protection elsewhere and recall his minister from the Russian court.

At this time, the whole direction of Paul's foreign policy was undergoing a radical change. From nonintervention in the affairs of Europe, he was veering toward a policy more militant than any conceived by Catherine the Great. His hatred of Jacobinism took on unprecedented violence. The French occupation of Malta, and the appeal for help by the Knights of St. John of Jerusalem, focused

[3] Butkov, *Materialy,* II, 446; A. A. Tsagareli, *Gramoty,* II, Part 2, 184.

[4] The British Ambassador Malcolm describes this episode as follows in a dispatch of the year 1800, on the basis of information supplied to him by an Armenian from Tiflis: "Nearly two years ago Khaujeh Aratoon Isaiah said that Baba Khaun sent one of his Generals Soliman Khaun Khajar to Hoin [Khoi] in Aderbijan, and that General dispatched a person to demand the submission of the new Wuli; Geourgeen [Gurjin, i.e., Giorgi] having just obtained the Government and being hardly fixed in power temporized: he wrote an Arzee to the King of Persia and evaded a demand of one of his sons as a hostage but sent one of his confidential servants with an ornamented watch of extraordinary value, which he desired to be given to Baba Khaun. Before this servant had advanced far, intelligence was received of Soliman Khaun's retreat from Hoin, and the Wuli's agent returned to Teflis" (archives of the Indian Office, London: Persia, XXII, 220–21).

[5] Dubrovin, *Georgii XII,* p. 59.

Paul's attention on Mediterranean affairs. Napoleon's invasion of Egypt in July, 1798, combined with the consequent Russian rapprochement with Turkey, meant that Paul could no longer affect indifference to developments in the Caucasus. Soon, the Russian fleet was on the way to the Bosphorus to join forces with the Turkish navy. Plans were already on foot for the coalition between Russia, Turkey, Austria, and England that was, so Paul hoped, to bring France to her knees and destroy the forces of revolution. But first it was essential to check Napoleon's advance in the Middle East. Once Napoleon had conquered Egypt and Syria, his next objectives might well be Anatolia and Persia. To protect Russia's Black Sea and Caspian possessions, the reoccupation of Georgia was an obvious precautionary measure, all the more so since the Russian army would be entering a friendly country at the invitation of its ruler.[6]

It is likely also that the military talent of King Giorgi's son David Batonishvili had made a good impression on Paul, and disposed him favorably toward the Georgian royal family.

These considerations help to explain the renewed attention shown to Georgian affairs by the Russian government in the latter half of 1798. On August 8 the emperor gave orders to declare a renewal of the Russian protectorate over Georgia. On receipt of a formal request from Giorgi, a set of royal insignia were to be sent to Tiflis by special envoy, in accordance with the Treaty of Georgievsk. Two battalions from the Caucasian Line would garrison the country, and the shah of Persia was to be warned not to interfere with the Georgians and other Caucasian peoples under Russian protection.[7] The Russian minister at Istanbul, Tamara, further induced the Ottoman government, with which Russia was now in alliance, to forbid the pasha of Akhaltsikhe to harbor gangs of Lezghis and to indulge in raids on Georgian territory.[8]

[6] It is worth noting that Napoleon did make an abortive attempt to win over King Giorgi to the French cause. In April, 1799, it was learned at Tiflis that a French envoy had set out from Napoleon's camp for Georgia but had been intercepted and executed by the Pasha of Akhaltsikhe. (Letter of David Batonishvili to Bishop Joseph Argutinskii, April 15, 1799, in A. A. Tsagareli, *Gramoty*, II, Part 2, 203).

[7] Memorandum by Prince A. A. Bezborodko, in A. A. Tsagareli, *Gramoty*, II, Part 2, 194–95.

[8] Butkov, *Materialy*, II, 447.

Giorgi lost no time in sending Prince G. Avalishvili to St. Petersburg with formal notification of his accession to the throne and the request that his eldest son, David, might be officially recognized as heir-apparent. Although nothing was said in the Russo-Georgian treaty about imperial recognition of heirs-apparent to the throne of K'art'lo-Kakhet'i, Giorgi hoped by this move to counteract the maneuvers of the Queen Dowager Darejan in favor of his half-brother Yulon, and to nullify the revised order of succession which Erekle had been bullied into signing at the end of his reign. The king's request was favorably received at St. Petersburg and the Georgian throne guaranteed to Giorgi and his posterity by an imperial rescript of April 18, 1799, in which David Batonishvili was specifically recognized as heir-apparent.[9]

Now that Paul's interest in Georgia was aroused, he showed himself as jealous of Russia's influence there as he had earlier been indifferent. The terms of the instructions given to the imperial envoy, State Councilor Peter Ivanovich Kovalenskii, were more appropriate for a viceroy than a simple diplomatic agent. He was to guard against the intrigues of the queen dowager; to prevent border clashes on the Turkish frontier; to encourage the settlement of Armenian communities in Georgia under their own *meliks* or provosts, and to secure privileges for them from the Georgian king; to assist in the formation of a native militia on European lines, which would operate in concert with the Russian garrison to be sent to Tiflis; to improve the commercial situation of Transcaucasia; and to hinder the military resurgence of Persia, and draw the Moslem khans of the Caucasus into the Russian orbit. He was to supervise the king's conduct of affairs, and see that "nothing was ever done contrary to the interest of the Imperial court."[10]

The internal and external state of K'art'lo-Kakhet'i was going from bad to worse. The Lezghian raids did not abate. The khan of

---

[9] A. A. Tsagareli, *Gramoty*, II, Part 2, 204–5; Avalov, *Prisoedinenie Gruzii k Rossii*, pp. 174–75. To avoid the precipitation of a civil war on Erekle's death, Giorgi had signed an undertaking that the throne would pass, after his own decease, to Yulon Batonishvili. By securing Paul's recognition of David as heir, Giorgi hoped to nullify this undertaking. See Document of December 8, 1797, in T'aqaishvili, ed., *Sak'art'velos sidzveleni*, I, Part 1 (1920) 223.

[10] Berzhe and others, eds., *Akty sobrannye Kavkaz.*, I, 93–96. Kovalenskii's instructions are dated April 16, 1799.

Shusha renounced his traditional allegiance to the Georgian crown in order to make his peace with the new shah. A Persian envoy arrived at Tiflis to browbeat the king into submission to the shah, and, to quote a report of the time, "was amused from day to day with promises, till the arrangement, now about to be carried into effect, was made with the Emperor Paul." [11] Giorgi was obliged to take several thousand Lezghians into his service, but their unruly behavior only made security deteriorate still further. In his own household, it is alleged that even his consort Mariam deceived him, and that when the king used to give his favorite child the royal seals to play with, the queen was not above borrowing them to send out forged charters in the king's name. Relations between Giorgi and his stepmother and half-brothers grew so bad that he became fearful for his life.[12]

Abandoned by virtually all the royal house except his sons David, Ioane, and Bagrat, and faced with the threat of civil war, Giorgi was forced to the conclusion that something more than a formal protectorate was needed to insure the kingdom's survival. He decided to throw himself on the emperor's magnanimity, in the hope that Paul would consent to incorporate the country into the Russian Empire while respecting the national traditions and dynastic prerogatives of K'art'lo-Kakhet'i. In instructions given to his representatives G. Avalishvili and E. P'alavandishvili on September 7, 1799, Giorgi wrote:

Surrender my kingdom and domains immutably and according to Christian truth, and place them not under the protection of the Imperial Russian throne, but give them into its full authority and complete care, so that henceforth the kingdom of Georgia may be within the Russian Empire on the same footing as the other provinces of Russia.

Then humbly request the Emperor of all the Russias that, while taking the kingdom of Georgia under his complete authority, he will furnish me with his most gracious written undertaking that the royal dignity will not be removed from my house, but be transmitted from generation to generation as in the time of my ancestors.

[11] Report of Captain John Malcolm, in the archives of the India Office, London: Persia, XXII, 221.

[12] Sokolov, "Puteshestvie v Imeretiiu, 1802," in *Chteniia v Imp. Obshchestve,* Bk. IV, pp. 88–89; Dubrovin, *Georgii XII,* p. 64.

Likewise you are to submit to the Most Gracious Emperor a most humble petition for the bestowal upon me and my children, within the borders of the Russian Empire, of an appropriate grant of landed property, in complete hereditary possession, which grant will serve for me as a token of final submission.[13]

It will be seen from this document that Giorgi had in mind a conditional incorporation of K'art'lo-Kakhet'i into Russia, with purely nominal royal authority retained by the Bagratid dynasty under the supreme authority of the emperor. The position as he envisaged it would have resembled that prevailing in the later Safavi period, when the monarch was simultaneously king (*mep'e*) of his people, and from the Persian shah's point of view, viceroy (*vali*) of the Georgian provinces. The settlement Giorgi desired has often been achieved in other imperial systems. It would have been comparable to the status an Indian rajah held during the period of British rule of India. Indeed, the concept of such a division of spheres between the occupying power and the local potentate has long since become a commonplace of colonial practice. Under the Emperor Paul, however, this concept had no chance of acceptance in the Russian autocratic system, where the presence of any other royal power besides that of the emperor could never be tolerated.

Georgia at this time was in no position to hold out for terms. As a Russian statesman admitted in 1801, "the simple protectorate which Russia granted Georgia in 1783 had dragged this unfortunate land into an abyss of misfortune which led to its complete exhaustion." [14]

The Russian Resident Kovalenskii arrived at Tiflis on November 8, 1799, and was followed on the twenty-sixth by a Jäger regiment under Major General Ivan Petrovich Lazarev. The troops were enthusiastically welcomed by the populace. Giorgi received the resident in state, and donned the insignia of royalty sent to him by the emperor.[15]

[13] A. A. Tsagareli, *Gramoty,* II, Part 2, 287; Avalov, *Prisoedinenie Gruzii k Rossii,* pp. 289–90. There are unimportant divergences between the two readings. This document was not immediately transmitted to St. Petersburg. Kovalenskii, jealous of his position and authority as Russian resident, forced the king to recall his representatives pending further discussions at Tiflis. (Sokolov, "Puteshestvie v Imeretiiu, 1802," in *Chteniia v Imp. Obshchestve,* Bk. IV, p. 90.)

[14] *Arkhiv Gosudarstvennogo Soveta,* III, Part 2 (1878), 1197.

[15] Berzhe and others, eds., *Akty sobrannye Kavkaz.,* I, 98–99. Captain Malcolm,

Kovalenskii found the kingdom divided into several factions. There was the loyalist party, favoring the king's policy of conditional annexation by Russia, with Giorgi's son David to follow his father as hereditary viceroy under Russian suzerainty; there was the party of the Queen Dowager Darejan, with her sons Yulon, Wakhtang, and P'arnavaz, who stood for the maintenance of Georgian independence under a nominal Russian protectorate, the throne to go to Yulon after Giorgi's death; there was the extreme anti-Russian faction headed by Alexander Batonishvili, who fled the country in 1800 and took the side of Persia; and finally there were some dissidents who wished the Bagratid dynasty to be abolished altogether.

Kovalenskii's character and behavior did not help to restore concord. The resident soon showed himself to be a bureaucrat of overbearing disposition. Besides insulting members of the royal family, he quarreled openly with the Russian military commander.[16]

The king was nevertheless glad to be relieved of some of his responsibilities. Kovalenskii took over the conduct of Georgia's foreign relations with Persia and the Caucasian khans. He sent Ensign Merabov to inform the shah of his arrival in Tiflis, and to warn him to refrain from molestation of Georgia. The emperor sincerely desired friendship with Persia, but this must be conditional on the latter power's renunciation of all claims on K'art'lo-Kakhet'i.[17] As may be imagined, the shah was by no means gratified at the tenor of this communication. Merabov was received with threats, and had to return incognito to Tiflis via Resht and Baku. In the reply sent to Kovalenskii by Hajji Ibrahim, the Persian grand vazir, Georgia was categorized as an inalienable part of the Persian realm. Should Russia persist in her policy, Tiflis would be trampled beneath the feet of 60,000 of Persia's victorious warriors.[18]

The British ambassador to Persia, Malcolm, followed these exchanges with interest, and gives further details in his report to the government of India:

---

then on his first mission to Persia, reported that already, "it was universally said, Georgia was placed under the protection and had in fact become a province of Russia" (archives of the India Office, London: Persia, XXII, 145–46).

[16] Berzhe and others, eds., *Akty sobrannye Kavkaz.*, I, 99–102.

[17] Butkov, *Materialy,* II, 451–52.

[18] Berzhe and others, eds., *Akty sobrannye Kavkaz.*, I, 96–97.

The General Commanding at Teflis had sent a Russian officer to the King of Persia who was instructed to demand restoration of the Christian prisoners taken by his predecessor Aga Mohammad Khan from Georgia in the year 1795 and a reimbursement of the expenses which that act of violence had obliged the Russian Government to incur. . . . The King when informed of the message was so enraged that he wished to put the officer to death but had been diverted from that by his Minister who persuaded him to send an answer importing that he could not acknowledge the authority of the Russian General to send him any message, that the Emperor of Russia was a Sovereign as well as himself, and that if he had any wishes or demands he should make them known through an Ambassador properly accredited.[19]

In spite of the asperity of the Persian reply, great uneasiness was felt at Teheran. Nor was the British administration in India indifferent to the menace presented by the Russian advance in Transcaucasia. In July, 1801, Malcolm wrote to Wellesley:

At the time of my arrival in Persia, the French were in possession of Egypt, and the Russians had taken Georgia, and threatened further attack. Both of these nations had made overtures to the existing Governments of Persia and it was likely that both would make further attempts to connect themselves closely with that state, in which if they succeeded it was easy to foresee consequences most dangerous to the British interests in India might arise.[20]

It becomes clear from the same source that the Armenians of Tiflis placed great hopes for benefits in the Russian occupation, and that these hopes were deliberately fostered by the Russian government. An Armenian who had been in Tiflis in November, 1799, at the time of Kovalenskii's arrival, told Malcolm:

Two chief Armenians, Mulekee Jumsheed, son of Mulekee Shah Nasir, and Mulek Feridoon, son of Mulekee Begler, who had gone to the Court of Russia after the army was recalled on the death of the Empress, had come to Teflis fifteen days before Khaujeh Aratoon Isaiah [i.e., the informant] left it. They had received from the Emperor blue ribbons, which they wore round their necks, and by a golden chain fastened to each was suspended the picture of the Emperor Paul. This Khaujeh Aratoon saw; he learnt that they had been treated with great notice,

[19] Archives of the India Office, London: Persia, XXII, 437.
[20] Archives of the India Office, London: Persia, XXII, 580.

that each received an annual pension of 3,000 dollars, and they were told to return to Teflis and that they would find . . . that a favourable ear was given to their requests. Khaujeh Aratoon did not precisely know what these requests were, but believed that they were for the Emperor to extend his relief to the distressed and oppressed Armenians. He added that all the inhabitants of Georgia were rejoiced at the prospect of Russia granting them open and avowed protection and that they already esteemed themselves subjects of the Emperor.[21]

From Russian sources, it emerges that Paul had promised these Meliks that an Armenian national home would be established in Georgia under Russian patronage to provide a refuge for Armenians from Persia and Turkey. This settlement would be granted autonomy within the Georgian state.[22] Such a project naturally led the Armenians to look for support to the Russian authorities rather than the Georgian king. In this they were encouraged by the new Armenian catholicos, Joseph Argutinskii, who was devoted to Russian interests.[23] The Armenians' allegiance to the reigning dynasty of Georgia had already been undermined by Erekle's failure to provide the security necessary for peaceful prosecution of trade. When the time came for abolishing the monarchy, it was from the country nobility and peasantry rather than the Armenian-dominated urban burgess class that resistance arose.

The arrival of Russian forces enabled Giorgi to put into effect the course of action on which he had decided several months previously, namely to place his kingdom under the direct authority of the emperor. In April, 1800, an embassy consisting of Garsevan Tchavtchavadze, Giorgi Avalishvili and Eleazar P'alavandishvili set out for St. Petersburg bearing a memorandum of sixteen clauses, known as Prositel'nye Punkty, or Petitionary Articles, to which it was hoped the emperor would give his consent in return for Georgia's voluntary submission to the empire. The main provisions of these Punkty provided that Giorgi and his successors retain the title of king and

[21] Archives of the India Office, London: Persia, XXII, 220. The son of this Khoja (Khaujeh) Aratiun is mentioned by Sir Robert Ker Porter in his *Travels in Georgia, Persia, etc.,* I, 115.

[22] Butkov, *Materialy,* II, 450.

[23] *Ibid.,* 455; Sokolov, "Puteshestvie v Imeretiiu, 1802," in *Chteniia v. Imp. Obshchestve,* Bk. IV, p. 110.

continue to administer KʻartʻLo-Kakhetʻi—according to the laws of
the Russian state; that Russia maintain 6,000 men in the country and
garrison its strategic fortresses; that Russia send skilled artisans to
exploit Georgia's resources in precious metals; that the Turkish
frontier pashas be prevented from raiding the Georgian borderlands;
that all Georgian subjects, including nobility, clergy, merchants, and
artisans, enjoy the same rights and obligations as Russian subjects.[24]

While these envoys were en route, the shah's emissary arrived in
Tiflis with the Persian reply to Kovalenskii's representations. The
king refused him a private audience, and received him in the Russian resident's presence, declining to accede to the shah's demands.
Some ten thousand Persian troops, commanded by the shah's young
son ʻAbbas Mirza and the Sardar Sulayman Qajar, had concentrated
near Tabriz and marched on Maku with the intention of advancing
on Erivan and Tiflis. This news caused consternation in the Georgian capital. Kovalenskii conceived the futile plan of digging a
trench around the city walls to improve the defenses, but this only
resulted in uncovering the corpses of plague victims, leading to an
outbreak of pestilence.[25]

In July, 1800, the Russians' most determined opponent among the
Bagratid princes, Alexander Batonishvili, fled the country and
joined the Persian army in Azerbaijan. He brought encouraging reports of Georgian weakness and dissension, as a result of which the
Persians crossed the Araxes and moved toward the Kʻartʻlian frontier. Alexander's brothers Yulon, Wakhtang, and Pʻarnavaz, under
pretense of warding off the Persians, collected three thousand of
their followers and occupied the outskirts of Tiflis. In reality, they
planned to effect the escape of their mother, the queen dowager,
from the capital, where she was under surveillance, and to raise the
standard of revolt in the outlying provinces. Prompt action by the
Russian authorities in setting a guard over the queen's house prevented her from leaving the city. The princes' patriotic zeal now
left them. Disbanding their followers, they retired to their domains.[26]

On July 10, 1800, the emperor ordered General Knorring to send

[24] Berzhe and others, eds., *Akty sobrannye Kavkaz.*, I, 105, 179–81; Butkov,
Materialy, II, 461–62; Avalov, *Prisoedinenie Gruzii k Rossii*, pp. 291–97.

[25] Berzhe and others, eds., *Akty sobrannye Kavkaz.*, I, 105; Sokolov, "Puteshestvie
v Imeretiiu, 1802," in *Chteniia v Imp. Obshchestve*, Bk. IV, p. 92.

[26] Berzhe and others, eds., *Akty sobrannye Kavkaz.*, I, 108; Butkov, *Materialy*,

fresh troops to Georgia from the North Caucasian Line. In the event of a Persian invasion, the expeditionary force was to be increased to ten squadrons of cavalry and nine battalions of infantry, with artillery. This advance by the Persians did not materialize ultimately, for the shah's army retired in August from Erivan to Tabriz. The arrival of General Guliakov in Georgia with the Kabardian Musketeer regiment helped in September to restore Georgian morale.[27]

The king's illness was approaching its last phase. He was now virtually bedridden with dropsy. "The king," General Lazarev reported, "owing to the weakness of his health, shows himself rarely to his people, and is surrounded by men intent on indulging in ever increasing abuses. He brings on himself growing popular dissatisfaction."[28] In the summer of 1800, Giorgi was driven to appoint Kovalenskii and Ioane Batonishvili, the king's second son, administrators of the realm. Giorgi's last months were further saddened by estrangement from his eldest son and heir, David, which occurred, it appears, largely because of David's ill-fated love match with an Armenian commoner, contracted against the king's will.[29] He came to rely more on his second son, Ioane, a prince of high intelligence and courage, who now drew up a plan for reform of the monarchy, calling for a thorough overhaul of the financial and administrative system and a campaign for the extension of education. This project had the full support of the king, but the disintegration of the body politic had gone too far for it to be effected.[30]

Danger of invasion from another quarter was becoming imminent. Although Omar Khan of Avaria had been receiving a substantial annual contribution from Georgia in the guise of protection money, he decided to take advantage of the Persian threat to stage an invasion of Kakhet‘i. At the same time, he craftily applied to General

---

II, 453. General Lazarev commented in August, 1800: "The royal prince-magnates, brothers of the king, are striving with indecent eagerness toward a course of insubordination, collecting into a faction those discontented with the government, and directing matters toward revolt, disorder and anarchy" (Berzhe and others, eds., *Akty sobrannye Kavkaz.*, I, 143).

[27] Berzhe and others, eds., *Akty sobrannye Kavkaz.*, I, 134–36, 154–55.

[28] Berzhe and others, eds., *Akty sobrannye Kavkaz.*, I, 140.

[29] Article "David" in Polovtsov, *Russkii Biograficheskii Slovar'*.

[30] Lang, "Prince Ioann of Georgia," in *American Slavic and East European Review*, XI, 275.

Knorring for Russian protection and thereby lulled the suspicions of that bluff soldier. When the Persians retreated from Erivan, Alexander Batonishvili went over to Omar's camp and persuaded him to continue with his campaign plans. Alexander was also in touch with his disaffected brothers Yulon, Wakhtang, and Pʻarnavaz. It was arranged that Omar and Alexander would occupy Sagarejo in Kakhetʻi while the other princes manned the Dariel Pass and prevented Russian reinforcements from reaching Tiflis. The expeditionary corps could then be annihilated, and Yulon, Alexander, and their brothers would divide up the kingdom amongst themselves.

This grand strategy was fruitless because of the resolution of Generals Lazarev and Guliakov and the courage of Giorgi's sons Ioane and Bagrat. The Georgian army, with its artillery commanded by Ioane, together with two Russian battalions, joined battle with Omar on November 7, 1800, near the junction of the Rivers Iori and Alazan. Omar Khan was completely routed, leaving fifteen hundred men dead on the battlefield. Russian and Georgian losses were small. Alexander Batonishvili was wounded, while Omar Khan died some weeks after of chagrin combined with the effects of dipsomania. For this notable victory the two Russian generals and the Princes Ioane and Bagrat were decorated with the order of St. John of Jerusalem.[31]

The three Georgian envoys, Tchavtchavadze, Avalishvili, and Pʻalavandishvili, had reached St. Petersburg in the summer and had entered into negotiations with the College of Foreign Affairs.[32] The presence of this embassy at the Russian capital was considered to render Kovalenskii's mission redundant, especially as Tchavtchavadze gave an unfavorable account of his activities. The Russian resident was recalled by an imperial rescript dated August 3, 1800, and relations with the Georgian court were entrusted to General Lazarev.[33]

[31] Butkov, *Materialy*, II, 456–59; Berzhe and others, eds., *Akty sobrannye Kavkaz.*, I, 163–77.

[32] Note of the Georgian plenipotentiaries, dated June 24, 1800, in A. A. Tsagareli, *Gramoty*, II, Part 2, 292–94.

[33] Berzhe and others, eds., *Akty sobrannye Kavkaz.*, I, 109; A. A. Tsagareli, *Gramoty*, II, Part 2, 216.

Discussions of Giorgi's terms for having K'art'lo-Kakhet'i placed under the immediate authority of Russia lasted from June until November. They were conducted mainly by the president of the College of Foreign Affairs, the able but autocratic Count Fedor Vasil'evich Rostopchin, who was later to become celebrated as governor of Moscow in 1812.[34]

It must be borne in mind that these months were marked by extraordinary convulsions in Russian foreign policy, due principally to Paul's increasing megalomania, not to mention his general mental derangement. His admiration for Napoleon Bonaparte, combined with indignation at the British seizure of Malta, seat of his grand mastership, led him to break off relations with England in October, 1800. He planned to partition the Ottoman Empire with Napoleon. The Don Cossacks were to invade India by marching straight across the deserts of Central Asia. To offset the loss of their Mediterranean headquarters, Paul apparently planned to transfer the grand priory of the Knights of Malta to Georgia. These fantasies of the autocrat help to explain the peculiar and erratic fashion in which the Georgian question was handled during the last months of his reign.[35]

On November 15, 1800, the emperor wrote to General Knorring asking how many troops he could spare to garrison Georgia. He was ordered to take all practicable steps to reinforce the detachment already there. Finally, and very significantly, the emperor wrote: "The weakening of the king's health gives grounds for expecting his decease; you are therefore immediately to dispatch, as soon as this occurs, a proclamation in Our name that until Our consent is received no action should be taken even to nominate an heir to the Georgian throne."[36] In view of Paul's guarantee to King Giorgi, this measure shows a distinct lack of good faith.

Nothing of course was said to the Georgian delegation about these

---

[34] See the biography of Rostopchin in Polovtsov, *Russkii Biograficheskii Slovar'*. It is to be noted that Rostopchin was a personal friend of the future commander in chief of the Caucasus, General Pavel Dimitrievich Tsitsianov (Tsitsishvili), whose forebears had come to Russia with Wakhtang VI in 1724.

[35] In October, Paul was on the point of having Georgia evacuated once more (Butkov, *Materialy*, III, 324).

[36] Berzhe and others, eds., *Akty sobrannye Kavkaz.*, I, 177–78. These instructions were duly passed on to General Lazarev at Tiflis.

instructions to General Knorring. On November 19, they were notified of the emperor's approval of the conditions set forth in the Prositel'nye Punkty, including the provision that the title of King of K'art'lo-Kakhet'i should be retained by Giorgi and his posterity forever. Count Rostopchin signified to the envoys the emperor's desire that the document embodying these clauses be taken back to Tiflis for ratification by both the sovereign and the representatives of the Georgian nation. The delegates were then to return to St. Petersburg as plenipotentiaries not only of the king, but of the entire Georgian nation, to be present at the conclusion of a solemn bilateral act by which K'art'lo-Kakhet'i would be voluntarily incorporated into the Russian Empire.[37]

It is obvious that if the formalities for concluding the annexation had been carried through according to the procedure outlined above, no question would have arisen as to its legality and voluntary character. A mutual agreement would have been effected between two states in which the one was merged into the other with the consent, or at least the outward semblance of consent, of sovereign and people, with the local dynasty maintained as titular rulers. Had this been done, Georgian national pride would have been spared humiliation, and history would not have been confronted with a controversial problem of international law.

Leaving Prince Tchavtchavadze in St. Petersburg, Avalishvili and P'alavandishvili set out for Tiflis at the end of November, 1800, to secure official ratification and to rally public opinion in favor of the Prositel'nye Punkty. Recommending the envoys to the care of General Knorring, Count Rostopchin sent the latter instructions on precautions to be taken to insure the successful outcome of the project, concluding sententiously: "And thus we shall have the pleasure of participating in a transaction so pleasing to God and to the Emperor." [38]

During the first half of December, Paul suddenly decided to throw overboard the elaborate and, on the whole, quite admirable machinery devised by Rostopchin for Georgia's incorporation. With his usual impetuosity, he now insisted that the kingdom must be declared annexed forthwith and unilaterally.

---

[37] Butkov, *Materialy*, II, 461–63; Avalov, *Prisoedinenie Gruzii k Rossii*, p. 195.
[38] Berzhe and others, eds., *Akty sobrannye Kavkaz.*, I, 181–82.

GIORGI XII, LAST KING OF KʻARTʻLO-KAKHETʻI

DAVID BATONISHVILI, PRINCE-REGENT OF GEORGIA

Several factors contributed to this change of attitude. Prominent among these was the report of Count Apollo Musin-Pushkin, the eminent geologist, who had gone to Georgia to examine the country's mineral resources. Musin-Pushkin saw enough to convince him of the land's enormous potentialities, of which he sent a glowing description to the emperor, later fully substantiated, be it noted, by the industrial development of Georgia in the last hundred years. At the same time, Musin-Pushkin stressed the dangers confronting the country from civil strife and external foes, as well as the extensive opposition to the heir-apparent, David Batonishvili. He added a number of reflections on the advantages which Russia could expect to derive from the development of trade relations with Persia and India from Tiflis; on the importance of building up military bases there as a bastion against Turkey and Persia; and on the extent to which occupation of Transcaucasia would help in encircling Daghestan and securing the North Caucasian Line. If the emperor decided on annexation, Musin-Pushkin added, urgent action must be taken in view of Giorgi's approaching death.[39]

Reports in similar vein reached St. Petersburg from General Lazarev at Tiflis. According to him, the king's authority was reduced to the vanishing point. His heir, David, had made himself unpopular with the aristocracy by marrying beneath himself. The intrigues of the queen dowager threatened to provoke civil war. The people were discouraged from working by the prevailing insecurity and the exactions of the tax-farmers. The treasury could not pay the salaries of government officials, who therefore lived by extortion. Through the raids of the Persians and Lezghis, the population of Kʿartʿlo-Kakhetʿi had sunk to a catastrophically low level.[40]

The Russian government was aware that the Georgian delegates could not complete the journey from St. Petersburg to Tiflis and back in less than three months, especially in view of the lateness of the season. By this time, King Giorgi might well have died. There was no guarantee that the faction of Prince Yulon would not have seized

---

[39] Butkov, *Materialy,* II, 464–65; III, 329.

[40] Berzhe and others, eds., *Akty sobrannye Kavkaz.,* I, 184–86. General Knorring estimated in 1801 that the population of Kʿartʿlo-Kakhetʿi amounted to barely 35,000 families.

power, or at least prevented the king's Prositel'nye Punkty from being endorsed by the Georgian nation.

On December 17, 1800, the Imperial Council of State was summoned to deliberate on Count Musin-Pushkin's memorandum on Georgia, referred to the meeting by the emperor through the Procurator-General Peter Khrisanfovich Obol'ianinov. The majority of its members were against outright and unilateral annexation. When the minutes of the session were being written up in this sense, Obol'ianinov told the secretary of the council that the emperor's mind was already made up on the subject, and that he would be well advised to alter the minutes accordingly. Count Rostopchin, the foreign minister, agreed with this. The secretary therefore recorded that the Council of State, on account of King Giorgi's petition and the threat of civil war, resolved that "it depends on the supreme consent of His Imperial Majesty to establish peace in those lands, either by extending His intervention in local affairs, or by the complete annexation of the above-mentioned realm into His dominions." This utterly spurious minute was authenticated by the heir-apparent, Alexander Pavlovich.[41]

On the following day, the emperor signed a manifesto declaring K'art'lo-Kakhet'i annexed to the Russian crown. Nothing was said about the retention of the Bagratid dynasty as titular rulers, though all classes of Georgian society were promised the same privileges under Russia as they had enjoyed under their own kings.[42] Nevertheless, Paul let it be known that he intended to place Giorgi's heir at the head of the new administration, provided the latter could command popular allegiance. The emperor also was intent on carrying through the formal ceremony marking the union of Georgia with Russia on the return of the delegates from Tiflis, and had replicas of the state robes of the Georgian kings made for him to wear on this occasion. He also signified his pleasure that the leading Georgian nobles be made counts or barons of the Russian Empire.[43]

---

[41] Butkov, *Materialy*, III, 333–34; Avalov, *Prisoedinenie Gruzii k Rossii*, pp. 211–12; *Arkhiv Gosudarstvennogo Soveta*, II (1888), 881–82.

[42] *Polnoe Sobranie Zakonov*, No. 19,721. This manifesto was made public at St. Petersburg on January 18, 1801, and at Tiflis the following month.

[43] Butkov, *Materialy*, III, 334; Dubrovin, *Georgii XII*, pp. 177–80.

At Tiflis, the dying king impatiently awaited the arrival of his plenipotentiaries.[44] He was well aware of the likelihood that civil war would break out when he was dead, unless the executive power was assumed by the emperor. "Our land belongs to His Imperial Majesty," he wrote to General Lazarev on December 7, 1800, "and we have sworn this to the last drop of blood."[45] But Giorgi did not live to confirm the Act of Incorporation with Russia. While Avalishvili and P'alavandishvili were still on the North Caucasian steppes, King Giorgi died on December 28.[46]

[44] Sokolov, "Puteshestvie v Imeretiiu, 1802," in *Chteniia v Imp. Obshchestve*, Bk. IV, p. 100.

[45] Berzhe and others, eds., *Akty sobrannye Kavkaz.*, I, 183.

[46] Berzhe and others, eds., *Akty sobrannye Kavkaz.*, I, 188.

13

The Liquidation of the Monarchy in Eastern and Western Georgia 1800-1810

O N the death of King Giorgi at Tiflis, General Lazarev carried out the instructions he had received from St. Petersburg, and announced that no successor to the throne was to be installed for the time being. He set up a temporary administration consisting of himself, Ioane Batonishvili, and the secretary (*mdivani*) Egnate T'umanishvili.[1]

This action commended itself neither to Giorgi's heir, David Batonishvili, nor to the late king's half-brothers headed by Yulon. David's interests were ably served by his secretary, Prince Solomon Leonidze, who now set about organizing David's supporters and agitating for him to be formally proclaimed king.[2]

Yulon and P'arnavaz broke into open revolt, and started ravaging the domains of pro-Russian nobles and the supporters of David. Wakhtang Batonishvili stationed himself at Dushet'i, where he

[1] A. A. Tsagareli, *Gramoty,* II, Part 2, 296-97.

[2] Leonidze's grandfather was a Lezghian who had settled in Georgia and been baptized, his father, a priest at T'elavi. Leonidze had an aptitude for languages, and became secretary to Princess Anna, sister of Erekle II, and then to Erekle himself. For his public services he was made a prince and rewarded with extensive properties, but certain intrigues in which he was involved led to his disgrace. His eclipse continued through the reign of King Giorgi, and it was only at the latter's death that Leonidze returned to the political arena (Dubrovin, *Zakavkaz'e ot 1803-1806 goda,* pp. 177-78). See the biography by Tchitchinadze, *Solomon Leonidze.*

intercepted couriers passing between Tiflis and North Caucasia and threatened Russian military communications. The rural districts generally tended to support Yulon rather than David, and prayers for the former were offered up in many country churches.[3]

During this chaotic week, the delegates Avalishvili and P'alavandishvili were toiling over the Dariel Pass on their way to Tiflis. Arriving there on January 8, 1801, they duly presented to David Batonishvili, as King Giorgi's son and heir, the rescripts addressed by the Emperor Paul to the late monarch. The Russian government had after all recognized David as the rightful heir, so this was certainly the correct course of action. They could not know of the *volte-face* which had since occurred in the emperor's mind.

The arrival of the envoys reinforced David's position. On the strength of the emperor's letters to King Giorgi, David issued on January 15 a proclamation stating that he had been authorized to draw near to the throne of his fathers. Following Giorgi's policy, David and General Lazarev drafted a fresh set of conditions for the incorporation of K'art'lo-Kakhet'i into Russia, to which members of the aristocracy and prominent citizens flocked to affix their signature. On January 18 the delegates set out on their return journey to the Russian capital. But just as they had failed to find their king alive when they returned to Tiflis, so they were not fated to see the Emperor Paul on their arrival at St. Petersburg. They had just reached Moscow when he was assassinated on the night of March 11–12, 1801.[4]

The manifesto of December 18, 1800, declaring the kingdom of K'art'lo-Kakhet'i annexed to Russia, was received and published in Tiflis on February 16 and 17 of the following year. David Batonishvili was naturally bewildered and resentful at this high-handed action. At the same time, the uncertainty which conflicting instructions had produced in General Lazarev's mind permitted David to remain for several months the effective prince-regent of Georgia.[5]

[3] Sokolov, "Puteshestvie v Imeretiiu, 1802," in *Chteniia v Imp. Obshchestve*, Bk. IV, pp. 102–6.

[4] Butkov, *Materialy*, II, 470–72; Sokolov, "Puteshestvie v Imeretiiu, 1802," in *Chteniia v Imp. Obshchestve*, Bk. IV, pp. 104–5; A. A. Tsagareli, *Gramoty*, II, Part 2, 217–21.

[5] Berzhe and others, eds., *Akty sobrannye Kavkaz.*, I, 297; Sokolov, "Puteshestvie v Imeretiiu, 1802," in *Chteniia v Imp. Obshchestve*, Bk. IV, p. 115.

The Georgian question was one of the first problems to demand the attention of the Emperor Alexander I. His father, as we have seen, had categorically declared Kʻartʻlo-Kakhetʻi annexed. On the other hand, the delegates from the princes and people of Georgia had now arrived to ask for the country to be incorporated by mutual agreement, on condition that the Bagratid dynasty were maintained as vassal rulers, with a mixed Russo-Georgian administration under the imperial aegis. Strangely enough, this obvious and equitable solution did not commend itself to Alexander and his advisers, and the matter was discussed during the ensuing six months without the participation of the Georgian delegation.[6]

The Georgian problem was deliberated in the Imperial Council of State on April 11 and 15, 1801. The new procurator general, N. A. Bekleshov, informed the meeting of the tsar's aversion to appropriating a territory to which he had no title, and thereby wronging the legitimate heir, David Batonishvili. The council responded by expressing respect for the tsar's honorable scruples, but recommended that Paul's manifesto of annexation should nevertheless be kept in force. The retention of Georgia, it was urged, was essential to the prestige of the Russian monarchy; feuds in the Georgian royal family and the threat of invasion from Persia and Daghestan made such action essential for the preservation of the Georgian people; it was important to safeguard the North Caucasian Line from Turkish infiltration into Transcaucasia; according to the report of Count Musin-Pushkin, Russia would derive great wealth from the land's unexplored mineral resources. It is noteworthy that the meeting deferred on these points to the judgment of Generals Platon and Valerian Zubov, both members of the Council of State, and both former active participators in Catherine's expansionary policy in the Near East.

The council accordingly resolved that "the protection which Russia

[6] A. A. Tsagareli, *Gramoty*, II, Part 2, 226–40; Butkov, *Materialy*, II, 485; Akaki Papava, "Sakʻartʻvelos sakitʻkhi da rusetʻis sakhelmdsipʻo sabtcho," in *Mamuli*, No. 4 (Buenos Aires, 1951), p. 105. It is noteworthy that the head of the Asiatic Department of the College of Foreign Affairs, S. L. Lashkarev, was a supporter of incorporation by negotiation and mutual consent, though his advice was ignored (A. A. Tsagareli, *Gramoty*, II, Part 2, 224–25). Lashkarev was descended from the Georgian family of Lashkʻarashvili, of the Gori district of Kʻartʻli.

formerly accorded to Georgia has so many mutual disadvantages that there is no middle way between complete abandonment of the country and making it subject to the Empire." It recommended that General Knorring be sent to Tiflis to set up a temporary administration, and that he report back on the situation of the land. To satisfy the emperor's scruples, he was to find out whether in fact the population was unanimous in wishing to become subject to Russia.[7]

General Knorring arrived at Tiflis on May 22, 1801. Finding the Prince-Regent David wielding virtually despotic power, he at once removed him from all authority and set up a provisional government of four Georgian noblemen under the presidency of General Lazarev. "Four rogues and one fool are governing the whole country," David wrote soon after to Prince Beglar Orbeliani, "Get them to remove this son of a dog [i.e., Lazarev] from us."[8]

The commander in chief was in a great hurry to complete his mission and did not attempt to organize a properly conducted plebiscite. He summoned members of various social groupings to sound them out on their dispositions, and hastened back to St. Petersburg. A soldier without political experience, Knorring was not the ideal person for so delicate a commission. Having already taken a prominent part in Paul's annexation of Georgia, it was hardly to be expected that he would let this acquisition slip from his grasp, especially when he had every reason to expect that Georgia would come under his own command. Knorring's report therefore underlined the desperate state of the country and the joy of the more enlightened sections of the community at the prospect of being taken under direct Russian rule. He expressed a low opinion of the qualities of the heir to the throne, David Batonishvili, even casting doubt on his constitutional right to the succession.[9]

In the meantime, the Council of State had received petitions from the Queen Dowager Darejan asking that Georgia be left under a simple protectorate as provided by the Treaty of 1783, and from David Batonishvili, requesting that he be permitted to inherit the throne of his ancestors. David also wrote personally in this sense to

[7] *Arkhiv Gosudarstvennogo Soveta,* III, Part 2 (1878), 1189–94.

[8] Sokolov, "Puteshestvie v Imeretiiu, 1802," in *Chteniia v Imp. Obshchestve,* Bk. IV, pp. 117–21; Dubrovin, *Georgii XII,* pp. 216–17.

[9] Butkov, *Materialy,* II, 476–84.

Platon Zubov, the most ardent advocate of unconditional annexation. The Council of State shelved these applications until Knorring's recommendations had been considered.[10]

On July 24, 1801, four days before Knorring presented his report, the tsar received from two of the most respected Russian statesmen of the day, Counts A. R. Vorontsov and Viktor Kochubei, a carefully reasoned memorandum in which the arguments of the Zubov–Musin-Pushkin group were subjected to strong criticism. Vorontsov was a veteran liberal who had suffered disgrace for his opinions under Catherine the Great; Kochubei, a member of Alexander's Neglasnyi Komitet, or Confidential Committee, had been vice chancellor under Paul, and was subsequently minister of the interior.

According to the two statesmen's memorandum, the strategic necessity for liquidating the monarchy of K'art'lo-Kakhet'i was much exaggerated, as were the profits to be gained from the country's mineral resources. It would be both just and feasible to constitute K'art'lo-Kakhet'i a vassal kingdom under Russian sovereignty and military protection, with one of the royal princes as titular ruler. The authors of the memorandum pointed out that Alexander had renounced the chimerical Eastern projects of his father and grandmother, and had no need to extend his vast dominions. Furthermore, the emperor's honor would be compromised by the perpetration of a flagrant wrong toward the Bagratid house.[11]

On August 8, the Council of State met to consider Knorring's report and the memorandum of Vorontsov and Kochubei. The majority professed themselves convinced by Knorring's arguments, notably that neither David nor Yulon could command unqualified allegiance in K'art'lo-Kakhet'i, that the vast majority of the people desired Russian rule, and that "the internal and external situation of this country is indeed such that it cannot by its own strength either withstand the ambitious encroachments of Persia, or repel the raids of the mountain tribes surrounding it." The council considered that it would be impracticable and humiliating for Russia to retreat from

[10] *Arkhiv Gosudarstvennogo Soveta,* III, Part 2 (1878), 1195–96; A. A. Tsagareli, *Gramoty,* II, Part 2, 299–300.

[11] *Arkhiv Gosudarstvennogo Soveta,* III, Part 2 (1878), 1200–7; Avalov, *Prisoedinenie Gruzii k Rossii,* pp. 226–34.

a position to which she was already committed by Paul's manifesto of annexation. Vorontsov and Kochubei dissenting, the tsar was advised to abolish entirely the monarchy of K'art'lo-Kakhet'i.[12]

Still Alexander was not convinced, and continued, as was his wont, to vacillate between idealistic impulses and realistic considerations. To add to his perplexity, the Zubovs prepared a fresh memorandum on the subject, designed to discredit the arguments of Vorontsov and Kochubei. The emperor decided to refer the whole question to his group of intimate advisers, the Neglasnyi Komitet.[13] The relevant papers were passed to Novosil'tsov and Stroganov for their comments.

The question was discussed at a meeting of the emperor with his committee on August 13, 1801. According to the record of the proceedings kept by Count Stroganov, the tsar recounted to his advisers the motives that had impelled the Council of State to advocate unconditional annexation. Kochubei retorted that these motives were of dubious validity: the population's wishes had not been clearly ascertained, and the interests of both countries could be perfectly well served by a protectorate. This protectorate, Kochubei added, had been illusory hitherto only because it had been the will of Catherine the Great to render it so: her aim was to carve a route to attack the Ottoman Empire, and it had been to her advantage to weaken the Georgians and make them incapable of defending themselves. Kochubei challenged the veracity of Musin-Pushkin's estimate of Georgia's natural resources.

The tsar said that he was satisfied that Georgia's resources were as Musin-Pushkin stated. He conceded, however, that General Knorring had privately admitted to having colored his report so as to give the strongest grounds for annexing K'art'lo-Kakhet'i, thinking that this would be pleasing to the emperor. Alexander told the committee that the worthy general had been quite astonished to find his imperial master so reluctant to seize this opportunity. On being pressed, Knorring had admitted that if the tsar so desired, it would be perfectly feasible to establish a simple protectorate.

[12] *Arkhiv Gosudarstvennogo Soveta*, III, Part 2 (1878), 1196–99; Avalov, *Prisoedinenie Gruzii k Rossii*, pp. 237–40.

[13] The Committee's members were Count P. A. Stroganov, N. N. Novosil'tsov, Count V. P. Kochubei, and Prince A. A. Czartoryski.

"As for us," Count Stroganov concludes his record of this discussion,

we persisted in the idea that it was essential to avoid uniting this country to the Russian crown, and the Emperor continued to remain undecided between the advice of his Council of State and the opposite course, for which he seemed to have a personal preference.[14]

After all this procrastination, it was the proposal of the Zubov–Musin-Pushkin group which won the emperor's final assent. He accepted the recommendation of the Council of State that the kingdom of K'art'lo-Kakhet'i be abolished once and for all and the Bagratid line removed from power. This decision is an excellent example of the duality in Alexander's character. While professing genuine zeal for liberal and high-minded ideals, when it came to the point of decision, Alexander had a way of adopting courses of action quite inconsistent with his avowed principles, and of even throwing to the wolves, as in the case of Speranskii, his idealistic advisers and friends. With regard to the Georgian question, he showed himself more autocratic even than his father. To the very end of his life, Paul had intended to go through the face-saving ceremonial of concluding a solemn bilateral agreement with the Georgian delegation, and of leaving the Bagratid line at least the shadow of royal dignity.

The manifesto confirming the annexation of K'art'lo-Kakhet'i to the Russian scepter was drafted by Platon Zubov. It is a model of its kind. The defenseless state of the country and the threat of civil war, together with the unanimous desire of the population, were cited as the reasons why Russia was now induced to undertake the burden of governing Georgia. The manifesto took pains to refute any accusation of self-interest on the part of the Russian government. The tsar was going to turn over all the country's revenue to its own use, and to observe the prerogatives and rights of every class of the community. The oath of allegiance to the tsar was to be taken by each social order as a pledge of fidelity.[15] The manifesto was published

---

[14] These minutes of the meetings of the Neglasnyi Komitet were published by the Grand-Duke Nikolai Mikhailovich, in *Graf Pavel Aleksandrovich Stroganov* (St. Petersburg, 1903), Vol. II. The session of August 13, 1801, is recorded on pages 90–95.

[15] *Polnoe Sobranie Zakonov*, Vol. XXVI, No. 20,007; Butkov, *Materialy*, II, 485–88; Avalov, *Prisoedinenie Gruzii k Rossii*, pp. 303–7; Dubrovin, *Zakavkaz'e ot 1803–1806 goda*, pp. 27–30.

at Moscow on September 12, 1801, three days before the emperor's coronation.

Simultaneously there was made public the new system of administration for Eastern Georgia, drafted by Platon Zubov and P. G. Butkov. The country was divided into five districts or *uezdy* on the Russian model, three in K'art'li and two in Kakhet'i, with administrative centers Tiflis, Gori, Dushet'i, T'elavi, and Sighnaghi. The commander in chief of the Caucasian Line was the supreme head of the central government at Tiflis, with executive authority vested in a council of Russian and Georgian officials headed by the commander in chief's deputy, the administrator, or *pravitel'*, of Georgia. The administration was divided into four "expeditions," the executive, the financial, and the criminal and civil judiciaries. Each "expedition" was to be headed by a Russian official over four Georgian councilors. Corresponding local administrations were to be set up in the country districts under Russian *kapitan-ispravniki*, or district officers. The mountain P'shavs, Khevsurs, and T'ushians, and the Tatar nomads of the southern borderlands, continued to be governed by Georgian *mouravs*. For civil litigation, the code of King Wakhtang remained in force, while criminal cases were to be judged according to Russian law.[16]

The unilateral abolition of kingship in K'art'lo-Kakhet'i did not pass without protest. Ioane Batonishvili, who had come to St. Petersburg, secured a copy of the manifesto of September 12 before it was published and sent it to his brother, David Batonishvili. Ioane advised him to organize a national petition to the emperor to have the royal title maintained in the Bagratid line. Ioane's letters were intercepted by the Russian authorities and his efforts rendered abortive.[17] The Georgian plenipotentiaries Tchavtchavadze, Avalishvili, and P'alavandishvili expressed their regret at the emperor's unilateral and high-handed action in a note which they addressed to the vice chancellor, Prince Kurakin. The envoys complained with justification that they had not even been notified of the tsar's

[16] Butkov, *Materialy*, II, 488–94; Khachapuridze, *K istorii Gruzii pervoi poloviny*, pp. 56–57.

[17] Berzhe and others, eds., *Akty sobrannye Kavkaz.*, I, 306; *Arkhiv Gosudarstvennogo Soveta*, III, Part 2 (1878), 1210. David also attempted to enlist the aid of the khan of Erivan in support of his cause, promising him the district of Pambak' if he would help him to regain power.

decision before the Manifesto was promulgated, in spite of the fact that they had been instrumental in setting the negotiations in motion. As a result of the Russian government's action, the envoys had been exposed to the reproach of disloyalty to their country, and to the abuse of their compatriots.[18]

It was now too late to modify the course of events. For over two hundred years, the tsars of Russia had styled themselves "Lords of the Iberian land and the Georgian kings," and now this honorific title had become reality with a vengeance. Petitions continued to be received, urging the claims of David or Yulon to be head of the Georgian administration, but the emperor stuck to his decision. No one can blame the Georgians for desiring to retain at least some vestige of self-government within the framework of the Russian Empire. Nor is it easy to censure Alexander for taking steps to incorporate the former kingdom so thoroughly as to shield it permanently from its hostile neighbors and make impossible the recurrence of the tragedy of 1795. The Russian concept of bureaucratic and centralized government had collided headlong with the Georgian idea of loose-knit, feudal relations, and the stronger party prevailed.

On April 12, 1802, Knorring published in Tiflis the imperial proclamation of September 12, 1801, confirming Paul's earlier decree and declaring K'art'lo-Kakhet'i part of the Russian Empire. When administering to the princes and notables of Georgia the oath of allegiance to the tsar, the general saw fit to surround the audience hall with armed guards and make it clear that refractory individuals might expect rigorous treatment. A few persons who gave voice to their resentment at this abuse of force were taken into temporary custody. Such action naturally offended the representatives of a nation deemed to have voluntarily placed itself under Russian suzerainty.[19]

In the following month, the new central and regional administration was formally installed.[20] Knorring's deputy, the *pravitel'* of Georgia, was the same Kovalenskii who had made himself so unpopular as resident at the Georgian court under Giorgi XII.

During the first two years of Russian rule, the internal situation

[18] A. A. Tsagareli, *Gramoty*, II, Part 2, 300–301.
[19] Khachapuridze, *K istorii Gruzii pervoi poloviny*, p. 60.
[20] Butkov, *Materialy*, III, 350–52.

left much to be desired. The Queen Dowager Darejan continued to intrigue in favor of Yulon's cause. In July, 1802, sixty-nine members of the nobility of Kakhet'i issued a statement professing loyalty to the tsar but requesting Yulon's installation as head of the Georgian government. The Russian authorities interpreted this as a threat of insurrection, and made a number of arrests. Marauding parties of Lezghis on their agile mountain horses continued to roam about the countryside, defying the less mobile Russian garrisons. The Ossetes inhabiting the Caucasian mountain fastnesses in the vicinity of the Dariel Pass held up travelers and convoys at will. Trade was virtually at a standstill, and the peasantry scarcely ventured out to till the fields.[21]

With the fall of the Eastern Georgian monarchy, the only remaining king in Transcaucasia was Solomon II of Imeret'i. The court of K'ut'ais now became a hotbed of anti-Russian intrigue. Leonidze, the leading partisan of the former Prince-Regent David, was appointed secretary to King Solomon. The royal princes Yulon, P'arnavaz, and Alexander, uncles of the king, made their headquarters in Imeret'i.

Prince Zurab Tseret'eli, the king's lord chamberlain and principal minister, and a former envoy to Russia, attempted without success to restrain his master from a policy which could lead only to disaster. Solomon was deaf to his advice. In March, 1802, bribed by Sherif Pasha of Akhaltsikhe, Solomon and Alexander Batonishvili treacherously murdered a rival claimant to that governorate, Sabid Pasha, who had taken refuge in Imeret'i. Sabid Pasha had been known to favor friendship with Russia. In the same year an emissary, A. E. Sokolov, was sent by the Russian court to induce Solomon to free Constantine, the son of the former King David of Imeret'i, who was being held as a prisoner of state. David's widow had sought the intercession of the tsar as Solomon was thought to be planning to put the young prince to death. Solomon refused to free Constantine, though the threat of armed force, combined with judicious bribery of his courtiers, later made him change his mind.[22]

[21] Report of Count A. Musin-Pushkin, August 20, 1802, in *Arkhiv Gosudarstvennogo Soveta,* III, Part 2 (1878), 1220–33.

[22] Sokolov, "Puteshestvie v Imeretiiu, 1802," in *Chteniia v Imp. Obshchestve,* Bk. IV, pp. 29–30, 65–77; Dubrovin, *Zakavkaz'e ot 1803–1806 goda,* pp. 188–89.

In the autumn of 1802, Solomon was concerting plans with Alexander Batonishvili, now in Azerbaijan, and the Persian General Pir-Quli-Khan, for a joint invasion of Eastern Georgia. The arrival of Russian reinforcements as well as the lack of cohesion among the anti-Russian groupings brought these plans to nought.[23]

Seeing little improvement in the state of the country, the people began to lose faith in the Russian administration. Kovalenskii was not the man to restore it. Insufferable in his relations with the late King Giorgi, he now showed himself to be a dishonest and autocratic administrator. He set out to enrich himself by disreputable speculations in the Tiflis bazaar, and allotted key positions in the government to his relatives and friends. The Georgian councilors provided for in the imperial statute were not appointed, and corruption and abuse of authority went unchecked. Russian official documents of the time show that rape and other acts of violence were committed by Russian functionaries and soldiery. Knorring's successor, Prince Tsitsianov, alludes in one of his reports to "the crying abuses of authority committed by the former *pravitel'* of Georgia," which had "gone beyond the Georgian people's limits of patience."[24] Even the official Russian historiographer of the Caucasus, A. P. Berzhe, remarks that

Kovalenskii and Company did not remove, but aggravated the abuses from which the Georgian people so grievously suffered. . . . Disappointed hope for improvement turned into ill-will, discontent, and impotent resentment, in fact the very impulses from which derive rebellion and revolt against supreme authority.[25]

But Kovalenskii could not prevent rumors of his nefarious activities from reaching St. Petersburg. Count Kochubei reported to the tsar in a meeting of the Neglasnyi Komitet that Knorring and his deputy "were committing great exactions; that they were maintaining discord among the peoples of the country in order to be able to pillage them with more ease; and all kinds of similar horrors."[26] Alexander realized the need for a governor who com-

---

[23] Butkov, *Materialy*, II, 544–45.
[24] Dubrovin, *Zakavkaz'e ot 1803–1806 goda*, pp. 49–53; Berzhe, "Prisoedinenie Gruzii k Rossii," in *Russkaia Starina*, XXVIII, 8.
[25] Berzhe, "Prisoedinenie Gruzii k Rossii," in *Russkaia Starina*, XXVIII, 7, 381.
[26] Grand-Duke Nikolai Mikhailovich, *Stroganov*, II, 171.

bined courage and integrity with knowledge of local conditions and decided to replace Knorring and Kovalenskii with General Pavel Dimitrievich Tsitsianov. A scion of the K'art'lian princely family of Tsitsishvili, Tsitsianov was an officer with a distinguished record in the Russian army and had been commandant of Baku during Valerian Zubov's campaign of 1796. He was a distant relative of the widow of Giorgi XII, Queen Mariam, who had been a Princess Tsitsishvili. In the letter of appointment addressed to Tsitsianov on September 8, 1802, Alexander directed him to introduce order and prosperity into the country and to show the Georgian people that "it would never have cause to repent of having entrusted its destiny to Russia." He was given full powers to annul the arbitrary measures put into force by Kovalenskii, and instructed to take immediate steps to persuade—if necessary by force—the former Georgian royal family to settle in Russia and thus put an end to agitation for Bagratid restoration.[27]

Tsitsianov arrived at Tiflis on February 1, 1803. His first task was to remove the remaining members of the Bagratid line. On February 18, the former Prince-Regent David and his Uncle Wakhtang Batonishvili, set out for St. Petersburg under military escort. A few days later, T'eimuraz, the fourth son of King Giorgi, succeeded in escaping to Persia, though in 1810 he voluntarily returned and joined the émigré group in Russia. In April, Tsitsianov learned that Giorgi's widow Mariam was preparing to flee to the mountain strongholds of Khevsuret'i. He sent General Lazarev to warn the queen that her plan had been revealed and that she would shortly be sent to Russia. Infuriated at the humiliations that she had suffered at the hands of the Russian authorities, the queen drew a dagger and stabbed the general to death. She was arrested and sent the same day to expiate her deed by seven years' incarceration in the Belogorodskii Convent at Voronezh. The Queen Dowager Darejan, the most determined and resourceful adversary of the occupying power—"that Hydra," as Tsitsianov termed her—managed to hold out until October, when she too was forced to leave. Her sons Yulon and P'arnavaz were captured by force in 1804 and sent to

[27] Dubrovin, *Zakavkaz'e ot 1803–1806 goda,* pp. 54–58. For the biography of Tsitsianov, see the account in Polovtsov, *Russkii Biograficheskii Slovar'.* Tsitsianov's grandfather Paata had served in the Georgian Hussar regiment of the Russian army.

Russia the following year. Their brother Alexander was the only prominent member of the royal family permanently to evade being sent to Russia; he remained in Persia, often at the shah's court and army headquarters, until his death in 1844.[28]

Except for Queen Mariam, the members of the late ruling house were generously and honorably treated by the emperor. Substantial pensions were allotted to them, and every encouragement was held out to the royal princes to enter or resume service in the Russian army and administration. David, the former prince-regent, was promoted to lieutenant general and made a senator. Of David's younger brothers, Bagrat was also appointed a senator, while T'eimuraz was elected an honorary member of the Imperial Academy of Sciences. Their Uncle Mirian Batonishvili also became a senator.[29]

During the first year of Tsitsianov's viceroyalty, Russian power rapidly expanded its grip on Transcaucasia. In the spring of 1803, General Guliakov attacked and subdued the Lezghian tribesmen of Jaro-Belakani. Intervention in the affairs of Armenia resulted in the elevation of the Catholicos Daniel to the Patriarchal See of Echmiadzin in defiance of the khan of Erivan's support for the rival candidate, Archbishop David. In Western Georgia, the hostilities carried on by King Solomon II against his former loyal supporter, Grigol Dadian of Mingrelia, forced the latter to sue for Russian help. The principality of Mingrelia, a ruler of which had first sworn fealty to Russia as long ago as 1638, was finally taken under direct protection in December, 1803. In contrast to Eastern Georgia, the local administration was left to the princely house, which retained control under Russian supervision until the Dadianate was finally abolished in 1857.[30]

King Solomon of Imeret'i, though irreconcilably hostile to Russia,

[28] Dubrovin, Zakavkaz'e ot 1803–1806 goda, pp. 80–90; 146, 209, 371.

[29] See the genealogical tables drawn up by M.-F. Brosset as a supplement to Histoire de la Géorgie, Vol. II, Part 1, and Toumanoff's article "Materialy k genealogii Bagratidov," Novik (New York), 1950.

[30] Dubrovin, Zakavkaz'e ot 1803–1806 goda, pp. 91–101, 151; extracts from the manuscript chronicle by Nikoloz Dadiani, published by E. T'aqaishvili, ed., in Sbornik Materialov dlia Opisaniia Mestnostei i Plemen Kavkaza, XXXI, 71–73. Grigol Dadian died suddenly in 1804 and was succeeded by his son Levan.

now thought it best to feign submission in order to prevent the Dadian from invoking military intervention against him. Leonidze was sent to St. Petersburg with a set of conditions on which Solomon was ready to accept Russian suzerainty. These proved unacceptable and were rejected, especially as it was learned that Solomon had murdered one of the Dadian's representatives to Russian headquarters. After much procrastination, Tsitsianov threatened to invade Imeret'i if Solomon did not give in. Some of the foremost court officials accepted Russian gold in return for exerting their influence on the obstinate monarch. Finally Solomon capitulated, and his dominions were placed under the Imperial aegis in 1804 under a guarantee similar to that given to the Dadian.[31]

Meanwhile, the storming of Ganja by Prince Tsitsianov on January 3, 1804, had delivered into Russian hands one of the key fortresses of Azerbaijan. Javat Khan, a bitter enemy of Erekle and a participant in Agha Mohammed's invasion of Georgia in 1795, was killed on the battlements. The town was renamed Elizavetpol'. This success enhanced Russian prestige to such an extent that for the time being, to use Dubrovin's metaphor, the potentates of neighboring khanates took on a demeanor of lamb-like meekness.[32]

Tsitsianov now judged the moment ripe for an expedition against Erivan, especially as it was learned that the Persians were massing a large army around Tabriz in preparation for an assault on Russia's Transcaucasian possessions. On June 20, a Russian detachment some 5,000 strong under the commander in chief routed 20,000 Persians under Crown Prince 'Abbas Mirza near Echmiadzin, and laid siege to Erivan. Harried by Persian light cavalry and often cut off from their sources of supply, the besiegers made little progress. At the beginning of September, a council of war decided, Tsitsianov dissenting, to abandon the siege.[33]

A contributory cause of the failure of this expedition was the rising which had broken out along the Georgian military highway. This is notable as the first of many spontaneous mass revolts against

[31] Dubrovin, *Zakavkaz'e ot 1803–1806 goda*, p. 528; Manvelishvili, *Ruset'i da Sak'art'velo*, I, 266–72.

[32] Dubrovin, *Zakavkaz'e ot 1803–1806 goda*, pp. 231–42.

[33] A full account of the campaign is given in Dubrovin, *Zakavkaz'e ot 1803–1806 goda*, Chapter XVII, and in Baddeley, *Russian Conquest of the Caucasus*, p. 69.

Russian rule; it bore an unmistakably popular character which distinguished it from earlier movements of disaffection confined to the
royal house and the aristocracy. The immediate reason for the outbreak was the brutality of the Russian commandants in the Dariel
Pass and Ananuri sectors. The Ossete mountaineers and the villagers of Mt'iulet'i had been treated like slave laborers and beasts
of burden. Those who refused to toil on the roads without payment
were brutally beaten, some dying from their injuries, while others
perished from cold in clearing away snowdrifts. Driven to desperation, the peasants murdered the town commandant of Ananuri. The
insurgents were joined by contingents of the Khevsurs and other
mountain clans. Encouraging messages were sent to them from
Prince Yulon and the shah of Persia. They defeated a regiment of
Don Cossacks sent from the North Caucasian Line, cut communications with Russia, and menaced Gori. The onset of autumn and the
arrival of fresh forces gradually strengthened Tsitsianov's hand, and
the revolt was, little by little, brought under control. Brutal reprisals
ensued, a number of families imprisoned in the fortress of Gori
being left to die of hunger and cold.[34]

Amidst all these warlike activities, Tsitsianov found time to at-
tend to the reorganization of Georgian civic and economic life.
With regard to the social order, little fundamental change was attempted in the prevailing class structure. The nobility were confirmed in their privileges and given the same powers over their serfs
as exercised by Russian landowners. Members of the aristocracy
whose estates had been confiscated by the Georgian royal family
were reinstated in them. The bourgeoisie of the towns were afforded
special protection and encouragement in view of the need to stimu-
late commerce and the beginnings of industry. Tsitsianov clearly
envisaged the urgency of improving trade and communications generally in order to feed and clothe the Russian garrison, increase the
customs and excise revenues, and make the country self-supporting.
For some years, however, wars and internal disturbances discouraged
infant enterprises, and the occupation was a substantial drain on the
Russian treasury. In 1811, a million silver rubles had to be sent to pay

[34] Khachapuridze, *K istorii Gruzii pervoi poloviny,* pp. 85–88; Manvelishvili, *Ruset'i
da Sak'art'velo,* I, 227–32.

the troops and civil servants. Count Musin-Pushkin's mining operations cost the government over forty thousand rubles in 1805, and the returns amounted to only three thousand.

Tsitsianov also turned his attention to education and public welfare. He founded a school at Tiflis for the sons of the aristocracy, with provision for some of them to continue their education at Moscow University. Medical studies were encouraged by special scholarships. The Georgian printing press which had been operating at Tiflis until destroyed by Agha Mohammed was now rebuilt. A state-owned apothecary's shop was opened, as well as a botanical garden. Public buildings on the European model began to make their appearance in the capital, while the citizens were enabled to proceed with the restoration of the ruins of old Tiflis.[35]

With regard to administrative policy, Tsitsianov was opposed to overhasty Russification of the governmental and judicial system. In his reports to the central authorities, he described the abuses resulting from his predecessor's attempt to impose the methods of Russian bureaucracy on a people with no knowledge of the Russian language or of European methods of administration. He advocated a more gradual transition from the old oral method of administering justice to the formalities of the Russian judicial system and the retention of the Georgian language as the medium of transaction of local official business. At the same time, he was opposed to any concession to Georgian national aspirations. When Kochubei, Alexander's liberal-minded minister of the interior, wrote to him in 1804 to ask whether one of the royal princes might not after all be set up as nominal ruler of K'art'lo-Kakhet'i under Russian tutelage, Tsitsianov at once stifled the project.[36]

To add to Tsitsianov's preoccupations, a full-scale war with Persia broke out in 1805. Owing to Russia's heavy commitments in the struggle against Napoleon in Europe, there was no hope of reinforcements. With greatly inferior numbers, Tsitsianov held out against determined thrusts by 'Abbas Mirza against Elizavetpol' and the

[35] Dubrovin, *Zakavkaz'e ot 1803–1806 goda,* pp. 123–30, 448–58; Khachapuridze, *K istorii Gruzii pervoi poloviny,* pp. 68–72; "Quelques notions sur la Géorgie," in the archives of the French Foreign Ministry, Mémoires et Documents, Russie, Vol. X; Freygang, *Letters from the Caucasus and Georgia,* pp. 128–29.

[36] Dubrovin, *Zakavkaz'e ot 1803–1806 goda,* pp. 460–65, 541–42.

Karabagh, until finally the shah's main forces retired in discouragement without joining battle. Tsitsianov now judged the time ripe for the seizure of Baku and the Caspian littoral. When the Russians appeared under the walls of Baku, the khan feigned submission and promised to deliver up the keys of the city. On February 8, 1806, Tsitsianov with only two members of his suite rode out to meet the khan and his followers. At a sign from the khan, Tsitsianov was shot down by the khan's entourage. The artillery of the citadel opened fire, and forced the Russians to withdraw.[37]

During his three years' viceroyalty, Tsitsianov laid the effective foundations of Russian power in Transcaucasia. He showed himself a distinguished military leader, and won back most of the territory and dependencies which had belonged to Georgia in Erekle's time. Mingrelia and Imeret'i were, nominally at least, reunited with Eastern Georgia. In the eyes of many of his compatriots, Tsitsianov was a renegade. He showed himself unswervingly attached to Russia's imperial interests and hostile to any recrudescence of Georgian nationalism. Nevertheless, it cannot be denied that his rule was a great improvement on that of Knorring and Kovalenskii, and that Georgia benefited in the long run from his stern, even at times harsh conduct of affairs.

Tsitsianov was succeeded by General Ivan Vasil'evich Gudovich, the same commander who had failed to secure Tiflis from the onslaught of Agha Mohammed in 1795. Gudovich was now well advanced in years and "had become capricious, tyrannical and vain to a degree." [38] Operations against the Persians were resumed, and Derbent and Baku occupied later in 1806 after negligible resistance, though a second attack on Erivan in 1808 ended in costly failure. The shah was now receiving support from Napoleon. The French envoy Amédée Jaubert arrived at Teheran in 1806, and was followed by General Gardane with a large military mission. By the Treaty of Finkenstein, signed on May 4, 1807, Napoleon undertook to assist Fath-'Ali Shah to recover Georgia and drive the Russians back beyond the Caucasus.[39] Gardane and his staff set about reform-

[37] Baddeley, *Russian Conquest of the Caucasus*, pp. 69–71.
[38] Baddeley, *Russian Conquest of the Caucasus*, p. 75.
[39] A. de Gardane, *Mission du Général Gardane en Perse*, p. 73.

ing the Persian army along European lines with a view to creating a diversion against Russia and invading British India. The Franco-Russian pact at Tilsit led to the withdrawal of Gardane. He was soon replaced by British military advisers, whose active intervention in the Russo-Persian conflict lasted until Napoleon invaded Russia in 1812.[40]

The outbreak of another war against Turkey increased the difficulties confronting the Russian army in Georgia. In 1807, Gudovich failed disastrously in an attempt to capture Akhalk'alak'i, but redeemed this setback by a victory over the Seraskier Yusuf Pasha near Gumri (Alexandropol'). Gudovich was replaced in 1809 by General Alexander Tormasov. The war with Turkey took a more favorable turn: P'ot'i fell in 1809, Sukhum-Kaleh in 1810, and Akhalk'alak'i in the following year.

The remaining independent potentates of Western Georgia accepted Russian suzerainty. In 1809, Safar Bey Sharvashidze, the lord of Abkhazia, was received under Russian protection and confirmed in his principality. Prince Mamia Gurieli was officially taken under the Russian scepter in 1811, receiving insignia of investiture from the emperor.[41]

While the rulers of Mingrelia, Abkhazia, and Guria gave support to Russia in the war against Turkey, this was far from the case with the king of Imeret'i. Solomon had never intended to observe the oath of allegiance which had been extorted from him in 1804 by force of arms. He now entered into secret relations with the Turkish *seraskier*. In 1809 the Imeret'ians ambushed and annihilated a Russian convoy proceeding to the siege of P'ot'i. This did not prevent the Russian force under Prince Orbeliani from capturing the port later in the year. Solomon's dominions were now encircled by Russian troops, and the commander in chief, Tormasov, decided that the time had come to remove the fractious monarch altogether.

Solomon's position was not a strong one. He had alienated the Mingrelian Dadian and the prince of Guria by his attempts to deprive them of their territorial possessions. Although most of the

---

[40] Baddeley, *Russian Conquest of the Caucasus*, pp. 178–80.
[41] Khachapuridze, *K istorii Gruzii pervoi poloviny*, pp. 101–3; Manvelishvili, *Ruset'i da Sak'art'velo*, I, 309–12, 391–95.

common people were faithful to him, several of the grandees of his court, led by Zurab Tseret'eli, were devoted to Russian interests. In January, 1810, Tormasov dispatched an ultimatum, demanding that Solomon hand over some members of the Imeret'ian nobility and his heir, Constantine,[42] as hostages, and that he reside permanently under Russian surveillance at K'ut'ais. Solomon refused the Russian demands. Reinforcements were sent from Tiflis and Solomon's partisans defeated by Colonel Simonovich with the help of the Dadian and the Gurieli. The king was declared deposed, and soon afterwards was captured in the hills and escorted to Tiflis.[43]

A few weeks after, the king staged a dramatic escape from house arrest by the following ingenious stratagem: His devoted servant, Ioane Saralidze, was in the habit of going daily to the banks of the Kura to fetch water. Some of the king's supporters, including members of the Tseret'eli, Erist'avi, and Abashidze clans, made their way to Tiflis under various pretexts. On a prearranged day, Solomon changed clothes with his retainer, took the bucket and himself went as if to fetch water from the river. Mounting a swift horse brought by his partisans, the king was soon with the Turkish pasha at Akhaltsikhe. Saralidze was sent to Siberia by the Russian authorities, but was pardoned after ten years of exile.[44]

Inspired by this daring exploit, the people of Imeret'i rose against the occupying power. Ten fierce engagements were fought between the Russians and the Imeret'ian nationalists. To make matters worse, famine and plague broke out, causing an estimated total of 30,000 deaths. The insurgents were eventually crushed. A Russian administration was set up at K'ut'ais under an administrator or *pravitel'*, with councilors appointed from the local nobility and Russian assessors. The country was divided into four districts or *okrugs*, and placed under martial law.[45]

[42] After the emperor and Prince Tsitsianov had taken a great deal of trouble to induce Solomon to release Constantine from prison, Constantine had voluntarily returned to Imeret'i to become heir to the throne as Solomon was childless.

[43] See the contemporary documents, including correspondence between Tormasov and Zurab Tseret'eli, printed in the journal *Moambe*, III (Tiflis, 1896), under the title "Mep'e Solomon meoris drois dserilebi"; Butkov, *Materialy*, III, 392–93; Nikoloz Dadiani's chronicle, T'aqaishvili ed., p. 87.

[44] K. A. Borozdin, "Imeretinskaia Tsaritsa Mar'ia," *Niva* (St. Petersburg), 1893, pp. 622–23.

[45] Khachapuridze, *K istorii Gruzii pervoi poloviny,* pp. 98–99.

Solomon turned for support to foreign powers, namely Turkey, Persia, and France. He went to Erivan to enlist the shah's aid, but was given only a small subsidy and advised to apply to the sultan for direct military help. Accordingly, Solomon sent to Istanbul a mission headed by his general, the Sardar K'aikhosro Tseret'eli, with letters to both the Ottoman court and the French embassy there. On March 5, 1811, the French chargé d'affaires, Latour-Maubourg, reported to his government that the Imeret'ian delegation had been well received by the Turks and had been promised a force of twenty to twenty-five thousand men to reconquer Solomon's kingdom.[46]

A few weeks later, Latour-Maubourg transmitted to the Duc de Cadore, the head of the French Foreign Ministry, a personal letter from Solomon to the Emperor Napoleon. This letter had been translated from Georgian into Turkish by a Georgian priest, and then into French by the Oriental Counselor Ruffin. (It is incidentally worth noting that Solomon had been following Napoleon's career with keen attention: when the Russian emissary Sokolov visited him in 1802, Solomon plied him with questions about Napoleon's invasion of Egypt and the aid given to Turkey by Russia and England.[47] No doubt Solomon now had an inkling of the impending breach between France and Russia, and hoped to turn it to his advantage.) The following is a translation of his letter to Napoleon, rendered from Ruffin's contemporary translation:[48]

Translation of the Turkish version of a dispatch addressed in the Georgian tongue to His Majesty the Emperor by the Prince Salomon, who signs himself King of Imirette.

January 6, 1811
Heading: To His Imperial Majesty, the very sublime, very great, very powerful monarch, the emperor of great Rome, the Caesar of the French, Napoleon, the great dominator of the whole Occident, Emperor most merciful.

Very august, very merciful Emperor, after God, King of Kings,

[46] Archives of the French Foreign Ministry, Correspondance Politique, Turquie, CCXXI, "Bulletin du 5 mars 1811," p. 153.

[47] Sokolov, "Puteshestvie v Imeretiiu, 1802," in *Chteniia v Imp. Obshchestve,* Bk. IV, p. 47.

[48] Archives of the French Foreign Ministry, Mémoires et Documents, Russie, X, 287–90.

After the unanimous will of the republic called you to the noble imperial crown of France, we hastened to submit to you some humble petitions.[49]

In these we represented to Your Majesty, as being the supreme head of Christendom, that the emperor of Moscow had unjustly and illegally stripped us of our royal estate; that this emperor had no legal title whatever; that, since we ourselves had neither the strength to set up armed resistance to the invasion of our domains, nor any means of obliging the usurper to restore them to us by recourse to law, therefore this double impotence served to excuse our failure to take effective action; and that it belonged to Your Imperial Majesty alone to take cognizance of the act of pitiless brigandage committed against us by the above mentioned emperor of Moscow; since Your Imperial Majesty, with God's help and according to the laws of nature and of men, has united in his hands alone the power, strength and authority of all the sovereigns of the earth, the Divine Creator having placed you upon earth solely for the purpose of establishing order through the power and justice with which He has Himself endowed you, consequently you are the supreme overlord of all the sovereigns. Can it be that our appeal to your legitimate authority could fail to be accepted and granted? For every one of us earthly potentates beneath the sun recognizes Your Imperial Majesty alone as the universal arbiter who rights all wrongs, regulates the compensations which are to be exacted and protects the weak against the strong.

It is in these circumstances, my very august, very potent emperor, and supreme lawgiver, that I prostrate myself humbly before Your Imperial Majesty. May Your Majesty increase from day to day, from hour to hour, in dignities and happiness! May Your Majesty add to your glorious titles that of Emperor of Asia! But may you deign to liberate me, together with a million Christian souls, from the yoke of the pitiless emperor of Moscow, either by your lofty mediation, or else by the might of your all-powerful arm, and set me beneath the protective shadow of your guardianship!

Accept the homage of my continual prayers and of the profound respect with which I am,

Very clement, very generous Emperor,
Your Imperial Majesty's poor servant,
The King of Imirette and of its domains.
[Impression of royal seal]

[49] These earlier letters to Napoleon, to which Solomon here refers, have not so far come to light.

Written the 6th of January, 1811.

The legend on the seal is: Salomon, King of Imirette.

Translated from the Turkish version by me, the undersigned, Counselor of Embassy, former Chargé d'Affaires of His Majesty the Emperor of the French, King of Italy, etc., etc., accredited to the Ottoman Porte. At Pera by Constantinople, June 28, 1811.

Signed: RUFFIN

The international situation soon took a direction which dashed Solomon's hopes of foreign intervention. The Russo-Turkish peace treaty signed at Bucharest in May, 1812, restored P'ot'i and Akhal-k'alak'i to Turkey, but made no provision in favor of Solomon. Napoleon's Russian campaign, which if successful would probably have led to the collapse of Russian power in Transcaucasia, ended in disaster. By the Treaty of Gulistan, concluded between Russia and Persia in 1813 through the mediation of Sir Gore Ouseley, Persia recognized Russia's acquisition of both Eastern and Western Georgia.[50]

Solomon ended his life at Trebizond on February 19, 1815, in his forty-first year. He was buried in the cathedral of St. Gregory of Nyssa. The Georgian verses carved on his mausoleum end with these poignant lines:

Overcome by sorrow, struck down by sickness, after confessing my sins and receiving the Holy Sacrament from my confessor Iese, priest of the Court of Imeret'i, I have been laid to rest in a hallowed place, where my sepulchre will be sprinkled every month with holy water.

Stranger, see where a stranger is buried, visit here a king. Whoever of my family comes to Trebizond, see a king, a king lying here. Ask forgiveness for him, and the Kingdom of Heaven.[51]

It is recorded of Solomon that he had been generally popular among the mass of his subjects. "His appearance," according to one account, "produced a favorable impression: he looked like an amiable man. He was of small stature, below the average, with a

[50] Baddeley, *Russian Conquest of the Caucasus,* pp. 87–90; Butkov, *Materialy,* III, 398.

[51] M.-F. Brosset, "Variétés géorgiennes," in *Mélanges Asiatiques,* V (1864–68), 736–41. According to a report published in the Paris Georgian journal *Bedi K'art'lisa,* No. 8 (1950), pp. 1–3, the mausoleum was recently demolished by the Turkish authorities.

full figure and a round white and rosy face. His large dark blue eyes were full of life and good nature, and he had a pleasant, cordial smile." [52] These good qualities, however, were offset by a fundamental weakness of character, allied with a vein of ruthlessness and cunning. Such acts as the murder of Sabid Pasha and that of the Dadian's representative, and the slaughter of the Russian convoy in 1809, brought him no ultimate advantage and contributed to his ruin. In his relations with Russia, he neglected the wiser course of conciliation. When all failed, he relied on the support of Russia's foes to restore his position. As this proved worthless, there was nothing left for him but to die in exile.

[52] This description is taken from the article "O tsare Solomone II i byvshem pri nem upravlenii," in *Kavkazskii Kalendar'*, XIV (Tiflis, 1858), 423.

14

Epilogue: The Consolidation
of Russian Power, 1810-1832

THE present narrative might properly conclude with the abolition
of the West Georgian monarchy in 1810, but it may be useful to
add at least a brief survey of the period leading up to the abortive
conspiracy of the K'art'lian nobility in 1832, the failure of which
marks the end of Georgian monarchist hopes.

The constant wars fought during the years 1800 to 1810 by the
Russian forces in Georgia had placed an intolerable burden on the
peasantry. It was little consolation for them to know that such wars
were being waged against Georgia's traditional enemies. They were
called upon to furnish transport, fodder, and supplies, often at artificially low rates, and were subjected to forced labor. The plague and
famine of 1810–12 added to their desperate situation. Russian occupation began to seem just as onerous as the invasions of Persia
and Turkey in the old days. True to their tradition of guerrilla
warfare, the peasants of Kakhet'i broke into revolt in the spring
of 1812. The garrison of Sighnaghi was wiped out and T'elavi
blockaded. The insurgents proclaimed as king of Georgia the young
Bagratid Prince Grigol, son of Ioane Batonishvili, and grandson of
Giorgi XII. In answer to the ultimatum addressed to them by the
Marquis Philip Paulucci, the commander in chief, the insurgents replied:

We know how few we are compared with the Russians, and have no
hope of beating them. We wish rather that they would exterminate us.

We sought the protection of the Russian Tsar, God gave it to us, but the injustices and cruelty of his servants have driven us to despair. We have suffered long! And now, when the Lord has sent us this terrible famine, when we ourselves are eating roots and grass, you violently seize food and forage from us! We have been expelled from our homes. Our storerooms and cellars have been plundered, our stocks of wine uncovered, drunk up and wantonly polluted by the gorged soldiery. Finally our wives and daughters have been defiled before our eyes. How can our lives be dear to us after such ignominy? We are guilty before God and the Russian Tsar of steeping our hands in Christian blood, but God knows that we never plotted to betray the Russians. We were driven to this by violence, and have resolved to die on the spot. We have no hope of pardon, for who will reveal our condition to the Emperor? Do we not remember that when we called on the Tsar's name, our rulers would answer: God is on high, the Emperor far away.[1]

The rebellion extended also to the Ananuri district, and even the Russian authorities at Tiflis felt themselves menaced. Alexander Batonishvili arrived from Persia to join in the struggle. But the fight was an unequal one, and the rebels could not hold out against Russian reinforcements which hastened to the scene. By the summer of 1812 the insurrection had been quelled. In October, Alexander Batonishvili invaded Kakhet'i with a horde of Lezghians, but was defeated near Sighnaghi.[2]

The year 1812 is also memorable in Georgian history for the heroic death of General Prince P. Bagration, a scion of the House of Mukhran, who fell at the battle of Borodino.

The insurrection of 1812 convinced Paulucci's successor as commander in chief, General N. F. Rtishchev, that some revision of policy toward the local population was indicated. The Georgian gentry were given a larger share in the administration. Magistrates and *smotriteli* or overseers of the peasantry were appointed from them. Traditional customs were treated with more consideration and a halt called to arbitrary Russification. The Russian senate set to work to prepare an official version of the laws of Wakhtang VI for use in the Georgian provinces.[3]

---

[1] Khachapuridze, *K istorii Gruzii pervoi poloviny,* pp. 114–15.

[2] "Smuty v Gruzii" (Disorders in Georgia), in *Akty sobrannye Kavkaz.,* V, (1873), 59–88, 459–67; Baddeley, *Russian Conquest of the Caucasus,* pp. 84–88.

[3] Khachapuridze, *K istorii Gruzii pervoi poloviny,* p. 117. A memorandum drawn

Although temporal sovereignty over virtually all Georgia had been in the hands of Russia since 1810, she had still to gain control of the autocephalic Georgian Orthodox Church. The catholicos patriarch was Antoni II, the son of King Erekle II. The inviolability of the church had been guaranteed by each Russian autocrat from Catherine the Great onwards. But now that organized political opposition had been eliminated, the Russian authorities found to their annoyance that the church remained a stronghold of national feeling. In 1811, therefore, the Catholicos Antoni II was sent into enforced retirement at St. Petersburg. He was replaced by a representative of the Russian synod, the Metropolitan Varlaam, with the title of exarch of Georgia.

Varlaam belonged to the family of the Erist'avs of the K'sani. He did not adopt a policy sufficiently subservient to the views of the synod, and was soon replaced by a Russian, Archbishop Theophilact Rusanov, quite alien to Georgian ways. Theophilact and his successors did what they could to reduce the Georgian Church to the same subordination to the state that had long prevailed for the Russian Church in Russia. Attempts were made to replace the Georgian liturgy with the Slavonic in churches of the principal towns.[4] These efforts were never entirely successful in spite of repressive measures taken against the more patriotic of the clergy, and the Church remained the symbol of Georgian popular solidarity.

The Exarch Theophilact encountered the strongest opposition in Western Georgia, which had had until the late eighteenth century a separate head, the catholicos of Abkhazia. In 1820, the archbishops of Gelat'i and K'ut'ais, staunch opponents of the Russification of the church and other changes introduced by Theophilact, were arrested. Archbishop Dositheus of K'ut'ais, stabbed and maltreated by Russian cossacks, died soon after. These incidents led to spontaneous uprisings in Imeret'i. The insurgents planned to restore the monarchy

up in 1815 by Colonel Rottiers, a Belgian officer in the Russian service, recommends that Russian officials be removed altogether from service in Georgia. Rottiers describes them as notoriously venal and inefficient, and attributes the recent disturbances in Kakhet'i to their unheard-of extortions. He also recommends that a Georgian governor general be set at the head of the civil administration ("Mémoire sur la Géorgie," in *Akty sobrannye Kavkaz.*, V, 980).

[4] Khachapuridze, *K istorii Gruzii pervoi poloviny*, p. 150; Makharadze, *Vosstanie v Imeretii 1819–20 gg.*, p. 55.

under either Prince Ioane Abashidze or Alexander Batonishvili, who was summoned from Persia. The district of Ratcha was the scene of particularly bitter resistance. Many of the aristocracy, however, had by now been won over to Russian interests, and cooperated in quelling the disturbances. The movement then spread to Guria and Mingrelia. An outbreak of civil war in Abkhazia in 1821 further complicated the situation, and the unrest was not finally crushed until 1822.[5]

Meanwhile, the nomination of A. P. Ermolov as commander in chief of the Caucasus in 1816 marked the opening of a new epoch in the consolidation of Russian power. Ermolov made Georgia the headquarters for a vigorous campaign of military conquest against Daghestan, while the Chechens were subjected to ceaseless pressure from the North Caucasian Line. The submission of Avaria, Ghazi-Ghumuq, and Qaraqaitaq brought some of Georgia's hereditary enemies, at least for the moment, to heel. Ermolov also pursued an aggressive policy toward the remaining autonomous khanates of Transcaucasia, resulting in the absorption of Shekki (1819), Shirvan (1820), and the Karabagh (1822).[6]

From 1813 until 1826, Russia was at peace with Iran, but this did not mean that the shah had abandoned hope of recovering his lost provinces. With the help of British advisers, the Crown Prince 'Abbas Mirza was busily reorganizing the Persian army with a view to staging a counterattack. In this he was spurred on by Alexander Batonishvili of Georgia, "a prince," as the British traveler Sir Robert Ker Porter wrote, "whose bold independence of spirit still resists all terms of amity with Russia." Ker Porter met Alexander at Tabriz in 1819 and recalled that,

It was impossible to look on this intrepid prince, however wild and obdurate, without interest; without that sort of pity and admiration, with which a man might view the royal lion hunted from his hereditary

---

[5] Khachapuridze, *K istorii Gruzii pervoi poloviny*, pp. 151–56; Tseret'eli, *Perezhitoe*, p. 34; A. P. Ermolov, "Zapiski . . . 1816–1827," in *Chteniia v Imp. Obshchestve* (1866), Bk. II, pp. 84–86, 106–13; Dubetskii, "Zapiski," in *Russkaia Starina*, LXXXIII, 119–37.

[6] On the history of Ermolov's viceroyalty, see Baddeley, *Russian Conquest of the Caucasus*, 92–163, in addition to Ermolov's own "Zapiski . . . 1816–1827," in *Chteniia v Imp. Obshchestve*, Bks. II–III (1866), and Bks. III–IV (1867).

wastes, yet still returning to hover near, and roar in proud loneliness his ceaseless threatenings to the human strangers who had disturbed his reign.[7]

Alexander's chance came in 1826. Without declaration of war, the Persian army under 'Abbas Mirza launched a surprise attack against Georgia and the Karabagh. Pambak', Shuragel, and Borchalo were overrun and Elizavetpol' captured. Tiflis itself seemed menaced. Alexander Batonishvili accompanied the Persian advanced headquarters.

At first, Ermolov showed something of the unpreparedness and masterly inactivity that Gudovich had displayed in 1795. The courage of Prince Madatov soon turned the tide at the battle of Shamkhor in September. The arrival of Paskevich resulted in the Persian army's complete collapse. Erivan, Tabriz, and Ardebil fell, and the Treaty of Turkmanchai in 1828 established Russia's frontier on the River Araxes, where it has ever since remained.

War with Turkey broke out the same year. In a series of brilliant operations Paskevich captured Akhaltsikhe, Kars, and Erzerum. The Treaty of Adrianople (1829) provided for the retention of only P'ot'i, Akhalk'alak'i, and Akhaltsikhe. Since the princess-regent of Guria, Sofia, had sided with the Turks and fled to Trebizond, the principality was placed under direct Russian rule.

With regard to the internal condition of Georgia, Ermolov's administration resulted at least in the return of a measure of public security. A police force was organized in Tiflis. Bands of Lezghis could no longer carry off villagers at will and make trade hazardous. Military and post roads were built, with benefits to trade and communications generally. Ermolov had some of the streets of Tiflis paved and the bazaar roofed over. The erection of villas and other European buildings began to modernize the town's appearance. Similar developments occurred in K'ut'ais, now the Russian administrative center for Western Georgia.[8]

[7] Ker Porter, *Travels in Georgia, Persia, etc.*, II, 521; for the Russian view of Alexander, see Ermolov, "Zapiski . . . 1816–1827," in *Chteniia v Imp. Obshchestve*, II (1866), 15–16.

[8] Ker Porter, *Travels in Georgia, Persia, etc.*, I, 116–53; Ermolov, *A. P. Ermolov, Biograficheskii ocherk*, pp. 92–96; Eichwald, *Reise in den Kaukasus*, II, 76–77, 214. Griboedov, who served in the Caucasus under Ermolov and Paskevich, drew up in

The unification of the lands between the Caspian and Black Seas facilitated transit trade between eastern and western Transcaucasia. Odessa was now linked by sea with Redut-Kaleh in Mingrelia. From there, goods from Russia and Western Europe could be transported readily via Tiflis to Baku, Tabriz, and beyond. To encourage the development of trade and the investment of capital in Georgia, an edict of 1821 granted Russian and foreign concerns in business there special customs concessions and other privileges for ten years.[9] Tiflis merchants began to establish connections with Marseilles, Trieste, and Germany, and to reexport European goods to Persia. In 1825, Georgian and Armenian traders made purchases totaling over a million rubles at the Leipzig fair; in 1828, the figure exceeded four million. The demand for European articles was stimulated by the presence of a large number of Russian officers and administrators and their families. In 1830 an officer of the finance department reported from Tiflis that trade was in the most flourishing condition.[10]

Domestic industry did not prosper to anything near the same extent. In 1824 there were operating at Tiflis one small alum factory, 24 tanneries, 30 brick kilns, and 4 pottery works, all on a more or less primitive basis. The mining enterprises on which the late Count Musin-Pushkin had expended so much energy were in a far from prosperous state, except for the productive copper mine in Borchalo.[11] In Western Georgia, the only industrial enterprises were three distilleries. Of course, handicrafts such as carpet-making, fine metal work, shoemaking, and all the trades practiced in the bazaars of the East flourished as they had done for centuries. In 1827 there were over two thousand skilled craftsmen and artisans operating workshops in the various centers of Eastern and Western Georgia.[12]

1827 a project for replanning Tiflis on improved lines ("Zapiska o luchshikh sposobakh vnov' postroit' gorod Tiflis," in Griboedov, *Polnoe Sobranie Sochinenii*, Piksanov, ed., III [Petrograd, 1917], 251–52).

[9] Ermolov, "Zapiski . . . 1816–1827," in *Chteniia v Imp. Obshchestve*, III (1867), 144–48.

[10] Khachapuridze, *K istorii Gruzii pervoi poloviny*, pp. 132–34; Eichwald, *Reise in den Kaukasus*, II, 104–6; Rozhkova, *Ekonomicheskaia politika tsarskogo pravitel'stva na srednem vostoke vo vtoroi chetverti XIX veka i Russkaia burzhuaziia*, pp. 52, 76.

[11] Eichwald, *Reise in den Kaukasus*, II, 444–45.

[12] *Ibid.*, p. 101; Khachapuridze, *K istorii Gruzii pervoi poloviny*, pp. 129–31.

With regard to agriculture and plantations, Ermolov made efforts to increase the land's resources. The French consul, the Chevalier de Gamba, was granted a concession in Imeret'i to exploit the country's vast timber resources and start cotton plantations.[13] Five hundred families from Württemberg arrived in 1818 to set up model farmsteads. The cultivation of silk was encouraged in Kakhet'i, though it did not reach the same scale there as in the Shamakhi area. In 1827 an experimental silk factory was opened at Tiflis, but it failed to prosper.[14] Kakhet'i, always renowned for its wine, derived a steady flow of wealth from viticulture.[15]

However, the Russian government's aim to make the Georgian provinces self-supporting was far from being fulfilled. The growth of an unrestricted transit trade was not accompanied by a corresponding growth of native industries. As it was, the revenues collected by the central government from Georgia, amounting to only about 580,000 rubles in 1825, did not even pay for the maintenance of the local garrison and administration.[16] With regard to the first decades of Russian rule, nothing could be farther from the truth than to suppose that vast revenues flowed into St. Petersburg from the proceeds of colonial exploitation of Transcaucasia.

Among those who turned their attention at this period to the need for making a better use of the country's natural riches was the dramatist A. S. Griboedov, author of the famous comedy *Gore ot Uma,* or *Woe from Wit,* and a prominent official in the administration of Georgia. Following the peace treaty with Persia in 1828, Griboedov drafted a far-reaching plan for the foundation of a Russian Transcaucasian Company under imperial charter, along the lines of the European East India companies. Such a corporation would provide capital for the development of plantations and factories, and thus could supply Russia with a wide range of products hitherto imported at vast expense from tropical countries abroad. In his

[13] See the article "Gamba" in Michaud, *Biographie Universelle.* The records of the former French consulate at Tiflis, now preserved in the archives of the French Foreign Ministry in Paris, give abundant details of Gamba's operations and projects.

[14] Rozhkova, *Ekonomicheskaia politika tsarskogo pravitel'stva,* pp. 135–36.

[15] Eichwald, *Reise in den Kaukasus,* II, 98.

[16] Khachapuridze, *K istorii Gruzii pervoi poloviny,* p. 129; Eichwald, *Reise in den Kaukasus,* II, 107–13. The latter source gives an analysis of income and expenditure in the various Russian Caucasian provinces.

memorandum Griboedov gives a remarkably frank account of the factors which hindered the economic progress of Georgia under the first years of Russian rule:

Having traversed the Caucasus, the Russians were primarily concerned with establishing themselves on a firm footing in Georgia, which had herself solicited the protection of our monarchs, and in the Khanates acquired by the force of Imperial arms. To this end it was necessary to ensure the external security of the new subject peoples and be perpetually prepared for repulsing ceaseless raids and attacks. Wars in Europe prevented the government from fully deploying means adequate to subdue simultaneously her external foes in Asia: the Persians and Turks. Within the newly acquired provinces, there occurred disorders resulting from the introduction of a new system, from official relationships of an unfamiliar nature, from the punctiliousness of an administration which demanded immediate execution of orders and an unheard-of degree of subordination, and in general from changes to which no nation would voluntarily submit. Communications with Russia could be established only gradually and with great difficulty. By military action, access was gained to the ports of two seas, the Black and the Caspian, and every step along the Georgian Military Highway was at first imprinted with Russian blood.

In such circumstances, it was impossible to give consideration either to new administrative arrangements or to the drafting of laws to fit local customs, for the study, collection, and checking of which, and their incorporation into a codex, critical attention, leisure, and calm are essential. The same applied to the drawing up of a cadastral survey. Most landed estates have remained and are still the subject of dispute. The administration grew up on a day-to-day basis, on an exclusively military footing, except for Georgia in the narrow sense, where the system introduced at the start according to the Edict on Governorates [17] was later combined in the regional administration with a special type of civil government made necessary by the country's military situation.

The financial system followed similar lines. There was no time to think about the fair assessment and equitable collection of taxes. It was imperative to provide for the quartering and provisioning of the army and the transport of supplies to depots and units on active service. In this way all kinds of impositions have received the force of law. The inhabitant of Transcaucasia has had no time to think of the improvement

[17] That is, Catherine the Great's Uchrezhdenie o Guberniiakh of 1775.

of his husbandry: his house, domestic utensils, horse trappings, cart, cattle, and almost all his immovable property might any minute be requisitioned for the public service in the course of troop movements and so on. The result was that he not only failed to give any thought to the future, but he also took no interest in his present possessions. We are not taking into account the malversations of any particular officials, but simply mentioning the inevitable misfortunes of war, which can often be neither foreseen or prevented.

The Treaty of Bucharest, and soon after, that of Gulistan, did not have such a beneficial effect on this land as might have been expected. Since then, the thunder of guns has not ceased in the fight to subdue the mountaineers and other rebellious clans, sometimes on the Caucasian Line, the command over which is concentrated in the same hands as that of Transcaucasia, at other times in Daghestan or the western maritime provinces. All the attention of the governors of that period was absorbed by these events. Little was done for education. Prince Tsitsianov, of unforgotten fame, opened one school for three hundred pupils; for a long time, no progress has been made beyond these weak beginnings.

Trade has been somewhat encouraged by the edict of 1821. Since then some of the Tiflis merchants have been traveling to Leipzig for their wares, selling them profitably at home or in Persia and accumulating substantial capital. But this has had no effect on the well being of landowners and peasants, who are most of all weighed down with government levies, nor has it encouraged the growth of native industry: not one factory was started, nor have agriculture or husbandry prospered. The nomad Tatars roaming over their fertile pastures still do not know of any other use for the splendid wool of their sheep than as barter for commodities they need in their semisavage pastoral existence. In several years not more than two or three foreign ships have anchored off the coast of Mingrelia, and that has been solely to try out a new outlet for their wares, without taking on board a cargo of local products, since these, through their trifling quantity and poor quality, are unsuitable for European use. Furthermore, while the Tiflis bazaar abounds with items of imported merchandise, the observer's gaze will seek in vain for home-produced wares or products for which these might be exchanged.

Finally, the recent invasion by the Persians, avenged by Count Paskevich-Erivanskii with so much glory for Russia, and the triumphs which he is now winning in the Turkish pashaliks, have cost the Transcaucasian provinces enormous sacrifices, and above all Georgia, which has borne a war burden of exceptional magnitude. It is safe to say that from the year

1826 up to the present time, she has suffered in the aggregate heavier losses in cereals, pack animals and beasts of burden, drovers, etc., than the most flourishing Russian province could have sustained, while in population and extent she equals only three *uezdy* of the Governorates of Great Russia.[18]

This project, which would have given the company extensive political authority in Transcaucasia, did not appeal to Paskevich, so it was dropped, although a concern called the Transcaucasian Trading Depot was set up in 1830 by Griboedov's associate Zavaleiskii.[19]

During the 1820s, the influence of Count Kankrin and the agitation of Moscow manufacturers had led to the triumph of protectionism in Russia. On the expiration of the local ten-year concessions granted for Georgia and neighboring areas by the edict of 1821, it was decided not to renew them but to impose on goods entering Transcaucasia the same high tariffs as were leviable at Russia's other frontiers. In the absence of any large-scale local enterprises, this return to protectionism merely served to impoverish the Tiflis merchants. The growth of Tiflis as an entrepôt was abruptly checked, and European goods were soon reaching Persia via Trebizond and Erzerum.[20]

Until the advent of Prince Vorontsov in 1845, the government of Georgia continued to bear a military stamp. Georgia was regarded first and foremost as a base for operations against Daghestan, Persia, and Turkey. Nevertheless, a certain improvement in the local administration resulted from the appointment of an official of Georgian descent, E. Chiliaev (E. Chilashvili), as procurator at Tiflis in 1822. He was a cultured and able man, educated in Russia, and equally conversant with Russian and Georgian ways. The Russian version of the code of Wakhtang VI was finally printed and issued in 1828, which helped to improve the dispensation of justice, though misunderstandings still arose through disparities between Russian and Georgian conceptions of jurisprudence.[21]

---

[18] Griboedov, *Sochineniia,* ed. Orlov (Leningrad, 1945), pp. 563–65.

[19] Rozhkova, *Ekonomicheskaiia politika tsarskogo pravitel'stva,* pp. 52–56; Shaduri, *Russkie pisateli o Gruzii,* I, 485.

[20] The plan of this work permitting only summary treatment of Russian economic policy in Georgia, reference should be made to M. V. Rozhkova's monograph, "Iz istorii ekonomicheskoi politiki Rossiiskogo tsarizma v Zakavkaz'e," in *Istoricheskie Zapiski,* XVIII (Moscow, 1946).

[21] Khachapuridze, *K istorii Gruzii pervoi poloviny,* pp. 127–28.

Little was done for public health during the first three decades of Russian rule. The civilian hospital at Tiflis had only twelve beds, and in all Georgia there were only a handful of properly qualified doctors. Most of the population entrusted their health to Persian quacks and local wise women.[22]

Education until 1830 was in a sadly neglected state, with most of the old Georgian church schools closed down. In 1817, however, an Orthodox seminary was opened in Tiflis. Through the 1820s not more than 10,000 rubles were spent annually on public education in all Transcaucasia, but in 1830 a great step forward was taken: the Tiflis school for sons of the nobility established by Tsitsianov was elevated into a gymnasium. Government schools were opened in T'elavi, Sighnaghi, Gori, and K'ut'ais, and a *pension* for daughters of the aristocracy was founded at Tiflis. The educational budget was increased to 135,000 rubles a year.[23]

A Georgian newspaper, *Sak'art'velos gazet'i,* the first ever issued, was published from 1819 until 1822.[24] The Russian-language *Tiflis- skie vedomosti* began to appear in 1828, with a Georgian section entitled *T'pilisis udsqebani.* The latter was edited for a time by the brilliant publicist and philosopher Solomon Dodashvili (Dodaev-Magarskii), who had attended courses at the University of St. Peters-burg. After his return he taught at the government school at Tiflis. He was one of the most independent and inquiring minds of his generation in Russia. Also prominent in the intellectual life of Georgia was Alexander Tchavtchavadze (1787–1846), son of Erekle's ambassador Garsevan and father-in-law of Griboedov. His house at Tiflis was a meeting place for the élite of Georgian and Russian society. He was eminent as a lyric poet, as was Prince Grigol Orbeli-ani (1800–1883), both of them high ranking officers in the Russian service.[25]

Further links between the literary and intellectual life of Russia and Georgia were established through the use of the Caucasus as a milder alternative to Siberia for political offenders. The Decembrist

[22] Eichwald, *Reise in den Kaukasus,* II, 158–75, 181–84.

[23] Khachapuridze, *K istorii Gruzii pervoi poloviny,* pp. 259–61; Eichwald, *Reise in den Kaukasus,* II, 130–34.

[24] Veidenbaum, "Pervaia Gruzinskaia gazeta," in *Kavkazskie etiudy* (Tiflis, 1901).

[25] Khachapuridze, "K voprosu o kul'turnykh sviaziakh Rossii i Gruzii v pervuiu polovinu XIX veka," in *Voprosy Istorii,* Nos. 5–6 (Moscow, 1946), pp. 76–89.

poets Kiukhel'beker and Odoevskii and the novelist Bestuzhev-Marlinskii all drew inspiration from their confinement in Georgia and the Caucasus. In the Russian administration Griboedov and even Ermolov himself were known to be in sympathy with the Decembrists. As Belinskii observed, "The Caucasus seems to have been fated to become the cradle of our poetic talents, the inspiration and mentor of their muses, their poetic homeland!" [26] In one of his lyrics, Griboedov describes the charm of Kakhet'i, "where the Alazan meanders, indolence and coolness breathe, where in the gardens they collect the tribute of the purple grape"; he also embarked on a romantic tragedy, *Gruzinskaia noch'* (*Georgian Night*) based on a theme from national legend. Pushkin was in Georgia in 1829 and wrote several lyrics on Georgian subjects. His travel journal, *Puteshestvie v Arzrum,* contains vivid glimpses of Georgian life, music, poetry, and scenic beauty. Some of Lermontov's most brilliant inspiration came to him from Georgia. The great poems "Mtsyri" and "Demon" have a Georgian setting, while his ballad "Tamara" presents a picturesque though unhistoric image of the great queen. In the poetic dialogue between Mounts Kazbek and Elbruz, "Spor," Lermontov sketches a portrait of the drowsy Georgian countryman, recumbent in the shade of a plane tree, languidly sipping the mellow wine of Kakhet'i.

Although Russian poets might lay stress on the langorous and exotic charm of the Georgian scene, any semblance of torpor in Georgian society at this period was a deceptive one. The Georgians had by no means forgotten their chivalrous days of old, and after the Decembrists in Russia, Georgia too had her phase of romantic revolt. All the elements were there: a proud aristocracy not yet reconciled to the ways of Russian autocracy; a ruling house in exile, imperfectly resigned to exclusion from power; and a generation of young poets, military officers, and thinkers imbued with high-minded and quixotic ideals. The example of the Decembrists themselves, together with the liberation of Greece, the Paris Revolution of 1830, and the general insurrection in Poland, all tended to arouse in Georgia a wave of patriotic sentiment and to encourage illusory hopes of moral and material support from Western Europe. Al-

[26] Shaduri, *Russkie pisateli o Gruzii,* I, 124-60, 288-96.

though one of the Decembrists, A. S. Gangeblov, was of Georgian descent,[27] there is no evidence to suggest that the movement of revolt among the Georgian aristocracy was connected in anything but spirit with the Decembrists in exile. But the romantic ideology of the Georgian conspirators,[28] their lack of any real contact with the masses of the population, and their rash and ill-conceived strategy recall corresponding features of the Decembrist rising.

Of the Bagratid princes in exile, few were still alive in 1830 who remembered the old days of the K'art'lo-Kakhet'ian monarchy. The Prince-Regent David had died in 1819; according to one version, his death was due to chagrin at a reprimand by the Emperor Alexander, who learned that David had been expressing discontent to certain foreign ambassadors at St. Petersburg on Russia's treatment of Georgia. David's brother Ioane, and Ioane's son Grigol, the latter prominent in the Kakhet'ian revolt of 1812, died in 1830. Of the other sons of King Giorgi XII, Bagrat and T'eimuraz occupied honored positions in Russian society, and were not personally involved in the nationalist movement. Their younger brother, Ok'ropir, however, was an active spirit in the revival of national pride in the Georgian community in Russia. He and his cousin Prince Dimitri Yulonovich used to hold gatherings of Georgian students at Moscow and St. Petersburg and attempt to inspire them with patriotic and monarchist doctrines. Alexander Batonishvili, now an elderly man, was still living in Persia and always on the alert for the chance to take action against Russia.[29]

Among the Georgian aristocracy's immediate grounds for discontent with the Russian administration on the spot may be included certain curtailments of the landlords' feudal jurisdiction over their peasants; the tendency to eliminate the nobility from participation in local government in favor of Russian bureaucrats; delays in verifying the titles of nobility of many Georgian families, resulting

[27] It is interesting to note that Gangeblov was exiled back to Georgia. In 1830, he records in his memoirs, gatherings of former Decembrists took place at his home in Tiflis. Those present included the Bestuzhevs and the Musin-Pushkins, Pushchin, Orzhitskii, Kozhevnikov, and Vyshnevskii (A. S. Gangeblov, *Vospominaniia*, pp. 102–3).

[28] Grigol Orbeliani and Solomon Dodashvili, for example, were admirers of the revolutionary verse of Ryleev.

[29] Khachapuridze, *K istorii Gruzii pervoi poloviny*, pp. 278, 293–96.

sometimes in extreme hardship; rumors that the Andronikashvilis, the Orbelianis, and the Bagration-Mukhranskii and Eristov-Ksanskii families were to be deported to Russia; and, in the case of the Eristovs, the confiscation of certain Ossete villages which they used to possess.[30]

The movement began to take definite shape in 1830, when Prince Ok'ropir Giorgievich visited Tiflis. A secret society was formed to work for the reestablishment of an independent kingdom under Bagratid rule. The principal conspirators were Elizbar Erist'avi, Alexander Orbeliani, other members of the Erist'avi (Eristov) and Orbeliani clans, and the publicist Solomon Dodashvili. They hoped to enlist the cooperation of T'eimuraz Lort'k'ip'anidze, who had been prominent in the revolt of 1820 in Imeret'i, to start a parallel movement in Western Georgia. The young Constantine Sharvashidze, a scion of the ruling house of Abkhazia, was also believed sympathetic. It does not appear, however, that the society ever made any real headway in Western Georgia.

It would be useless to seek for any signs of republican ideology among the Georgian conspirators of 1830-32. Their outlook was monarchist and nationalist, combined with a strong tinge of romantic patriotism and the desire to resurrect Georgia's past glories. Their projected plan of action was something of a mixture of the Sicilian Vespers and the tactics of the Russian uprising of December 14, 1825: the governor general, Baron Rosen, and other members of the garrison and administration were to be invited to a grand ball at Tiflis and assassinated at a given signal. The Dariel Pass would be seized to prevent reinforcements arriving from Russia, while Alexander Batonishvili would return from Persia to be proclaimed king. Plans for seizing the arsenal and barracks were drawn up, as was the composition of a provisional government.[31]

This spectacular and rather bloodthirsty plan failed to commend itself to several of the secret society's members, and deterred a number of waverers who might otherwise have joined the movement. Many of the Georgian nobility had relatives or close friends among the Russian residents, and were against a wholesale massacre. Solo-

---

[30] Khachapuridze, *K istorii Gruzii pervoi poloviny*, pp. 281-83.
[31] Khachapuridze, *K istorii Gruzii pervoi poloviny*, pp. 359-79, 392-95.

mon Dodashvili left the society altogether, though without betraying it to the authorities. Alexander Tchavtchavadze, an ardent patriot, refused to join in a scheme which depended for success on the support of Alexander Batonishvili and the infidel Persians, the murderers of his son-in-law Griboedov.[32] But Tchavtchavadze, too, kept his knowledge to himself.

The fall of Warsaw in 1831 and the crushing of Polish resistance gravely alarmed the conspirators. Nevertheless, they continued to plan their coup. The ball at which the Russian officers were to be assassinated was scheduled for November 20, 1832, the day of the meeting of Georgian princes and nobles at Tiflis for the election of deputies for the Provincial Assembly of the Nobility. This session was unexpectedly postponed first to December 9, and then to December 20.

On December 9, the plot was revealed to the authorities by one of the conspirators, E. P'alavandishvili. Extensive arrests were made. Commissions of inquiry were set up at Tiflis and St. Petersburg. Ten of the accused, including E. Erist'avi, A. Orbeliani, and Solomon Dodashvili, were sentenced to death by quartering, but then reprieved and deported, either to other parts of Russia or into enforced military service. The two Bagratid princes, Ok'ropir and Dimitri, were exiled to Kostroma and Smolensk, respectively. Alexander Tchavtchavadze was sent for a few years to Tambov as a penalty for his silence.[33]

The Emperor Nicholas's policy toward Georgia was based on enlisting the maximum cooperation from the local gentry, and he ordered a thorough investigation into the basic causes of discontent among the landed aristocracy. Those of the conspirators who belonged to leading families were treated with great leniency, and were almost all allowed to return home in a few years and resume their military or official careers in the tsar's service. Prince Grigol Orbeliani rose to the dignity of governor general of Tiflis. The harshest fate befell Dodashvili, who, already suffering from tuberculosis, was posted as a punishment to Viatka. Permission to transfer

[32] Griboedov was appointed minister to Persia in 1828. The following year, he and the staff of the Russian embassy were murdered by a fanatical mob in Teheran.

[33] See "Delo o Gruzinskom zagovore" (The Dossier on the Georgian Conspiracy), in *Akty sobrannye Kavkaz.*, VIII (1881), 391–423.

to a more temperate climate was refused, and he died there in 1836.

The failure of the conspiracy of 1830–32 brought about the final eclipse of monarchist hopes. The return of stability to Europe, lasting until the convulsions of 1848, enabled the tsarist government to concentrate its energies on subduing the tribes of Daghestan and Circassia and on consolidating its position in Transcaucasia generally. Tiflis became more and more an international city as better communications were established with Constantinople and Western Europe on the one hand, and with Baku, Astrakhan, and St. Petersburg on the other. The conciliatory policy of Prince Vorontsov, viceroy of the Caucasus from 1845 until 1854, tended to encourage the cultural and intellectual rebirth of the country, and helped to reconcile Georgian public opinion to the loss of political sovereignty. The growth of industry, an urban proletariat, and the Social Democratic movements toward the end of the century, the establishment of the Georgian republic in 1918, and the eventual crushing of Georgian independence by Soviet armed force in 1921, belong to another historical phase.

To sum up the conclusions of the foregoing chapters, it is clear that the fall of the Georgian monarchy was not solely due to the onward march of tsarist imperialism as many writers have asserted. The undeniable fact is that by the year 1800, the process of disintegration of the Georgian state had reached a critical stage. A fusion of Eastern and Western Georgia was as far away as ever, and the centrifugal forces in Georgia's political life had triumphed, banishing the very concept of centralized royal power and an ordered system of administration. The royal family of K'art'lo-Kakhet'i was divided against itself, while Western Georgia was convulsed internally by civil war between Imeret'i and Mingrelia. The essential conditions for evolving a sound body politic—internal and external security, and a reasonably prosperous economy—were absent. The persistence of feudal institutions, combined with isolation from the Western world, paralyzed social and political reform. The population of Western and Eastern Georgia combined had sunk below half a million. The raids of the Lezghis imposed a constant drain on the country's meager resources. Turkey and Persia, egged on by France and England, were making strenuous attempts to subjugate Transcaucasia and retain the Caucasian range as a barrier against the advancing might of Russia.

The unilateral decision of Alexander I to abolish the monarchy of K'art'lo-Kakhet'i was scarcely defensible legally, and was carried out in a manner least calculated to spare the Georgians' legitimate national pride. But it must be conceded that the system of vassal suzerainty which the Georgians desired never had any place in the Russian autocratic system, if we except the not always happy experiments in Poland and Finland. Centralized, absolutist government on the St. Petersburg model was something very different from the elastic hierarchy of khanates and pashaliks that made up the Persian and Ottoman empires. An autonomous Georgia within the Asiatic dominions of the Russian state would have been an anachronism, a fact which the Georgian people, understandably enough, could never bring themselves to appreciate.

Left to itself, it is doubtful whether the Georgian nation would even have been assured of physical survival. The country would have been ravaged and depopulated, as so often before, by Turkish and Persian armies, now strengthened by European instructors and equipment. It may be objected that Russia was bound by treaty to afford the Georgian kingdom protection without usurping direct rule over it. Indeed, there can be little doubt that Catherine the Great and her successors committed flagrant violations of their promises, but could Russia reasonably have been expected to wage ceaseless wars against Turkey and Persia and to engage in more than half a century's embittered struggle with the clansmen of Daghestan and Circassia in a purely disinterested fashion? Is it likely that Russian troops would have stayed in Georgia during the Napoleonic invasion of 1812 if the country had not been a Russian province? Following the absorption of Georgia, tens of millions of rubles and scores of thousands of Russian lives were expended in fighting the traditional enemies of Georgia. In return, the Georgian people had to suffer a century and a half of Russian rule, which often seemed to them onerous and intolerable.

Together with many humiliations, Russia assured the Georgian people their corporate physical survival. Behind a ring of Russian bayonets, the population had risen by the 1830s to three quarters of a million, and at the present day it is approaching the three million mark. Had events taken a different course, the Georgian nation might well have vanished from the face of the earth, relegating to the past a tradition of chivalry and of striking achievement in many spheres of art, literature, and Christian civilization generally.

Appendix

Chronological Tables of the Last Kings of Georgia

Principal authorities: M.-F. Brosset, "Tables généalogiques et statistiques des dynasties géorgiennes," in *Histoire de la Géorgie,* Vol. II, Part 1, Addition IX. A. Gugushvili, "The Chronological-Genealogical Table of the Kings of Georgia," in *Georgica,* Vol. I, Nos. 2–3 (London, 1936). Berdzenishvili, Javakhishvili, and Janashia, *Istoriia Gruzii* (2d ed.; Tiflis, 1950).

KINGS OF K'ART'LI

K'ART'LIAN BAGRATID LINE

1632–58	Rostom (or Khusrau-Mirza)
1658–76	Bakhuta-Beg, Prince of Mukhran (of the collateral branch, the Bagratids of Mukhran), adopted son of Rostom, reigned as King Wakhtang V, otherwise known as Shahnavaz I
1676–88	Giorgi XI (first reign)
1688–1703	Erekle I or Nazar-'Ali-Khan, of the Bagratids of Kakhet'i
1703–9	Giorgi XI (second reign); Prince Wakhtang, regent
1709–11	K'aikhosro, nephew of Giorgi XI; Prince Wakhtang, regent
1711–14	Wakhtang VI, nephew of Giorgi XI and formerly regent

1714–16, 1724–27	Iese or 'Ali-Quli-Khan, later known as Mustafa Pasha, brother of Wakhtang VI
1717–19	Bak'ar, son of Wakhtang VI
1719–23	Wakhtang VI, reinstated under the title of Husayn-Quli-Khan
1723–35	Turkish occupation: various Georgian puppet rulers
1735–44	Persian dictator Nadir Shah: various Georgian and Persian puppet rulers
1744–62	T'eimuraz II, of the Bagratids of Kakhet'i

KINGS OF KAKHET'I

KAKHET'IAN BAGRATID LINE

|

1606–16, 1623–32, 1634–48	T'eimuraz I
1648–64	Interregnum: Persian governors
1664–75	Archil, son of King Wakhtang V, of the Bagratids of K'art'li
1675–1703	Interregnum: Persian governors
1703–22	David II or Imam-Quli-Khan, great-grandson of T'eimuraz I
1722–32	Constantine II or Mohammed-Quli-Khan, brother of David II
1732–44	T'eimuraz II, brother of Constantine II (married Princess T'amar, daughter of King Wakhtang VI of K'art'li)

|

1744–62	Erekle II

KINGS OF UNITED K'ART'LI AND KAKHET'I

KAKHET'IAN BAGRATID LINE

|

1762–98	Erekle II, son of T'eimuraz II

|

1798–1800	Giorgi XII

|

1800–1801	David Batonishvili, regent

KINGS OF IMERET'I (WESTERN GEORGIA)

IMERET'IAN BAGRATID LINE

|

1639–60	Alexander III

1660, 1664–78, 1679–81	Bagrat IV
1661, 1668	Wakhtang, consort of Queen Dowager Darejan, widow of Alexander III
1661–63, 1678–79, 1690–91, 1695–96, 1698	Archil, son of King Wakhtang V of K'art'li
1663–64	Demetre, Prince of Guria
1681–83	Giorgi III, Prince of Guria
1683–90, 1691–95	Alexander IV, son of King Bagrat IV
1696–98	Giorgi IV Bagration, nicknamed Gotchia
1699–1700	Simon, son of King Alexander IV
1701–1702, 1711, 1713	Mamia, Prince of Guria
1702–7	Prince Abashidze (usurper)
1707–20	Giorgi V, son of King Simon
1720–52	Alexander V, son of King Giorgi V
1752–65, 1768–84	Solomon I
1765–68	T'eimuraz, cousin of Solomon I
1784–89	David, cousin of Solomon I
1789–1810	Solomon II, nephew of Solomon I and grandson of Erekle II of K'art'lo-Kakhet'i

Chronological Table of the Last Catholicos-Patriarchs of All Georgia

(RESIDING AT MTSKHET'A)

Principal authorities: B. Lominadze, "Masalebi Sak'art'velos XVII–XVIII saukunet'a istoriis k'ronologiisat'vis," in *Materialy po Istorii Gruzii i Kavkaza,* Vol. 29 (Tiflis, 1951). M. Tamarati, *L'Église géorgienne* (Rome, 1910), pp. 408–9 (which also gives a provisional list of the patriarchs of Abkhazet'i).

1616–22	Christopher
1623–30	Zak'aria Jorjadze
1630–37	Evdemoz Diasamidze
1638–60	Christopher Urdubegashvili
1660–76	Domenti K'aikhosros-dze Mukhran-Batoni
1678–88, 1691–96	Nikoloz Iot'amis-dze Amilakhoris-shvili
1688–91, 1696–1700	Ioane Diasamidze

1701–5	Evdemoz Diasamidze
1705–25, 1739–41	Domenti Levanis-dze Batonishvili
1725–37	Besarion Orbelishvili
1737–39	Cyril
1741–44	Nikoloz Kherkheulidze
1744–55, 1764–88	Anton Ieses-dze Batonishvili
1755–64	Joseph Jandierishvili
1788–1811	Anton Erekles-dze Batonishvili

Bibliography

BIBLIOGRAPHICAL GUIDES

Abuladze, I., *see* State Museum of Georgia.

Abzianidze, G., and others. K'art'uli zhurnalebisa da krebulebis analitikuri bibliograp'ia (Analytical Bibliography of Georgian Journals and Symposia). Vol. I–. Tiflis, 1940–. [In progress.]

Academies, Tiflis, Book Palace of Georgia. Dsignis matiane. SSSR sakhelmdsip'o bibliograp'iis organo, Sak'art'velos dsignis palatis qovelt'viuri biuletini (The Book Chronicle. Government Bibliographical Organ of the USSR, Monthly Bulletin of the Book Palace of Georgia). 11 vols. Tiflis, 1926–35. [? No more issued. The first number lists works published in Georgia from 1917 to 1925.]

Beridze, Shalva. "Bibliographie française de la Géorgie," *Revue des Bibliothèques*. Vols. 38–39. Paris, 1931–32.

Bianu, I., and N. Hodoş. Bibliografia Românéscă Veche (Ancient Rumanian Bibliography). Vol. I. Bucharest, 1903.

Bleichsteiner, Robert. The library of the late Robert Bleichsteiner (E. J. Brill, Catalogue No. 202). Leiden, 1955.

Brosset, Laurent. Bibliographie analytique des ouvrages de Monsieur Marie-Félicité Brosset. St. Petersburg, 1887.

Gizetti, A. Bibliograficheskii ukazatel' sochineniiam i stat'iam o voennykh deistviiakh Russkikh voisk na Kavkaze (Bibliographical Index to Works and Articles on the Military Operations of Russian Armies in the Caucasus). St. Petersburg, 1901.

Grigolia, K. Akhali K'art'lis tskhovreba (The New Georgian Annals). Tiflis, 1954. [A study of the continuations and various redactions of the Georgian chronicles.]

—— *see* State Museum of Georgia.

Houtsma, M. T., and others, eds. The Encyclopaedia of Islam. 4 vols. and Supplement. Leyden and London, 1913–38.

Janashia, S. N., *see* State Museum of Georgia.

Javakhishvili, I. A. Dzveli k'art'uli saistorio mdserloba—V–XVIII s.s. (Ancient Georgian Historical Literature—5th–18th Centuries). Tiflis, 1916.

Kekelidze, K. S., *see* State Museum of Georgia.

Kiknadze, G. I., gen. ed. K'art'uli dsigni, bibliograp'ia. (The Georgian Book, a Bibliography). Vol. I, 1629–1920. Tiflis, 1941.

Lang, David Marshall. "Georgian Studies in Oxford," in Oxford Slavonic Papers. Vol. VI. Oxford, 1955.

Melik'set'-Begi, L. Sak'art'velos istoriis dserilobit'i dsqaroebis publikatsiebi: Katalogi I (Publications of the Written Sources of Georgian history: Catalogue No. 1). Tiflis, 1949.

Mezhov, V. I. Bibliografiia Azii (Bibliography of Asia). 2d series. St. Petersburg, 1891–94.

Miansarov, M. Bibliographia Caucasica et Transcaucasica. Vol. I. St. Petersburg, 1874–76. [Only one volume published.]

Orbeli, R. R. "Sobranie gruzinskikh rukopisei Instituta Vostokovedeniia Akademii Nauk SSSR" (The Collection of Georgian manuscripts in the Oriental Institute of the Academy of Sciences of the USSR), in Uchenye Zapiski Instituta Vostokovedeniia (Bulletin of the Oriental Institute). Vol. IX. Moscow, 1954.

Polievktov, M. A. Evropeiskie puteshestvenniki po Kavkazu (European Travelers in the Caucasus). 2 vols. Tiflis, 1935–46. [Vol. I, to end of 18th century; Vol. II, 1800–1830.]

Qip'shidze, I. Ukazatel' k stat'iam i materialam v gruzinskoi periodicheskoi pechati, 1852–1910 (Index to Articles and Materials in the Georgian Periodical Press, 1852–1910). Petrograd, 1916.

State Museum of Georgia, Tiflis. Opisanie gruzinskikh rukopisei Gosudarstvennogo Muzeia Gruzii (Description of the Georgian Manuscripts in the State Museum of Georgia). Comp. and ed. by I. Abuladze, S. N. Janashia, K. S. Kekelidze, and others. Vol. I–. Tiflis, 1946–. [In progress.]

—— Sak'art'velos sakhelmdsip'o muzeumis dzvel khelnadsert'a satsavebis gzamkvlevi (Guide to the Ancient Manuscript Collections of the State Museum of Georgia). Comp. by a group of scholars and ed. by K. Grigolia. Tiflis, 1951.

T'aqaishvili, E. "Opisanie rukopisei biblioteki Obshchestva Rasprostraneniia Gramotnosti sredi Gruzinskogo Naseleniia" (Description of the Manuscripts in the Library of the Society for the Spreading of Education among the Georgian Populace), in Sbornik Materialov dlia Opisaniia Mestnostei i Plemen Kavkaza (Collection of Materials for the Description of the Localities and Tribes of the Caucasus). Vols. 31–41. Tiflis, 1903–10.

Toumanoff, Prince Cyril Leon. "Medieval Georgian Historical Literature," in Traditio. Vol. I. New York, 1943.

Tsagareli, A. A. Svedeniia o pamiatnikakh gruzinskoi pis'mennosti (Information on the Monuments of Georgian Literature). 3 vols. St. Petersburg, 1886–94.

ARCHIVE MATERIALS (MANUSCRIPT)

No attempt has been made to list archive material relating to Georgia in Soviet collections not at present open to Western scholars. Much of this material has, however, been printed, and will be found listed in the next section, Contemporary Works, below.

Istanbul. Prime Minister's Archives. Dossiers Nos. 897/418 and 900/831, dated A. H. 1140/1727–28 A.D., comprise a *mufassal* or detailed census for tax purposes of the city of Tiflis, at that time under Ottoman occupation. In the same archives there are four other registers covering the province of Gurjistan (Georgia) apart from Tiflis. (I owe this information to the kindness of my colleague, Professor B. Lewis.)

London. East India Company. Persia and Persian Gulf records, preserved in the India Office Library, London. See in particular Persia Factory Records, Vol. 22: John Malcolm's Embassy to Persia, 1799–1801.

Palermo. Biblioteca Comunale. Albums of drawings and impressions of Georgia by the seventeenth-century Italian missionary Cristoforo Castelli. A number of the drawings are reproduced in Allen, *History of the Georgian People*, and Tamarati, *L'Église géorgienne*. The accompanying text, written in Latin, is unpublished; a copy was made for Mr. W. E. D. Allen, who has kindly communicated it to me. The copyist has furnished the following details of the manuscript: "Nel manoscritto del Padre Cristoforo de Castelli che si conserva nella Biblioteca Comunale di Palermo ai segni 30q E 94 e che ha per titolo: Miscelaneo di personaggi praticati in Oriente, che non conoscono Dio, che l'ha creato, per mancamento de' ministri evangelici.— Ritratti di principi e regi orientali, nostri benefattori, et altre cose curiose.— Ritratti delle donne, che li principi Giorgeani et il re diedero alli padri nostri acciò li servissero.—Ms. del secolo XVII, in fog.—Da pag. 118 a 141 si legge quanto segue: [Chapter headings:]
   [a] De Iberia Orientalis Regni eiusque recentulis Bellis
   [b] De Regione Colchidea eiusque situ
   [c] De Colchico Principe eiusque Descendentia
   [d] De Laboribus quos patiuntur Clerici Regulares in Iberia, et Colchide pro Christi Fide praedicatione susceptis

Paris. Ministère des Affaires Étrangères.
Archives Consulaires: Tiflis.
Archives Diplomatiques, Correspondance Politique: Perse, Russie, Turquie.
Mémoires et Documents: Perse, Russie.

CONTEMPORARY WORKS

Works and documents written before 1832 but published after that date are also included in this section.

Akty sobrannye Kavkazskoiu Arkheograficheskoiu Kommissieiu, *see* Berzhe, A. P., and others.

Allerneueste Staat von Casan, Astracan, Georgien und vieler andern Landschaften, der. Nuremberg, 1723.

Amilakhori, Alek'sandre. Georgianuli istoria (Georgian History), tr. from the Russian by G. K'ik'odze, in the journal *Mnat'obi* (The Light), No. 8 (Tiflis), 1939.

Archil, King of Imeret'i and Kakhet'i. Archiliani (The Archiliad). Ed. by A. Baramidze and N. Berdzenishvili. 2 vols. Tiflis, 1936–37.

—— *see* Golovin, N. G.

Arkhiv Gosudarstvennogo Soveta (Archives of the Council of State). 5 vols. St. Petersburg, 1869–1904.

Artemii (Bogdanov, A.), of Mount Ararat. Lebensgeschichte seiner Jugend, etc. Halle, 1821.

—— Memoirs of the Life of Artemi, of Wagarschapat, near Mount Ararat, in Armenia: From the Original Armenian Written by Himself. London, 1822.

—— Zhizn' Artemiia Araratskogo (Life of Artemii of Ararat). 2 parts. St. Petersburg, 1813.

[On this Armenian memoirist, see N. Y. Marr, in *Zapiski Vostochnogo Otdeleniia Imp. Arkheologicheskogo Obshchestva* (Bulletin of the Oriental Division of the Imperial Archaeological Society), IX (St. Petersburg, 1896), 311–13.]

Avril, Père Philippe. Voyages en divers états d'Europe et d'Asie. Paris, 1692. Another ed., Paris, 1693.

Baert-Duholant, Baron C. de, ed. Mémoires historiques et géographiques sur les pays situés entre la Mer Noire et la Mer Caspienne. 3 parts. Paris, 1797.

Bagrat Batonishvili, Prince of Georgia. Akhali mot'khroba (Narrative of Modern Times). Ed. by T.' Lomouri. Tiflis, 1941. [Published together with *Akhali istoria* by David Batonishvili.]

Bak'radze, D. Z., *see* Wakhtang VI.

Baramidze, A., *see* Archil, King of Imeret'i and Kakhet'i; Gabashvili, Besarion; Guramishvili, D.; Ioane Batonishvili; Wakhtang VI, King of Georgia.

Barat'ashvili, Iese. Barat'ashvilis tskhovreba-anderdzi (The Life and Testament of Iese Barat'ashvili). Ed. by A. Ioseliani. Tiflis, 1950. [Forming Vol. 28 of *Materialy po Istorii Gruzii i Kavkaza*.]

Begichev, K. N., *see* Burnashev, S. D.

Berdzenishvili, N. A. Dokumentebi Sak'art'velos sotsialuri istoriidan, tom. I, II: Batonqmuri urt'iert'oba XV–XIX s.s. (Documents from Georgian Social History. Vols. I and II: Feudal Relationships from the Fifteenth to the Nineteenth Century). Tiflis, 1940–53.

—— Masalebi Sak'art'velos ekonomiuri istoriidan (Materials on Georgian Economic History). 2 vols. Tiflis, 1938–53.

—— *see* Archil, King of Imeret'i and Kakhet'i; Wakhusht, Prince.

Berzhe, A. P., and others, eds. Akty sobrannye Kavkazskoiu Arkheograficheskoiu Kommissieiu (Official Documents Collected by the Caucasian Archaeographical Commission). 12 vols. Tiflis, 1866–1912.

Bogdanov, A., see Artemii.

Botchoridze, G., ed. "P'urtselaant'euli k'ronika" (The P'urtseladze Chronicle), in Saistorio Moambe (Historical Bulletin). Book I. Tiflis, 1925.

Breitenbauch, G. A. von. Geschichte der Staaten von Georgien. Memmingen, 1788.

Bronevskii, S. Noveishie geograficheskie i istoricheskie izvestiia o Kavkaze (Latest Geographical and Historical Data on the Caucasus). 2 vols. Moscow, 1823.

Brosset, M.-F. Chronique Géorgienne. Paris, 1830.

—— Collection d'historiens arméniens. 2 vols. St. Petersburg, 1874–76.

—— "Documents originaux sur les relations diplomatiques de la Géorgie avec la France, vers la fin du règne de Louis XIV," Nouveau Journal Asiatique. Vol. IX. Paris, 1832.

—— "Explication de quelques inscriptions géorgiennes," in Mémoires de l'Académie des Sciences, 6th series, Sciences Politiques, Vol. IV. St. Petersburg, 1840.

—— Histoire de la Géorgie depuis l'Antiquité jusqu'au XIXme siècle. Vol. II, Parts 1 and 2: Histoire Moderne, and Introduction. St. Petersburg, 1856–58.

—— "Inscriptions tumulaires géorgiennes," in Mémoires de l'Académie des Sciences, 6th series, Sciences Politiques, Vol. V. St. Petersburg, 1845.

—— "Notice sur une lettre géorgienne du roi Artchil à Charles XII," in Mélanges Asiatiques. Vol. II. St. Petersburg, 1856.

—— Perepiska na inostrannykh iazykakh Gruzinskikh Tsarei s Rossiiskimi Gosudariami, 1639–1770 (Correspondence in Foreign Languages of the Georgian Kings with the Russian Emperors). St. Petersburg, 1861.

—— see Chkheidze, Sekhnia; Chubinov, D.; Giorgijanidze, P'arsadan; Kherkheulidze, Oman; Orbeliani, Papuna; Wakhusht, Prince.

Burnashev, S. D. Kartina Gruzii (Depiction of Georgia). Kursk, 1793. New edition. Tiflis: K. N. Begichev, 1896.

Burnashev, S. N. Novye materialy dlia zhizneopisaniia S. D. Burnasheva (New Materials for the Biography of S. D. Burnashev). St. Petersburg, 1901.

Busbecq, Ogier Ghiselin de. The Turkish Letters of Ogier Ghiselin de Busbecq, tr. and ed. by E. S. Forster. Oxford, 1927.

Butkov, P. G. Materialy dlia novoi istorii Kavkaza, 1722–1803 (Materials for the Modern History of the Caucasus, 1722–1803). 3 vols. St. Petersburg, 1869.

Chardin, Chevalier J. Voyages en Perse. 10 vols. Amsterdam, 1711. 4 vols. Amsterdam, 1735. Nouvelle édition, ed. Langlès. 10 vols. and atlas. Paris, 1811.

Chkheidze, Sekhnia. Chronicle of, trans. and ed. M.-F. Brosset, in Histoire de la Géorgie, Vol. II, Part 2.

Chubinov (Chubinashvili), David, and M.-F. Brosset, ed. K'art'lis tskhovreba (The Life of Georgia). Vol. II. St. Petersburg, 1854.

Churchill, A. and J., *see* Gemelli-Careri, G. F.

Clairac, Louis André de la Mamye. Histoire de Perse depuis le commencement de ce Siècle. 3 vols. Paris, 1750.

Council of State, Imperial, *see* Arkhiv.

Dapper, O. "Het Landschap van Georgie," in Asia . . . beneffens een volkome Beschryving van geheel Persie, Georgie, Mengrelie, etc. Amsterdam, 1672.

David Batonishvili, Prince-Regent of Georgia. Akhali istoria (Modern History). Ed. by T'. Lomouri. Tiflis, 1941.

—— "Dve zapiski tsarevicha Davida 'O luchshem ustroistve Gruzii' " (Two Memoranda of Prince David "On Improved Administration of Georgia"), ed. by I. K. Enikolopov, in Materialy po Istorii Gruzii i Kavkaza (Materials for the History of Georgia and the Caucasus). Part I. Tiflis, 1942.

—— Kratkaia istoriia o Gruzii (Brief History of Georgia). St. Petersburg, 1805.

—— Masalebi Sak'art'velos istoriisat'vis shekrebili Batonishvilis Davit' Giorgis-dzisa da misi dzmebisagan, 1744–1840 (Material on Georgian History Collected by Prince David, Son of Giorgi, and His Brothers). Ed. by M. Janashvili. Tiflis, 1906.

—— "Shedegi Kakhet'is tskhovrebisa" (Continuation of the History of Kakhet'i), in K'art'lis tskhovreba, ed. Chubinov and Brosset. Vol. II. St. Petersburg, 1854.

—— *see* Reineggs, J.

Dondua, V. D., *see* Ioane Batonishvili.

Dubetskii, I. P. "Zapiski" (Memoirs), in Russkaia Starina (Russian Antiquity). Vol. LXXXIII. St. Petersburg, 1895.

Dubrovin, N. T., ed. Bumagi Kniazia G. A. Potemkina-Tavricheskogo, 1774–1788 gg. (Papers of Prince G. A. Potemkin-Tavricheskii, 1774–1788). St. Petersburg, 1893.

Du Cerceau, Father J.-A., *see* Krusinski, Father J. T.

Egnatashvili, the Monk. Akhali K'art'lis tskhovreba (The Modern Georgian Annals). Ed. by I. A. Javakhishvili. Tiflis, 1940. [A continuation of the Georgian Chronicle up to the beginning of the 18th century.]

Eichwald, E. Reise in den Kaukasus. Bd. II. Stuttgart, 1837.

Ellis, G. Memoir of a Map of the Countries Comprehended between the Black Sea and the Caspian; with an Account of the Caucasian Nations. London, 1788.

Emin, Emin Joseph. The Life and Adventures of Joseph Emin, an Armenian, Written by Himself. London, 1792. New edition. Calcutta, 1918.

Enikolopov, I. K., *see* David Batonishvili; Reineggs, J.

Enuk'idze, T'., *see* Wakhtang VI.

Erekle II, King of Georgia. "Mep'e Erekle meoris dokumentebi" (Documents of King Erekle II), *Moambe* (The Messenger). Tiflis, 1894.

Eristov-Sharvashidze, N. Kniga o pridanom tsarevny Niny Georgievny, pamiatnik 1791 goda (The Book of the Dowry of Queen Nina Georgievna, a Document of 1791). Moscow, 1916.

Ermolov, General A. P. "Zapiski vo vremia upravleniia Gruziei, 1816–1827" (Memoirs during his Governorship of Georgia, 1816–1827), in Chteniia v Imp. Obshchestve Istorii i Drevnostei Rossiiskikh (Readings in the Imperial Society of Russian History and Antiquities). Moscow, 1866 (Books II–III) and 1867 (Books III–IV).

Estreicher, K., see Krusinski, Father J. T.

Eugenius, Metropolitan of Kiev. Istoricheskoe izobrazhenie Gruzii (Historical Depiction of Georgia). St. Petersburg, 1802. Georgien, oder historisches Gemälde von Grusien, tr. by F. Schmidt. Riga and Leipzig, 1804.

Ferrières-Sauveboeuf, Comte de. Mémoires historiques, politiques et géographiques des voyages faits en Turquie, en Perse, etc. 2 vols. Paris, 1790.

Ferriol, Marquis de. Correspondance du Marquis de Ferriol, Ambassadeur de Louis XIV à Constantinople. Ed. by E. Varenbergh. Anvers, 1870.

Forster, E. S., see Busbecq.

Francklin, W. Observations Made on a Tour from Bengal to Persia. 2d ed. London, 1790.

Frenkel, A. S., see Wakhtang VI, King of Georgia.

Freygang, F. von. Letters from the Caucasus and Georgia. London, 1823.

—— Lettres sur le Caucase et la Géorgie. Hamburg, 1816.

[And versions in several other languages.]

Gabashvili, Besarion, known as Besiki. T'khzulebat'a sruli krebuli (Complete Collection of Works). Ed. by A. Baramidze and V. T'op'uria. 3d ed. Tiflis, 1932.

Gamba, Chevalier J. F. de. Voyage dans la Russie méridionale. 2 vols. and atlas. Paris, 1826.

Gemelli-Careri, G. F. Voyage round the World, in Churchill, Collection of Voyages and Travels. Vol. IV. London, 1732.

Ghoghoberidze, E., see Orbeliani, Sulkhan-Saba.

Gilanents, Petros di Sargis. "Dnevnik osady Ispagani Afganami" (Diary of the siege of Isfahan by the Afghans), ed. by K. Patkanov, in Zapiski (Bulletin) of the Imperial Academy of Sciences, Vol. XVII, Appendix 3. St. Petersburg, 1870.

Giorgijanidze, P'arsadan. Chronicle of, trans. and ed. by M.-F. Brosset, in Histoire de la Géorgie, Vol. II, Part 1.

—— P'arsadan Giorgijanidzis istoria (History of P'arsadan Giorgijanidze). Ed. by S. Kakabadze. Tiflis, 1926. Reprinted from Saistorio Moambe (Historical Bulletin). Vol. II. Tiflis, 1925.

Golovin, N. G., ed. Pis'ma Imeretinskogo tsaria Archila k boiarinu Fedoru Alekseevichu Golovinu (Letters of King Archil of Imeret'i to the Boyar Fedor Alekseevich Golovin). Moscow, 1856.

Grabsch, G. "Account of the Attempt Made by the Brethren at Sarepta, near

Grabsch, G. (*Continued*)
Astrachan, to Spread the Gospel among the Tartar Tribes Inhabiting Mount Caucasus," Extracted from the Periodical Accounts relating to the Missions of the Church of the United Brethren, and reprinted as an appendix to Klaproth, *Travels in the Caucasus and Georgia,* tr. Schoberl. London, 1814.

Griboedov, A. S. Polnoe Sobranie Sochinenii (Complete Collection of Works). Ed. by Piksanov. Vol. III. Petrograd, 1917.

Güldenstädt, J. A. Reisen durch Russland und im Caucasischen Gebürge . . . herausgegeben von P. S. Pallas. 2 vols. St. Petersburg, 1787–91.

—— Reisen nach Georgien und Imerethi. Ed. by H. J. von Klaproth. Berlin, 1815.

Guramishvili, D. Davit'iani: T'khzulebat'a sruli krebuli (The Lay of David: Complete Collection of Writings). Ed. by A. Baramidze and others. Tiflis, 1955.

Hanway, Jonas. The Revolutions of Persia. 2 vols. London, 1753.

Herbert, Sir T. Somes Yeares Travel into Africa and Asia. 4th ed. London, 1677.

Hinz, W., *see* Kaempfer, E.

Imperial Council of State, *see* Arkhiv.

Ioane Batonishvili. Kalmasoba (The Alms-Collecting Tour). Ed. by K. Kekelidze and A. Baramidze. 2 vols. Tiflis, 1936–48. Russian trans. by V. Dondua. Tiflis, 1945.

Iordanishvili, S., *see* Orbeliani, Sulkhan-Saba.

Ioseb Tp'ileli (Saakadze). Did-Mouraviani (The Lay of the Grand Constable). Ed. by G. Leonidze. Tiflis, 1939.

—— Velikii Mouravi: Poema XVII veka o Georgii Saakadze (The Grand Constable: A 17th Century Poem about Giorgi Saakadze). Tr. by G. Tsagareli. Moscow, 1945.

Ioseliani, A., *see* Barat'ashvili, I.

Janashvili, M., *see* David Batonishvili.

Javakhishvili, I. A., *see* Egnatashvili, the Monk.

Jean de Luca, Father. "Relation des Tartares du Crim, des Nogais, des Circasses, et des Abassas," in M. Thévenot, Relations de divers voyages curieux. Vol. I. Paris, 1696.

Kaempfer, Engelbert. Am Hofe des persischen Grosskönigs. Tr. and ed. by W. Hinz. Leipzig, 1940.

Kakabadze, S., ed. Istoriuli sabut'ebi (Historical Documents). Books I–V. Tiflis, 1913.

—— *see* Giorgijanidze, P'arsadan.

Karbelashvili, P. "Amilakhvart'a sagvareulos istoriuli gujrebi" (Historical Charters of the Amilakhvari Family), in Dzveli Sak'art'velo: L'ancienne Géorgie. Vol. II. Tiflis, 1913.

Karst, J., *see* Wakhtang VI, King of Georgia.

Kekelidze, K. S., *see* Ioane Batonishvili.

Ker Porter, Sir Robert. Travels in Georgia, Persia, Armenia, Ancient Babylonia, etc. 2 vols. London, 1821–22.

Kherkheulidze, Oman. "Tskhovreba mep'is Irakli meorisa" (Life of King Erekle II), in K'art'lis tskhovreba, ed. Chubinov and Brosset. Vol. II. St. Petersburg, 1854.

—— "Vie du roi Eréclé II," tr. and ed. by M.-F. Brosset, in Histoire de la Géorgie, Vol. II, Part 2.

Khoubov, Georg Melk'isedek. Opisanie dostopamiatnikh proizshestvii v Armenii . . . ot Patriarshestva Simeonova 1779 g. do 1809 goda (Description of Memorable Events in Armenia from the Patriarchate of Simeon in 1779 until 1809). St. Petersburg, 1811.

Khubua, M. Sak'art'velos muzeumis sparsuli p'irmanebi da ok'mebi (The Persian Firmans and Administrative Documents in the Georgian Museum). Tiflis, 1949.

K'ik'odze, Geronti, *see* Amilakhori, A.

Klaproth, H. J. von. Reise in den Kaukasus und nach Georgien. 2 vols. Halle-Berlin, 1812–14.

—— Tableau historique, géographique, ethnographique et politique du Caucase. Paris, 1827.

—— Travels in the Caucasus and Georgia. Tr. from the German by F. Schoberl. London, 1814.

—— Voyage au Mont Caucase et en Géorgie. 2 vols. Paris, 1823.

—— *see* Güldenstädt, J. A.

Krusinski, Father Judas Thaddeus. Histoire de la dernière révolution de Perse. Ed. by Du Cerceau. 2 vols. Paris, 1728.

—— History of the Revolutions of Persia. 2d ed. 2 vols. London, 1740.

—— Tragica Vertentis belli Persici Historia. Lemberg, 1740.

[For other editions and versions of Krusinski's works, *see* K. Estreicher, *Bibliografia Polska,* Vol. XX, Cracow, 1905.]

La Mamye Clairac, *see* Clairac.

Lamberti, Father Arcangelo. "Relation de la Mengrellie," in M. Thévenot, Relations de divers voyages curieux. Vol. I. Paris, 1696.

Lang, David Marshall. "Count Todtleben's Expedition to Georgia, 1769–1771, According to a French Eyewitness" in Bulletin of the School of Oriental and African Studies, London. Vol. XIII. 1951.

Langlès, L. M., *see* Chardin, Chevalier J.

Leandro di Santa Cecilia. Persia, ovvero Secondo Viaggio dell'Oriente. Rome, 1757.

Lebedeva, Olga, *see* Macarius III, Patriarch of Antioch.

Leonidze, G., *see* Ioseb Tp'ileli.

Likhachev, D. S., ed. Puteshestviya Russkikh poslov XVI–XVII vv. (Travels of Russian Ambassadors of the 16th and 17th Centuries). Moscow, 1954. [Contemporary reports, including that of the Russian Embassy to Mingrelia.]

Lomouri, T'., see Bagrat Batonishvili; David Batonishvili; Wakhusht, Prince.

Lovell, A., see Simon, R.

Macarius III, Patriarch of Antioch. Histoire de la Conversion des Géorgiens. Arabic text ed. and tr. by Olga Lebedeva. Rome, 1905.

Malcolm, Sir John. The History of Persia. 2 vols. London, 1815. 2d edition. London, 1829.

Manstein, General C. H. Memoirs of Russia. London, 1770.

Marr, N. Y., see Artemii.

Martens, G. F. de. Recueil de Traités. . . . des Puissances et États de l'Europe. 2d ed. 8 vols. Göttingen, 1817–35.

Melik'set'-Begi, L., ed. Corpus Juris Armeniaci, versio Georgica. Tiflis, 1927.

Meskhia, Shot'a, ed. Masalebi K'art'l-Kakhet'is samep'os samokheleo dsqobis istoriisat'vis (Materials on the Administrative Organization of the Monarchy of K'art'lo-Kakhet'i). Tiflis, 1948. [Forming Vol. 26 of Materialy po Istorii Gruzii i Kavkaza.]

Minorsky, V., ed. Tadhkirat al-Muluk: A Manual of Safavid Administration. London, 1943.

Mohammed Taher, see P'ut'uridze, V.

Novikov, N. I. Drevniaia Russkaia Vivliotheka. (Ancient Russian Library). Moscow, 1788–91. [Volumes of these years contain reports of Russian embassies to Georgia.]

Olearius, Adam. Voyages and Travels. 2d ed. London, 1669. [And other editions in various languages.]

Olivier, G. A. Voyage dans l'Empire Othoman, l'Egypte, et la Perse. 3 vols. and atlas. Paris, 1801–7.

Orbeliani, Papuna. Chronicle of, tr. and ed. by M.-F. Brosset, in Histoire de la Géorgie, Vol. II, Part 2.

Orbeliani, Sulkhan-Saba. The Book of Wisdom and Lies. Tr. by Sir J. O. Wardrop. Kelmscott Press, London, 1894. Kniga Mudrosti i Lzhi. Russian trans. by A. A. Tsagareli. St. Petersburg, 1878. O Mudrosti Vymysla. Russian trans. by E. Ghoghoberidze. Moscow, 1951. Die Weisheit der Lüge. German trans. by M. Tseret'eli. Berlin, 1933.

—— Mogzauroba Evropashi (Travels in Europe). Ed. by S. Iordanishvili. Tiflis, 1940.

Ozell, J., see Tournefort, Pitton de.

Pallas, P. S., see Güldenstädt, J. A.

Perry, J. The State of Russia under the Present Czar. London, 1716.

Peter the Great, Tsar of Russia. Pis'ma i bumagi (Letters and Papers). Vol. I–. St. Petersburg, 1887–. [In progress.]

—— see Tumanskii, Th.

Peyssonnel, C. C. de. Essai sur les troubles actuels de Perse et de Géorgie. Paris, 1754.

—— Traité sur le Commerce de la Mer Noire. 2 vols. Paris, 1787.

Piksanov, N. K., *see* Griboedov, A. S.

Pitton de Tournefort, *see* Tournefort.

Polievktov, M. A., ed. Posol'stvo Kniazia Myshetskogo i D'iaka Kliuchareva v Kakhetiiu, 1640–43 (Embassy of Prince Myshetskii and the Secretary Kliucharev to Kakhet'i, 1640–43). Tiflis, 1928.

—— Posol'stvo stol'nika Tolochanova i d'iaka Ievleva v Imeretiiu, 1650–52 (Embassy of the Cup-Bearer Tolochanov and the Secretary Ievlev to Imeret'i, 1650–52). Tiflis, 1926.

Potemkin, Prince G. A., *see* Dubrovin, N. T.

P'urtseladze, D. P. Gruzinskie dvorianskie gramoty (Charters of the Georgian Nobility). Tiflis, 1881.

—— Gruzinskie krest'ianskie gramoty, krepostnye i sudebnye akty, gramoty i pis'ma gruzinskikh i persidskikh tsarstvennykh osob (Georgian Peasant Charters, Deeds Relating to Serfs, and Judicial Decisions, Charters, and Letters of Georgian and Persian Royal Personages). Tiflis, 1882.

P'ut'uridze, V. "Mohamed T'aheris tsnobebi Sak'art'velos shesakheb" (The Information of Mohammed Taher concerning Georgia), in Materialy po Istorii Gruzii i Kavkaza. Vol. 30. Tiflis, 1954.

Reineggs, J. Allgemeine historisch-topographische Beschreibung des Caucasus. 2 vols. Gotha, Hildesheim, and St. Petersburg, 1796–97.

—— "Kurzer Auszug der Geschichte von Georgien" in Neue Nordische Beyträge zur Erd- und Völkerbeschreibung, Bd. III. St. Petersburg and Leipzig, 1782.

[Concerning Reineggs and his works on Georgia, see I. K. Enikolopov, "Tsarevich David o Reinegse" (Prince David on Reineggs), in *Materialy po Istorii Gruzii i Kavkaza* (Materials on the History of Georgia and the Caucasus). Vol. 29. Tiflis, 1951.]

Rottiers, Colonel B. E. A. Itinéraire de Tiflis à Constantinople. Brussels, 1829.

Sanson, Father P. Voyage de Perse. Paris, 1695.

Sauveboeuf, *see* Ferrières-Sauveboeuf.

Schmidt, F., *see* Eugenius, Metropolitan of Kiev.

Schoberl, F., *see* Klaproth, H. J. von.

Schweigger, Salomon. Ein newe Reyssbeschreibung auss Theutschland nach Constantinopel und Jerusalem. Nuremberg, 1608.

Simon, R. The Critical History of the Religions and Customs of the Eastern Nations . . . Now Done into English, by A. Lovell. London, 1685.

Soimonov, Th. Opisanie Kaspiiskogo Moria (Description of the Caspian Sea). St. Petersburg, 1763.

Sokolov, A. E. "Puteshestvie v Imeretiiu, 1802" (Journey to Imeret'i, 1802), in Chteniia v Imp. Obshchestve Istorii i Drevnostei Rossiiskikh (Readings in the Imperial Society of Russian History and Antiquities). Book IV. Moscow, 1873.

Solomon II, King of Imeret'i. "Mep'e Solomon meoris drois dserilebi" (Letters

Solomon II, King of Imeret'i (*Continued*)
of the time of King Solomon II), *Moambe* (The Messenger). Part III. Tiflis, 1896.

T'aqaishvili, E., ed. "K'snis kheobis statistikuri aghdseriloba" (Statistical Description of the K'sani Valley), in Shromebi (Works) of Tiflis State University. Vol. 45. Tiflis, 1951.

—— Masalani Sak'art'velos statistikuri aghdserilobisa met'vramete saukuneshi (Materials on the Statistical Description of Georgia in the 18th Century). Tiflis, 1907.

—— Sak'art'velos sidzveleni: Les antiquités géorgiennes. (A Collection of Georgian Historical Charters.) 3 vols. Tiflis, 1899–1910. [Vol. I, Part 1, reprinted at Tiflis in 1920; supplement to Vol. III published at Tiflis, 1926.]

—— *see* Tlashadze, I.

Tavernier, J.-B. Les six voyages de Monsieur Jean-Baptiste Tavernier en Turquie, en Perse, et aux Indes. Nouvelle édition. 6 vols. Paris, 1713. [And other editions in various languages.]

Tchqonia, T'., *see* Wakhtang VI, King of Georgia.

T'eimuraz Batonishvili. Istoria dadsqebit'gan Iveriisa, ese igi Giorgiisa, romel ars sruliad Sak'art'veloysa (A History of Iveria, That Is, Georgia, Comprising the Entire Land of Sak'art'velo, from the Beginning). St. Petersburg, 1848.

Thévenot, M., *see* Jean de Luca; Lamberti, A.

Tlashadze, Iese. Kat'alikoz-Bak'ariani (The Poem of Catholicos Domenti and Prince Bak'ar). Ed. by E. T'aqaishvili. Tiflis, 1895.

T'op'uria, V., *see* Gabashvili, Besarion.

Tournefort, Pitton de. Relation d'un Voyage du Levant. 2 vols. Paris, 1717.

—— A Voyage into the Levant. [Translated by J. Ozell.] 3 vols. London, 1741.

Tsagareli, A. A. Gramoty i drugie istoricheskie dokumenty XVIII stoletiia otnosiashchiesia do Gruzii (Charters and Other Historical Documents of the 18th Century Relating to Georgia). 2 vols. in 3 parts. St. Petersburg, 1891–1902.

—— *see* Orbeliani, Sulkhan-Saba.

Tsagareli, G., *see* Ioseb Tp'ileli.

Tseret'eli, M., *see* Orbeliani, Sulkhan-Saba.

Tsintsadze, I. Z. "Ori sabut'i Ruset'-Sak'art'velos urt'iert'obis istoriidan, 1768–1774 ds. ds. Ruset'-T'urk'et'is omshi" (Two Documents on the History of Russo-Georgian Relations during the Russo-Turkish War of 1768-1774), in Bulletin de l'Institut Marr, Vol. V–VI. Tiflis, 1940.

Tumanskii, Th. Sobranie raznykh zapisok o zhizni Petra Velikogo (Collection of Various Memoirs on the Life of Peter the Great). Vol. V. St. Petersburg, 1787.

Umikashvili, P., *see* Wakhtang VI, King of Georgia.

Vakhtangi, *see* Wakhtang VI, King of Georgia.

—— "Guriis samt'avros sotsialur-ekonomiuri vit'areba XIX saukunis pirvel mesamedshi" (The Social and Economic Condition of the Principality of Guria in the First Third of the 19th Century), in Materialy po Istorii Gruzii i Kavkaza. Vol. 30. Tiflis, 1954.

—— Istorikosi Dimitri Bak'radze (The Historian Dimitri Bak'radze). Batum, 1950.

Enikolopov, I. K. Griboedov v Gruzii (Griboedov in Georgia). Tiflis, 1954.

Ermolov, A. A. P. Ermolov: Biograficheskii ocherk (A. P. Ermolov: Biographical Sketch). St. Petersburg, 1912.

Esadze, B. S., ed. Letopis' Gruzii, iubileinyi sbornik. (Chronicle of Georgia, a Jubilee Symposium). Tiflis, 1913.

Ezov, G. Snosheniia Petra Velikogo s armianskim narodom (Relations of Peter the Great with the Armenian People). St. Petersburg, 1898.

Gabashvili, V. N. "Dasturlamalis 1729 ds. khelnadseri" (A Manuscript of the Dasturlamali of the Year 1729), in Materialy po Istorii Gruzii i Kavkaza. Vol. 30. Tiflis, 1954.

—— "Ioseb k'art'veli, XVIII s-is diplomati da istorikosi" (Joseph the Georgian, an 18th Century Diplomat and Historian), in Materialy po Istorii Gruzii i Kavkaza. Vol. 32. Tiflis, 1955.

—— "Sakhelmdsip'o dsqobilebis sakit'khisat'vis gvianp'eodalur Sak'art'veloshi" (On the Question of State Organization in Late Feudal Georgia), in Mimomkhilveli (The Observer). Vol. II. Tiflis, 1951.

—— "Sat'at'ro gamosaghebeli gvianp'eodalur Sak'art'veloshi" (The Tatar Tax in Late Feudal Georgia), in Mimomkhilveli (The Observer). Vol. III. Tiflis, 1953.

Gamqrelidze, G. Khelosneba Tp'ilisshi (Trades and Crafts in Tiflis). Tiflis, 1926.

Gardane, A. dc. Mission du Général Gardane en Perse. Paris, 1865.

Ghoghoberidze, E., see Tseret'eli, Akaki.

Gibb, H. A. R., and H. Bowen. Islamic Society and the West. Vol. I. Oxford, 1950.

Gogebashvili, A. "The Battle of Aspindza," in Georgica. Vol. I. Nos. 4–5. London, 1937.

Gomiashvili, A. and Gvetadze, R. Khalkhuri poezia (Popular Poetry). Tiflis, 1950.

Gorgadze, A. Sak'art'velos me-XVIII saukunis samkhedro istoriis masalebi (Material on the Military History of Georgia in the 18th Century). Tiflis, 1927.

Gotsadze, M. K. K'art'uli zhurnalistikis istoria (History of Georgian Journalism). Vol. I. Tiflis, 1954.

Gozalishvili, G. 1832 dslis shet'k'muleba (The Conspiracy of 1832). Tiflis, 1935.

Grekov, B. D., S. V. Bakhrushin, and V. I. Lebedev. Istoriia SSSR. (History of the USSR). Vol. I. 2d ed. Moscow, 1947.

Grigolia, A. Custom and Justice in the Caucasus: The Georgian Highlanders. Philadelphia, 1939.

Grigorovich, N. Kantsler Kniaz' Aleksandr Andreevich Bezborodko (Chancellor Prince A. A. Bezborodko). 2 vols. St. Petersburg, 1879–81.

Grishashvili, I. Sayat'nova da dzveli Tp'ilisi (Sayat'nova and Old Tiflis). Tiflis, 1918.

Grunwald, C. de. Trois siècles de diplomatie russe. Paris, 1945.

Gugushvili, A. "The Chronological-Genealogical Table of the Kings of Georgia," in Georgica. Vol. I, Nos. 2–3. London, 1936.

—— "Ethnographical and Historical Division of Georgia," in Georgica. Vol. I, Nos. 2–3. London, 1936.

—— see Allen, W. E. D.

Gvritishvili, D. "Epizodi sat'avadoebis urt'iertobis istoriidan" (An Episode from the History of Relations between the Principalities), in Materialy po Istorii Gruzii i Kavkaza (Materials for the History of Georgia and the Caucasus). Part 2. Tiflis, 1951.

—— Goris istoria (History of Gori). Tiflis, 1954.

—— "K'art'veli khalkhis brdzolis istoriidan t'urk' da spars dampqroblebis dsinaaghmdeg XVIII s. pirvel nakhevarshi: Givi Amilakhvaris ajanqeba" (From the History of the Georgian People's Struggle against Turkish and Persian Rule in the First Half of the 18th Century: The Insurrection of Givi Amilakhvari), in Mimomkhilveli (The Observer). Vol. III. Tiflis, 1953.

—— P'eodaluri Sak'art'velos sotsialuri urt'iert'obis istoriidan: K'art'lis sat'ava-doebi (From the History of the Social Relationships of Feudal Georgia: The K'art'lian Principalities). Tiflis, 1955.

—— "Zemok'art'lis sadrosho" (The Banner or Military District of Upper K'art'li), in Shromebi (Works) of Tiflis State University. Vol. 41. Tiflis, 1950.

Gvritishvili, D., and S. Meskhia. T'bilisis istoria (History of Tiflis). Tiflis, 1952.

Hammer-Purgstall, Baron J. von. Geschichte des Osmanischen Reiches. 10 vols. Budapest and Vienna, 1827–35.

Haxthausen, A. von. Transcaucasia. London, 1854.

—— Transkaukasia. 2 vols. Leipzig, 1856.

Herbette, M. Une Ambassade persane sous Louis XIV. Paris, 1907.

Holldack, Felix. Zwei Grundsteine zu einer Grusinischen Staats- und Rechts-geschichte. Leipzig, 1907.

Ioannisian, A. R. "Armianskoe natsional-osvoboditel'noe dvizhenie v 60-kh gg. XVIII stoletiia" (The Armenian National-liberation Movement in the '60s of the 18th Century), in Izvestiia Akademii Nauk SSSR, Ser. ist. fil. (Bulletin of the Academy of Sciences of the USSR, Historico-Philosophical Series), Vol. III (1946), No. 2.

Ioseliani, Platon. Goroda, sushchestvovavshie i sushchestvuiushchie v Gruzii (Towns Formerly and Now Existing in Georgia). Tiflis, 1850.

—— Istoricheskii vzgliad na sostoianie Gruzii pod vlastei Tsarei-Magometan (Historical Survey of the State of Georgia under the Rule of the Moham-medan Kings). Tiflis, 1849.

—— A Short History of the Georgian Church. Tr. by the Reverend S. C. Ma-lan. London, 1866.

—— Tskhovreba Giorgi metsametisa (Life of Giorgi XIII). Tiflis, 1936.

Jamburia, G. D. K'art'uli p'eodaluri urt'iert'obis istoriidan: Somkhit'-Sabarat'-ianos sat'avadoebi (From the History of Georgian Feudal Relations: The Principalities of Somkhit'-Sabarat'iano). Tiflis, 1955.

Janashia, S. N. "K'art'uli patronqmobis bunebisa da dsarmoshobis sakit'khisat'-vis" (On the Problem of the Nature and Formation of Georgian Feudalism), in Shromebi (Collected Works). Vol. II. Tiflis, 1952.

—— "Shekheduleba p'eodaluri aghzrdisa da ganat'lebis shesakheb da mat'i dsesebi XVII saukunis Sak'art'veloshi" (Conceptions of and Regulations for Feudal Education and Enlightenment in 17th-Century Georgia), in Shromebi (Collected Works). Vol. II. Tiflis, 1952.

—— "Vakhushti k'art'uli p'eodalizmis shesakheb" (Wakhusht on Georgian Feudalism), in Shromebi (Collected Works). Vol. II. Tiflis, 1952.

—— see Berdzenishvili, N. A.

Janashvili, M. G. "Sak'art'velos deda-k'alak'i Tp'ilisi" (Georgia's Mother-City Tiflis), in Krebuli (Literary Symposium). 9 parts. K'ut'ais, 1899.

Javakhishvili, I. A. Damokidebuleba Ruset'sa da Sak'art'velos shoris me-XVIII-e saukuneshi (Russo-Georgian Relations in the 18th Century). Tiflis, 1919.

—— "K'alak'ebi, sak'alak'o dsesdsqobileba da tskhovrebis vit'areba Sak'art'-veloshi XVII–XVIII ss." (Towns, Urban Administration, and Town Life in Georgia in the 17th and 18th Centuries). Extract from the journal Promet'e (Prometheus), No. 1. Tiflis, 1918.

—— K'art'uli samart'lis istoria (History of Georgian Law). 2 vols. 2d ed. Tiflis, 1928–29.

—— K'art'veli eris istoria (History of the Georgian People). Rev. ed. 4 vols. Tiflis, 1941–51.

—— Sak'art'velos ekonomiuri istoria (Economic History of Georgia). 2 vols. 2d ed. Tiflis, 1930–34.

—— Sak'art'velos sazghvrebi (The Frontiers of Georgia). Tiflis, 1919.

—— see Berdzenishvili, N. A.

Kakabadze, S. Cherty feodal'nogo stroia i krest'ianskie povinnosti v Gruzii v kontse srednykh vekov (Features of the Feudal System and Peasant Dues in Georgia at the Close of the Middle Ages). Tiflis, 1912.

—— Dserilebi da masalebi Sak'art'velos istoriisat'vis (Articles and Materials on Georgian History). Book I. Tiflis, 1914.

—— Dsvrili shtudiebi Sak'art'velos istoriis sakit'khebis shesakheb (Short Essays on Questions of Georgian History). Tiflis, 1914.

Kakabadze, S. (*Continued*)
—— Kratkii obzor istorii Gruzii (Brief Survey of the History of Georgia). Sukhum, 1941.
—— Kvleva-dziebani Sak'art'velos istoriis sakit'khebis shesakheb (Researches on Questions of Georgian History). Tiflis, 1920.
—— Saeklesio rep'ormebisat'vis Solomon pirvelis dros (On the Church Reforms of the Time of Solomon I). Tiflis, 1913.
—— Saistorio dziebani (Historical Researches). Tiflis, 1924.
—— Saistorio krebuli (Historical Miscellany). 4 vols. Tiflis, 1924–29.
—— Sak'art'velos mokle istoria: Akhali saukuneebis epok'a (Short History of Georgia: Modern Period). Tiflis, 1920.
—— "Sap'asis istoriisat'vis Sak'art'veloshi" (History of Price Changes in Georgia), in Saistorio Moambe (Historical Bulletin). Vol. II, Part 1. Tiflis, 1925.
—— "Sasiskhlo sigelebis shesakheb" (Concerning Wergild Charters), in Saistorio Moambe (Historical Bulletin). Vol. I, Part 2. Tiflis, 1924.
Kapanadze, D. G. Gruzinskaia numizmatika (Georgian Numismatics). Moscow, 1955.
—— K'art'uli numizmatika (Georgian Numismatics). Tiflis, 1950.
Kapterev, N. F. Kharakter otnoshenii Rossii k pravoslavnomu vostoku v XVI i XVII stoletiiakh (The Nature of Russian Relations with the Orthodox East in the 16th and 17th Centuries). 2d ed. Sergiev Posad, 1914.
Karitchashvili, D. K'art'uli dsignis betchdvis istoria (History of Georgian Book Printing). Tiflis, 1929.
Karst, J. Armenisches Rechtsbuch. 2 vols. Strasbourg and Venice, 1905–6.
—— Littérature géorgienne chrétienne. Paris, 1934.
—— Précis de numismatique géorgienne. Paris and Strasbourg, 1938.
—— "Recherches sur l'histoire du droit ecclésiastique Carthvélien," in Archives d'Histoire du Droit Oriental. Vols. I–II. Brussels, 1937–38.
Kavkazskii Kalendar' (Caucasian Calendar). Tiflis, annually from 1846.
Kekelidze, K. S. Dzveli k'art'uli mdserlobis istoria (History of Ancient Georgian Literature). 2 vols. 3d ed. Tiflis, 1951–52.
—— K'art'uli literaturis istoria. II tomi: saero mdserloba XI–XVIII s. (History of Georgian Literature. Vol. II: Profane Literature from the 11th to the 18th Century). Tiflis, 1924.
Kekelidze, K. S. and A. Baramidze. Dzveli k'art'uli literatura, V–XVIII ss. (Ancient Georgian Literature, 5th–18th Centuries). (Vol. I of History of Georgian Literature in Four Volumes.) Tiflis, 1954.
Khachapuridze, G. V. K istorii Gruzii pervoi poloviny XIX veka (On the History of Georgia in the First Half of the 19th Century). Tiflis, 1950.
—— "K voprosu o kul'turnykh sviaziakh Rossii i Gruzii v pervuiu polovinu XIX veka" (On the Question of the Cultural Links between Russia and Georgia during the First Half of the 19th Century), *Voprosy Istorii* (Questions of History), Nos. 5 and 6, Moscow, 1946.

Khakhanov (Khakhanashvili), A. S. Aperçu géographique et abrégé de l'histoire et de la littérature géorgienne. Paris and Tiflis, 1900.

—— "K'art'velt' mep'et'a tituli, kurt'kheva da regaliebi" (The Title, Coronation, and Regalia of the Georgian Kings), *Moambe* (The Messenger). Tiflis, 1895.

Khant'adze, Sh. A. "Sakhelmdsip'o puris gadasakhadi (sursat'i) K'art'l-Kakhet'shi me-19 saukunis damdegs" (The State Bread Tax, Known as Sursat'i, in K'art'lo-Kakhet'i at the Beginning of the 19th Century), in Materialy po Istorii Gruzii i Kavkaza. Vol. 32. Tiflis, 1955.

K'ik'odze, Geronti. Iraklii vtoroi (Erekle the Second). 2d ed. Tiflis, 1948.

Kikvidze, A. Ia. Glekht'a ajanqeba Kakhet'shi 1812 ds. (The Peasant Rising in Kakhet'i in 1812). Tiflis, 1941.

—— Sak'art'velos istoria, XIX saukune (History of Georgia in the 19th Century). Tiflis, 1954.

Kosarik, D. David Guramishvili. Kiev, 1951. [A biography of this 18th-century Georgian poet.]

Kovalevskii, M. Zakon i obychai na Kavkaze (Law and Custom in the Caucasus). 2 vols. Moscow, 1890.

Krachkovskii, I. Y. "Opisanie puteshestviia Makariia Antiokhiiskogo" (Description of the Travels of Macarius of Antioch), in Sovetskoe Vostokovedenie (Soviet Orientalism). Vol. VI. Moscow, 1949.

Kudriavtsev, K. Sbornik materialov po istorii Abkhazii (Collection of Materials on the History of Abkhazia). Sukhum, 1922.

Lambton, A. K. S. Landlord and Peasant in Persia: A Study of Land Tenure and Land Revenue Administration. Oxford, 1953.

Lang, David Marshall. "Georgia and the Fall of the Safavi Dynasty," in Bulletin of the School of Oriental and African Studies, London, Vol. XIV, Part 3, 1952.

—— "Georgian Relations with France during the Reign of Wakhtang VI, 1711–1724," *Journal of the Royal Asiatic Society* (London), October, 1950.

—— "Prince Ioann of Georgia and his 'Kalmasoba,' " American Slavic and East European Review, Vol. XI, Dec. 1952.

—— Studies in the Numismatic History of Georgia in Transcaucasia. (American Numismatic Society Notes and Monographs, No. 130.) New York, 1955.

Langlois, Victor. Essai de classification des suites monétaires de la Géorgie. Paris, 1860.

Lebedev, V. I. "Posol'stvo Artemiia Volynskogo v Persiiu" (The Embassy of Artemii Volynskii to Persia) in Izvestiia Akademii Nauk SSSR, Ser. Ist. Fil. (Bulletin of the Academy of Sciences of the USSR, Historico-Philosophical Series), Vol. V (1948), No. 6.

—— *see* Grekov, B. D.

Lockhart, L. Nadir Shah. London, 1938.

Lominadze, B. R. "Iese Barat'ashvilis tskhovreba-anderdzis akhali gamotsemis

Lominadze, B. R. (*Continued*)
gamo" (Concerning the New Edition of the Life and Testament of Iese Barat'ashvili), in Materialy po Istorii Gruzii i Kavkaza. Vol. 32. Tiflis, 1955.
—— "Masalebi dasavlet' Sak'art'velos XVII–XVIII s-t'a istoriis k'ronologiisat'vis" (Materials for the Chronology of Western Georgian History in the 17th and 18th Centuries) [Being a list of the Patriarchs of Western Georgia during this period], in Materialy po Istorii Gruzii i Kavkaza (Materials for the History of Georgia and the Caucasus). Vol. 31. Tiflis, 1954.
—— "Masalebi Sak'art'velos XVII–XVIII saukunet'a istoriis k'ronologiisat'vis" (Materials for the Chronology of Georgian History in the 17th–18th Centuries), in Materialy po Istorii Gruzii i Kavkaza. Vol. 29. Tiflis, 1951.
—— "P'eodaluri meurneobis organizatsiis istoriidan gvianp'eodalur Sak'art'veloshi" (From the History of the Organization of the Feudal Economy in Late Feudal Georgia), in Materialy po Istorii Gruzii i Kavkaza. Vol. 30. Tiflis, 1954.
—— "P'eodaluri midsismp'lobelobis istoriidan 'sadsinamdzghvro'" (On the History of Feudal Land Tenure Termed Sadsinamdzghvro), in Materialy po Istorii Gruzii i Kavkaza. Vol. 31. Tiflis, 1954.
Lort'k'ip'anidze, Iason. K'vemo K'art'li me-XVIII saukunis pirvel meot'khedshi: Nizhniaia Kartliia v pervoi chetverti XVIII stoletiia (Lower K'art'li in the First Quarter of the 18th Century). 4 parts in 2 vols. Tiflis, 1935–38. [Georgian and Russian texts.]
Makharadze, N. B. Vosstanie v Imeretii 1819–20 gg. (The Rebellion in Imeret'i in 1819–20). Tiflis, 1942. [Forming Part 3 of *Materialy po Istorii Gruzii i Kavkaza* for the year 1942.]
Manvelishvili, A. Histoire de Géorgie. Paris, 1951.
—— Ruset'i da Sak'art'velo, 1801–1951 (Russia and Georgia, 1801–1951). Vol. I. Paris, 1951.
Markova, O. P. Vosstanie v Kakhetii 1812 g. (The 1812 Revolt in Kakhet'i). Moscow, 1951.
Materialy po Istorii Gruzii i Kavkaza (Materials for the History of Georgia and the Caucasus). Tiflis, 1937–. [In progress.]
Meskhia, Shot'a. "Masalebi klasobrivi brdzolis istoriisat'vis XVIII s. Sak'art'velos k'alak'ebshi" (Materials on the History of the Class Conflict in the Towns of 18th-Century Georgia), in Materialy po Istorii Gruzii i Kavkaza. Vol. 32. Tiflis, 1955.
—— "Masalebi Sak'art'velos ekonomiuri istoriisat'vis" (Materials for the Economic History of Georgia), in Materialy po Istorii Gruzii i Kavkaza. Vol. 30. Tiflis, 1954.
—— "Vakhushti da dzveli k'art'uli saistorio mdserloba" (Wakhusht and Ancient Georgian Historical Writing), in Analebi (Annals), a recueil published by the Ivane Javakhishvili Historical Institute. Vol. I. Tiflis, 1947.
—— *see* Gvritishvili, D.

Miklukho-Maklai, N. D. "Zapiski S. Avramova· ob Irane kak istoricheskii istochnik" (The Notes of S. Avramov on Iran as a Historical Source), in Uchenye Zapiski Leningradskogo Gosudarstvennogo Universiteta (Learned Papers of Leningrad University), No. 128. Leningrad, 1952. (Series of Oriental Studies, Part 3.)

Minorsky, V. "Tiflis," in Encyclopaedia of Islam. Leyden and London, 1913–38.

Muskhelishvili, L. "Dasavlet' Sak'art'velos glekhobis sotsialur-ekonomiuri kategoriebi XV–XVII ss." (Social-Economic Categories of the Western Georgian Peasantry in the 15th–17th Centuries), in Bulletin de l'Institut Marr. Vol. V–VI. Tiflis, 1940.

Nat'adze, G. Y. "Krest'iane 'Sakhaso' v vostochnoi Gruzii v kontse XVIII stoletiia" (The "Sakhaso" Peasantry in Eastern Georgia at the End of the 18th Century), in Materialy po Istorii Gruzii i Kavkaza. Part V. Tiflis, 1937.

—— Sak'art'velos istoriis mokle sotsialogiuri mimokhilva (Short Sociological Survey of the History of Georgia). 2 vols. K'ut'ais, 1925.

—— Sulkhan Baratov kak istorik Gruzii (Sulkhan Baratov as a Historian of Georgia). Tiflis, 1934.

Natroev, A. Mtskhet i ego sobor Sveti-Tskhoveli (Mtskhet'a and Its Cathedral of the Living Pillar). Tiflis, 1900.

Nikolai Mikhailovich, Grand-Duke. Graf Pavel Aleksandrovich Stroganov. (Count P. A. Stroganov). 3 vols. St. Petersburg, 1903.

Nolde, Boris. La formation de l'Empire Russe. Vol. II. Paris, 1953.

Okun', S. B. Istoriia SSSR, 1796–1825 (History of the USSR, 1796–1825). Leningrad, 1948.

Olonetskii, A. A. Iz istorii velikoi druzhby (From the History of a Great Friendship). Tiflis, 1954. (Studies in the History of Russo-Georgian Relations in the First Half of the 19th Century).

Orbeliani, A. V. Jambakurian-. "Agha-Mamad-Khanis shemosvla Tp'ilisshi" (Agha Mohammed Khan's Assault on Tiflis), Moambe (The Messenger). Tiflis, 1895.

Papava, T'amar. Didi sakheebi patara charchoebshi (Great Figures in Small Frames). 2 vols. Paris and Buenos Aires, 1937–53. (Georgian Historical Biographies).

Petit-Dutaillis, C. The Feudal Monarchy in France and England. 2d ed. London, 1949.

P'irtskhalaishvili, A. G. "Imeretiia i Guriia v period 1804–1840 g." (Imeret'i and Guria in the Period 1804–1840), in Materialy po Istorii Gruzii i Kavkaza (Materials for the History of Georgia and the Caucasus). Tiflis, 1942. Part 1.

Polievktov, M. A. Ekonomicheskie i politicheskie razvedki Moskovskogo gosudarstva XVII veka na Kavkaze (Economic and Political Reconnaissance by the Muscovite State in the Caucasus during the 17th Century). Tiflis, 1932.

—— "K voprosu o snosheniiakh Rostoma Kartalinskogo s Moskvoiu" (On

Polievktov, M. A. (*Continued*)
the Question of the Relations of Rostom of K'art'li with Moscow), in
Bulletin de l'Institut Marr. Vol. V–VI. Tiflis, 1940.

Poole, R. S. Catalogue of the Coins of the Shahs of Persia in the British
Museum. London, 1887.

Potto, General V. A. Kavkazskaia voina (The Caucasian War). 3d ed. St.
Petersburg, 1897–98.

—— *see* Beliavskii, N. N.

P'roneli, A. Ambokheba Kakhet'isa 1812 ds. (The 1812 Revolt in Kakhet'i).
Tiflis, 1907.

Rabino, H. L. Coins, Medals, and Seals of the Shahs of Iran. London, 1945.
With Album. Oxford, 1951.

Radiani, Sh., *see* Baramidze, A.

Ratchvelishvili, K'ristep'ore. Sak'art'velos mokle istoria (Brief History of
Georgia). Tiflis, 1925.

—— Sak'art'velos p'eodalizmis istoria (History of Georgian Feudalism). Tiflis,
1926.

Rogava, A. Sakhalkho ganat'leba Erekle meoris khanis K'art'l-Kakhet'shi da
Anton pirveli (Popular Education in K'art'li and Kakhet'i during the Reign
of Erekle II, and the Role of Catholicos Antoni I). Tiflis, 1950.

Rozhkova, M. K. Ekonomicheskaia politika tsarskogo pravitel'stva na srednem
vostoke vo vtoroi chetverti XIX veka i Russkaia burzhuaziia (The Economic
Policy of the Tsarist Government in the Near East during the Second
Quarter of the 19th Century and the Russian Bourgeoisie). Moscow, 1949.

—— "Iz istorii ekonomicheskoi politiki Rossiiskogo tsarizma v Zakavkaz'e"
(From the History of the Economic Policy of Russian Tsarism in Transcaucasia), in Istoricheskie Zapiski (Historical Essays). Vol. XVIII. Moscow,
1946.

Salia, K., ed. Bedi K'art'lisa. Le Destin de la Géorgie: Recueil historique,
scientifique et littéraire géorgien. Paris, 1948–. [In progress.]

Salomon, R. La politique orientale de Vergennes, 1780–1784. Paris, 1935.

Sanders, A. (pseud. Alexander Nikuradze). Kaukasien, geschichtlicher Umriss.
Munich, 1942.

Sbornik Imperatorskogo Russkogo Istoricheskogo Obshchestva (Collected Publications of the Imperial Russian Historical Society). 148 vols. St. Petersburg
and Iuriev, 1867–1916.

Sbornik Materialov dlia Opisaniia Mestnostei i Plemen Kavkaza (Collection of
Materials for the Description of the Localities and Tribes of the Caucasus).
44 vols. Tiflis, 1881–1915. (Vols. 45 and 46 published after 1920 at Makhach-
Kala.)

Shaduri, V. Russkie pisateli o Gruzii (Russian Writers on Georgia). Vol. I.
Tiflis, 1948. [An anthology.]

Shanidze, A. Dzveli k'art'uli ena da literatura (Ancient Georgian Language and Literature). 9th ed. Tiflis, 1947.

Sharashidze, K'. "Sak'art'velos istoriis masalebi XV–XVIII ss." (Material for Georgian History during the 15th–18th Centuries), in Materialy po Istorii Gruzii i Kavkaza. Vol. 30. Tiflis, 1954.

Shay, M. L. The Ottoman Empire from 1720 to 1734, As Revealed in Despatches of the Venetian Baili. Urbana, Ill. 1944.

Solov'ev, S. M. Istoriia Rossii s drevneishikh vremen (History of Russia from the Most Ancient Times). 2d ed. 6 vols. St. Petersburg, 1894.

Soloveytchik, G. Potemkin. 2d ed. London, 1939.

Sorel, A. La question d'Orient au XVIIIme siècle. Paris, 1878.

Soselia, O. N. "Klasobrivi brdzolis istoriidan gvianp'eodalur dasavlet' Sak'-art'veloshi" (From the History of the Class Conflict in late Feudal Western Georgia), in Mimomkhilveli (The Observer). Vol. III. Tiflis, 1953.

—— "Masalebi agraruli urt'iert'obis istoriisat'vis gvianp'eodalur dasavlet' Sak'art'veloshi" (Materials for the History of Agrarian Relationships in Late Feudal Western Georgia), in Materialy po Istorii Gruzii i Kavkaza. Vol. 31. Tiflis, 1954.

—— "Masalebi dasavlet' Sak'art'velos sat'avadoebis mmart'velobis istoriisat'vis" (Materials for the History of the Administration of the Western Georgian Principalities), in Materialy po Istorii Gruzii i Kavkaza. Vol. 31. Tiflis, 1954.

—— "P'eodaluri Sak'art'velos politikuri dashlis istoriidan" (From the History of the Disintegration of Feudal Georgia), in Materialy po Istorii Gruzii i Kavkaza. Vol. 30. Tiflis, 1954.

—— "Saglekho valdebulebani dasavlet' Sak'art'veloshi XVII s." (Peasant Dues in Western Georgia in the 17th Century), in Materialy po Istorii Gruzii i Kavkaza. Vol. 32. Tiflis, 1955.

Sumbadze, L. Z. Gori (The Town of Gori). Moscow, 1950.

Sumner, B. H. Peter the Great and the Emergence of Russia. London, 1950.

Surguladze, Iv. Sak'art'velos sakhelmdsip'osa da samart'lis istoriisat'vis (On the History of the Government and Law of Georgia). Tiflis, 1953.

—— "Sakhelmdsip'o gadasakhadebi K'art'lis samep'oshi me-18 s. dasadsqisshi" (State Revenue in the K'art'lian Kingdom at the Beginning of the 18th Century), in Shromebi (Works) of the Institute of Economics of the Georgian Academy of Sciences, Tiflis. Vol. VI.

Tamarati (T'amarashvili), M. L'Église géorgienne des origines jusqu'à nos jours. Rome, 1910.

—— Istoria katolikobisa k'art'velt'a shoris (History of Catholicism among the Georgians). Tiflis, 1902.

T'aqaishvili, E. "Georgian Chronology and the Beginnings of Bagratid Rule in Georgia," in Georgica. Vol. I, No. 1. London, 1935.

T'aqaishvili, E., ed. Dzveli Sak'art'velo: L'ancienne Géorgie (Organ of the

T'aqaishvili, E., ed. (*Continued*)
   Georgian Society of History and Ethnography). 4 vols. Tiflis, 1909–15.
Tatishvili, V. Chapter on the Georgian colony in Moscow, in S. V. Bakhrushin,
   Istoriia Moskvy (History of Moscow), Vol. II. Moscow, 1953.
—— Gruziny v Moskve, istoricheskii ocherk, 1653–1722 (The Georgians in
   Moscow, Historical Sketch, 1653–1722). Tiflis, 1950.
Tchitchinadze, Z. K'art'vel mep'et' drois k'art'veli respublikanelebi da mep'e
   Erekles dserilebi Venetsiis respublikuri mt'avrobis dsinashe (Georgian Re-
   publicans under the Georgian Kings, and King Erekle's Letters to the
   Venetian Republican Government). Tiflis, 1917.
—— Mister Oliver Uordropi da Inglisis kavshiri Sak'art'velost'an 1780 ds.
   (Mister Oliver Wardrop and the English Link with Georgia in 1780). Tiflis,
   1920.
—— Sak'art'velos batonqmobis p'aktiuri masalebi (Data on Georgian Serf-
   dom). Tiflis, 1924.
—— Solomon Leonidze. Tiflis, 1910. [A biography of Solomon Leonidze.]
—— Vakhtang mep'is dserilebi Sap'ranget'is mep'est'an da mep'is Erekles
   midser-modsera Inglisis dsarmomadgenelt'an (King Wakhtang's Letters to
   the King of France and King Erekle's Correspondence with the English
   Representative). Tiflis, 1895.
Tchqonia, T'. "Gorkis olk'shi aghmochenili k'art'uli sidzveleni" (Georgian
   Antiquities Discovered in the Gorki District), in Literaturuli dziebani
   (Literary Researches). Vol. IV, Tiflis, 1948.
Toumanoff, Prince Cyril Leon. "The Early Bagratids: Remarks in Connexion
   with some Recent Publications," in Le Muséon. Vol. LXII. Louvain, 1949.
—— "Kniazia Bagrationy-Mukhranskie, Rodoslovie" (The Princes Bagration-
   Mukhranskii, a Genealogy), in the journal *Novik*. New York, 1951.
—— "Materialy k genealogii Bagratidov" (Materials for the Genealogy of the
   Bagratids), *Novik*. New York, 1950.
—— "Poslednie tsari Imeretii i ikh potomstvo" (The Last Kings of Imeret'i
   and Their Descendants), *Novik*. New York, 1953.
Tschotschia, Schalwa. Agrarverfassung und Landwirtschaft in Georgien. Leip-
   zig, 1927.
Tseret'eli, Akaki. Perezhitoe (Reminiscences). Tr. by E. Ghoghoberidze. 2d
   ed. Moscow, 1950.
Tsintsadze, I. Z. "XVIII saukunis Ruset'-Sak'art'velos urt'iert'obis istoriis
   ark'ividan" (From the Records of Russo-Georgian Relationships in the 18th
   Century), in Materialy po Istorii Gruzii i Kavkaza. Vol. 32. Tiflis, 1955.
—— "Ramdenime akhali tsnoba XVIII saukunis K'art'lis istoriisat'vis" (Some
   New Data on the History of K'art'li in the 18th Century), in Materialy po
   Istorii Gruzii i Kavkaza (Materials for the History of Georgia and the
   Caucasus). Tiflis, 1942. Part 4.
Tsitsishvili, S. A. Dzveli Sak'art'velos anu Giorgias ruka (Map of Ancient
   Georgia). Paris, 1935–36.

Uchaneishvili, D. "K voprosu ob ekonomicheskom razvitii vostochnoi Gruzii vo vtoroi polovine XVIII veka" (On the Question of the Economic Development of Eastern Georgia during the Second Half of the 18th Century), in Materialy po Istorii Gruzii i Kavkaza. Part V. Tiflis, 1937.

Vacheishvili, A. Narkvevebi k'art'uli samart'lis istoriidan (Researches in the History of Georgian Law). Vol. I, Tiflis, 1946.

Vasiliev, A. A. Histoire de l'Empire Byzantin. 2 vols. Paris, 1932.

Veidenbaum, E. G. Kavkazskie etiudy (Caucasian studies). Tiflis, 1901.

—— Khizany v Gruzii ("Khizani" Peasants in Georgia). Tiflis, 1913.

—— Putevoditel' po Kavkazu (Guidebook to the Caucasus), Tiflis, 1888.

Vermishev, Kh. "Khizany i khizanstvo" (Khizani Peasants and Their Status), in Trudy (Works) of the Imperial Caucasian Society of Agriculture. Vol. II–III. 1885.

"Wanderer," pseud. Notes on the Caucasus. London, 1883.

Wardrop, Sir J. O. The Kingdom of Georgia. London, 1888.

Weidenbaum, see Veidenbaum.

Zhghenti, V., see Baramidze, A.

Zhuze, P. Gruziia v 17 stoletii po izobrazheniiu Patriarkha Makariia (Georgia in the 17th Century according to the Description of the Patriarch Macarius). Kazan, 1905.

Index

DATE DUE